MUSIC MAKING IN IRAN FROM THE FIFTEENTH TO THE EARLY TWENTIETH CENTURY

Music and Performance in Muslim Contexts

Published in Association with the Aga Khan University Institute for the Study of Muslim Civilisations and the Aga Khan Music Programme

Series Editors: Theodore Levin and Jonas Otterbeck

This series presents innovative scholarship in music, dance, theatre, and other performative practices and varieties of expressive culture inspired or shaped by Muslim artistic, cultural, intellectual, religious and social heritage, including in new creative forms. Bringing together outstanding new work by leading scholars from a variety of disciplines across the humanities and social sciences, the series embraces contemporary and historical cultural spheres both within Muslim-majority societies and in diasporic subcultures and micro-cultures around the world.

Published and forthcoming titles

The Awakening of Islamic Pop Music
Jonas Otterbeck

From Rumi to the Whirling Dervishes: Music, Poetry and Mysticism in the Ottoman Empire
Walter Feldman

Music Making in Iran from the Fifteenth to the Early Twentieth Century
Amir Hosein Pourjavady

edinburghuniversitypress.com/series/mpmc

CONTENTS

List of Illustrations vii
List of Tables xi
Note on Transliteration and Translation xiii
Acknowledgments xv
Preface xvii

Part I Historical and Social Contexts

1 Centers of Musical Patronage between the Fifteenth and Eighteenth Centuries 3
2 Courtesans and Concubines in Early Modern Iran 63
3 Musical Life in the Nineteenth Century 98

Part II Music Theories and Practices

4 The Modal System 165
5 Rhythm 231
6 Musical Genres 276

Appendix 1: The Systematist Texts 319
Appendix 2: The Non-Systematist Texts 321
Appendix 3: An Account of the Modal System and Rhythmic Cycles in Non-Systematist Treatises 322

Glossary 327
Works Cited 339
Index 356

ILLUSTRATIONS

Figures

1.1	Koyuk (r. 1246–1248) the grandson of Genghis Khān, from a copy of *Tārikh-e jahāngoshā* by ʿAṭā Malek Jovayni	5
1.2	Timur (r. 1246–1248) in a royal ceremony, from the *Ẓafar-nāma*, also called the *Tārikh-e jahāngoshā-ye Timur*	8
1.3	Abu al-Fatḥ Pir Budāq, the governor of Shiraz (1456–1460), sitting under a brightly colored canopy as attendants serve food	10
1.4	Shāhrokh (r. 1405–1447), the son of Timur at his enthronement, with many courtiers and artists including ʿAbd al-Qāder Marāghi	12
1.5	Bāysonghor (1397–1433), the son of Shāhrokh	13
1.6	A binding of the *Divān* of Amir ʿAlishir Navāʾi showing him sitting in a garden with the literati and musicians of Herat	15
1.7	Map of the Safavid domains	19
1.8	Ḥamza Mirzā entertained	23
1.9	European musicians sent to the Safavid court from Frederick II, Duke of Holstein-Gottorp	39
1.10	Shah ʿAbbas II (r. 1642–1666) and his courtiers	40
1.11	Shah Solaymān (r. 1666–1694) with attendants serving food and drink while musicians perform in the foreground	41

1.12	Two Georgian dancing boys, Isfahan, 1654	44
1.13	Tombstones of two Armenian musicians, Zādur (d. 1741) and Hovasap (d. 1712) in the New Julfa cemetery in Isfahan	45
1.14	Drawings of the above tombstones made by Abraham Gurgenian (1908–1991)	46
2.1	Harem of Solṭān-Ḥosayn Bāyqarā, Herat, dated 1481	66
2.2	Painting of Shah Ṭahmāsb made for his brother Bahrām Mirzā. Tabriz or Herat, 1520s	69
2.3	"*Shāhedbāz* and *qavvāl*," from the Kaempfer album, 1684–1685	70
2.4	Courtesan with a long-necked lute, Isfahan, *c.* 1600–1610	74
2.5	Detail of a pen-box showing a courtesan making love with a member of the gentry, Isfahan, dated 1712	79
2.6	Map of Nāder's camp (1741–1747) as originally drawn by Père Louis Bazin	81
2.7	"Shākha Nabāt," a courtesan of Shiraz who became Karim Khan's mistress	83
2.8	A pasteboard showing courtesans entertaining a patron, Shiraz, dated 1775	85
2.9	Mirror case with shutter showing courtesans entertaining a patron, Tehran, *c.* 1840	86
2.10	An acrobat of *dastgāh-e bāzigar-khāna*, Tehran, *c.* 1820	88
2.11	A courtesan playing the *kamāncha* associated with the *dastgāh-e bāzigar-khāna*, Tehran, *c.* 1820	89
2.12	A courtesan playing the *santur* associated with the *dastgāh-e bāzigar-khāna*	89
2.13	A courtesan playing the *setār*, Tehran, *c.* 1820	90
2.14	Two courtesans associated with the *dastgāh-e bāzigar-khāna*, Tehran, *c.* 1811–1814	91
3.1(a–d)	"Court *bāzigars*," three courtesans dancing and one concubine holding a frame drum.	103
3.2	Painting by the prominent court painter Ṣani' al-Molk (1814–1866) depicting Āqā 'Ali-Akbar with a group of young musicians and performers	109
3.3	Court male musicians in 1863, seated from left to right in descending order of rank	110

3.4	Court male musicians in 1863	111
3.5	A performance of *rawża* for the wives and concubines of the shah at the Golestān Palace in 1885	112
3.6	The ceremony of *āshpazān* (making soup), October 9, 1894	113
3.7	Moḥammad Ṣādeq Khān with his two sons, Moṭalleb and 'Abdollāh, and his brother, Mirzā Shafi'	119
3.8	Mirzā 'Abdollāh and his disciples	121
3.9	A troupe of rural musicians and *bāzigar*s	124
3.10	Karim Shira'i and his troupe of *moqalled*s	125
3.11	Esma'il Bazzāz and his troupe of *moqalled*s and musicians	126
3.12	Female musicians at the *andarun* of Nāṣer al-Din Shah	128
3.13	Anis al-Dawla, the favorite wife of Nāṣer al-Din Shah	128
3.14(a–b)	Two photographs of the troupe of 'Aziz and 'Aṭā	132
3.15	A postcard showing a troupe of male musicians and a dancing boy, including Dāvud Kalimi Shirāzi (*tār*) and Aqā Jān (*dombak*)	133
3.16	Ghazāl (dancer), 'Aziz Shashlulband (*tār*), and Marāl (dancer)	135
3.17	Herati musicians at the Qajar court	136
3.18	Āqā Ḥosayn-Qoli and his students in the house of the luthier Yaḥyā	137
3.19	The *dasta-ye shāhi*, the royal court ensemble	139
3.20	Ḥosayn Bālā Raqqāṣ and Qorbān-'Ali Beg Jalawdār	140
3.21	The court military band, as drawn by Alexey Saltykov in the 1830s	141
3.22	Alfred Jean-Baptiste Lemaire and 'Ali-Akbar Mozayyen al-Dawla surrounded by their students at the Dār al-Fonun	143
3.23	"Garden party at the Anjoman-e Okhovvat." The musician playing the *kamāncha* is Ḥosayn Khān Esmā'ilzāda	146
3.24	The Multiplex Grand Phonograph technicians beginning to record with permission from Moẓaffar al-Din Shah	148
4.1	Four *dastgāh*s as represented in a hierarchical set of modal entities together with their appropriate rhythmic cycles	208
5.1	The *dik dak* drum patterns in a late Safavid musical text	243
6.1	A folio with *kolliyāt* attributed to 'Abd al-Qāder Marāghi	286

Musical Examples

4.1	The basic heptatonic scale presented in the *Taqsīm al-naghamāt*	185
4.2	Melodic contours of *maqāms* and *sho'bas* in the *Taqsīm al-naghamāt*	190
4.3	The seven modes using basic scale degrees	192
5.1	The six basic rhythmic cycles in the Qajar period	266
5.2	A *taṣnif* in *se-żarb-e sangin* beginning in the third beat	267
5.3	Two mnemonic patterns used for didactic purposes in the late Qajar period	268

TABLES

1.1	The sixteenth-century composers mentioned in Safavid *tadhkeras*	31
1.2	The seventeenth-century composers whose compositions or names are mentioned in the codex of Amir Khān Gorji	36
4.1	Musical sources written between the fifteenth and twentieth centuries	174
4.2	The twelve *parda*s and their related *sho'ba*s in the treatise of Nayshāburi	178
4.3	The fourteen *parda*s and their cosmological affiliations in the treatise of 'Alā' al-Din Bokhāri	180
4.4	Names of scale degrees in Persian and Ottoman musical sources between the sixteenth and eighteenth centuries	202
4.5	Lists of *dastgāh*s in six eighteenth- and nineteenth-century musical sources	213
5.1	The rhythmic cycles mentioned by Safavid music theorists throughout the sixteenth and seventeenth centuries	244
5.2	The rhythmic cycles mentioned in the Anonymous Treatise and the *Bahjat al-ruḥ* and comparing them with the accounts of the first and last Safavid musical treatises	246
6.1	The names of various sections of vocal and instrumental compositions between the fifteenth and twentieth centuries	311

A3.1 The twelve *pardas* and their number of *bāngs* in non-Systematist treatises 323
A3.2 The *sho'ba/āvāz* in non-Systematist treatises 324
A3.3 The account of rhythm in non-Systematist treatises 325

NOTE ON TRANSLITERATION AND TRANSLATION

I have used the transliteration system of the *Encyclopaedia Iranica* with seven simple modifications:

ث	th
خ	kh
چ	ch
ذ	dh
ژ	zh
ش	sh
غ	gh

Arabic names, technical terms, and titles are transliterated according to the above Persian system except for the vowels. The short vowels are represented by:

a e o in Persian
a i u in Arabic
("two" in Persian is always represented by *dō*)

The long vowels are represented by:

ā i u in Persian
ā ī ū in Arabic

Final silent Persian ه and Arabic ة are always represented by "a" and و is represented in Persian by "v" and in Arabic by "w."

All translations of Persian texts are my own, with the exception of a few cases that are indicated.

For translations of some paragraphs from Eskandar Beg Turkamān's *Tārikh-e 'ālamārā' 'Abbāsi*, I primarily use the English translation of Roger Savory, but changed in accordance with the Persian text in certain instances where it was inaccurate. I did the same with the English translation of the *Ā'in-e Akbarī* by H. Blochmann.

ACKNOWLEDGMENTS

This book would not have been possible without the contributions of the teachers, colleagues and friends who have assisted me in the last few years. Above all, I must thank my mentor and dissertation advisor Stephen Blum for the time, attention, and thought he has given to my work, which has profited immeasurably from his detailed criticisms and suggestions. Special thanks are also due to my long-time teacher Eckhard Neubauer who has taught me to cultivate a painstaking approach to reading and analyzing music treatises and historical texts. I must further acknowledge my debt to Owen Wright and Peter Manuel, whose critical reading of my chapters and dialectical approach to ethnomusicology encouraged and inspired me throughout the many stages of the book. Likewise, Jean During, Martin Stokes, Walter Feldman, Robert Simms, and Sasan Fatemi's insightful questions and indispensable critique helped me to refine some of the arguments presented in these pages. I also want to thank Theodore Levin, co-editor of the series Music and Performance in Muslim Contexts at Edinburgh University Press for providing encouragement and feedback, and for editing the entire manuscript.

The late Dariush Safvat, my first music teacher, gave me training in *setār* playing and the *radif*. I owe to him my understanding of Persian music. I also benefited immensely from hours of conversations and interviews with Taqi Binesh, Mohammad Taghi Massoudieh, Ali Tajvidi, Hasan Kasai, Hatam Askari, Mohammad-Reza Lotfi, Hossein Alizadeh, Dariush Talai, Hooman

Asadi, Manuchehr Sadeghi, Alireza Miralinaqi, Ramin Jazayeri, and Farid Kheradmand.

I should also thank Houman Sarshar, Mehdi Farahani, and Manuel Sánchez for giving me some of the paintings and photographs of musicians. Finally, George Murer kindly reviewed all chapters, offering suggestions concerning grammar and helping me with the translation of some paragraphs from French and German to English. Last but not least, I would like to acknowledge the loving support of my wife Shādi and my son Sohrab, who had to share me with this book for more than five years.

Amir Hosein Pourjavady

PREFACE

This book comprises a study of music in Iran from the Timurid period in the fifteenth century up until the end of the Qajar period at the beginning of the twentieth century. It examines many aspects of music making in this span of time, including centers of musical patronage, the role of patrons, music theorists, music treatises, the social organization of musicians, courtesan and concubine culture, and performance contexts. It also compares descriptions of musical sessions and performance formats from different periods and considers Western influence, socio-political developments, and contact with other musical cultures. *Music Making in Iran* also scrutinizes the emergence and evolution of modal entities, rules for modulation, the formation of court repertoires, the development of rhythmic structures, vocal and instrumental genres, and forms of composition.

From the perspective of ethnicity, "Iranian" is the generic term for peoples of Iranian descent who speak an Iranian language. Some of these peoples, most notably, Persians, an ethnonym derived from Parsa, the ancient name for the territory that corresponds to the current-day Fars province, are demographically centered in Iran itself. Other Iranian peoples, for example, Baloch and Kurds, are represented by significant populations both within Iran and in neighboring countries. And still other Iranian peoples, for example, Pashtuns, Ossetians, and Yaghnobis, reside principally outside Iran. If, however, "Iranian" is not defined ethnolinguistically but in the socio-political sense of an inhabitant of Iran, then it would also include Turkic-speaking Iranians such as Azeris, Qashqais, and Turkmens.

By the sixth century BCE, ethnic Persians had expanded their area of settlement far beyond their native territory of Parsa and dominated all Iranian lands as well as adjacent territories. Over time, the Persian language and identity were assimilated throughout Iran and, until 1935, the nation of Iran was known in the Western world as Persia. Most pre-1935 European documents, especially travel accounts, refer to the country as "Persia" and its people as "Persians," but following the practice of Iranians themselves, I use "Iran" to refer to the geographical territory ruled by the Safavid, Afshar, and Qajar dynasties. I use Persia and Persian, however, like Westerners do, to refer to elements of Iranian culture such as music, poetry, and miniature paintings.

In discussing the culture of what one could call Greater Iran, I use the term "Persianate," coined in the 1960s by the historian of Islamic civilization Marshall Hodgson to describe the sphere of Iranian cultural influence extending from Central Asia, Xinjiang, and India in the east to the Caucasus, Anatolia, and the southern Balkans in the west.

In the past two decades, thanks to new discoveries of documents ranging from music treatises and song–text collections to travel accounts, biographies, musicians' diaries and interviews, musical notations, paintings, photographs, and early recordings, the nature of musical research in Iran and the Muslim world in general has evolved enormously and scholars are now in a better position to examine the historical development of Persian music. Meanwhile, several scholarly studies have appeared recently that elucidate the significant changes that occurred in some aspects of music making in the Persianate world.

Three monographs in English have been published in the last three years that mark notable contributions to the field of Persian music history: Owen Wright's *Music Theory in the Safavid Era: The taqsīm al-naġamat*; Ann Lucas' *Music of a Thousand Years: A New History of Persian Musical Traditions*; and Margaret Caton's *A Persian Ode: Musical Life in Safavid and Qajar Iran*. Wright's book is particularly oriented toward the analysis of a theoretical treatise from the mid-sixteenth century which contains descriptive accounts of modes, modulatory sequences, and rhythmic cycles. In addition to a detailed commentary on the text, Wright scrutinizes the treatise in relation to a range of music treatises of the Timurid and Safavid periods, providing a more comprehensive discussion of music theory throughout the sixteenth and seventeenth centuries. Lucas' book addresses a larger timespan (1100–1950) and divides the history of Persian music into two periods: the culture of *maqām* and the culture of *dastgāh-radif*. After examining some of the treatises on the *maqām* and *dastgāh* systems, she argues that while the world of twelve-*maqāms* was more universal, timeless, aloof from ethnonational delineations, and related to polyglot populations and dynastic centers of power, the world of *dastgāh-radif* was engaged in a modern negotiation of Iran's national identity and thus provides evidence for the nation's legitimacy in the modern world. Lucas centers her discussions of Persian music on the modal system and select song genres and compositional forms. Caton's book focuses on a wealth of reports on music and society in the Safavid and Qajar periods and is largely based on European travel accounts. While the book lacks theoretical discussions of music, its eight chapters consider many topics including, but not limited to, music in rural contexts, music in daily life, rites of passage, religions and music, ceremonial music, European music presence and influence, and the court and aristocracy. One of the major benefits of her book is the collection of images that are either reproduced from travel accounts or obtained from the Golestān Palace Museum and the Central Library of Tehran University.

Two Iranian scholars, Sāsān Fāṭemi and Sayyed Ḥosayn Maythami, have provided important studies on music of the premodern and modern periods. In the second chapter of his book, *Jashn va musiqi dar farhanghā-ye shahri-ye Irāni* (*Celebration and Music in Iranian Urban Cultures*), Fāṭemi examines the role and social status of hereditary male and female performers from the Safavid to the end of the Qajar period. Maythami's book *Musiqi-ye ʿaṣr-e Ṣafavi* (*Music in the Safavid Era*) also contains a wealth of information on various aspects of life, theory, and musical performance practice during the Safavid period. Both authors have published valuable articles on different musical topics relating to the Safavid, Zand, and Qajar periods.

While the present book is indebted to all these studies, it draws on examination of data collected from many other primary and secondary sources, and in many cases takes different analytical approaches to the subjects at hand. *Music Making in Iran* aims to answer questions that have been frequently raised by both indigenous and Western scholars about how the music of Iran evolved from the fifteenth century onward. Why was music banned during the Safavid period, and when it was banned, what was the long-term impact on music making? What was the *maqām* system, how late was it practiced and how did it finally evolve into a set of seven or twelve *dastgāh*s? What was the rhythmic organization of Persian music before the twentieth century? What were the common musical genres in the Safavid period, and how did they evolve or decline after the seventeenth century? How and when was the concept of *radif* formed? And, above all, what were the socio-cultural forces behind these developments?

Music Making in Iran is divided into two parts, each consisting of three chapters. Part I addresses the historical and social context of music. Chapter 1 introduces centers of musical patronage between the thirteenth and eighteenth centuries, with its main focus on musical life in the Timurid and Safavid periods. This chapter looks at the major and minor courts, focusing on the tastes, roles, and contributions of patrons, courtly music institutions, prominent performers, composers, music theorists, and musical settings.

Chapter 2 provides a background to the roles and classes of professional female performers, including both concubines and courtesans. Beginning with an introduction devoted to the life of courtesans and the dynamics within courtesan salons in the fifteenth and sixteenth centuries, this chapter subsequently examines the emergence of upper-class courtesans in Isfahan during the seventeenth century and further discusses the reasons why music and dance were variously stigmatized and banned during the Safavid period. It also illustrates how upper-class courtesans were settled in Shiraz toward the end of the eighteenth century and later found their way into the Qajar court, where they were trained systematically in music and dance by master court musicians.

Chapter 3 examines the lives and roles of male and female musicians in the nineteenth century, focusing on various classes of musicians and entertainers (instrumentalists, singers, accompanists, dancing boys and girls, buffoons) at the Qajar court, with further attention paid to the wider urban musical life in the capital. The chapter introduces the role and size of prominent male and female ensembles in Tehran that largely performed in the houses of the aristocracy and were also occasionally invited to perform at the court. It also discusses the introduction and development of Western military music, the establishment of the music division of the Dār al-Fonun (Iran's first European-style institution of higher learning), the introduction of Western instruments, the advent of recording technologies and accounts of recording sessions, and, finally, the impact of modernization of traditional practices.

Part II concerns music theories and practices. Chapter 4 first provides an overview of musical texts devoted to modal theory between the sixteenth and twentieth centuries, and then summarizes what can be inferred from theoretical treatises and literary sources about early Persian modal entities such as *dastān*, *khosravāni*, *al-ṭurūq al-mulūkiyya*, *parda*, and *shadd*. In this summary, I build on the monumental work of Owen Wright on the modal system of Arab and Persian music in the fourteenth century described in his 1978 monograph *The Modal System of Arab and Persian Music, A.D. 1250–1300*. Subsequently, this chapter considers in more detail the function, structures, organization, and interrelations among the twelve *maqām*s, six *āvāza*s, and twenty-four *sho'ba*s. The consolidating of the modal system into the *dastgāh* in the eighteenth century and its development in the Qajar period constitute the final part of the chapter, which also examines the concepts of *āvāz*, *gusha*, and *radif*.

Chapter 5 presents theoretical discussions of rhythmic–metric concepts and accounts of rhythmic cycles. Beginning with an outline of the early concepts of rhythm and the structure of meters in Arabic and Persian traditions, it surveys accounts of rhythmic cycles in the Timurid and Safavid periods pertaining to both art music and the *naqqāra-khāna*. The chapter further considers the development of rhythm and meter in the eighteenth and nineteenth centuries, mainly through examinations of musical texts, collections of *taṣnif*s, early recordings, and interviews with senior master performers.

Finally, Chapter 6 is a survey of musical genres. It commences with accounts of early Arabic and Persian genres and goes on to discusses the structure of Timurid and Safavid genres in light of descriptions in music treatises and representations found in song–text collections. The last part of the chapter offers speculations regarding the transmission of these genres in the eighteenth century, while examining the structure and development of vocal and instrumental genres that came to be associated with or developed within the *dastgāh* system.

While all six chapters work together to comprise an integrated whole, they also stand as a collection of studies devoted to separate topics that can be consulted individually. That said, readers interested, for example, in the modal system, rhythm, or musical genres may find it useful to read earlier chapters that provide historical background.

In the case of Chapter 3, 'Musical Life in the Nineteenth Century', the structure of subheadings may give the chapter an encyclopedic rather than a narrative character. This is mostly because of the nature of the available sources, since, for no other period of Iranian music history do we possess such detailed accounts of different types of performers. Nonetheless, there is a paucity of accounts of music in urban centers other than Tehran, especially Isfahan, Shiraz, Kāshān, and Tabriz.

Throughout the book, I use such terms as "classical musicians" or "classically trained musicians." While the epithet "classical" may seem inappropriate or anachronistic when applied to musicians of the fifteenth to nineteenth centuries, by "classical" I essentially mean the category of musicians who enjoyed a high level of skill and sophistication, and who mostly performed at the courts or in the homes of the aristocracy. This category of musicians may well be what in the fifteenth century 'Abd al-Qāder Marāghi (d. 1435) labels as *mobāsherān-e fann* (commissioners of the art), adept in both *'elm* and *'amal* (theoretical and practical knowledge) who performed at the *majāles* of sultans and *amirs*.[1] In the nineteenth century, *'amala-ye ṭarab-e khāṣṣa*, the solo specialists who enjoyed the highest esteem at the Qajar court and were masters of *dastgāh*s and the *radif*, could well fit into the category of classical musicians, whereas *maddāh*s, *moṭreb*s (hereditary professional musicians), and courtesans who were exponents of religious genres, light songs, and dance tunes could be grouped as semi-classical musicians or entertainers.

I also employ the taxonomy of classical/semi-classical/light in reference to musical genres, melodic modes, and rhythmic cycles. In Chapter 4, I show that while classical modes were characteristically performed at the court and in urban musical centers and were set to *ghazal*s of classical poets, semi-classical or vernacular modes were associated mainly with folk-regional genres and were typically set to *dōbayti*s (quatrains).[2] Classifying vocal genres or rhythmic cycles as light was also a phenomenon common among Persianate music theorists. For instance, Marāghi characterized *havā'i* as *akhaff-e aṣnāf-e taṣānif* or the lightest genre of *taṣnif*s, and Mir Ṣadr al-Din Moḥammad recognized *awfar* as less respected (*ḥaqirtar*) in relation to other cycles.[3]

An attempt to reconstruct the historical development of a domain of music certainly involves a considerable amount of conjecture and necessarily raises more questions than it can answer. One always must be mindful of the gap between theory and practice and the fact that the mentalities of music theorists and practicing musicians were different from those of their respective audiences and readerships. While music theorists frequently emphasize structure, classification, concepts, and terminology, in performance practice, corners usually get cut and nomenclature is often absent.

In the second part of the book, musical analysis is mostly based on information gathered from technical treatises whose interpretation can sometimes be complicated and perplexing. For one thing, descriptions of terms and concepts are not always readily intelligible. Furthermore, musical treatises rehash accounts found in earlier texts as though the information they contain has retained its validity intact. And finally, the relationship between theory and practice is often ambiguous; for instance, the extent to which the classification of modes, rhythms, and genres spelled out in theoretical writings is maintained by practicing musicians is often unclear.

I hope that addressing these issues will resolve some of the ambiguities that currently beleaguer attempts to clarify the terminology of Persian music, particularly modal concepts such as *maqām*, *āvāz* and *dastgāh*, which tend to overlap or take on multiple meanings. In the course of their evolution, these musical concepts have indeed become protean and polysemous, and some terms, such as *gusha,* had a different connotation in the nineteenth century or earlier than what they mean in the modern practice of Persian music. While the concept of *dastgāh* as it is known today is primarily a nineteenth century development, *dastgāh* as a musical term evidently predates the Qajar period (1785–1925) and did not emerge out of a vacuum. Rather, it should be seen as a recent variant of a long line of earlier counterparts.

In the course of chronicling the history of Iranian music, *Music Making in Iran* also illuminates historical links between Persian music and cognate musical systems in neighboring regions, such as the Azeri *mugham*. Likewise, some of the methodologies used in this book could be applied to the study of historical developments of other large-scale ordered repertoires in the Middle East and Central Asia such as the Iraqi *maqām*, Tajik-Uzbek *shashmaqom*, and Uyghur *on ikki muqam*.

Notes

1. See ʿAbd al-Qāder Marāghi, *Jāmiʿ al-alḥān: khātema*, ed. Taqi Binesh (Tehran: Mo'assesa-ye Moṭāleʿāt va Taḥqiqāt-e Farhangi, 1993), 201–204.
2. In an interview I conducted with Moḥammad-Reżā Loṭfi he also opined that the *āvāz*s of *radif* that are set to *dōbayti*s were predominantly rooted in regional-folk music of Iran.
3. See ʿAbd al-Qāder Marāghi, *Sharḥ-e advār*, ed. Taqi Binesh (Tehran: Markaz-e Nashr-e Dāneshgāhi, 1991), 342; for further discussion on this subject. see Sāsān Fāṭemi, "*Taṣnif-e moʿāṣer*," *Māhur* 40 (2008): 85–112.

PART I

HISTORICAL AND SOCIAL CONTEXTS

1

CENTERS OF MUSICAL PATRONAGE BETWEEN THE FIFTEENTH AND EIGHTEENTH CENTURIES

For most of its history, Iran has experienced an unusually high level of foreign invasion, violence, chaos, and socio-historical disruption. Although this persistent adversity has tended to hinder the development of the rich tradition of court music, contacts with Arabic, Mongolian, Turkish, Indian, and Caucasian cultures have led to musical syncretism. While we may trace a continuous tradition of Persian court poetry as far back as the tenth century, the same cannot be said about a tradition of court music being entirely created and upheld by Persian musicians. Before the twelfth century, court compositions were predominantly written in Arabic, though vernacular songs were certainly in Persian. After the eleventh century, when Persian achieved literary prominence, court compositions began to appear in Persian. Nonetheless, from that point on some of the most prominent court musicians in Tabriz, Herat, Qazvin, Shiraz, and Isfahan were of Turkic origin, and they composed and performed songs in Turkish dialects. Likewise, in the seventeenth and eighteenth centuries, several musicians and dancers, particularly in Isfahan, were brought from Georgia and Armenia and became major exponents of Caucasian dance tunes and compositions. During the sixteenth and seventeenth centuries, Persian musicians frequently traveled between Iran and India and subsequently, in the eighteenth and nineteenth centuries, many Indian and Afghan musicians were brought to Iran. The names of modal entities or melody types in music treatises and in the nineteenth-century repertoire of the *radif* clearly exhibit traces of some of these contacts with other cultures.

The Mongol Period and its Aftermath

The invasion of Genghis Khān (d. 1227) and his descendants marks the beginning of a new chapter in Iranian history. In the middle of the thirteenth century, Hülegü (d. 1265), the grandson of Genghis Khān, invaded Iran with an army of about 130,000. He subjugated the rebellious tribes and moved with the bulk of his army to Azerbaijan, where he established the Ilkhanid dynasty in 1256. Two years later, he seized Baghdad and subsequently put an end to the caliphate that had been the central Islamic political institution since the death of the Prophet Moḥammad in 632.

Following the conquest of Baghdad, Ṣafī al-Dīn al-Urmawī (d. 1294), the celebrated music theorist and calligrapher at the court of al-Mustaʿṣim bi-Allāh (r. 1242–1258), was taken captive. He later continued his career in the service of Hülegü and his *ṣāḥeb divān* (vizier and minister of finance), Shams al-Din Jovayni (d. 1284), who, along with his historian brother, ʿAṭā Malek Jovayni (d. 1283), was a prominent patron of fine arts, literature, and music in the second half of the thirteenth century. Al-Urmawī became the tutor to Shams al-Din Jovayni's two sons, Bahā' al-Din and Sharaf al-Din Hārun, and even dedicated his second music treatise, *Risāla al-Sharafiyya* to the latter. Two other polymaths and music theorists, Khᵛāja Naṣir al-Din al-Ṭusi (1201–1274) and his brilliant student, Qoṭb al-Din Shirāzi (1236–1311), were also associated with the court of Hülegü. Shirazi wrote an encyclopedic oeuvre in Persian titled *Durrat al-tāj* (*Pearl of the Crown*), whose chapter on music came to be the most significant commentary on al-Urmawī's *Risāla al-Sharafiyya*.[1]

Except for Maḥmud Ghāzān (r. 1295–1304), most of the Ilkhanid rulers were ardent patrons of music. Öljaitü (r. 1304–1316) displayed more fondness for the fine arts and wine-drinking than administering his kingdom. Abu Saʿid Bahādor Khān (r. 1316–1335) studied composition and *ʿud* (short-necked lute) playing with his court composer and boon companion, Kamāl Tawrizi. Another famous musician at his court, Neẓām al-Din b. Ḥakim (d. *c.* 1360) was an eminent singer who later continued in favor under Musā Khān (r. 1336–1337) as well (Figure 1.1).[2] The Mongols also developed the custom of accumulating female musicians and dancers in their conquests of various

Figure 1.1 Koyuk (r. 1246–1248) the grandson of Genghis Khān, from a copy of *Tārikh-e jahāngoshā* by ʿAṭā Malek Jovayni. British Museum 1948,1211,0.5.

towns. Likewise, among the tributes they sent along with an envoy on diplomatic missions to another ruler, they often included female performers.[3]

In the first half of the fourteenth century, the Jalāyirids (1335–1432) came to power and promoted various forms of art and literature in the two courts of Tabriz and Baghdad. The most famous ruler of this dynasty, Shaykh Ovays (r. 1356–1377), was a talented painter and musician himself. He patronized the composer Khᵛāja Rażi al-Din Reżvānshāh and the music theorist Shihāb al-Dīn al-Ṣayrafī al-Tabrīzī, who dedicated his treatise on music, *Khulāṣat al-afkār fī maʿrifat al-adwār*, to Shaykh Ovays.[4]

The reign of Solṭān-Ḥosayn Jalāyer (r. 1377–1382) was also a remarkable period in the history of Persian music. He frequently hosted poets and musicians at his court, the most celebrated among whom was the composer and music theorist ʻAbd al-Qāder Marāghi (d. 1435). In *Jāmiʿal-alḥān* (*Compiler of Melodies*), Marāghi relates the story of a courtly musical gathering, referring to the musical figures and specific standards of courtly composition in Tabriz in the second half of the fourteenth century as follows:

> On January 10, 1377, in the city of Tabriz at a courtly gathering of Sultan Jalāl al-Din Ḥosayn Khān b. Sultan Shaykh Ovays, may God illuminate their proof, the Great Shaykh al-Islām Khᵛāja Shaykh al-Kojoji and the grand vizier Amir Shams al-Din Zakariyā and other grandees and learned men of the time were present. Those who wrote commentaries on the *Kitāb al-adwār* and *Sharafiyya* such as Mawlānā Jalāl al-Din Fażlollāh al-ʻObaydi, Mawlānā Saʿd al-Din Kuchak, and Mawlānā ʻOmar Tāj Khorāsāni were also present. The great singers, master composers, and authorities of the time such as the composer Khᵛāja Rażi al-Din Reżvānshāh, Ostād ʻOmarshāh, Ostād Buka, and Nurshāh and other players of wind and stringed instruments were also present at that gathering, discussing both theoretical and practical aspects of music. The composers maintained that the compositional form *par excellence* is the *nawbat-e morattab* and it cannot be composed in the period of less than a month, for each section of the *nawbat*, when composed, needs to be memorized and rehearsed in intervals. Some people said that this is possible when the composer is well-grounded and adept. I said I would compose thirty *nawbat-e morattab*s within one month, God willing. They unanimously maintained that this would be unlikely. I said, now, in this month of Ramażān, I will compose one *nawbat-e morattab* every day and submit it to you. On the day of *ʿarafa* I will ask you to return all thirty *nawbat*s to me, God willing.

> The commentators of the *Kitāb al-adwār* and the masters of the time, especially the eminent Kh^{v}āja Reżvānshāh and the performers of the wind and stringed instruments unanimously maintained that this would be unlikely. Kh^{v}āja Reżvānshāh, who was the master and authority of the time, said he may have composed them in advance and now simply wants to present them. I asked them to choose the verses of *nawbat*s as well as the rhythmic and melodic cycles every day, and I would promise them to compose the *nawbat*s according to their preferred technique (*ṣan'at*) of various forms of modulation (*tarkibāt-e moshakkala*) and present them, provided there would be no objection from their side. Thus, Solṭān-Ḥosayn ordered Shaykh [Kojoji], Amir Zakariyā, Mawlānā Jalāl al-Din Fażlollāh 'Obaydi and Kh^{v}āja Salmān Sāvaji to choose the verses of the *nawbat*s, and also ordered master composers to determine technicalities of melodies and rhythms in collaboration with Kh^{v}āja Reżvānshāh each day.[5]

The above report clearly exhibits the significance of Tabriz as a center of musical activities in the northwest of Iran where the most prominent composers and music theorists of the time, especially those who wrote commentaries on al-Urmawī's *Kitāb al-adwār*, were sustained by the Jalayirid court. The most eminent court composer in this period was Kh^{v}āja Rażi al-Din Reżvānshāh, who once composed a *nawbat-e morattab* incorporating the entire set of twelve *maqām*s, six *āvāza*s, and twenty-four *sho'ba*s.[6] His compositions brought him a tremendous reputation, which lasted many years, until he was eventually outshone by Marāghi, who composed his set of thirty *nawbat*s.

The *nawbat-e morattab* was the most respected form of courtly composition and performance format in this period, consisting of four sections, namely, *qawl*, *ghazal*, *tarāna*, and *forudāsht*.[7] Marāghi also mentions that in his time the *ṭanbur-e shervāniyān*, a two-stringed long-necked lute, was exclusively played in Tabriz, and the rhythmic cycle of *chanbar* was frequently used by the *qavvālān* (probably courtesans) and *moghanniyān* (male musicians) of that city.[8]

Solṭān-Ḥosayn was succeeded by his brother Solṭān-Aḥmad, who ascended the throne in Tabriz in 1382. According to Dawlatshāh Samarqandi, he composed poetry in both Arabic and Persian and was trained in painting, calligraphy, and inlay working. As a student of Marāghi, he had a profound knowledge of music theory and even wrote some essays on this subject. Solṭān-Aḥmad composed several *taṣnif*s that came to be popular with contemporary musicians.[9] Persian and Ottoman song-text collections include some *taṣnifs* attributed to Solṭān-Aḥmad or Solṭān-Aḥmad Baghdādi, which suggests that his compositions continued to be performed as late as the seventeenth century.[10]

In 1383, Timur (r. 1370–1405) began his conquests in Persia. He attacked Tabriz three years later, forcing Solṭān-Aḥmad to flee to Baghdad. While the music schools of Tabriz and Baghdad continued to be active throughout the fifteenth century, Samarqand and—most notably—Herat emerged as other prominent centers of musical patronage (Figure 1.2).

After Timur's conquest of Baghdad in 1393, Marāghi, who was in the service of Solṭān-Aḥmad Jalāyer, was captured and brought all the way to Samarqand, where he served as the distinguished court composer of Timur for five years.[11] Later, in 1398, he returned to Tabriz and resumed his career at the court of Mirānshāh, the third son of Timur, who was by then the governor of Azerbaijan. Mirānshāh took far less interest in administering his territory than in spending time with the inner circle of his intimates and

Figure 1.2 Timur (r. 1246–1248) in a royal ceremony, from the *Ẓafar-nāma*, also called the *Tārikh-e jahāngoshā-ye Timur*. British Library, London MS. IO Islamic 137, f. 326r.

musicians. During his reign, Tabriz once again flourished as an outstanding hub of high caliber performers. Among Mirānshāh's most eminent musicians were Mawlānā Moḥammad Quhestāni, Qoṭb al-Din Nā'i, Ḥabib 'Udi, and 'Abd al-Mo'men Guyanda, who accompanied him frequently on most occasions inside and outside of the court.[12]

In Shiraz, the Inju and Mozaffarid courts vied with Baghdad and Tabriz in their patronage of art and science. Jamāl al-Din Abu Esḥāq Inju (r. 1342–1356) commissioned the Shi'ite mathematician 'Emād al-Din Yaḥyā b. Aḥmad Kāshi to write a commentary on the *Kitāb al-adwār*. Shams al-Din Maḥmud Āmoli (d. 1352) also wrote his encyclopedic *Nafā'is al-funūn fī 'arā'is al-'uyūn* for the same ruler, which contained a chapter on music.[13] Two fourteenth-century books are also associated with the court of Shah Shojā' Moẓaffari (r. 1358–1384), the patron of the great Persian poet, Ḥāfeẓ, yet both texts have been erroneously attributed to Mir Sayyed Sharif Jorjāni (d. 1413). While the first text is a broad commentary on the *Kitāb al-adwār* written by a certain Mobārakshāh, the second is a lexicon of scientific terms titled *Maqālīd al-'ulūm* (*Keys to the Sciences*) that contains a short chapter on music.[14] A prominent musician and composer at the beginning of the fifteenth century in Shiraz was Ḥaydar (1378–1450), who traveled to Syria and Egypt in 1421 where he was known as Ḥaydar al-'Ajami and later became the founder of the Rifā'ī Sufi order.[15] In 1456, Abu al-Fatḥ Pir Budāq, the son of Jahānshāh Qara Qoyunlu (r. 1438–1467), became the governor of Shiraz. He was a poet himself and seems to have maintained a group of male and female musicians at his court (Figure 1.3).

In the second half of the fifteenth century, under the Turkmen Āq Qoyunlus, Tabriz once again rose in stature as an important literary and artistic center. Uzun Ḥasan (r. 1453–1478) and his two sons Khalil and Ya'qub (r. 1478–1490) built splendid monuments in Tabriz and made their court the resort of artists and poets. The most notable ruler of the Āq Qoyunlu dynasty was Sultan Ya'qub, who created the garden of Hasht Behesht (lit. "eight paradises") and patronized many men of letters, including the Herati poet and musician 'Ali b. Moḥammad Me'mār, better known as Bannā'i (d. 1513). Awḥadi Balayāni declares that Sultan Ya'qub wrote a letter to Solṭān-Ḥosayn Bāyqarā in Herat requesting that he send him a roster of accomplished literary figures and leading masters in every field of artistry and knowledge, but instead of all the persons requested, Bāyqarā just sent him Bannā'i, who was a

Figure 1.3 Abu al-Fatḥ Pir Budāq, the governor of Shiraz (1456–1460), sitting under a brightly colored canopy as attendants serve food and musicians and a dancing girl perform in the foreground. Present whereabouts unknown.

polymath and master artist in every possible field.[16] Bannā'i stayed in the court of Sultan Ya'qub until the end of the latter's reign and finished his treatise on music in 1484, which is to say, during his years in Tabriz. According to the Ottoman biographer Qenālizāda, the *'ud* and *chang* (harp) player Zayn al-'Ābedin, who had already served at two Ottoman courts in Amasya and Manisa, later found his way to the court of Sultan Ya'qub.[17] The Bukharian music theorist and biographer Darvish-'Ali Changi further claims that Zayn al-'Ābedin was originally from Anatolia and later studied music in Herat under Darvish Shādi. He also refers to Zayn al-'Ābedin's three *pishraw*s, which were considered ideal models of composition at the time.[18]

The Timurid Period

In the fifteenth century, the city of Herat grew to be the outstanding center of cultural activities in the east of Iran. Before his death, Timur appointed his fourth son, Shāhrokh Mirzā, as the governor of Khorasan (the large historical region in southwest Central Asia) with his administrative capital in Herat. After Timur's death, Shāhrokh (r. 1405–1447) established himself as his father's sole heir, gradually turning Herat into a dazzling metropolis where learning, literature, poetry, painting, calligraphy, and the performing arts became matters of great concern for the rulers. Meanwhile, Marāghi moved to Herat, where he completed much of his writing and eventually died in 1435 (Figures 1.4 and 1.5).[19]

The last Timurid potentate in Herat was Solṭān-Ḥosayn Bāyqarā (r. 1469–1506), who ruled before the invasion of the Uzbeks. During his long reign, he displayed more fondness for calligraphy, painting, poetry, music, dance, and epicurean pleasure in general than for the tedium of administering his kingdom. Together with Mir 'Alishir Navā'i (1441–1501), who served as his advisor and the custodian of the royal seal, he elevated the fine arts to an unprecedented standard of excellence. Early sixteenth-century historical texts such as *Badāyi' al-waqāyi'* (*The Marvels of the Events*) and the *Bābur-nāma* provide ample information about the musical life of Herat at the turn of the sixteenth century, and mention numerous singers, instrumentalists and dancers in the city who were commonly invited to perform at various courtly musical gatherings.

Zayn al-Din Vāṣefi, the author of *Badāyi' al-waqāyi'*, introduces Qāsem-'Ali Qānuni, Chakar Changi, Ostād Sayyed Aḥmad Ghejaki, Moḥebb-'Ali Balabāni, Ostād Ḥasan 'Udi, Ostād Ḥosayni Kuchak Nā'i, Mir Khᵛānanda, Ḥāfeẓ Baṣir, and Maqṣud-'Ali Raqqāṣ as the most celebrated musicians of Herat, who were invited to perform frequently at the court in the late fifteenth and early sixteenth centuries.[20] He further designates a handful of patrons among the nobility and literati who venerated and supported some of these musicians. For instance, the prominent poet and Sufi master of Herat, 'Abd al-Raḥmān Jāmi (d. 1492), was presumably fond of Ostād Sayyed Aḥmad Ghejaki and wrote a *ghazal* praising the physical beauty and musical talent of this performer. Likewise, the Uzbek ruler Moḥammad Shaybāni Khān (r. 1507–1510) was particularly attracted to Moḥebb-'Ali Balabāni and even admired his artistic *balabān* playing in a couplet he wrote for him.[21]

Music was mostly performed in a formal or convivial *majles* at the court or in an exquisite garden. In a formal gathering, the musical setting was much more splendid and the performance was arranged in a sequence of pieces called *faṣl*, rendered on various instruments such as *qānun*, *'ud*, *kamāncha*, and *nay*,

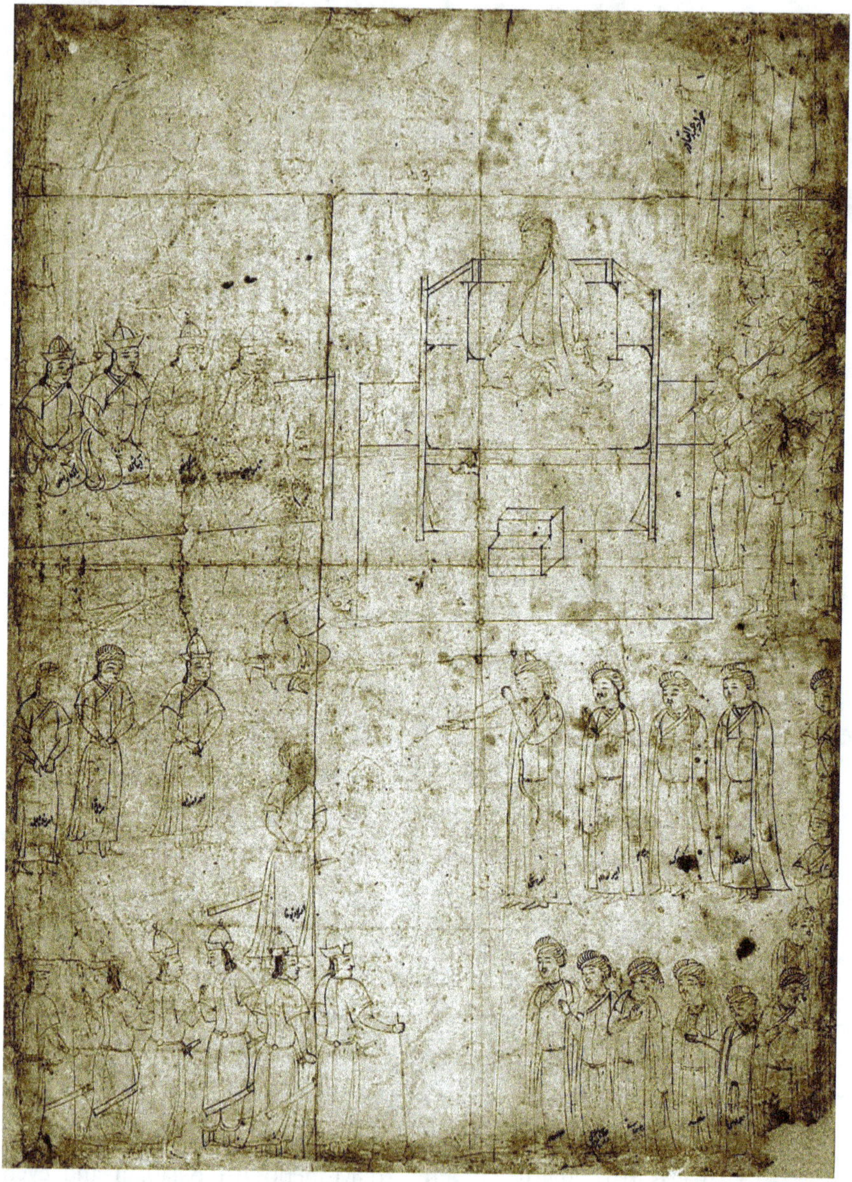

Figure 1.4 Shāhrokh (r. 1405–1447), the son of Timur at his enthronement, with many courtiers and artists, including 'Abd al-Qāder Marāghi. Courtesy of Staatsbibliothek zu Berlin. Preussischer Kulturbestiz, Orientabteilung. MS Diez A. f. 74.

Figure 1.5 Bāysonghor (1397–1433), the son of Shāhrokh. Courtesy of the Topkapı Palace Museum, Istanbul, R. 1022, f. 4.

and accompanied mostly by male singers and dancers. The musical session was often followed by the drinking of wine, the exchange of witticisms, the narration of anecdotes, and the recitation and discussion of poetry.[22]

Dancing was by no means confined to the realm of female performers, for in the second half of the fifteenth century dancing boys were evidently more sought after and renowned than women (Figure 1.6). Vāṣefi mentions Maqṣud-'Ali Raqqāṣ as the most prominent dancing boy who performed at the gatherings of the nobility in the late fifteenth century.[23] He also reports on a musical gathering taking place in Herat right after the accession of the Safavid Shah Esmā'il I (r. 1501–1524) where Ṭāherchaka and Māhchubak were dancing.[24]

Ẓahir al-Din Moḥammad Bābur, the first Mughal emperor, visited Herat in 1506 and later compiled his monumental memoir, the *Bābur-nāma* in which he gives a significant account of scholars, poets, painters, calligraphers, musicians, and composers who were associated with the court of Solṭān-Ḥosayn Bāyqarā. Of the musicians he writes:

> Among the musicians no one could play the *qānun* the way 'Abdollāh Morvārid did, as has been mentioned. There was also Qol-Moḥammad the *'ud* player. He played the *ghaychak* beautifully and added a third string to the instrument. No musicians and instrumentalists composed so many *pishraws* as did he. Even aside from *pishraws*, there are none like him.
>
> Shaykhi Nā'i played both the *'ud* and the *ghaychak* well. From the age of twelve and thirteen on he played the *bāznay* (reed) well. Once, at a gathering at Badi' al-Zamān Mirzā's, he played a composition (*kār*) on the *nay* very well. Qol-Moḥammad, who could not reproduce that composition on the *ghaychak*, said "The *ghaychak* is a deficient instrument." Shaykhi immediately took the *ghaychak* from Qol-Moḥammad's hand and played the composition beautifully, without flaw, on the *ghaychak*. They also related something else about Shaykhi: he had a very good command of melodies such that every time he heard a new melody, he would say that a certain melodic nuance or phrase from another piece is similar to this one. Nonetheless, he did not leave many compositions, only one or two *naqshs* are attributed to him.
>
> Shāh-Qoli was a *ghaychak* player from 'Eraq[-e 'ajam] who came to Khorasan. He played instruments and made admirable progress. He has composed a number of *naqshs*, *pishraws*, and *kārs*.
>
> Ḥosayn 'Udi performed on the *'ud* and sang in a charming style. He could tune all the strings of an *'ud* to one note and play the instrument. His flaw lay

Figure 1.6 A binding of the *Divān* of Amir 'Alishir Navā'i showing him sitting in a garden with the literati and musicians of Herat. Courtesy of the British Library, London, OR. 1374.

> in his reluctance to play. Once Shaybāni Khān ordered him to play. He made a big fuss about it and not only played badly, but also brought not his own instrument but a deficient instrument. Shaybāni Khān caught on and ordered him to be severely beaten right in the assembly. This was the one good thing that Shaybāni Khān did in this world. Really, he did a good thing: such temperamental fellows deserve such punishment.
>
> Among the composers was Gholām Shādi, the son of Shādi the singer. Although he could play instruments well, he was not in the same league as the aforementioned instrumentalists. He came up with decent *ṣawt*s and alluring *naqsh*s. At that time no one composed as many *ṣawt*s and *naqsh*s as he did. In the end, Shaybāni Khān sent him to the Khān of Kazan, Moḥammad Amin Khān. He was never heard from again.
>
> Mir ʿAzzu did not play an instrument, he was a composer. Although he composed very little, what he did compose was charming. Bannāʾi was also a composer who composed decent *naqsh*s and *ṣawt*s.
>
> Another unrivaled figure was Pahlavān Moḥammad Bu Saʿid, an outstanding wrestler who also wrote poetry and composed *ṣawt*s and *naqsh*s. He composed a good *naqsh* in *chahārgāh*. He was good company, and to have such accomplishments and be a wrestler as well is a marvel.[25]

In the second half of the fifteenth century, a few music theorists were also associated with the Timurid court who, one way or another, were all adherents of the theoretical norms established a few decades earlier by Marāghi. In his *Khamsat al-mutaḥayyirīn*, Mir ʿAlishir Navāʾi refers to five music theorists of Herat as follows:

> When I realized that a theoretical treatise needed to be compiled on the art [of music], I commissioned Mawlānā ʿAlishāh Buka, an unrivaled master in this art, to write something on the subject. While, as the result of excessive addiction to opium, he was unable to think and write properly, he composed a book called *Aṣl al-waṣl*. Mir Mortāż and Khᵛāja Shehāb al-Din ʿAbdollāh Morvārid and Mawlānā Bannāʾi also wrote treatises on this art, but since they all strove to boast of their own talents, a novice can hardly gain benefit from their writings. Eventually, Mawlānā [ʿAbd al-Raḥmān Jāmi] who was always gentle and kind to me, wrote a treatise on music and *advār* than which no other treatise is more useful and complete.[26]

ʿAbdollāh Morvārid was a poet, calligrapher, composer and, above all, a celebrated *qānun* player. He received a high-status position at the court of Solṭān-Ḥosayn Bāyqarā and later even took over the post of Navāʾi as the keeper of the great seal.[27] After the Safavid conquest of Herat, ʿAbdollāh Morvārid was treated with the utmost respect by Shah Esmāʿil's officials and he was even offered a prestigious position in the shah's administration, though he rejected the offer.[28] ʿAlishāh Buka Awbahi was a scholar and music theorist of Turkic descent who lived in the second half of the fifteenth century in Herat. He first wrote a more complex musical treatise titled *Uṣūl al-wuṣūl* and later on, mainly at Navā'i's request, compiled his second treatise, called *Muqaddimat al-uṣūl*, which was presumably an abridged version of the former text.[29] ʿAli b. Moḥammad Meʿmār, as mentioned previously, was one of the most famous poets of Herat and wrote a *divān* of *ghazal*s and also composed several *math-navi*s. According to Bābur, his father Ostād Moḥammad was a mason (*bannā*), hence his pen name Bannā'i.[30]

Solṭān-Ḥosayn Bāyqarā died in 1506 and his capital finally fell into the hands of the Uzbek ruler, Moḥammad Shaybāni Khān (r. 1507–1510). Under the Timurids, Herat had reached its cultural apogee, but the sixteenth century would see the beginnings of its gradual decline.

The First Half of the Safavid Period

At the beginning of the sixteenth century, Shah Esmāʿil, the founder of the Safavid dynasty, came to power in Tabriz and proclaimed Twelver Shiʿism to be the official and compulsory religion of Iran. By 1510, he had conquered all of Iran along with Mesopotamia, eastern Anatolia, the eastern Caucasus, southern Dagestan, Armenia, and Khorasan, and had made the Georgian kingdoms of Kartli and Kaketi his vassals.

Shah Esmāʿil was a poet himself who composed Turkish verses under the pen name "Khaṭā'i." At the beginning of his campaign, he received a troop of female court musicians and dancers from Solṭān-Ḥosayn Bāyqarā, but he refused to accept them, claiming that as a defender of Twelver Shiʿism, he did not need to be entertained by such decadent companions. He maintained instead a group of Qizilbāsh musicians called *ozān*s, who performed Turkish *varsāqi* verses and accompanied themselves on the long-necked *chogur*.[31] Besides *varsāqi*, *arasbāri* was another Turkish genre that was vocal by nature but predominantly played on the *chogur*.[32]

In 1510, Shah Esmāʿil marched on a campaign to Khorasan. He defeated Moḥammad Shaybāni Khān and captured Herat, where he became heir to the great literary, artistic, and musical schools of the Timurids. In the wake of his campaign, he brought, among other men of arts and letters, a group of professional Herāti musicians to Tabriz who later played a seminal role in the expansion of Safavid, and subsequently, Ottoman, court music. In 1514, the Ottoman Sultan Selim (r. 1512–1520) set out on a campaign against the Safavids and defeated Shah Esmāʿil at the battle of Chalderan. His troops invaded Tabriz in that year, seized the treasure accumulated by the sovereigns, and carried off 1,000 skilled artists and craftsmen to Istanbul.[33] An important record of payments to musicians (*Cemāʿet-i muṭribān*) that has survived from the reign of Sultan Süleyman (r. 1520–1566) contains the names of musicians who were employed at the court eleven years after Chalderan. The document clearly mentions that a number of musicians had been brought to Istanbul by Sultan Selim and that during the reign of Süleyman, four performers were still active at the court, namely, Şah Kulu (*kamāncha* player), Yusuf bin Saka (singer), Siyahiç (singer), and Hasan (*nay* player).[34] In addition to these, Mawlānā Nāji Kermāni, another Herāti musician and poet, was brought to Azerbaijan and later taken to Istanbul.[35] Likewise, Moḥammad Ḥāfeẓ Eṣfahāni, the eminent muezzin (one who chants the call to prayer) of Tabriz, and his son Ḥasan Jān were both brought to Istanbul, where the latter became the chief of court musicians and the boon companion of both Selim I and Süleyman.[36]

After his defeat at Chalderan, Shah Esmāʿil's spirit changed significantly, and he began spending most of his time either at his court in Tabriz or at his summer encampment in Nakhjavān, where he engaged in hunting, wine-drinking, and the company of male and female entertainers.[37]

Shah Esmāʿil was succeeded by his son, Shah Ṭahmāsb (r. 1524–1576). As crown prince, Ṭahmāsb had studied painting and calligraphy in Herat and was surrounded by some of the most celebrated artists and musicians of his time. In 1533, he made great efforts to endorse *sharīʿa* law, which is to say, he relinquished all worldly pleasures and withdrew his patronage of music.[38] He banned music making of every kind except for the activities of musicians in the *naqqāra-khāna* (the ceremonial and military musical institution of the court) and ordered that anyone who played musical instruments should have a hand cut off.[39] During his reign, court music in Tabriz declined significantly, but Herat, Mashhad, Gilān, Sistān, and Ray remained centers of musical activity where musicians were patronized by Safavid princes and Qizilbāsh governors (Figure 1.7).

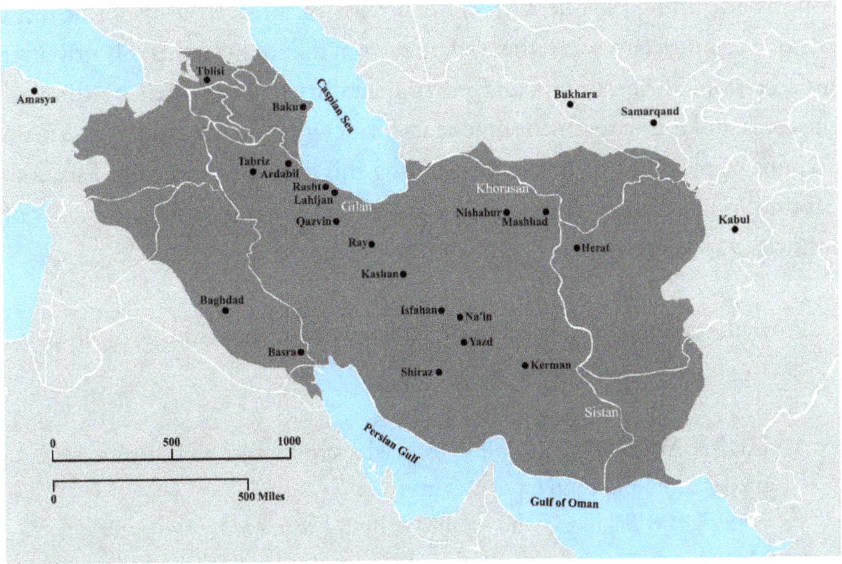

Figure 1.7 Map of the Safavid domains.

For the first half of the sixteenth century, the only account of musicians and musical life in Iran is provided in the *Toḥfa-ye Sāmi*, a *tadhkera* of poets completed in 1550 by Shah Ṭahmāsb's brother, Sām Mirzā (1517–1575). Alongside the poets he chronicles, Sām Mirzā refers to Vaṣli Tabrizi, Ḥāfeẓ Charkin, Mawlānā Ṣadr Khiyābān, and Ḥāfeẓ Majlesi, all of whom were involved in music making in Tabriz.[40]

Qazvin

In 1548, Shah Ṭahmāsb transferred the capital from Tabriz to Qazvin, where the situation for musicians initially deteriorated. He ordered the hanging of Khᵛāja Moḥammad Moqim, the unrivaled *ṭanbur* player in the employ of his son, Ḥaydar Mirzā.[41] Later he ordered the execution of the prominent *qānun* player Ostād Qāsem, who was the boon companion of his son-in-law Ebrāhim Mirzā in Mashhad.[42]

The ban on music expired with the death of Shah Ṭahmāsb and the accession of his son Esmāʿil II (r. 1576–1577). The eighteen-month reign of Esmāʿil II was marked by a serious tide of terror and merciless cruelty unparalleled even by the bloody standards of Safavid history, as he exterminated his brothers and cousins, including the celebrated Ebrāhim Mirzā.[43] Nevertheless, Esmāʿil II's attitude to musicians was rather different from that of his father. Shortly after his accession, all the singers and instrumentalists resumed their positions at the court and music regained some of its former glory in the capital. The main account of musical life in the court during this period comes from Eskandar Monshi in his chapter titled *asāmi-ye moṭrebān va ahl-e naghma* ("names of musicians and entertainers"):

> After the accession of Shah Esmāʿil II, however, musicians began again to gather at court. Among the *guyanda*s were:
>
> 1. [Ḥāfeẓ] Aḥmad Qazvini, who possessed a strong voice and surpassed his predecessors and contemporaries in *guyandagi*.
> 2. Ḥāfeẓ Jalājel Bākharzi, who excelled at both *khvānandagi* and *guyandagi*. He was appointed as the chief of the community of musicians in town (*chālchi-bāshi*) under Shah Esmāʿil II and continued in favor under Shah ʿAbbas I until his eventual death in Qazvin.
> 3. There was also Ḥāfeẓ Moẓaffar Qomi. People maintain that *khvānandagi* is the special forte of Khorasanis, and *guyandagi* is the forte of the people of Iraq. Although Ḥāfeẓ Moẓaffar came from Iraq, he used to do *khvānandagi* in the Khorasani style, in which art he was supreme in Iraq.
> 4. Ḥāfeẓ Hāshem Qazvini, although in the period we are speaking of he was not in the same class as the others, later he came into his own and was elevated in stature by Sultan Ḥamza Mirzā.
>
> Among the *sāzanda*s were:
>
> 1. Moḥammad Kamāncha'i—an unrivaled instrumentalist who played the *ʿud*. In the time of Shah Esmāʿil II, he performed at court and was the best of all.
> 2. Moḥammad Mo'men—an unrivaled *ʿud* player and a peerless instrumentalist whose playing style was distinguished by his sharp plucking and the sweetness and nuances [of his left hand]. Eventually he decided to enter into the service of Khān Aḥmad Gilāni, and he died in Gilān while still a young man.
> 3. Ostād Shāhsavār played the four-stringed *ṭanbur*. He used to brag about his uniqueness, but his playing technique lacked sweetness and character.

4. Ostād Shams Shetorghu'i—a master musician who was also a composer. He served at court during the time of Sultan Ḥamza Mirzā and continued to enjoy favor after the accession of Shah 'Abbas I.
5. Ostād Ma'ṣum Kamāncha'i, his brother, was an unrivaled performer on the *ghaychak*.
6. In the Varāmin district, a group of talented brothers became accomplished players, and the quality of musical entertainment there reached a high level through their efforts.
7. Ostād Solṭān-Moḥammad Tanburi was a skilled performer on the *ṭanbur*. He remained at Mashhad in the service of Sultan Ebrahim Mirza and did not travel elsewhere.
8. Mirzā Ḥosayn Tanburi was the champion *ṭanbur* player in Iraq.
9. Ostād Solṭān-Moḥammad Changi was a skilled *chang* player. Skilled musicians existed in other places too, but this brief list is sufficient.

Of the class of professional storytellers, *shāh-nāma* reciters, and the like, there was a considerable number, but I will just mention two or three:

1. Mawlānā Ḥaydar Qeṣṣa-khᵛān, who was unequaled in his art.
2. Mawlānā Moḥammad Khᵛarshid Eṣfahāni, also a good storyteller but not better than Mawlānā Ḥaydar;
3. Mawlānā Fatḥi, the brother of the preceding, unrivaled *shāh-nāma* reciter whose peerless voice carried—without exaggeration—for several miles, without any loss of quality.[44]

Male singers of the court belonged to two categories: professional *maqām* singers, known as *khᵛānanda*s, and *taṣnif* singers, referred to as *guyanda*s. Eskandar Monshi emphasizes that *khᵛānandagi* was mostly the specialty and domain of singers from Khorasan (eastern Iran), whereas *guyandagi* was more common among the singers of western Iran.[45] *Ḥāfeẓ* was a title often used for respected singers and professional composers of vocal genres. Other categories were *sāzanda* (instrumentalist), *moṣannef* (composer), *raqqāṣ* (dancer), and *qeṣṣa-khᵛān* (storyteller). The ranking of singers was presumably higher than that of instrumentalists, a phenomenon which was common in earlier periods as well.[46]

In the second half of the sixteenth century, another patron of musicians was Ḥamza Mirzā, the nephew of Esmā'il II and the first son of Moḥammad

Khodābanda (r. 1578–1587). When his father ascended to the throne, Ḥamza Mirzā was appointed *vakil* and served at his father's side for almost ten years until his murder in 1586. As a youth, Ḥamza Mirzā studied music with Mir Ṣadr al-Din Moḥammad Qazvini, who came to be his boon companion as well.[47] Two professional musicians, Ḥāfeẓ Hāshem and Ostād Shams Shetorghu'i, were in his service at Qazvin (Figure 1.8).[48]

Of the musicians who were associated with the court of Esmā'il II, none is mentioned as a composer. It is likely that in this period, when it came to court musicians, the ability to perform was more venerated than the ability to compose music. Vocal genres were certainly composed in Qazvin, but the task of composition was mostly the responsibility of poet-musicians. In the chapter on poets, Eskandar Monshi mentions two famous poets, Mir Vālahi Qomi and Mirzā Ḥesābi Naṭanzi, who were also notable for their musical knowledge and their ability to compose *taṣnif*s. Mir Vālahi Qomi was a *sayyed* of Qom who wrote *ghazal*s and vocal compositions in the *qawl* and *'amal* genres.[49] Mirzā Ḥesābi Naṭanzi was originally from Naṭanz, but he resided in Qazvin and his *naqsh*s were popular and performed frequently by the singers of western Iran.[50] Another poet-musician in Qazvin was Ḥarifi Moṣannef (d. 1607), a shoe- and sock-maker who composed *naqsh*s and *ṣawt*s while writing his own verses for his compositions.[51]

There is no reference to the composers of instrumental genres in the accounts of Sām Mirzā and Eskandar Monshi, hence it is not clear to what extent instrumental compositions were composed or even performed at the courts of Tabriz and Qazvin. Other sources attest to the popularity of *pishraw* in Herat and Gilān. Evidently the court repertoire could not have been vocal in its entire format, and it certainly included instrumental compositions of some sort. Nevertheless, even if instrumental compositions were performed at the Safavid courts, performers presumably rendered vocal compositions instrumentally or perhaps drew on the *pishraw*s of Herati musicians.

A remarkable development in the second half of the sixteenth century was the emergence of a circle of scholars in Qazvin engaged in music theory. The circle was associated with Mawlānā Mālek Daylami (d. 1562), a celebrated calligrapher and polymath who excelled in mathematics, geometry, astronomy, and music. He went with Ebrāhim Mirzā to Mashhad and became the head of his atelier (*ketāb-khāna*). Mawlānā Mālek was neither a performer nor a

Figure 1.8 Ḥamza Mirzā entertained. Courtesy of Boston Museum of Fine Arts, 14.587.

composer, yet he is the first person in this period who is identified as a music theorist from the medieval point of view, specializing mostly in sciences of the quadrivium. Furthermore, a handful of individuals associated with him later became celebrated as the best calligraphers, performers, composers, and music theorists of their time.[52] In addition to Ebrāhim Mirzā, who was primarily a pupil of Mawlānā Mālek, two other composer–music theorist–calligraphers—Mawlānā ʿAbd al-Hādi and Mir Ṣadr al-Din Moḥammad—belonged to this circle. They were both major figures in the composition of vocal genres and the establishment of theoretical knowledge in the second half of the sixteenth century in Qazvin. Mawlānā ʿAbd al-Hādi (d. 1569) was Mawlānā Mālek's student as well as his brother-in-law. Mir Aḥmad Monshi refers to him as a seeker of knowledge, an unrivaled scholar of mathematics and music theory, and a remarkable composer of *naqsh*.[53] Mir Ṣadr al-Din Moḥammad Qazvini (d. 1599) was even more renowned than his teacher and played a more distinguished role in the music of the Safavid court.[54] Coming from a family of jurists and literary figures, his grandfather, Qāżi Jahān Qazvini (d. 1553) was the *vakil* of Shah Ṭahmāsb and his father Mirzā Sharaf Jahān (d. 1561) was the court poet laureate.[55] Mir Ṣadr al-Din Moḥammad first served at the court of Sultan Moḥammad Khodābanda (r. 1577–1587) as a calligrapher, painter, poet, and composer, and also as the music tutor of Ḥamza Mirzā, later continuing his services and duties at the court of Shah ʿAbbās (r. 1587–1628).[56] Mir Aḥmad Monshi mentions him as a prolific composer of *ṣawt* and *naqsh*. Eskandar Monshi also confirms that he was a composer known for his novel compositions in the *qawl*, *ʿamal*, *kār*, and *naqsh* genres. According to his own testimony, he was planning to compose a *kolliyāt* (modulatory composition) toward the end of his life, but the weakness of his voice did not permit him to accomplish this task.[57] The most significant accomplishment of Mir Ṣadr al-Din Moḥammad was a treatise on music that he wrote toward the end of his life.

Herat

As the cultural glory of the Timurids began to decline in Herat, professional musicians and composers who had been patronized by the court of Solṭān-Ḥosayn Bāyqarā gradually dispersed and moved to other cities. Yet a group of musicians remained in town and later made significant contributions under the Uzbek rulers and Safavid governors.[58]

Following the Timurid tradition, the Safavid princes were often sent to other provinces to govern in the shah's name.[59] In this case, a Qizilbāsh *amir* was always appointed as the guardian (*lala*) of the prince and it was this guardian who wielded power. More often than not, the prince was accompanied by some of the best calligraphers, artists, poets, and musicians of the time who acted as his tutors. The crown prince was usually sent to Herat, the most important city after the capital. The governorship of Khorasan, and of its capital, Herat, was first in the hands of Prince Ṭahmāsb (1515–1521), but after his accession, his brothers Sām Mirzā (1521–1529 and 1533–1535) and Bahrām Mirzā (1530–1533), and his sons Moḥammad Mirzā (1537–1556 and 1556–1571) and Esmā'il Mirzā (1556), were all appointed to this position. These Safavid princes often had competence in music themselves, but above all they were enthusiastic supporters of musicians, and their continued lavish patronage sustained the musical life of Herat at least until the end of the sixteenth century.

When Sām Mirzā was appointed as the governor of Herat, a few musicians were in his service, including the *nay* player Moḥebb-'Ali.[60] His accounts of musicians in the *Toḥfa-ye Sāmi* also indicate that not only was he familiar with several performers but that he knew music well enough to consider himself a critical listener and to make judgments about these performers' musical skills and performance styles.

In 1530, Bahrām Mirzā became the governor of Herat for almost two years. Sām Mirzā refers to his brother as an unrivaled calligrapher and artist who "sometimes played music and held the *qānun* of talent in his hand," a statement that clearly suggests that the latter was familiar with playing the *qānun*.[61] In Safavid accounts, Bahrām Mirzā is also introduced as the patron of the Qizilbāsh poet-composer Nārenji-Solṭān.[62]

In 1536, Moḥammad Mirzā, later known as Sultan Moḥammad Khodābanda, became the governor of Khorasan and Moḥammad Sharaf al-Din Oghlu Takallu was made his guardian and *amīr al-umarā'*. The prince was sent to Herat where he remained for almost thirty-five years. Ṣādeqi Ketābdār confirms that Moḥammad Mirzā was proficient in painting, composing poetry, and music.[63]

In 1544, the Mughal emperor Homāyun sought asylum in Safavid territory, and after a short stay in Sistān, entered Herat. Upon his arrival, Shah Ṭahmāsb sent a *farmān* (decree) to Moḥammad Sharaf al-Din Oghlu ordering him to show Homāyun the utmost hospitality and to place all the royal facilities, including professional musicians and entertainers, at his disposal at all times.[64] The author of *Afżal al-tawārīkh*, reports that two or three days after the arrival of Homāyun a *majles* was held in his honor in the garden of Zāghān, for which the most eminent musicians of Herat, such as Ṣāber Qāq and Ostād Zaytun, were invited to perform.[65] Abu al-Fażl Mobārak, the author of *Akbar-nāma*, relates what is essentially the same story while emphasizing the musical content of the *majles* in more detail. As Abu al-Fażl relates, in this *majles* Ḥāfeẓ Ṣāber Qāq sang a *ghazal* by Amirshāhi Sabzavāri (d. 1452) in *maqām segāh* that was commensurate with the emotional condition and disposition of Homāyun at the time.[66] The *ghazal* was so powerful that Homāyun "was deeply affected and poured presents into the skirts of his hopes."[67] In another event that took place for the celebration of *nawruz* in the same year (March 21), a ceremony was held in which the nobles and courtiers of Herat offered Homāyun 8,000 *tumāns* as a gift, and subsequently Ṣāber Qāq and Yusof Mawdud Qazvini (another singer), together with Ostād Qāsem, arranged a musical performance for him.[68]

Ḥāfeẓ Ṣāber Qāq appears to have been the most prominent musician of Herat in the mid-sixteenth century.[69] The memory of this musician seems to have remained vivid for more than a century, for Darvish-'Ali Changi, in Bukhara, also wrote highly of his mastery in vocal music.[70] Meanwhile, Ostād Qāsem Qānuni was a renowned *qānun* player and composer who later became the music teacher of Ebrāhim Mirzā, the nephew of Shah Ṭahmāsb. Ostād Shāh-Moḥammad Surnā'i was presumably the *surnā* player of the *naqqāra-khāna* at that time. Finally, the last two musicians, Ostād Yusof Mawdud and Ḥāfeẓ Dust Moḥammad Khᵛāfi, left the city with Homāyun and later continued their careers at the Mughal court in Delhi.[71]

In 1577, Esmā'il II made 'Ali Qoli Khān Shāmlu (d. 1589) the Qizilbāsh *amir* of Herat, and he stayed in that city for several years both as the governor and the guardian of Prince 'Abbās. As an ardent patron of arts and literature, he gathered a number of poets and musicians to his office.[72] His steward (*sofrachi*), Dawra Beg Karāmi, was a composer and music theorist who compiled a treatise on music for his patron, titled *Resāla-ye Karāmiya*. Dawra Beg Karāmi was of Turkish descent, and he also wrote poetry and vocal compositions in both Chaghatai Turkish and Persian.[73]

The Safavids remained in control of Herat throughout the sixteenth and seventeenth centuries, with the notable exception of the period 1588–1598, when the Shaybanid ʿAbdollāh Khān II conquered Khorasan. During the seventeenth century, the city became the Safavid political and military base of operations against the Janid Uzbeks and the Mughals of India for control of Qandahār.[74]

Mashhad

Ebrāhim Mirzā (1540–1577), a son of Bahrām Mirzā and the favorite nephew and son-in-law of Shah Ṭahmāsb, was appointed governor of Mashhad in 1556. Ebrāhim Mirzā was accompanied to Mashhad by the most distinguished calligrapher and music theorist of his time, Mālek Daylami Qazvini, who became the head of his *ketāb-khāna*.[75] It was during this period that Ebrāhim Mirzā may have studied music theory with Mālek Daylami, and also *qānun*-playing with Qāsem Qānuni Herāti, the master *qānun* player of his time.[76] Eskandar Monshi and Qāżi Mir Aḥmad Monshi both mention that Ebrāhim Mirzā was adept at instrument-making (*sāz tarāshi*), as well as composing in the *naqsh*, *ṣawt*, *qawl*, and *ʿamal* genres.[77] Ṣādeqi Ketābdār also refers to one of Ebrāhim Mirzā's vocal compositions that came to be very famous during that time.[78] Ebrāhim Mirzā spent the last eighteen years of his life largely involved in literary and artistic activities in Khorasan. He was ultimately murdered by Esmāʿil II when the latter came to power in 1577.

An ardent patron of musicians, Ebrāhim Mirzā is associated with two outstanding performers of Khorasan, Qāsem Qānuni Herāti and Solṭān-Moḥammad Ṭanburi. Qāsem Qānuni was first active in Herat during the governorship of Moḥammad Mirzā, but later moved to Mashhad in1560 and remained in the service of Ebrāhim Mirzā for the rest of his life as both music teacher and boon companion. In 1571, Shah Ṭahmāsb issued a *farmān* to kill instrumentalists and singers in all cities and singled out Qāsem Qānuni in particular.[79] At this time Ebrāhim Mirzā secretly gave refuge to his teacher and strove to keep him hidden in the cellar of his house. A few days later, Qāsem Qānuni left the basement, only to meet his unfortunate death on the same day.[80] Even at the time Darvish-ʿAli Changi was writing his treatise, Ostād Qāsem Qānuni's reputation as a prolific composer of Mashhad with works in the *pishraw*, *naqsh*, and *ṣawt* forms remained well intact. According to Darvish-ʿAli, of all Qāsem Qānuni's compositions, two *pishraw*s reached a greater degree of popularity than the others: *nāz va ghamza* ("mincing and coquetry"), composed in *ḥosayni* and the rhythmic cycle *dō-yek*, and *davā-ye dard-e saram* ("a cure for the pain in my head") in *ḥejāz* and the rhythmic cycle *fākhta-żarb*.[81]

The second musician, Solṭān-Moḥammad, was a master *ṭanbur* player who remained with Ebrāhim Mirzā during his entire stay in Mashhad. As a composer, Solṭān-Moḥammad Ṭanburi produced a number of *pishraws* and *naqshs* and also trained many disciples, including Amir-Qoli Dōtāri and Moḥammad Ḥosayn 'Udi.[82] Dawra Beg Karāmi ascribes the invention of the rhythmic cycle *żarb al-aṣl* to Solṭān-Moḥammad and declares that he wrote several *pishraws* in that cycle.[83] According to Darvish-'Ali Changi, Solṭān-Moḥammad was put to death by order of 'Abd al-Mo'men Khān Bahādor when he captured Mashhad in 1589.[84]

Gilān

Gilān, a northern province of Safavid territory on the shores of the Caspian Sea, had been divided long before the Safavid period into two principalities comprising eastern and western sections. The eastern section was ruled by the Kārkiyā dynasty, with Lāhijān as their capital, whereas western Gilān, ruled by the Esḥāqvand dynasty, had its capital in the city of Fuman.

From the very beginning of the Safavid period, the Kārkiyā dynasty attracted the most outstanding literary figures, poets, artists, and musicians of the time and hence their provincial court became a center of cultural splendor. During the reign of Sultan Aḥmad Kārkiyā (r. 1506–1534), a few musicians, notably Ostād Dust Moḥammad (d. 1543), were sustained at his court.[85] However, it was in the second half of the sixteenth century under Sultan Aḥmad Kārkiyā's grandson Khān Aḥmad Gilāni (r. 1537–1568) that musical patronage in eastern Gilān really flourished. Khān Aḥmad Gilāni was an unrivaled *'ud* player and composer of *pishraw*. Darvish-'Ali Changi indicates that several *pishraws* of Khān Aḥmad were highly venerated, and Kh^{v}orshāh b. Qobād Ḥosayni confirms that Khān Aḥmad was adept at playing most instruments, as well as having an adequate talent for writing poetry.[86] As a patron of music, Khān Aḥmad was associated with many musicians, including Moḥammad Mo'men 'Udi, Qoli Beg 'Udi, Ostād Zaytun Kamāncha'i, and Ostād Kheżrshāh Sornā'i.[87]

Ostād Zaytun was a highly professional court composer and *kamāncha* player who began his career in Herat and subsequently came to Lāhijān and

Rasht, where he became a *chālchi-bāshi*. At some point, he was appointed as the general of the cavalry (*sepahsālār*) of Tulem, a town in Gilān, but Khān Aḥmad later asked him to return to Rasht and serve at the court.[88] Darvish-'Ali Changi refers to him as a prolific composer of *pishraw*. Together with his brother, Qāsem, they once wrote two separate *pishraws* in *maqām ḥosayni* and the rhythmic cycle *thaqil*, and later combined them into a single piece that they named *chupān-o rama* ("shepherd and the flock").[89]

Moḥammad Mo'men 'Udi, whose father Ostād Ḥosayn 'Udi had been the most eminent *'ud* player of Herat, was another musician employed at the court of Khān Aḥmad Gilāni.[90] He was appointed the *chālchi-bāshi* in Gilān at some point, a position previously held by Ostād Zaytun.[91] According to Eskandar Monshi, Moḥammad Mo'men was an unrivaled *'ud* player whose techniques of right-hand plucking and left-hand fingering were so extraordinary that no one could surpass him.[92]

In the first half of the sixteenth century, western Gilān was ruled by Amira Dobbāj, who later received the title of Moẓaffar Sultan and married the daughter of Shah Esmā'il I. Following Moẓaffar Sultan, his son Sultan Maḥmud ruled western Gilān for some years, but later Khān Aḥmad Gilāni gained control over the entire region. An important music treatise, *Nasim-e ṭarab*, has survived from the sixteenth century and represents a tradition distinct from the mainstream Safavid sources. The treatise is undated, but the author praises his patron in a handful of verses, mentioning the names of both Moẓaffar and Maḥmud.[93]

Sistān

In 1555, Shah Ṭahmāsb dispatched his nephew and son-in-law, Badi'al-Zamān Mirzā, to the Nimruz district of Sistān, where he became the governor until the end of his uncle's reign.

Information about the musical life of Sistān is primarily provided by Malek Shāh-Ḥosayn b. Ghiyāth al-Din Moḥammad, the author of *Iḥyā' al-mulūk* (*The Revival of Kings*). He states that when Badi' al-Zamān Mirzā arrived in Sistān, he asked for four outstanding musicians of Herat—Ḥāfeẓ 'Arab, Ḥāfeẓ Moḥammad Moqim Jibra'ili, Kamāl al-Din 'Udi, and Moḥammad Ḥosayn Ṭanburi—to join him in his court. Celebrated largely for singing in the same style as Ostād Ṣāber Qāq, Ḥāfeẓ 'Arab (d. 1590) was famous for singing 300 lines of *mathnavi* (poetic form) in a high register.[94] Likewise, Ḥāfeẓ Moḥammad Moqim had a warm and rapturous voice and was adept at both *khᵛānandagi* and *guyandagi*.[95] Another singer, Ḥāfeẓ Moḥebb ʿAli, came to Sistān in 1595 and stayed there for seven months.[96] Finally, Malek Shāh-Ḥosayn's brother Malek Maḥmud (d. 1601) was a respected scribe, calligrapher, and poet in the service of Badiʿ al-Zamān Mirzā; he was also proficient in both music theory and practice and played the *kamāncha* and *ṭanbur* equally well.[97]

Ray

Ray was the birthplace of a number of poets, singers, and composers during the sixteenth century. Nonetheless, the existence of an institution supporting musicians in this city is doubtful.[98] In the first half of the sixteenth century, Sām Mirzā mentions the poet Ghafuri from Ray who had a solid grounding in singing as well.[99] In the second half of the sixteenth century, Ray emerges as a more prolific center of musical activity. During this period, Mosayyeb Khān Takallu, son of Moḥammad Khān Sharaf al-Din Oghlu and nephew of Solṭānom (Shah Ṭahmāsb's wife), was the Qizilbāsh *amir* of this city. He was a poet, calligrapher, and composer of note whose compositions acquired a considerable reputation during that period.[100] Two renowned composers of Ray in this period were Qāżi ʿAbdollāh Rāzi and Mir Sadid Rāzi, who had a lively musical rapport with the court musicians of Qazvin.[101]

Kāshān and Naṭanz

Kāshān was home to many poets and literary figures, including the eminent panegyrist Moḥtasham Kāshāni (1528–1588). Many sixteenth-century writers of *qaṣida*s and *ghazal*s are mentioned in the *Toḥfa-ye Sāmi* as natives of Kāshān, with some remaining in that city and others relocating to Tabriz or Qazvin, where they achieved considerable fame through the royal patronage of the Safavid princes and sovereigns. One of the outstanding poets of the second half of the sixteenth century was Mirzā Ḥesābi Naṭanzi, who received his early education in Kāshān and subsequently went to Qazvin. He had a thorough knowledge of most sciences of his time, including medicine, mysticism, and music. While Eskandar Monshi refers to Mirzā Ḥesābi Naṭanzi as a celebrated composer of *naqsh*, Taqi Kāshi mentions him as a composer of the more complex vocal genres of *kār* and *'amal*.[102] Another eminent musician of Kāshān in the late sixteenth century was Mollā Afżal Dōtāri, a student of Mirzā Ḥesābi Naṭanzi, who was renowned as an unparalleled player of *dōtār* and *chahārtār* (long-necked lutes) in Kāshān and Naṭanz. As a follower of the Noqṭavi Messianic movement, Mollā Afżal Dōtāri was eventually accused of heresy and persecuted by Qizilbāsh officers in 1586.[103]

Table 1.1 The sixteenth-century composers mentioned in Safavid *tadhkira*s

Composer	Place of Origin	Patrons/Active Period
Nārenji-Solṭān	Tabriz	Bahrām Mirzā
Vaṣli	Tabriz	first half of 16th century
Ḥāfeẓ Charkin	Tabriz	first half of 16th century
Ebrāhim Mirzā	–	–
'Āsheqi	Khorasan	–
Qāsem Qānuni	Herat	Ebrāhim Mirzā
Solṭān-Moḥammad Ṭanburi	Herat	Ebrāhim Mirzā
Khān Aḥmad Gilāni	Gilān	–
Ostād Zaytun	Herat (active in Gilān)	Khān Aḥmad Gilāni
Mawlānā Rashki	Hamadān (active in Qazvin)	second half of 16th century
Mir Vālahi	Qom (active in Qazvin)	second half of 16th century
Mirzā Ḥesābi	Naṭanz (active in Qazvin)	second half of 16th century
Mir Ṣadr al-Din Moḥammad	Qazvin, Isfahan	Ḥamza Mirzā, Shah 'Abbās I
Moṭrebi Qazvini	Qazvin	Shah 'Abbās I
Ḥarifi	Qazvin	late 16th/early 17th centuries

The Second Half of the Safavid Period

In 1587, Shah 'Abbās I, the grandson of Shah Ṭahmāsb, ascended the throne in Qazvin and subsequently made significant reforms in the implementation of social policies and in fiscal planning in Iran. He restored the country's preeminent position in international trade; reasserted its political supremacy over its neighbors; and encouraged justice throughout the land and learning among its inhabitants. Upon his accession, he put an end to the military domination of the Qizilbāsh Turkmen tribes and made peace with the Ottomans and Uzbeks.

Among all the Safavid shahs, Shah 'Abbās I was the most distinguished patron of arts and culture, most strikingly in architecture, but also, albeit to a lesser degree, in music making. An ardent connoisseur of music, Shah 'Abbās reportedly possessed a decent competence himself, both as a performer and composer. Evidence of Shah 'Abbās' musical acumen is provided by different sources. His secretary Eskandar Monshi, for instance, reports that in the composition of *qawl* and *'amal*, the shah was celebrated above everyone else.[104] Another contemporary historian, Awḥadi Balayāni (1565–1631), admired Shah 'Abbās' talent in composing songs and stated that he "reached in music to such a level that all the composers of his time were keen to learn his style."[105] While these statements seem like sheer exaggeration, they show that the shah must have had some interest in composing melodies. In the Ottoman song–text collection of Hâfiẓ Post a *naqsh* has survived which is attributed to Shah 'Abbās.[106]

At the beginning of the reign of Shah 'Abbās, Ḥāfeẓ Jalājel Bākharzi was the chief of the community of musicians in Qazvin and later joined the circle of the close companions of the shah.[107] Other singers, including Ḥāfeẓ Hāshem Qazvini and Ḥāfeẓ Moẓaffar Qomi, were also active at the court. Of the instrumentalists, Eskandar Monshi reported only that Shams Shetorghu'i, a composer and master *shetorghu*-player in the service of Hamza Mirzā, continued to enjoy patronage under Shah 'Abbās.[108] Likewise, Moṭrebi Qazvini, a gifted musician who often attracted the inhabitants of Qazvin to his small shop by composing and performing *taṣnif*s, achieved recognition as a court composer.[109]

Isfahan

Shah 'Abbās transferred his seat of power to Isfahan in 1598 and soon after began to make great efforts to establish a centralized state in Iran. He reformed his armed forces by creating a standing army and abolishing the autonomy of tribal leaders. He also transferred 3,000 Armenian families and 20,000 Georgians to Isfahan, and soon this new population with its skills in various crafts and mercantile expertise made a significant contribution to the economic and cultural life of the new capital. Notably, Shah 'Abbās called on the services of the architects and artists from this population to develop a specifically Safavid style of architecture and urban planning in Isfahan.

Historical sources in this period refer to various groups of performers, including professional court musicians as well as urban musicians and entertainers, who were presumably active in public places such as *sharāb-khānas* (taverns), *bayt al-lotfs* (brothels), *qomār-khānas* (gambling houses), *qavvāl-khānas* (courtesan houses), and coffeehouses.

Earlier in the reign of Esmā'il II, court music was revived and all performers, including master male musicians, musicians of the *naqqāra-khāna*, courtesans, dancers, and entertainers, came to be supervised by a chief musician called the *chālchi-bāshi*, who was usually selected from among the most celebrated singers (*ḥāfeẓes*) or court composers. The *Dastur al-moluk*, a manual of the Safavid government, describes the character of the *chālchi-bāshi* in the following words:

> He is the white-bearded elder (*rishsefid*) of the entire community of performers and musicians and responsible for training a group of musicians, singers, and instrumentalists qualified and adept at performing at the gatherings of the shahs. He is required to be present in the service of the shah when he is traveling as well as when he is resident at his court. The salaries and stipends of the *chālchi-bāshi*'s subordinates are paid in accordance with his suggestion and the approval of his excellency, the *nāẓer-e boyutāt* and pending the grand vizir's consent. He receives 50 *tumāns* as annual salary from the custom revenues (*'oshur*).[110]

Ḥāfeẓ Jalājel Bākharzi remained in the office of *chālchi-bāshi* for a few decades and was succeeded by Āqā Ḥaqqi, who, as Pietro Della Valle confirms, came to be the *chālchi-bāshi* and superintendent of courtesans.[111] In the early seventeenth century, three singers, Efendi Khᵛānanda, Ḥāfeẓ Thāni, and Ḥāfeẓ Jāmi, were employed at the court. In 1608, Shah 'Abbās ordered houses to be built for them in an Isfahan neighborhood that would come to be known as the *maḥalla-ye naghma* (the musicians' quarter).[112] Among the court instrumentalists was Mawlānā Aḥmad, a *kamāncha* player, who had earlier been in the service of Akbar in India but later moved to Isfahan, where he became a court musician to Shah 'Abbās.[113]

Shah 'Abbās not only patronized musicians lavishly but occasionally appointed them to court offices, a practice that was uncommon among his predecessors. One musician who received great recognition in this period was Mir Fayżollāh (d. 1610), who, Eskandar Monshi relates, Shah 'Abbās I elevated to the position of vizier of *gholāmān* (servants).[114]

The main *tadhkera* of poets containing references to composers in the first half of the seventeenth century was written by Moḥammad Ṭāher Naṣrābādi (1617–1677). The author introduces 1,000 poets and provides samples of their poetry up until the end of the reign of Shah Solaymān (r. 1666–1694). Naṣrābādi particularly specifies Shāh-Morād Moṣannef and Madhāqi Nā'ini as the two outstanding court composers in the first half of the seventeenth century, as well as many subsequent court composers who also achieved recognition as poets.

Shāh-Morād Moṣannef, a native of Khᵛānsār, was the most celebrated composer at Shah 'Abbās I's court in Isfahan. He was a versatile composer who wrote his own verses for his compositions, and who composed in all vocal genres, but most conspicuously in *qawl* and *'amal*. Shāh-Morād once composed a modulatory *taṣnif* in the three modes of *dōgāh*, *nawruz*, and *ṣabā* that found favor at the court and brought him remarkable fame and rewards.[115] Some compositions in Demetrius Cantemir's collection are attributed to Shāh-Morād, though an authoritative musicological monograph on Ottoman music misattributes them to Sultan Murad IV (r. 1623–1640).[116]

Madhāqi Nā'ini was a draper (*bazzāz*) by profession. He came to Isfahan during the reign of Shah 'Abbās I and acquired tremendous fame for his fine vocal compositions.[117] Awḥadi Balayāni declared that "from Nayshābur to Irāq and Ḥejāz, and from Tabriz to Isfahan and Nehāvand, he was superior to all musicians."[118] Naṣrābādi introduces Madhāqi Nā'ini as a composer of *ṣawt* and *'amal* and gives a sample of his Persian poems.[119] Amir Khān Gorji also records one of his vocal compositions set to a Turkish text, suggesting that Madhāqi must have composed both Persian and Turkish *taṣnif*s.[120]

Āqā Mo'men was another composer and music theorist who entered the court of Shah 'Abbās I around 1622, and he remained the most celebrated *moṣannef* and the head of the community of musicians through the entire reign of Shah Ṣafi (r. 1629–1642) and the first phase of the reign of Shah 'Abbās II (r. 1642–1666). During his career at the court, he accompanied the shahs on their many expeditions as well as to their summer quarters, and wrote at least fifty-four vocal compositions for different courtly occasions. Among his compositions are fourteen laudatory songs that he wrote in praise of his patrons and also five victory songs that he composed after the capture of neighboring regions. Āqā Mo'men's entire collection of *taṣnif*s and his musical treatise have survived as part of the codex of Amir Khān Gorji, an established composer during the reign of Shah Solaymān, and probably earlier. A few instrumental compositions attributed to Āqā Mo'men are also included in the collection of Demetrius Cantemir; these were most likely vocal compositions later turned into *pishraws*.[121]

Among the most celebrated composers active in the coffeehouses of Isfahan was Shams Tishi. He was originally from Shiraz but later came to Isfahan and found his own way to the court of Shah 'Abbās I, who eventually bought a coffeehouse and tavern for him in the Chahārbāgh district.[122] Naṣrābādi venerates Shams Tishi as a great composer of *ṣawt* and *'amal*, who once set a *ghazal* of Amir Khosraw Dehlavi to the mode *bayāt* and the rhythmic cycle *samā'i*.[123] Amir Khān Gorji also included a composition by Shams Tishi in his collection of *taṣnifs*.[124]

Another renowned composer and music theorist was 'Abd al-Bāqi Nā'ini (d. *c.* 1658), better known by his pen name Bāqiyā. He grew up in Nā'in, spent some years in Isfahan, Mashhad, and Herat, and subsequently migrated to India in 1614, where he stayed in the service of Jahāngir (r. 1605–1627) and Prince Khorram (later crowned as Shāhjahān) for several years and also wrote a music treatise titled *Zamzama-ye vaḥdat* (*Murmur of Unity*).[125] During his stay in India, Bāqiyā Nā'ini studied *rāgs* and, following in the footsteps of Indian and Persian composers as well as his brother Fatḥi, composed many *rikhtas* and *naqshs*.[126]

Fatḥi Moṣannef or Fatḥā (his pen name) was the brother of Bāqiyā Nā'ini. He accompanied his brother to India where he made a reputation as a composer. In his codex, Amir Khān Gorji mentions a *taṣnif* by Fatḥā set to a text in four languages.[127]

Two other court composers, Mir Ṣawti (d. 1669) and Ṣāber Shirāzi, received significant recognition in this period. Mir Ṣawti, a composer of *naqsh* and *'amal*, was in the service of Shah 'Abd al-Baqā, the local governor of his home town, Yazd; he later went to Isfahan where he found his way to the court of 'Abbās II.[128] Ṣāber Shirāzi was also a humble poet-composer with an engaging and easy-going temperament whose character was manifested in his delicate compositions. He moved to India where he died in the 1660s.[129]

Amir Khān Gorji also included compositions of some other seventeenth-century composers, among them Ḥabibā Tanbāku-forush (a tobacco seller by profession), Aḥmad, 'Ayshi, Ebrāhim Golpāyegāni, Moẓaffar Golpāyegāni, Sharif Hamadāni, and Ḥāfeẓ Moḥammad Kāẓem.[130] Moḥammad Kāẓem was the *chālchi-bāshi* of Isfahan at some point and he set his compositions to both Persian and Turkish verses.[131] Ebrāhim Golpāyegāni was the nephew and presumably a disciple of Shāh-Morād Moṣannef in mid-seventeenth century Isfahan.[132]

Throughout the sixteenth and seventeenth centuries, Baṣra was intermittently under the control of the Safavid court, and there seem to have been close cultural affinities among Qazvin, Isfahan, and Baṣra. Around the turn of the sixteenth century, a group of musicians and composers were gathered in the local court of the Ottoman governor, 'Ali Pāshā, who was himself a musician and composer. Amir Khān Gorji records a few *taṣnifs* composed by 'Ali Pāshā, Shaykh 'Abd al-'Ali Baṣri, Ḥabibollāh Baṣri (a disciple of 'Abd al-'Ali Baṣri), and Ḥasan Chalabi, clearly indicating that at the beginning of the eighteenth century, these compositions were still known in Isfahan.[133]

Another highly accomplished composer in the early seventeenth century was Jalāl Beg Moṣannef, whose compositions, according to Awḥadi Balayāni, were frequently sung and transmitted orally by people in public.[134]

Table 1.2 The seventeenth-century composers whose compositions or names are mentioned in the codex of Amir Khān Gorji

Composer	Place of Origin	Patrons	No. of Compositions
'Ali Pāshā	Baṣra		1
Shāh-Morād	Khᵛānsār	'Abbās I	–
Madhāqi	Nā'in	'Abbās I	1
Shams Tishi	Shiraz	'Abbās I	1
Āqā Mo'men	Isfahan	'Abbās I, Ṣafi, 'Abbās II	54+5
Shaykh 'Abd al-'Ali	Baṣra	–	2
Ḥabibollāh	Baṣra	–	1
Ḥasan Chalabi	–	–	1
Aḥmad	–	–	1
Ḥabibā	–	–	1

Composer	Place of Origin	Patrons	No. of Compositions
ʿAyshi	–	–	1
Ebrāhim	Golpāyegān	–	1
Moẓaffar	Golpāyegān	–	1
Sharif	Hamadān	–	2
ʿAbd al-Bāqi (Bāqiyā)	Nā'in	–	1
Fatḥi (Fatḥā)	Nā'in	–	1
Mir Ṣawti (d. 1669)	Yazd	ʿAbbās II	5
Ṣāber (d. 1660s)	Shiraz	ʿAbbās II	2
Ḥāfeẓ Moḥammad Kāẓem	–	Solaymān	4
Morteżā-Qoli Beg	Georgia	Solaymān, Solṭān-Ḥosayn	1
Amir Khān Gorji	Georgia	Solaymān, Solṭān-Ḥosayn	10

The *qahva-khānas* (coffeehouses) were also major venues for the cultivation of sung poetry, music, and dance in the capital and other urban centers. Eskandar Monshi mentions a few *qeṣṣa-khᵛāns* and *shāh-nāma-khᵛāns* (reciters of Ferdawsi's *Shāh-nāma*) who were active in Qazvin in the second half of the sixteenth century.[135] In the early seventeenth century, the number of storytellers and *shāh-nāma-khᵛāns* increased significantly in Isfahan, and Shah ʿAbbās I reportedly visited coffeehouses where he was entertained by such performers.[136]

Earlier, in the first half of the sixteenth century, the Safavids had begun to expand their territories by conquering the Caucasus. Shah Esmāʿil I sacked Baku in 1501 and captured Armenia and Dagestan between 1500 and 1502. While the wars with the Ottomans continued throughout the reign of Shah Ṭahmāsb, the cities of Shamākhi, Ganja, and Baku were later occupied by the Ottomans in the 1580s. Shah ʿAbbās managed to repel the Ottomans and recapture the entire Caucasus in 1603–1604 and 1616, and meanwhile imported up to 300,000 Caucasians into Iran. To diminish the Qizilbāsh's capacity to interfere in internal affairs, he continued the policy instituted by his predecessors of fully integrating the Caucasus and its various groups into Persian society.

He did so largely by creating substitute military and administrative elites. He raised the profile of the *gholām* institution and gave thousands of Georgians, Armenians, and Circassians positions in the royal house, civil administration, and military, where they served to counterbalance the Qizilbāsh as members of a standing army answerable directly to the shah himself.

Throughout the seventeenth century, the influence of Caucasian men and women was conspicuous at the Safavid court. The harem also became a multicultural environment where the queen, wives, concubines, and ladies-in-waiting were predominantly Georgian or Circassian. At the same time, Georgian, Armenian, and Circassian concubines and courtesans became major exponents of dance and acrobatics both inside and outside the court. Antonio de Gouvea, a Portuguese cleric who visited the court of Shah ʻAbbās I in 1603, reports that he was entertained by a group of eight Circassian female dancers.[137]

Shah ʻAbbās I was succeeded by his grandson, Shah Ṣafi (r. 1629–1642), whose mother was a Georgian woman. While Shah Ṣafi lacked the cultural sophistication and intellectual character of his grandfather, he displayed much fondness for smoking opium, meaning that the administration of his kingdom was largely left in the hands of a Tabrizi eunuch, Mirzā Moḥammad Taqi, better known as Sāru Taqi (1579–1645). The latter was appointed grand vizier in 1634 and subsequently became a significant patron of Georgian musicians and dancers.[138] During the reign of Shah Ṣafi, Āqā Mo'men was the *chālchi-bāshi* of Isfahan and composed more than forty *taṣnifs* for the celebration of various occasions, including the shah's coronation and the conquest of many regions.[139] The most prominent musician at the court of Shah Ṣafi was Ostād Moḥammad Mo'men, better known as Ḥāfeẓak. He was a singer and *ṭanbur* player who had earlier performed at the court of Shah ʻAbbās as well.[140]

In 1637, Shah Ṣafi received a trade delegation from Frederick II, Duke of Holstein-Gottorp, accompanied by the German mathematician and scholar Adam Olearius and a group of musicians. According to Olearius, the musicians, including performers on violin, bass-viol (viola da gamba), and bandore, together with a vocalist arrived in Isfahan in August of the same year after a long stay in the city of Shamākhi.[141] These musicians were received with admiration at the court and their images were depicted above the main entrance to the Qayṣariya bazaar in Isfahan; where they have survived to this day (Figure 1.9).

When ʿAbbās II (r. 1642–1666) came to the throne, he was only ten years old, hence his Circassian mother and his grand vizier, Sāru Taqi, assumed the role of regents, taking charge of governing the kingdom. Āqā Mo'men continued to be the most distinguished composer at the court and wrote at least seven *taṣnifs* for ʿAbbās II. Naṣrābādi also refers to Ṣafi Qoli Beg Eṣfahāni, a poet and player of the *ṭanbur-e chahārtār* (four-stringed lute) during the reign of ʿAbbās II, whose father had been *chāvosh* (chief herald) at the court of Shah ʿAbbās I (Figure 1.10).[142]

Jean Chardin (1643–1713) mentions the house of a group of Indian wind instrument and gigantic drum performers who were brought to Isfahan by ʿAbbās II after his conquest of Qandahār in 1648.[143]

The next ruler, Shah Solaymān (r. 1666–1694), was the son of a Circassian woman and was raised in the seraglio surrounded by the ladies of the

Figure 1.9 European musicians sent to the Safavid court from Frederick II, Duke of Holstein-Gottorp, whose images were depicted on the top of the main entrance to the Qayṣariya bazaar in Isfahan.

Figure 1.10 Shah ʿAbbas II (r. 1642–1666) and his courtiers. Courtesy of Institute of Aga Khan Museum, Toronto, AKM 110.

harem and Georgian eunuchs. Although little interested in administration, he was a great patron of the arts—specifically, painting and music. Two Georgian *gholāms*, Amir Khān Gorji and Morteżā-Qoli Beg, were prominent court composers in this period. The latter additionally served as keeper of the royal cellars.[144] Naṣrābādi also refers to Ḥāfeẓ Moḥammad Taqi, known as *ʿAndalib-e Kāshi* (nightingale of Kāshān), who was a court singer in this period. Likewise, among the instrumentalists were Samandar, a *kamāncha* player, and Ṭāher, who was celebrated both as a *chahārtār* player and composer (Figure 1.11).[145]

European travelers who visited Isfahan in the second half of the seventeenth century often offered significant information about the settings and performance practices of music at the court. In his official banquets and audiences, ʿAbbās II often requested the company of European residents of the city—people who represented Western nations or trading companies. On one occasion Daulier Deslandes (1621–1715), a French merchant who arrived in Isfahan in late 1664, indicated that several French and Dutch guests were invited to a gathering at the court, which began at nine in the

Figure 1.11 Shah Solaymān (r. 1666–1694) with attendants serving food and drink while musicians perform in the foreground. The Trustees of Chester Beatty Library, CBL Per 279, f.90r.

morning with wine-drinking. Here is his description of the entertainers at that gathering:

> The royal entourage passed by, engaged in the debauchery to be expected from a king who was so feared. The musicians did their best with lutes of various sorts, which they strummed nicely, and their one-string violins, with which they accompanied their voices, which were not at all unpleasant. A troupe of dancers who were in the paid service of the king, entertained the company with dances, in the manner of intermission performances at the theater. They danced in circles of perhaps seventeen or eighteen, performing nicely, and well dressed. They didn't join hands but performed a variety of gestures with their hands and bodies. Their voices were in tune with the instrumentalists and their steps were regulated by the sounds of a great tambourine, which an old woman seated off to the side beat slowly. There was also a small Georgian who was playing a harp not at all badly, and an Armenian who was making plenty of noise on an organ that had been given to the king.[146]

The French missionary and traveler N. Sanson, who visited Isfahan in the reign of Shah Solaymān, observed that during audiences, the heads of state, military leaders, diplomats, and directors of European trading companies and musicians were all seated in differing positions and varying proximity to the shah, while musicians were placed separately and were only assigned the duty of entertaining the invitees:

> E'temād al-Dawla (grand vizier) sits in the first row on the king's left side, which is the position of honor in Persia. The general or commander in chief of the army sits on the king's right side, and after him the viziers, *vālis*, *khāns*, ambassadors and the guests of the shah all sit in parallel rows one after another down the hall. The musicians form another row, sitting in a section of the hall across from the king's throne. Their musical performance continues throughout the audience preceding the mealtime, and they do this on purpose so that the invitees do not hear what is being discussed with the king. The forty ceremonial guards also stand with their sticks, preventing the invitees from seeing clearly what is happening in the audience hall.[147]

The German naturalist and physician Engelbert Kaempfer (1651–1716), who, in 1683, was offered the post of secretary to the Swedish ambassador to Iran, is more specific about the ensemble of court musicians and their instruments during the reign of Shah Solaymān:

> Among the locals there were 22 officials of medium rank, regular guests of royal feasts. Further, some *satrapes*, or governors and heads of cities, as well as men who had been recalled from these places for discussions. On the transversal row were seated, on each side of the entrance, 15 musicians and in this way their row was bisected and divided into two choirs. They played an unfamiliar music, alternating the flutes, cymbals and several types of string instruments, sometimes accompanied by a drummer who played lightly with one finger, more seldom a human voice sang. If you expect a judgment of the music? It was noise rather than music that did not respect any rule of harmony, but still it was neither without refinement nor charm. If I leave aside the voice, this music was rather charming and muffled so as not to hamper conversations and discussions in the Assembly, and yet still able to charm the ears and the hearts of the guests by the unfamiliar charm of its mixed sounds.[148]

Chardin reports that the instrumentalists found throughout the capital were poor and mostly dressed in rags except for those who were employed at the court and supervised by the *chālchi-bāshi*.[149] Overall, the social status of court musicians was presumably higher than that of regular musicians across the capital, but it was significantly lower than that of musicians in the preceding Timurid or Jalayirid periods. At the court of the Jalayirids in Tabriz, composers and musicians enjoyed a respected status and collaborated closely with the elite circle of the court, which included poets, literary figures, and members of the *'ulamā'*. In the second half of the seventeenth century, however, the attitude of the Shi'ite *'ulamā'* was conspicuously hostile toward music—evident from the body of literature condemning the performance practice of music and dance in this period.[150] Chardin further indicates that at court banquets, clerics used to leave the audience hall whenever musicians entered.[151]

Outside the court, music and dance were largely performed by male and female performers in coffeehouses and other public places such as taverns, houses for smoking hashish, gambling houses, courtesan salons, and brothels. The Italian traveler Pietro Della Valle (1586–1652) stated that dancing boys in women's clothes and accompanied by frame drummers frequently performed Persian, Uzbek, and Tatar dances in coffeehouses, where they were also engaged in "games" that incited the customers' libidinous desires.[152] Chardin described coffeehouses as places where one was served and entertained by attractive Georgian boys aged between ten and sixteen, dressed in lascivious women's clothes with their long hair let down (Figure 1.12). These places, so Chardin claimed, were veritable houses of sodomy that filled wise and virtuous people with horror.[153] In other public places, most notably, courtesan salons and brothels, music and dance were performed by courtesans and female entertainers who often had male or female accompanists.

In the second half of the seventeenth century, the influence of the Caucasus on Safavid court music was undoubtedly much greater than were the Timurid and Āq Qoyunlu models in the sixteenth century. Moreover, the *shetorghu* (a long-necked lute) and *chang* were no longer in vogue in Isfahan. In their place, a new set of instruments, including the *chahārtār*, *sanṭur* (hammer dulcimer), and *ṭuṭak* (small wooden flute), was introduced to the Safavid court. An organ was also sent as a gift to the court of 'Abbās II by the Russian ambassador and was used during the reign of Shah Solaymān as well.[154]

Armenian and Georgian male instrumentalists certainly played an important role in music making in both urban and rural centers, yet their affinities

Figure 1.12 Two Georgian dancing boys, Isfahan, 1654. The Trustees of Chester Beatty Library, Dublin, CBL. In 47.14.

with the Safavid court or the courtesan communities are not clearly mentioned in surviving documents. Nevertheless, one unique source of evidence indicating the existence of Armenian instrumentalists and their expertise is the presence of their tombstones in the New Julfa cemetery in Isfahan. Exquisitely designed, each tombstone contains an image of the musician together with the instruments on which he was adept. Instrumentalists whose tombstones survive include Hovasap (d. 1712), a performer of *kamāncha* and *surnā*; Tāsāle (d. 1732), the son of Megerdom and performer of *kamāncha*, *naqara*, *surnā*, and *dohol*; Ghul-Egāz (d. 1734), an *ʿāsheq* (bard) who played the *ṭanbur*; and Zādur (d. 1741), the son of Shamir and performer of *sanṭur*, *kamāncha*, and *surnā* (Figures 1.13 and 1.14).[155]

The last Safavid ruler, Shah Solṭān-Ḥosayn (r. 1694–1722), eventually submitted himself to the demands of religious authorities and theologians, especially his famous chaplain, Moḥammad Bāqer Majlesi (1627–1699), and issued royal decrees forbidding wine-drinking, gambling, the sport of pigeon racing, and ultimately limiting the performance of music.[156] Music making

Figure 1.13 Tombstones of two Armenian musicians, Zādur (d. 1741) and Hovasap (d. 1712) in the New Julfa cemetery in Isfahan. Photographs by Samvel Karapetyan, 2009.

Figure 1.14 Drawings of the above tombstones made by Abraham Gurgenian (1908–1991). Courtesy of Vank Cathedral in Isfahan.

was retained as part of the court service for much of the first half of the eighteenth century, but the performance of music in public places was reduced in many respects. Performers and composers of art music in this period frequently became members of various bureaucracies within the court and were no longer musicians employed under the supervision of the *naqqāra-khāna*. Nevertheless, in 1697, Shah Solṭān-Ḥosayn commissioned Amir Khān Gorji, a former Georgian servant at his court, to collect the repertoire of *taṣnif*s that had mostly been composed throughout the seventeenth century at the courts of his predecessors.[157]

Gilān

In the middle of the seventeenth century, Lāhijān emerged once again as a conspicuous center of cultural activities where a number of poets and musicians were supported by local dignitaries. The patron of poets and musicians in this period was a certain Mirzā ʿAbdollāh, the vizier. Naṣrābādi mentions Moḥammad Qoli Salim (d. 1647) as a prominent poet and Mollā Vāṣeb and Ḥosaynā (d.1687) as two musicians who were in his circle.[158] Mollā Vāṣef was a poet and musician originally from Qandahār who moved back and forth between Isfahan and Lāhijān. He had an in-depth knowledge of music and a captivating voice when performing *dōbaytis* (a musical genre).[159] Ḥosaynā was first a dervish in Khᵛānsār who spent some time in Tabriz before eventually moving to Lāhijān with Mollā Vāṣef, where he served at the local court of Mirzā ʻAbdollāh. He was adept at playing the *ṭanbur-e chahārtār* and reciting the *Shāh-nāma* and the story of Ḥamza. As a poet, he wrote his poems mostly in the *mathnavi* form.[160]

Musical Life in the Eighteenth Century

The invasion of the Afghan tribes in 1722 and the collapse of the Safavid dynasty in the following decade plunged Iran into a period of political and cultural disarray. Little is known about the status of music during the Afghan occupation (1722–1736). Before the Afghan invasion, a few musicians who were in the service of Ṭahmāsb II left the capital with him; nevertheless, the *naqqāra-khāna* of Isfahan fell into the hands of Maḥmud Afghan.[161]

Nāder Shah (r. 1736–1747) rose from a peasant family and, to a large extent, lacked the sophisticated taste and refinement of his Safavid predecessors. While his seat of power was Mashhad, he spent much of his reign marching across the country, and while on campaign he recruited a large number of urban and rural performers, including musicians, dancers, courtesans, acrobat dancers, comedians, and firework performers. He also received female performers and courtesans as gifts from his chieftains and governors as well as from foreign ambassadors.[162] Nāder's chronicler Moḥammad Kāẓem Marvi describes instances of festive occasions, including weddings, a coronation, victory celebrations, *ʻayd-e nawruz* (the first day of spring), and court banquets when music, dance, and acrobatics were performed either in Mashhad or in Nāder's encampment.[163]

In 1729, Nāder defeated the Afghans in a series of brilliant victories, after which he restored Ṭahmāsb II, the son of Shah Solṭān-Ḥosayn to the Iranian throne. He treated Ṭahmāsb II with the utmost respect, arranging a stunning musical ceremony in his honor and ordering the *naqqāra-khāna* to play for him for seven days. Nāder, who was aware of Ṭahmāsb II's excessive fondness for music, even had a number of remarkable musicians from Khorasan brought to him in Isfahan. According to Marvi, in the following months, Ṭahmāsb II spent his time largely in the company of his musicians and entertainers, but was deposed by Nāder in 1732 due to his excessive indulgence in sensual pleasures and immoral conduct. Subsequently Nāder dispatched Ṭahmāsb II along with his entourage and court musicians to Mashhad.[164]

After the fall of the Safavids, Isfahan's court musical activities came to an end. Nāder once again returned to Isfahan in 1735 to meet with some foreign envoys and in particular with an Ottoman embassy. The Swiss traveler Daniel Moginié (1710–1749), who visited the city at that time, reports that Nāder was reluctant to have the audience hall displaying the vestiges of the Safavid rulers. Therefore, he removed the extravagant furniture and equipment from the hall and replaced them with various types of weapons. He also removed fancy stringed musical instruments and instead hung drums, timpani, and trumpets on the walls.[165]

In 1738, the Ottoman-Armenian *ṭanbur* player Harutin came to Iran and stayed at Nāder's camp for a few years. He later wrote a music treatise as well as a travel account and makes references to some of the musical norms he observed during his stay in Iran.[166] Harutin indicates that the musicians in Nāder's camp were overseen by a superintendent, and that the instrumentalists were supervised by the *sāzanda-bāshi*, who had a tent separate from the courtesans and other performers. He further adds that the tents of musicians were off-limits to soldiers and other members of the camp.[167] Likewise, Abraham Kretatsi, the Armenian Catholicos, who visited Nāder on the Moghān plains in Azerbaijan preceding his coronation in 1736, reports that the shah had a troop of twenty-two dancing boys who were accompanied by performers on the *ṭanbur*, *kamāncha*, *qānun*, *sanṭur*, and *nutak*.[168] Nāder invaded India in 1739, and on his return he brought back several Indian musicians and dancers who remained in his encampment for four years and conveyed their knowledge of music and dance to their Iranian counterparts.[169]

Following the decline of court music, a few literary assemblies (*maḥfel*s) emerged in Isfahan where sung poetry and music were notably performed by poets, calligraphers, and amateur musicians. Among the notables of Isfahan was Mirzā ʿAbd al-Vahhāb Musavi (1761–1828), a polymath, poet, and calligrapher whose house was a hub for literary and artistic figures. Better known by his pen name, Neshāṭ, he later came to Tehran in 1803 and received a respected position at the Qajar court. Two celebrated poet-musicians in this period, Moshtāq 'Alishāh (1758–1791) and Mirzā 'Ali, were associated with the literary circle of Mirzā 'Abd al-Vahhāb Musavi. Moshtāq 'Alishāh was an eminent Sufi musician who added a fourth string to the three-stringed *setār*, which has been named after him ever since. Mirzā 'Ali was also an intelligent nobleman of Isfahan, educated in many sciences and, above all, an outstanding *chahārtār* player.[170]

Unlike the Georgians who gradually assimilated into the dominant Persian culture (adopting the Persian language and converting to Islam), Armenians maintained their own identities. Georgian boys trained in music and dance continued to perform in public places.[171] Armenian performers and luthiers instead contributed significantly to the professional music making of Isfahan and surrounding villages. The census conducted by the Armenian Church of houses in the suburb of New Julfa in 1789 lists a number of musicians, including Avud (instrumentalist), Gurgen (instrumentalist), Khāchik (*surnāzan*), Barsegh (*surnāzan*), and Antanes (luthier) among the residents of the neighborhood.[172] Likewise, a house is listed in the Chahārsu area as the workshop of luthiers (*chogur* makers).[173] New Julfa continued to be the most prominent center of instrument-making in Iran throughout the nineteenth and early twentieth centuries.

In the mid-eighteenth century, Shiraz, a city 300 miles southwest of Isfahan, came under the beneficent rule of Karim Khān Zand (r. 1751–1779), who served as a regent (*vakil*) for the last Safavid puppet kings. Shiraz was already a political and economic urban center with a cultural flavor of its own, and a substantial courtesan community especially trained in music and dance had already existed in this city during the sixteenth and seventeenth centuries.[174]

Karim Khān established a red-light district known as *maḥalla-ye khayl* (the army's quarter) in the *kharābāt* quarter of Shiraz where he gathered and even imported 5,000–6,000 urban and rural courtesans and dancing boys catering to the tastes of the nobility and, specifically, of his military commanders. He wanted the latter to be immersed in lavish entertainment in order to keep them from interfering in the administration of the state or initiating aggressive political moves.[175] The author of *Rustam al-tawārīkh* names almost seventy courtesans of Shiraz and mentions that they were famous for their beauty, seductive manners, polished etiquette (*adab*), witty conversation, and, above all, that they were accomplished singers, dancers, and performers.[176] Karim

Khān was also well aware that taxes collected from courtesans and prostitutes were a source of prodigious revenue for the state and, unlike his Safavid predecessors, he felt no constraints in exhibiting his interest in supporting female musicians and dancers in the new capital.

During the reign of Karim Khān music making came to be ubiquitous and widespread in Shiraz, and musical instruments such as the *naqqāra*, *surnā*, *musiqār* (panpipe), *nay*, *daf*, *dombak* (goblet drum), *ṭanbur*, *kamāncha*, *sanṭur*, and *chahārtār* were all cultivated to an impressive extent.[177] Edward Scott Waring, a British traveler, visited Shiraz in this period and refers to two male accompanists who were "considered to be very superior players on an instrument very like a violin." He appreciates their musicality "much but could form no judgment on their performance." He further indicates that these men and their accompanying courtesans drank wine in enormous quantities, in a manner he found too public.[178] Waring adds that many of the prominent men kept sets of Georgian boys who were instructed to sing, play on various instruments, and perform feats of creativity.[179]

Mirzā Naṣir Eṣfahāni (d. 1777), a mathematician and poet of this period who later came to be the boon companion and physician of Karim Khān, was also well-versed in music theory and wrote a treatise on the affinities between music and medicine.[180]

Finally, evidence suggests that a sizeable courtesan community was also active in Isfahan in the second half of the eighteenth century, as some members of this community, including female performers and their male instructors and accompanists, were later transferred to Tehran.[181]

Summary

The sixteenth century witnessed the emergence of several princes and Qizilbāsh governors who came to be ardent patrons of music. While the capital was Tabriz (and later Qazvin), the crown prince was always sent to Herat, the second most important city in Safavid territory. Herat in this period still had its own cultural flavor, presumably marked by both Persian and Chaghatai characteristics. Outside the Safavid court, music and dance were performed by male and female performers mainly in coffee houses, taverns, houses for smoking hashish and opium, gambling houses, courtesan salons, and brothels. It was due to the association of music with houses of ill-repute that Shah Ṭahmāsb banned music and even ordered the cutting off of hands or hanging of musicians. In Tabriz and Herat, *naqsh*, *ṣawt*, *qawl*, and *'amal* were composed and performed by professional musicians, but composing *pishraw* was likely the specialty of Herati instrumentalists. The traditional instruments in vogue in the first half of the Safavid period include the *'ud*, *qānun*, *chang*, *kamāncha*, *shetorghu*, *nay*, and *ṭanbur*.

At the turn of the seventeenth century, the seat of power moved to Isfahan and subsequently a great number of men and women were brought from the Caucasus (Georgia, Armenia, Circassia, and Dagestan) to the new capital, where they became major exponents of music and dance at the court, in coffeehouses, courtesan salons, and other public places.

Beginning with Shah 'Abbās I, all seventeenth-century potentates had two or three composers at their courts who wrote laudatory songs on various festive occasions. The vocal compositions of some early seventeenth-century court composers such as Shāh-Morād, Āqā Mo'men, Moẓaffar Golpāyegāni, and Sharif Hamadāni later turned into *peşrev*s at the Ottoman court, transcriptions of which can be seen today in Cantemir's collection.[182] By the beginning of the eighteenth century, while the *'ud*, *chang*, and *shetorghu* were no longer part of the Safavid court instrumentation, the new instruments *chahārtār* (later called *tār*), *sanṭur*, and *nutak* had already been introduced to the musical scene in Isfahan, most likely representing the musical influence of the Caucasus.

With the dissolution of the Safavid court in Isfahan, music continued to be performed in literary assemblies by amateur poet-musicians and in public places by professional *sāzanda*s and courtesans. Meanwhile, Shiraz rose to prominence as the hub of various classes of courtesan. Chapters 2 and 3 address how upper-class courtesans and their accompanying male instructors in Shiraz and Isfahan were later brought to Tehran, where they contributed significantly to the formation and development of Qajar court music.

Notes

1. Eckhard Neubauer, "Musik zur Mongolenzeit in Iran und der angrenzenden Ländern," *Der Islam* 45 (1969): 246.
2. Ibid, 247–9.
3. Ibid., 250–251. For further information on music in the Mongol period, see Ernst Emsheimer, "Earliest Reports about the Music of the Mongols," trans. Robert Carroll, *Asian Music* 18/1 (1986): 4–9.

4. For further details, see Moḥammad Taqi Dāneshpazhuh, *Nemuna'i az fehrest-e āthār-e dāneshmandān-e Irāni va Eslāmi dar ghenā' va musiqi* (Tehran: Vezārat-e Farhang va Honar, 1976), 90.
5. ʿAbd al-Qāder Marāghi, *Jāmiʿ al-alḥān*, ed. Taqi Binesh (Tehran: Mo'assasa-ye Moṭāleʿāt va Taḥqiqāt-e Farhangi, 1987), 243–244. A slightly different version of this story is also related in Marāghi's *Sharḥ-e advār*, ed. Taqi Binesh (Tehran: Markaz-e Nashr-e Dāneshgāhi, 1991), 337–338.
6. Qażi Aḥmad Ghaffāri. *Tārikh-e negārestān*, ed. Morteżā Modarres Gilāni (Tehran: Ketābforushi-ye Ḥāfeẓ, 1962), 321.
7. Marāghi later added a fifth section (*mostazād*) to it, but it failed to gain general acceptance.
8. ʿAbd al-Qāder Marāghi, *Maqāṣid al-alḥān*, ed. Taqi Binesh, 2nd ed. (Tehran: Bongāh-e Tarjoma va Nashr-e Ketāb, 1977), 127–128; Marāghi, *Jāmiʿ al-alḥān*, 200–201.
9. Dawlatshāh Samarqandi, *Tadhkirat al-shuʿarā'*, ed. Edward Brown (Tehran: Asāṭir, 2003), 306.
10. A few compositions of Solṭān-Aḥmad are mentioned in a Persian musical treatise at the University of Tehran (Tehran) MS 1974, 25b; for the compositions of Solṭān-Aḥmad in Ottoman song-text collections, see Owen Wright, *Words without Songs, A Musicological Study of an Early Ottoman Anthology and its Precursors*, SOAS Musicology Series (London: School of Oriental and African Studies, 1992), 300.
11. Sharaf al-Din ʿAli Yazdi, *Ẓafar-nāma*, ed. Moḥammad ʿAbbāsi, 2 vols. (Tehran: Amir-Kabir, 1957), 1: 735.
12. Mirānshāh once fell from his horse and consequently suffered mental problems. When Timur returned to Tabriz, he was told that Mirānshāh's problem had been caused by his musicians who had kept entertaining him while he was on the horse until he eventually lost his balance and fell off. Upon hearing this news, Timur ordered that Moḥammad Quhestāni, Qoṭb al-Din Nā'i, Ḥabib ʿUdi, and ʿAbd al-Mo'men Guyanda be hung. For the details, see Sharaf al-Din ʿAli Yazdi, *Ẓafar-nāma*, 2: 1000; Dawlatshāh Samarqandi, *Tadhkirat al-shuʿarā'*, 330–331.
13. See Mohammad Taghi Massoudieh, *Manuscrits persans concernant la musique* (Munich: G. Henle Verlag, 1996), 18–31, 199–200.
14. The court of the Mozaffarid ruler Shah Shojāʿ (r. 1358–1384) was an important center of musical activities in Shiraz. Mobārakshāh Bokhāri, a music theorist at his court, wrote a commentary on the *Kitāb al-adwār* and dedicated it to his patron. For the critical editions, see ʿAbdollāh Anvār, *Tarjoma-ye sharḥ-e Mobārakshāh Bokhāri bar advār-e Ormavi dar ʿelm-e musiqi* (Tehran: Farhangestān-e Honar, 2013).

15. Cf. Eckhard Neubauer, "Zur Bedentung der Begriffe Komponist und Komposition in der Musikgeschichte der islamischen Welt," *Zeitschrift für Geschichte der Arabisch-Islamischen Wissenschaften* 11 (1997): 350.
16. Taqi al-Din Awḥadi Balayāni, *'Arafāt al-'āshiqīn wa 'araṣāt al-'ārifīn*, ed. Dhabiḥollāh Sāḥebkāri and Āmena Fakhr-Aḥmad, 8 vols. (Tehran: Markaz-e mirāth-e maktub, 2010), 2: 780.
17. See Ismail Hakkı Uzunçarşılı, "Osmanlılar Zamanında Saraylarda Musiki Hayatı," *Türk Tarih Kurumu* XLI (161): 82–83; as cited in Walter Feldman, *Music of the Ottoman Court: Makam, Composition and the Early Ottoman Instrumental Repertoire* (Berlin: Verlag für Wissenschaft und Bildung, 1996), 111.
18. For extensive biographies of Zayn al-'Ābedin and Gholām Shādi, see Darvish-'Ali Changi, *Tuḥfat al-surūr*, Institute of Written Heritage (Dushanbe) MS 264, 114a–115a, 105a–107b; Feldman, *Music of the Ottoman Court*, 41–44.
19. For further information, see Owen Wright, "On the Concept of a Timurid Music," *Oriente Moderno*, NS 15(76) no. 2 (1996): 665–681; John Baily, "The Music of the Timurids and its Legacy in Afghanistan," in *The Theory and Practice in the Music of the Islamic World: Essays in Honour of Owen Wright*, ed. Rachel Harris and Martin Stokes, SOAS Musicology Series (London: Routledge, 2018), 199–216; Will Sumits, "*Tawārīkh-i Mūsīqīyūn*: The 'Histories of Musicians' from Herat and Khotan According to a 19th Century Chaghatai Treatise from Eastern Turkestan," *Revue des Traditions Musicales* 10 (2016): 130–146.
20. Zayn al-Din Vāṣefi, *Badāyi' al-waqāyi'*, ed. Alexander Boldyrev, 2 vols. (Tehran: Bonyād-e Farhang-e Irān, 1971), 1: 19–23.
21. Ibid, 1: 20–21.
22. Ibid., 1: 22–23.
23. Ibid., 1: 22.
24. Ibid., 2: 245.
25. Zahiruddin Muhammad Babur, *Bâburnâma: Chaghatay Turkish Text with Abdul-Rahim Khankhanan's Persian Translation*, Turkish transcription, Persian edition and English translation by W. M. Thackston, Jr. (Cambridge, MA: Department of NELC, Harvard University, 1993), 378–381.
26. Mir 'Alishir Navā'i, "Khamsat al-mutaḥayyirīn," Persian translation from Chaghatai by Moḥammad Nakhjavāni, ed. Mehdi Farāhāni Monfared, *Nāma-ye farhangestān*, supplement 12 (2002): 36.
27. For further details on the life and works of Shehāb al-Din 'Abdollāh Morvārid, see *Munis al-aḥbāb: Majmu'a-ye, robā'iyāt-e Shehāb al-Din 'Abdollāh Morvārid*, ed. Sayyed 'Ali Mirafżali (Tehran: Markaz-e Asnād-e Majles-e Shorā-ye Eslāmi, 2011).

28. Sām Mirzā Ṣafavi, *Toḥfa-ye Sāmi*, ed. Vaḥid Dastgerdi (Tehran: Armaghān, 1935), 66.
29. See 'Alishāh b. Buka Awbahi, *Muqaddimat al-uṣūl*, ed. Moḥammad-Taqi Ḥosayni (Tehran: Farhangestān-e Honar, 2011).
30. Zahiruddin Muhammad Babur, *Bâburnâma*, 373.
31. A. D. Moẓṭar (ed.), *Tārikh-e jahāngoshā-ye khāqān* (Islamabad: Markaz-e Taḥqiqāt-e Fārsi-ye Irān va Pākestān, 1971), 222.
32. *Arasbār* refers to the region along the *Aras*/Araxes river.
33. Vladimir Minorsky and C. E. Bosworth, "Tabriz," *EI2*, 45.
34. For the list of musicians, see Uzunçarşılı, "Osmanlılar Zamsnında Saraylarda Musiki Hayatı," 84–86; Feldman, *Music of the Ottoman Court*, 45–56.
35. Mawlānā Nāji Kermāni was apparently a relative of 'Abdollāh Morvārid. For further details, see Sa'id Nafisi, *Tārikh-e naẓm va nathr dar adabiyāt va zabān-e fārsi tā pāyān-e qarn-e dahom-e hejri*, 2 vols. (Tehran: Forughi, 1984), 614–615.
36. Ḥasan Jān was the father of Mollā Sa'd al-Din Moḥammad Mo'allem, a literary figure at the court of Sultan Murad III (r. 1574–1595). For further details, see Ḥasan Rumlu, *Aḥsan al-tawārīkh*, 709; Feldman, *Music of the Ottoman Court*, 66, 515.
37. See *Travels to Tana and Persia by Josafa Barbaro and Ambrogio Contarini*, ed. Lord Stanley of Alderley, trans. William Thomas and S. A. Roy (London: Hakluyt Society, 1873), 2: 202.
38. Eskandar Beg Turkamān, *Tārikh-e 'ālamārā-ye 'Abbāsi*, 2 vols. (Tehran: Amir-Kabir, 1970), 1: 190; for English translation, see Eskandar Monshi, *History of Shah 'Abbas*, trans. Roger M. Savory, 2 vols. (Boulder, CO: Westview, 1978), 1: 280–281.
39. Ḥasan Rumlu, *Aḥsan al-tawārīkh*, 323. The text of Shah Ṭahmāsb's *farmān* was engraved in the stone of Mir 'Emād's Mosque in Kāshān. For the content of the *farmān*, see 'Abd al-Ḥosayn Navā'i, *Shah Ṭahmāsb Ṣafavi, Majmu'a-ye asnād va mokātabāt-e tārikhi hamrāh bā yāddāshthā-ye tafṣili* (Tehran: Bonyād-e Farhang-e Irān, 1971), 513–514.
40. Sām Mirzā Ṣafavi, *Toḥfa-ye Sāmi*, ed. Vaḥid Dastgerdi, 143, 82–84.
41. Qāżi Mir Aḥmad Monshi, *Golestān-e honar*, ed. Aḥmad Sohayli Khvānsāri (Tehran: Bonyād-e Farhang-e Irān, 1973), 113–114.
42. Ibid., 114.
43. *Tārikh-e 'ālamārā-ye 'Abbāsi*, 1: 209; *History of Shah 'Abbas*, 1: 311.
44. *Tārikh-e 'ālamārā-ye 'Abbāsi*, 1: 190; *History of Shah 'Abbas*, 1: 281.
45. Ibid.

46. Wright, "On the Concept of a Timurid Music," 671.
47. Moḥammad Yusof Vāla Eṣfahāni, *Khold-e barin*, ed. Mir Hāshem Moḥaddeth (Tehran: Bonyād-e Moqufāt-e Afshār, 1993), 462.
48. *Tārikh-e ʿālamārā-ye ʿAbbāsi*, 1: 190; *History of Shah ʿAbbas*, 1: 281.
49. *Tārikh-e ʿālamārā-ye ʿAbbāsi*, 1: 183; *History of Shah ʿAbbas*, 1: 277.
50. *Tārikh-e ʿālamārā-ye ʿAbbāsi*, 1: 185; *History of Shah ʿAbbas*, 1: 278.
51. Mollā ʿAbd al-Nabi Fakhr al-Zamāni Qazvini, *Tadhkera-ye maykhāna*, ed. Aḥmad Golchin Maʿāni (Tehran: Eqbāl, 1996), 902–903.
52. The most eminent student of Mawlānā Mālek is said to have been Mir ʿEmād Qazvini. Cf. Qāżi Mir Aḥmad Monshi, *Golestān-e honar*, 121.
53. Ibid., 105.
54. For the biography of Mir Ṣadr al-Din Moḥammad, see *Tārikh-e ʿālamārā-ye ʿAbbāsi*, 1: 171–172; *History of Shah ʿAbbas*, 1: 267–268.
55. Ibid., 1: 178; *History of Shah ʿAbbas*, 1: 274.
56. Moḥammad Yusof Vāla Eṣfahāni, *Khold-e barin*, 462.
57. Mir Ṣadr al-Din Moḥammad, "Resāla-ye ʿelm-e musiqi," ed. Āriyu Rostami. *Māhur* 18 (2003): 94.
58. Bābur names some musicians who were in Herat shortly after the reign of Solṭān-Ḥosayn Bāyqarā. See Zahiruddin Muhammad Babur, *Bâburnâma*, 372–381, 396–399; Feldman, *Music of the Ottoman Court*, 40–41.
59. For the complete list of the governors appointed to provinces of Iran in the sixteenth century, see: Klaus Michael Röhrborn, *Provinzen und Zentralgewalt Persiens im 16. und 17. Jahrhundert* (Berlin: Walter De Gruyter, 1966), 40–44.
60. Sām Mirzā Ṣafavi, *Toḥfa-ye Sāmi*, ed. Vaḥid Dastgerdi, 84.
61. Ibid., 9–10. For further information on the artistic patronage of Bahrām Mirzā, see Basil Gray, "The Arts in the Safavid Period," in *The Cambridge History of Iran*, ed. P. Jackson and L. Lockhart, vol. 6. (Cambridge: Cambridge University Press, 1986), 886.
62. Sām Mirzā Ṣafavi, *Toḥfa-ye Sāmi*, ed. Rokn al-Din Homāyun-Farrokh (Tehran: Asāṭir, 2005), 346–347.
63. Ṣādeqi Ketābdār, *Majmaʿ al-khawāṣṣ*, trans. from Chaghatai to Persian by ʿAbd al-Ḥosayn Khayyāmpur (Tabriz: Akhtar-e Shomāl, 1948), 9–10.
64. The original text of this *farmān* is published in ʿAbd al-Ḥosayn Navāʾi, *Shāh Ṭahmāsb-e Ṣafavi* (Tehran: Bonyād-e Farhang-e Irān, 1971), 51–61. Some parts of this *farmān*, especially the account of musicians, are also reproduced in Abu al-Fażl, ʿAllāmi ibn Mubārak, *Akbar Nāma*, trans. H. Beveridge, 3 vols. (Calcutta: Asiatic Society of Bengal, 1907–1939), 1: 427.

65. The account of this assembly is given in Sukumar Ray, *Humāyūn in Persia* (Calcutta: Royal Asiatic Society of Bengal, 1948), 11.
66. See also Abu al-Fażl, *Akbar Nāma*, 1: 214. For further information about Amirshāhi Sabzavāri and his collection of poems, see *Tuḥfat al-surūr*, 97a–98a; *Divān-e Amirshāhi Sabzavāri*, ed. Sa'id Hamidiān (Tehran: Ebn-e Sinā, 1969).
67. Abu al-Fażl, *Akbar Nāma*, 1: 433–434.
68. Ray, *Humāyūn in Persia*, 13.
69. According to Abu al-Fażl, *Akbar Nāma*, 1: 433, he was celebrated in both Khorasan and 'Erāq (i.e., in the east and west of the Safavid territory). In the music treatise *Dar bayān-e 'elm-e musīqi va dānestan-e sho'abāt-e ou*, Ḥāfeẓ Ṣāber Qāq is praised as the inventor of *maqām kuchak*, although this attribution was certainly an overstatement.
70. Darvish-'Ali Changi, *Tuḥfat al-surūr*, 186b.
71. Abu al-Fażl, *Ain i Akbari*, 681-682. For the account of Ostād Yusof Mawdud, see *Tuḥfat al-surūr*, 149b.
72. Ṣādeqi Ketābdār mentions a few persons associated with 'Ali Qoli Khān Shāmlu who were also poets, such as Yolqi Beg Shāmlu and Qāsem Beg Raghmi. See Ṣādeqi Ketābdār, *Majma' al-khawāṣṣ*, 107, 122.
73. A short biography of Dawra Beg Karāmi is provided in Ṣādeqi Ketābdār, *Majma' al-khawāṣṣ*, 122–123.
74. Indeed, the trading back and forth of control over Qandahār between the Mughals and the Safavids began in the sixteenth century, and Herat was always the Safavids' base for those campaigns.
75. Qāżi Mir Aḥmad Monshi, *Golestān-e honar*, 93–94.
76. Ebrāhim Mirzā was a student of Mālek Daylami and took calligraphy lessons from him for a while. For further detail, see ibid., 106.
77. For further details of the biography of Ebrāhim Mirzā, see *Tārikh-e 'ālamārā-ye 'Abbāsi*, 1: 209. As previously mentioned, I have edited Savory's English translation when necessary. For Savory's translation, see Eskandar Monshi, *History of Shah 'Abbas*, 1: 311.
78. Cf. Ṣādeqi Ketābdār, *Majma' al-khawāṣṣ*, 25–26.
79. Qāżi Mir Aḥmad Monshi, *Golestān-e honar*, 112–113.
80. Darvish-'Ali Changi mentions that Qāsem Qānuni was in love with Ebrāhim Mirzā, and upon hearing about their relationship Shah Ṭahmāsb sought to kill the musician. See *Tuḥfat al-surūr*, 185a.
81. Ibid.
82. Ibid.

83. Mehrdad Fallahzadeh, *Two Treatises–Two Streams* (Bethesda: Ibex, 2009), 68, 88, 94.
84. Darvish-'Ali Changi, *Tuḥfat al-surūr*, 185b.
85. Khᵛorshāh b. Qobād Ḥosayni, *Tārikh-e ilchi-ye Neẓāmshāh*, ed. Moḥammad Reżā Naṣiri and Koichi Haneda (Tehran: Anjoman-e Āthār va Mafākher-e Farhangi, 1990), 215; Sām Mirzā Ṣafavi, *Toḥfa-ye Sāmi*, ed. Vaḥid Dastgerdi, 83.
86. *Tuḥfat al-surūr*, 132a; Ḥosayni, *Tārikh-e ilchi-ye Neẓāmshāh*, 220; also see Ṣādeqi Ketābdār, *Majma' al-khawāṣṣ*, 12–13.
87. Feraydun Nurzād, ed., *Nāmahā-ye Khān Aḥmad Khān Gilāni* (Tehran: Bonyād-e Mawqufāt-e Maḥmud Afshār, 1994), 47, 112–114, 154–156.
88. Ibid, 156, 186.
89. Ibid, 131b–132a.
90. Moḥammad Yusof Vāla Eṣfahāni, *Khold-e barin*, 484.
91. Feraydun Nurzād, *Nāmahā-ye Khān Aḥmad Khān Gilāni*, 112–113.
92. *Tārikh-e 'ālamārā-ye 'Abbāsi*, 1: 191; for English translation, see *History of Shah 'Abbas*, 281.
93. See Nasimi, *Nasim-e ṭarab (The Breeze of Euphoria): A Sixteenth-Century Persian Musical Treatise*, ed. Amir Hosein Pourjavady (Tehran: Farhangestān-e Honar, 2007), ix–xii.
94. Malekshāh Ḥosayn b. Ghiyāth al-Din Moḥammad, *Iḥyā' al-mulūk*, ed. Manuchehr Sotuda (Tehran: Enteshārāt-e 'Elmi va Farhangi, 2004), 329, 217.
95. Ibid., 217.
96. Ibid., 337–339.
97. Ibid., 421.
98. Sām Mirzā Ṣafavi (*Toḥfa-ye Sāmi*, ed. Vaḥid Dastgerdi, 162–163) mentions a number of poets who were active in Ray and Ṭahran, such as 'Eshqi Ṭahrāni, Afżal Sārāni, Mawlānā Vaṣli, Ḥefẓi Ṭahrāni, Jāni Ṭahrāni, Dehqāni, Nisti, Ruḥi, Vafā'i Rāzi, Mawlānā 'Abdi, Ṣaḥrā'i, Mawlānā Ḥaqqi.
99. Ibid., 162.
100. Ṣādeqi Ketābdār, *Majma' al-khawāṣṣ*, 29–30.
101. Ibid, 51, 79.
102. See *Tārikh-e 'ālamārā-ye 'Abbāsi*, 1: 185; for English translation, see *History of Shah 'Abbas*, 278; Taqi al-Din Ḥosayni Kāshāni, *Khulāṣat al-ash'ār wa zubdat al-afkār*, Kitābkhāna-ye Majles-e Shorā-ye Eslāmi (Tehran) MS 334, 90–91.
103. Ibid., 209–211.
104. *Tārikh-e 'ālamārā-ye 'Abbāsi*, 2: 1109.
105. Awḥadi Balayāni, *'Arafāt al-'āshiqīn*, 5: 2882.

106. Ḥâfiẓ Post. *Güfte mecmuası*. Topkapı Sarayı Library (Istanbul) MS Revan 1724, 134b.
107. See Mollā Jalāl Monajjem, *Tārikh-e ʿAbbāsi*, ed. Sayfollāh Vaḥidniā (Tehran: Forughi, 1987), 71.
108. *Tārikh-e ʿālamārā-ye ʿAbbāsi*, 1: 191.
109. Awḥadi Balayāni, *ʿArafāt al-ʿāshiqīn*, 6: 4126.
110. Mirzā Rafiʿā, *Dastur al-Moluk*, ed. Moḥammad-Esmāʿil Marcinkowski (Tehran: Markaz-e Asnād va Tārikh-e Diplomāsi, 2006), 286–287.
111. For further information about Ḥāfeẓ Jalājel Bākharzi, see *Tārikh-e ʿālamārā' ʿAbbāsi*, 1: 190; Mollā Jalāl Monajjem, *Tārikh-e ʿAbbāsi*, 71. For Āqā Ḥaqqi, see Pietro Della Valle, *Les Fameux Voyages*, 4 vols. (Paris, 1663–1664), 3: 178; Willem Floor, *A Social History of Sexual Relations in Iran* (Washington, DC: Mage, 2008), 213.
112. Mollā Jalāl Monajjem, *Tārikh-e ʿAbbāsi*, 352.
113. Ḥasan Mashḥun, *Tārikh-e musiqi-ye Irān*, 2 vols. (Tehran: Simorgh-Fākhta, 1991), 330.
114. *Tārikh-e ʿālamārā-ye ʿAbbāsi*, 2: 828; for the English translation, see *History of Shah ʿAbbas*, 2: 1035.
115. Moḥammad Ṭāher Naṣrābādi, *Tadhkera-ye Naṣrābādi*, ed. A. Modaqqaq Yazdi (Yazd: Dāneshgāh-e Yazd, 1990), 482.
116. Seven compositions of Shāh-Morād are notated by Ali Ufuki and four by Cantemir. See Owen Wright, *Demetrius Cantemir: The Collection of Notations*, pt 1: Text, SOAS Musicology Series (London: School of Oriental and African Studies, 1992), 105, 154, 158, 350. The misattribution of these pieces to Sultan Murad IV occurs in Feldman, *Music of the Ottoman Court*, 358.
117. Mashḥun, *Tārikh-e musiqi-ye Irān*, 330.
118. Ibid.
119. *Tadhkera-ye Naṣrābādi*, 425–426.
120. Amir Khān Gorji, *Resāla*, Bibliothèque Nationale (Paris), MS Suppl. persan 1087, 27a–27b.
121. See Wright, *Demetrius Cantemir*, pt 1: Text, 274, 347, 360, 423.
122. *Tadhkera-ye Naṣrābādi*, 216.
123. Ibid.
124. Amir Khān Gorji, *Resāla*, 26b.
125. Bāqiyā Nā'ini, *Zamzama-ye vaḥdat*, Biruni Institute of Oriental Studies (Tashkent) MS 10226. For a biography of Bāqiyā Nā'ini, see Mollā ʿAbd al-Nabi Fakhr al-Zamāni Qazvini, *Tadhkera-ye maykhāna*, 872–875.

126. Ibid.
127. Amir Khān Gorji, *Resāla*, 19b–20a.
128. Moḥammad Mofid Mostawfi Bāfqi, *Jāme'-e Mofidi*, ed. Iraj Afshār (Tehran: Ketābforushi-ye Asadi, 1961), 440–441; *Tadhkera-ye Naṣrābādi*, 425–426.
129. Ibid.
130. Amir Hosein Pourjavady, 'The Musical Codex of Amir Khān Gorji (c. 1108/1697)" Ph.D. dissertation, University of California, Los Angeles, 2005, 299, 311, 314, 316; Amir Khān Gorji, *Resāla*, 11b, 13b, 24a. The *taṣnifs* of Moẓaffar Golpāyegāni and Sharif Hamadāni apparently turned into *peşrevs* at the Ottoman court. For a list of their compositions, see Owen Wright, *Demetrius Cantemir: The Collection of Notations*, pt. 2: Commentary, SOAS Musicology Series (Aldershot: Ashgate, 2000), 593.
131. Amir Khān Gorji mentions that Ḥāfeẓ Moḥammad Kāẓem was a *chālchi-bāshi*. See Pourjavady, "The Musical Codex of Amir Khān Gorji," 316.
132. Ibid., 299.
133. Ibid., 271, 284, 288, 302, 324.
134. Awḥadi Balayāni, *'Arafāt al-'āshiqīn*, 2: 1062.
135. *Tārikh-e 'ālamārā-ye 'Abbāsi*, 1: 190; *History of Shah 'Abbas*, 1: 281.
136. See *Tadhkera-ye Naṣrābādi*, 357, 465.
137. Antonio de Gouvea, *Jornada do arcebispo de Goa Dom Frey Aleixo de Menezes* (Coimbra: 1606), 145b.
138. Cf. Adam Olearius, *Vermehrte Newe Beschreibung der Muskowitischen und persischen Reyse* (Schleswig, 1656), ed. D. Lohmeier (Tübingen, 1971), 531, as cited in Rudi Matthee, "Prostitutes, Courtesans, and Dancing Girls: Women Entertainers in Safavid Iran," in *Iran and Beyond*, edited by Rudi Matthee and Beth Baron (Costa Mesa, CA: Mazda, 2000), 141.
139. For the life and compositions of Āqā Mo'men, see Pourjavady, "The Musical Codex of Amir Khān Gorji," 98–131.
140. Mashḥun, *Tārikh-e musiqi-ye Irān*, 1: 329.
141. Adam Olearius, *The Voyages & Travels of the Ambassadors Sent by Frederick Duke of Holstein, to the Great Duke of Muscovy, and the King of Persia: Begun in the Year M. DC. XXXIII, and Finish'd in M. DC. XXXIX: Containing a Compleat History of Muscovy, Tartary, Persia, and Other Adjacent Countries*, trans. John Davies (London: Thomas Dring & John Starkey, 1662), 211.
142. *Tadhkera-ye Naṣrābādi*, 57–58.
143. Jean Chardin, *Voyages du chevalier Chardin, en Perse, et autres lieux de l'Orient*, ed. L. Langlès, 10 vols. (Paris: Le Normant, 1811), 8: 61.

144. *Tadhkera-ye Naṣrābādi*, 66–67.
145. Moḥsen Ta'thir Tabrizi, *Divān-e Moḥsen Ta'thir Tabrizi*, ed. Amin Pāshā Ejlāli (Tehran: Markaz-e Nashr-e Dāneshgāhi, 1994), 165–166; as cited in Sayyed Ḥosayn Maythami, *Musiqi-ye 'aṣr-e Ṣafavi* (Tehran: Farhangestān-e Honar, 2010), 58.
146. A. Daulier Deslandes, *Les beautez de la Perse ou la description de ce qu'il y a de plus curieux dans ce royaume* (Paris, 1673), 31–32.
147. N. Sanson, *Voyages ou relation de l'éstat présent du royaume de Perse* (Paris, 1694), 65–66.
148. Engelbert Kaempfer, *Exotic Attractions in Persia, 1684–1688: Travels & Observations*, trans. and annot. Willem Floor and Colette Ouahes (Washington, DC: Mage, 2018), 186.
149. Chardin, *Voyages*, 5: 369–372.
150. See Reżā Mokhtāri and Moḥsen Ṣādeqi (ed.), *Ghenā' Musiqi*, 4 vols. (Qom: Nashr-e Merṣād, 1997).
151. Chardin, *Voyages*, 6: 51.
152. Pietro Della Valle, *Viaggi di Pietro della Valle. Il pellegrino descritti da lui medesimo in lettere familiari all'erudito suo amico Mario Schipano divisi in tre parti cioè: la Turchia, la Persia e l'India* (Brighton: G. Gancia, 1843), 1: 25.
153. Chardin, *Voyages*, 4: 69. For further detail on coffeehouses in the Safavid period, see Rudi Mattheee, *The Pursuit of Pleasure: Drugs and Stimulants in Iranian History, 1500–1900* (Washington, DC: Mage, 2005), 144–177.
154. See Daulier Deslandes, *Les beautez*, 30–36; Jean-Baptiste Tavernier, *Les six voyages de Jean-Bapt. Tavernier en Turquie, en Perse et aux Indes*, 2 vols. (Utrecht, 1712), 1: 544.
155. The images of these tombstones were later reproduced as drawings by the renowned painter and anthropologist Abraham Gurgenian (1908–1991), and they are currently preserved at the Vank Cathedral in Isfahan. I am grateful to Leon Minassian (1920–2012) who gave me his notes and the Gurgenian drawings during my visit to New Julfa (Isfahan) on January 27, 2007. Deciphering the names of musicians from tombstones was done by Leon Minassian.
156. Kathryn Babayan, "Sufis, Dervishes and Mullas: The Controversy over Spiritual and Temporal Dominion in Seventeenth-Century Iran," in *Safavid Persia: The History and Politics of an Islamic Society* (Cambridge: University of Cambridge, 1996), 117.
157. Pourjavady, "The Musical Codex of Amir Khān Gorji,", 96–168.
158. *Tadhkera-ye Naṣrābādi*, 338–339, 512, 545.

159. Ibid., 512.
160. Ibid., 545.
161. Moḥammad Moḥsen Mostawfi, *Zubdat al-tawārīkh*, ed. Behruz Gudarzi (Tehran: Bonyād-e Mawqufāt-e Maḥmud Afshār, 1996), 133.
162. For the musical life in the Afsharid period, see Amir Hosein Pourjavady, "Negāhi be ḥayāt-e musiqā'i-ye dawra-ye Afshāri," *Māhur* 31 (2006): 29–60.
163. Ibid, 41–58.
164. Cf. Mostawfi, *Zubdat al-tawārīkh*, 154; Rostam al-Ḥokamā', *Rustam al-tawārīkh*, ed. Moḥammad Moshiri (Tehran: Amir-Kabir, 1973), 194, 199–201; Moḥammad Kaẓem Marvi, *'Ālamārā-ye Nāderi*, ed. Moḥammad Amin Riyāḥi (Tehran: Nashr-e 'elm, 1990), 231; Pourjavady, "Negāhi be ḥayāt-e musiqā'i-ye dawra-ye Afshāri," 55–56.
165. Daniel Moginié, *L'illustre paisan, ou, Memoires et avantures de Daniel Moginié . . .: où se trouvent plusieurs particularités anecdotes des derniéres révolutions de la Perse & de l'Indostan & du règne de Thamas-Kouli-kan* (Lausanne: Au depens de la compagnie, 1761), 94.
166. See Eugenia Popescu-Judetz, *Tanburî Küçük Artin: A Musical Treatise of the Eighteenth Century* (Istanbul: Pan Yayıncılık, 2002).
167. Hārutin Ṭanburi, "Tārikh-e Ṭahmāsb-Qoli Khān," in *Sefāratnāmahā-ye Irān: gozāreshhā-ye mosāferat va ma'muriyat-e safirān-e Othmāni dar Irān* ed. Moḥammad Amin Riyāḥi (Tehran: Ṭus, 1989), 141–145.
168. Abrāham Gātoghikus, *Montakhabāti az yāddāshthā-ye Abrāhām Gātoghikus*, trans. 'Abd al-Ḥosayn Sepantā and Estiphan Hananian (Isfahan: Vaḥid, 1968), 50–51; Pourjavady, "Negāhi be ḥayāt-e musiqā'i-ye dawra-ye Afshāri," 45.
169. Mirzā Mehdi Astarābādi, *Tārikh-e jahāngoshā-ye Nāderi* (Tehran: Donyā-ye Ketāb, 1989), 430, 488; Pourjavady, "Negāhi be ḥayāt-e musiqā'i-ye dawra-ye Afshāri," 52–54.
170. See 'Abd al-Razzāq Beg Donbali, *Tajrubat al-aḥrār wa tasliyyat al-abrār*, ed. Ḥasan Qāżi Ṭabāṭabā'i, vol. 1 (Tabriz: Mo'assasa-ye Tārikh va Farhang-e Irān, 1970), 269; Loṭf-'Ali Beg Ādhar Bigdeli, *Ātashkada-ye Ādhar*, ed. Mir Hāshem Moḥaddeth, vol. 2 (Tehran: Amir-Kabir, 1999), 578, as cited in Sayyed Ḥosayn Maythami, "Musiqi-ye dawrān-e Zand," *Māhur* 68 (2015): 41–42.
171. Edward Scott Waring, *A Tour to Sheeraz, by the Route of Kazroon and Feerozabad* (London: T. Cadell & W. Davies, 1807), 53.
172. Harutiwn Ter Hovhaneants, *Tārikh-e Jolfā-ye Eṣfahān* [*History of New Julfa in Isfahan*], trans. from Armenian by Leon Minassian and M. A. Mussavi Feraydani (Isfahan: Nashr-e Zendarud, 2000), 274–278.

173. Ibid., 274.
174. During the Safavid period Shiraz hosted a considerable number of courtesans and musicians. The Portuguese traveler Tenreiro, visiting the city during the reign of Shah Esmā'il I, mentions a banquet organized by the governor in 1524 where he was entertained by female singers. A century later, Hubert Visnich, the director of the Dutch East India Company in Iran, relates how he was entertained by female musicians and dancers in the court of the governor of Shiraz, Emām Qoli Khān, who later that night dispatched the same courtesans to the room of the Dutchman for more amusement. See Ronald Smith, *The First Age of the Portuguese Embassies Navigations and Peregrinations in Persia (1507–1524)* (Bethesda, MD: Decatur Press, 1970), 67, 74; Hendrik Dunlop, ed., "Journal of Hubert Visnich, Nov. 1627–28 Dec.1628," in *Bronnen tot de geschiedenis der Oostindische Compagnie in Perzië 1611–1638* ('S-Gravenhage: Nijhoff, 1930), 271–272.
175. Rostam al-Ḥokamā', *Rustam al-tawārīkh*, 340.
176. Ibid., 341.
177. Ibid., 411–412.
178. Waring, *A Tour to Sheeraz*, 54.
179. Ibid., 53.
180. Mashḥun, *Tārikh-e musiqi-ye Irān*, 1: 360–361.
181. As will be discussed in Chapters 2 and 3, at the beginning of the Qajar period, the Armenian Sohrāb and his students Ostād Zohra and Ostād Minā, who were overseers and trainers of courtesans in the *dastgāh-e bāzigar-khāna,* were all from Isfahan.
182. It seems to have been usual to perform vocal compositions instrumentally in the Safavid court. Amir Khān Gorji mentions a *taṣnif* composed by Ḥāfeẓ Moḥammad Kāẓem that was rendered instrumentally as *pishraw-ye nāz*. See Amir Khān Gorji, *Resāla*, 24a. Likewise, *varsāqi* and *arasbāri*, the two Turkish vocal genres of the Safavid period, were rendered instrumentally in both Safavid and Ottoman courts. Amir Khān Gorji even emphasizes that by the end of the seventeenth century *arasbāri* was known only as an instrumental genre comparable to *pishraw*.

2

COURTESANS AND CONCUBINES IN EARLY MODERN IRAN

In the period between the fifteenth and nineteenth centuries in Iran, female performers as concubines and courtesans played a significant role in the dissemination of music and dance. Concubines were mostly slave women who were related to rulers, princes, or governors through temporary marriage and performed only in the harem or in the houses of the nobility when there were all-female gatherings. Courtesans were upper-class prostitutes in urban centers who entertained men with their music, dancing, culture, and wit in their own houses, and were also invited occasionally to perform at the courts of potentates or governors. However, because of their inferior social status as women and their stigmatized and disreputable character in particular, court chronicles make no direct references to their lives and careers, nor do they include women in their enumeration of prominent musicians. Nonetheless, European travelers who visited Persia on political or religious missions or for commercial purposes mention the activities of dancing girls and female entertainers in their travel accounts, and often provide valuable information about the courtesans and their reception in society.

The seventeenth century was the zenith of courtesan culture in Persia. Among the travelers who visited the Safavid court was the Italian composer and music theorist Pietro Della Valle (1586–1652), a cultivated man, proficient in Latin, Greek, classical mythology, medicine, and the sciences. While staying in Persia for six years (1617–1623), he traveled to many cities and wrote extensively on festivals, customs, pastimes, food, drink, dress, flora, corps, currency, drugs, spices, and, above all, Safavid legal and administrative systems. He is the first European traveler to provide scattered but detailed information about female entertainers in Iran in the seventeenth century. The other most eminent traveler was Jean Chardin, a Parisian merchant who undertook multiple visits to Persia (1673–1677) because of his father's position as a jeweler and shareholder in the French East India Company. He enjoyed royal patronage for many years and acquired a great command of the Persian language. In his ten-volume travel account, he frequently refers to courtesans in Isfahan and the amount of taxes they paid annually, also while describing their internal institution and relations with their patrons. During his nearly twenty-month stay in Isfahan (1684–1685), Engelbert Kaempfer also sought to collect as much information as possible to convey a complete picture of a foreign land and culture. He walked frequently through the capital, visited various districts, interviewed inhabitants, sketched views of people and objects, and described the buildings of the court, its palaces and gardens, the ladies' chambers, and, finally, the reception of the legation at the court. Kaempfer also reports frequently on courtesans and their activities in his travel journals.

It is customary for travel literature to entail the blending of different genres, and it may contain elements of exaggeration or distortion. In some cases, travelers attempt to combine reality and fiction so as to create a literary style to entertain a wider readership. Some travelers may also simply copy the accounts of their predecessors. After all, travelogues were written to sell, and they came to be among the most widely read books available in Europe, second in popularity only to romance. Nonetheless, most European travelers who visited Persia between the sixteenth and eighteenth centuries were mostly straightforward and attentive in writing their observations and ethnography. Rudi Matthee argues that the seventeenth-century travelogues are particularly notable in the authentic, detailed, and cross-cultural information they offer. The authors project neither the superiority of faith of their sixteenth-century predecessors, nor the orientalist approach of their late nineteenth-century successors. As Matthee writes, "intensely curious, the more perceptive ones sought to depict what they saw as faithfully and accurately as possible. They came to recognize and appreciate the intrinsic merits of Iranian society and culture. Most remarkably, the best ones show a willingness to test and even transcend the limitations of their culture and its assumptions."[1]

All in all, European travelers provide a great deal of information about courtesan culture, but certain aspects of their musical performance are still missing in travel accounts. These include descriptions of the types of poetry, music, and dance that were cultivated by various female performers. Even travelers like Chardin and Kaempfer, who deal in a more technical way with music, neglect to comment on the types of song that were typically performed by courtesans in the seventeenth century.[2] Nor did any traveler prior to the nineteenth century seek to assemble a collection of songs performed by female entertainers.[3]

Herat and Tabriz in the Late Fifteenth Century

Solṭān-Ḥosayn Bāyqarā lavishly patronized poets, musicians and dancers, and held poetic and musical gatherings (*bazms*) in the glorious gardens of Herat, to which a leisured class that included princes, noblemen, poets, calligraphers, painters, singers, and instrumentalists was frequently invited. He built a splendid music hall called Qaṣr-e Ṭarabafzā (lit. "euphoria-inducing palace") in the garden of Jahānārā, which came to be a major performance milieu for music and dance in the second half of the fifteenth century.[4] A group of female musicians and dancers was reportedly sustained by the court and the nobility during this period. In a short letter written by the famous calligrapher Solṭān-'Ali Mashhadi (1453–1520), a convivial gathering in the garden of Nurā is described in which, alongside male musicians, several female performers are enumerated as being in attendance.[5] The court also retained female performers from beyond the borders of Herat, most notably from other parts of Khorasan, Transoxiana, and Mongolia. A painting has survived in which Solṭān-Ḥosayn Bāyqarā is depicted sitting on the balcony of his palace, enjoying a troupe of Central Asian girls performing a round dance (Figure 2.1).[6]

The Āq Qoyunlu court of Tabriz was also an important center of musical patronage in the same period. The Italian traveler Josafa Barbaro, who visited the court of Uzun Ḥasan, describes an afternoon musical gathering at which female musicians and dancers performed for hours before the sunset.[7]

Figure 2.1 Harem of Solṭān-Ḥosayn Bāyqarā, Herat, dated 1481. Private collection of Abolala Soudavar. Currently on loan to the Arthur M. Sackler Gallery of the Smithsonian's National Museum of Asian Art, Washington, DC.

The Ban on Music

Following the conquest of Tabriz, Shah Esmāʿil I initially showed a hostile disposition toward female performers and even ordered 200 to 300 courtesans across the city to be killed.[8] He received a group of female harpists and dancers from Solṭān-Ḥosayn Bāyqarā, but dismissed them all as being an inappropriate tribute, claiming that as a defender of Twelver Shiʿism he did not need to be amused by such music-making beauties (*hurvashān-e naghmasāz*).[9] Later on, especially after his defeat at the battle of Chaldiran in 1514, his spirit changed significantly and thereafter he engaged in hunting, wine-drinking, and spending time in the company of dancing girls.[10] The Italian merchant Francesco Romano, who visited Tabriz during the reign of Shah Esmāʿil I, relates that courtesans frequented public places and they were bound to pay taxes based on their beauty. The more attractive and stylish they were, the higher the taxes they had to pay.[11]

It is during the reign of Shah Ṭahmāsb (r. 1524–1576) that we find a more extensive account of courtesans and their associated male instrumentalists. We are informed that when Shah Ṭahmāsb came to power, he withdrew his patronage of music and subsequently ordered the hands of everyone who played musical instruments in public to be cut off.[12] Eskandar Monshi, a chronicler of the Safavid court, appears to justify the shah's hostility to music as follows:

> Since Shah Ṭahmāsb always eschewed all practices forbidden by religious law, musicians found little favor with him. He fired most of those who already had employment at the court and retained only Ostād Ḥosayn Shushtari Balabāni and Ostād Asad, who was the *sornā* player in the royal *naqqāra-khāna* (drum house). Toward the end of his life, the Shah expelled from the court musicians such as Ḥāfeẓ Aḥmad Qazvini, who was renowned for his superb vocal techniques and graceful style of singing; Ḥāfeẓ Lālā Tabrizi; and others. The Shah had the idea that perhaps the royal princes, by associating with them, might begin to pay too much attention to music, and that they might corrupt the emirs who were their moral tutors and guardians and thus generate a general demand at court for such forbidden pleasures. Even Ostād Ḥosayn, the *sornā* player, was arrested, for he played in the public gatherings, and spent some time in prison. Finally, he swore a solemn oath that he would not play his *sornā* at any other place than the royal *naqqāra-khāna*.[13]

At first glance, the reaction of Shah Ṭahmāsb toward musicians seems perplexing, especially when we learn that as crown prince he was surrounded by some of the most outstanding musicians of his time. His fondness for music was so great that in one of his own paintings he depicted a *nay*-player and a male dancer who were likely in his service between 1515 and 1521 in Herat (Figure 2.2). Why, then, did Shah Ṭahmāsb abruptly turn his back on musicians and ban those who were affiliated with his court from performing in public places? And what were these public places? In Islamic law major offences such as burglary may be punishable by amputation and retribution for criminal activity, but were performers of instrumental music engaged in activities that would have rendered them deserving of such severe punishment? Evidently, the public gatherings to which Eskandar Monshi refers could not have been merely wedding ceremonies and annual festivities, for it is unrealistic to assume that a potentate such as Shah Ṭahmāsb would have shown such harsh reactions to the recreational and mundane social activities of common citizens.

Historical sources claim that in a gesture known as *tawba*, Shah Ṭahmāsb first repented in 1533 and later made a second and apparently more stringent declaration of *tawba* in the wake of the 1555 Treaty of Amasya, when he issued several decrees (*farmāns*) in an attempt to curtail forms of frivolous entertainment and recreation. These included activities associated with the *sharāb-khāna* (tavern), *bang-khāna* (house for smoking hashish), *ma'jun-khāna* (house for drinking a cocktail drug), *buza-khāna* (house for drinking rice beer), *bayt al-loṭf* (brothel), *qomār-khāna* (gambling house), and *qavvāl-khāna* (courtesan salon).[14] What stands apart in this list of public places is the *qavvāl-khāna*, and by extension, the word *qavvāl*. The *qavvāl-khāna* has been interpreted and identified imprecisely by historians of the Safavid period as a gathering place for performing music or storytelling. Yet *qavvāl* literally means a performer of *qawl*, which was a metric vocal composition; therefore, it should not be confused with the *naqqāl*, who is indeed a narrator or storyteller. The German physician Engelbert Kaempfer mentions that the term *qavvāl* referred specifically to a courtesan who made a living in brothels.[15] Furthermore, in a sketchbook that Kaempfer brought back from Isfahan, the drawing of a woman is described as "the archetypal image of *qavvālān* in Iran" (Figure 2.3).[16]

Unfortunately, the extant accounts shed little light on the *qavvāl-khāna* as a socio-cultural institution in Tabriz or Qazvin, the two Safavid capitals in the sixteenth century. Yet we can glean much information about the social organizations

Figure 2.2 Painting of Shah Ṭahmāsb made for his brother Bahrām Mirzā. Tabriz or Herat, 1520s. Courtesy of the Topkapı Palace Museum, Istanbul, H. 2154, f. 1b.

of courtesans and urban male musicians by examining unique records associated with the provincial court of the Kārkiyā dynasty in eastern Gilān.[17]

An appointment letter reveals that at some point Khān Aḥmad Gilāni invited the prominent *kamāncha* player of his time, Ostād Zaytun, to Lāhijān

Figure 2.3 "*Shāhedbāz* and *qavvāl*," from the Kaempfer album, 1684–1685. British Museum, London, inv., No. 1974 6-1701 (13).

and appointed him as the *chālchi-bāshi* for several years. In a similar letter, written a few years later, Ostād Moḥammad 'Udi was appointed to the same office and various classes of musicians and entertainers in Lāhijān were assigned to operate under his supervision.[18]

The letters first indicate that all musicians and entertainers formed a community known by officials and in court records as *ahl-e naghma* (lit. "people of music"). In one letter, four major groups of musicians are introduced as such, namely, instrumentalists (*sāzanda*s), courtesans (*qavvāl*s), musicians of military and ceremonial bands (*naqqārachi*s), and street entertainers who attract a circle (*maʿrekagir*s).[19] In the second letter, vocalists (*guyanda*s and *kh^{v}ānanda*s) and luthiers (*sāztarāsh*s) are also added to this list. On the order of Khān Aḥmad, the four groups of musicians had to abide by the rules and regulations set by the *chālchi-bāshi*. They had to seek his advice on most matters, resolve their fiscal and legal problems through him, and enter into or cancel deals and contracts under his authority. If they were arrested or convicted, it was the responsibility of the *chālchi-bāshi* to intervene and release them from jail. No claim or problem could be presented to the court unless it had already been heard by the *chālchi-bāshi*. In one instance, Khān Aḥmad directly ordered the *ṭavā'ef*, who appear to have been courtesans and musicians of tribal or rural background, to obey the order of the *chālchi-bāshi* and be at his service at all times.[20]

Ostād Zaytun, one of the most renowned instrumentalists of his time, was formerly based in Herat. After he served as *chālchi-bāshi* in Lāhijān, Khān Aḥmad appointed him as the commander-in-chief of a vast region in Gilān called Tolam.[21] A few years later, Shah Ṭahmāsb wrote a letter to Khān Aḥmad making remarks critical of the appointment and allocating an annual salary of 400 *tumān*s to Ostād Zaytun. The content of the letter reveals that Shah Ṭahmāsb was previously familiar with this musician, probably from Herat, and had a severely negative impression of him, referring to Ostād Zaytun as "an alcoholic instrumentalist of gypsy origin (*kawli*) who would incite a large number of Muslim men to adultery every year." Shah Ṭahmāsb further blames Ostād Zaytun for his lack of adherence to *shari'a* (Islamic law) and for being surrounded by aristocrats of that region who keep young Muslim boys as their companions and would commonly attend the latter's gatherings, engaging in music, gambling, and sexual dissipation.[22]

Among the four groups of musicians and entertainers mentioned in the letter, instrumentalists and courtesans seem to have been the major exponents of music in the town. We may assume that prominent soloists like Ostād Zaytun and the skilled courtesans had the opportunity to perform at the court or the *majles* of nobility; less esteemed *qavvāl*s and *sāzanda*s only performed in courtesan salons. In other words, most *sāzanda*s seem to have been associated with courtesan salons in one way or another. In the case of *ṭavā'ef*, the *sāzanda*s must have also been related to the courtesans either through familial or pedagogical ties, as was the case in later periods. All the accounts allude to the fact that it was the prior connection and experience of Ostād Zaytun with the courtesan community that brought him to Lāhijān. Likewise, we can infer that the hostility shown by Shah Ṭahmāsb toward instrumentalists and, more specifically, toward Ostād Zaytun was due to the latter's association with the courtesan community and prostitution. Taken together, these facts explain why the performance of music came to be banned during the reign of Shah Ṭahmāsb as well as, periodically, throughout the Safavid period in general.

In the court correspondence of Khān Aḥmad there is a short letter written by the *qavvālān* of Rudsar, a small town 16 miles east of Lāhijān, which reveals not only the existence of a courtesan community in Rudsar, but also that the courtesans of that town were highly literate and had a demonstrable command of witty conversation, an uncommon attribute of the average housewife in that period.[23]

Despite the ban, Shah Ṭahmāsb failed to eliminate *qavvāl-khānas* in the capital or in any other cities, although he assigned severe punishments to professional instrumentalists who performed in courtesan salons and houses of ill-repute. Many instrumentalists presumably supported themselves partially or entirely through teaching or accompanying the courtesans. Indeed, what Shah Ṭahmāsb managed to achieve in this period was chiefly to remove the position of *chālchi-bāshi* and abolish all taxes on courtesan salons and other public houses such as gambling dens and brothels. Yet he must have retained professional female performers in his own service or as part of his extensive harem. In 1566, he dispatched four dancing girls together with a group of musicians and a large collection of *naqqāra-khāna* instruments to the Ottoman ruler, Selim II (r. 1566–1574).[24] During the reign of Shah Ṭahmāsb, musical contact was also initiated with the Caucasus. Shah Ṭahmāsb invaded Georgia several times, and from his raiding expeditions he brought back a large number of men and women from that region. Georgian and Circassian women, who were often engaged in music and dance, later became omnipresent at the seraglio, and the royal practice of contractual marriages with them as concubines became widespread from that time on.

The Emergence of Upper-class Courtesans

When Shah 'Abbās I (r. 1581–1628) moved the capital to Isfahan in 1587, large contingents of performers, courtesans, artists, poets, craftsmen, and merchants migrated there. Pietro Della Valle, who visited Isfahan at that time, refers to the king's female performers and specifically mentions Felfel (lit. "Pepper"), a senior courtesan who commanded much respect from everyone at the court, even though by then she was old and unattractive.[25] The Armenian historian Zakaria Kanakertsi (1627–1699) also recounts the story of an Armenian dancer, Ghazāl, who was Shah 'Abbās' favorite performer despite never having converted to Islam. Later she repented and became a nun.[26] The Spanish envoy Don Garcia de Silva y Figueroa and Della Valle both refer to several instances where a group of twenty to twenty-five courtesans on horseback and without veils were present among the shah's retinue or as an entourage welcoming foreign ambassadors and envoys who had arrived from India, the Ottoman empire, Muscovy, and Spain.[27] Della Valle specifies that these respectable women were upper-class courtesans and entertainers who were selected directly by the shah (Figure 2.4).[28] Likewise an Augustinian cleric, Antonio de Gouvea, who traveled with Shah 'Abbās I from Mashhad to Isfahan, confirms that the king's entourage consisted of a number of women who rode horses and wore no veils.[29]

Every time Shah 'Abbās I undertook official visits to various places or traveled to other cities, he was accompanied by a group of professional courtesans who were led by an older, experienced woman. This senior courtesan served to organize the entire group and had influence with the shah. In the words of De Silva y Figueroa, "the shah and his courtiers indeed were lavish in their appreciation, which allowed these women to live luxuriously."[30]

We know from Della Valle that when Shah 'Abbās I conquered Qandahar in 1622, he had a group of courtesans led by Dallāla Chizi (= Qezi) enter the city first. This was done to humiliate the Mughal army, establishing a pretense that the fortress had been defeated by a group of soft women.[31] Āqā Mo'men, a leading composer of Isfahan, who later became the *chālchi-bāshi*, accompanied the king and the courtesans in the same expedition and wrote a victory song after the conquest of Qandahar.[32] It is therefore safe to assume that the victory song and probably the majority of laudatory songs in the surviving song–text collection of Āqā Mo'men, were compositions intended to be performed by courtesans in the first half of the seventeenth century.

Aside from those highly respected and select courtesans associated with the royal court and the gentry, there were less esteemed and even indigent female singers and dancers who were active in courtesan salons and caravanserais, and whose activities were always kept under some measure of control and supervision by the authorities. In urban centers, courtesans, along with other entertainers, were always monitored by the *dārugha* (chief of police) and they were called upon especially when the authorities wished to provide music and dance for an auspicious occasion.

At the beginning of the seventeenth century more than 12,000 prostitutes and courtesans were registered in Isfahan alone; a figure that would constitute 5 percent of the city's female population at that time.[33] These women and the

Figure 2.4 Courtesan with a long-necked lute, Isfahan, c. 1600–1610. Reproduced by permission of Los Angeles Museum of Art, the Nasli M. Heeramaneck Collection, gift of Joan Palevsky (M.73.5.457).

assorted courtesan salons would have certainly provided a large amount of tax revenue for the government. The taxes were collected by *mash'aldār-bāshi*, the chief of the royal department of lighting, who was primarily in charge of city lighting and official fireworks. Shah 'Abbās I was known to have been uncomfortable and doubtful about the revenues collected from brothels and courtesan salons, "fearing to sully his Treasury with money rais'd from so infamous a commerce, [he] order'd it should pass the Fire to purifie it, that is, be employ'd to defray the expense of Flambeaux, Illuminations, and other artificial fireworks that are made at the King's charges."[34] Nevertheless, Kaempfer confirms that at least in the second half of the seventeenth century the salaries of musicians at the court and the *naqqāra-khāna* were paid out of revenues collected from the *qavvāl*s.[35]

European travel accounts usually mention different classes of courtesan in this period, which were distinguished by their ethnicity, appearance and wealth, and by the amount of money they would charge their patrons. In 1637, Adam Olearius wrote that brothels and courtesan salons thrived in all cities except Ardabil and that they were protected by the authorities.[36] Shah 'Abbās I considered Ardabil, the burial place of his ancestor, Shaykh Ṣafi al-Din, a sacred city, and hence he banned the activities of courtesan salons there. However, this proscription did not have a lasting effect, for, in 1670, Struys reports that he saw several courtesans in Ardabil who composed religious epic songs in praise of 'Ali and Ḥosayn, and some were dancing before the governor.[37]

Once a courtesan danced so well at court that Shah 'Abbās II, who had become enamored, gave her a caravanserai as a reward for her performance, which is to say, a substantial property that yielded significant rental income. The following day the grand vizier advised the shah to cancel the gift and instead give her 100 *tumān*s. The courtesan at first insisted upon her right to the original award, but finally gave in when told that she would otherwise receive nothing.[38]

Chardin, who had indirect access to the internal establishments of the court, reports that there was a group of twenty-four female musicians and dancers at the service of Shah Solaymān and that these performers were celebrated as the most renowned and superior courtesans of the country. This group of upper-class and well-dressed women was supervised by a madam (*khānom*) who was herself a senior courtesan at the court. They used to live in different neighborhoods of Isfahan, and it was the responsibility of the madam to assemble them for each event or banquet. She would arrange for performances, settle disputes among them, punish them, if need be, protect them if they were insulted, and keep an eye on the finances of the troupe. Punishment was administered with a whip, and if the infraction was repeated, the girl would be expelled from the group. The madam also took care of their salaries; she had to make sure that they had proper dress, and appropriate furniture, in short that they were properly equipped for the tasks they had to perform. Chardin mentions:

> Each courtesan in the [royal] troupe had a support staff of two maids, a male servant, a cook, and a groom with two or three horses. If they traveled with the court, they had four additional horses for their luggage. The annual payment for the entire troupe was 1,800 francs. In addition to this, they received a certain quantity of fabrics for their dresses. Likewise, a sufficient food allowance was sent to them from the court. Some of them made as much as 900 *écus*; but the level of their salary depended on the shah's appreciation of their art. This was not their only source of income, for some nights they might be paid as much as 50 *pistoles*.
>
> Each member of this troupe was identified by the amount of money she demanded for each performance, such as the 10-*tuman* or 5-*tuman* or 2-*tuman* girl. Each *tuman* equals 15 *écus* in France. None of them asked less than one *tuman*, and when she could not command that much, she was let go and another took her place.
>
> As is customary in Iran, in order to invite these girls, one has to send them money in advance. If the invitation is only for dancing, one should talk to the madam and pay two *pistols* for each dancer. If one wants to have six, seven or eight girls, he has to pay twelve, fourteen and sixteen *pistols*. If the performance of dancers was enjoyable to the host, he would give them some gifts as well. But if the intention of the host is to receive other services, he has to pay girls in advance.[39]

In 1665, Chardin met two courtesans in outfits studded with precious stones, whose value he estimated at 10,000 *écus*.[40] Chardin further claims that there were 14,000 registered courtesans and prostitutes throughout the capital who paid the substantial amount of over 13,000 *tumāns* in taxes. He adds that the same number of courtesans went unregistered as they did not want to be labeled officially as public women.[41]

Non-Muslim and convert female performers, notably Georgian, Circassian, and Armenian concubines and courtesans, as well as Indian performers, are frequently mentioned in travelers' accounts, and they played a significant role in court musical life and certain urban centers in general during the seventeenth century. The Portuguese cleric Antonio de Gouvea describes how, during a visit with his men to the court of Shah 'Abbās I in 1603, he was entertained by a group of eight Circassian dancers.[42] Among the upper-class courtesans in the reign of Shah Solaymān (r. 1666–1694) there were reportedly six Georgian slave girls living in a single house in Isfahan where they were supervised by a madam.[43] Furthermore, during the campaign of Shah 'Abbās I to Armenia in 1604–1605, numerous women were purchased with the intention of putting them to work as public women in courtesan salons and brothels.[44] Thus, from all available evidence, it is safe to assume that most of the rulers retained Caucasian performers in their courts who were either concubines or upper-class courtesans invited occasionally for ceremonial and formal gatherings. Toward the end of the seventeenth century, the French missionary N. Sanson observed that Shah Solaymān's concubines were particularly trained in archery, horseback riding, and hunting at the court. He further reports that some concubines received professional training in singing and playing musical instruments as well.[45]

Moreover, Olearius reports that 12,000 Indians, including an envoy from the Mughal emperor and many affluent merchants, were settled in Isfahan around the middle of the seventeenth century, and he further mentions that on one occasion he was entertained by Indian courtesans in Sāru Taqi's house.[46] Chardin also informs us that a group of Indian musicians were moved by Shah 'Abbās II from Qandahar to Isfahan, where they were given a house by the shah.[47] These courtesans must have had a profound knowledge of Persian songs and poetry, for otherwise their arts might have seemed foreign, if not distasteful to a Persian clientele in seventeenth-century Isfahan.

Chardin claims that there were almost 1,000 gypsies (*kawli*s) in the capital in the second half of the seventeenth century, and that the majority were musicians of less esteemed social position. While the men of this community were mostly active as hereditary instrumentalists, the women were predominantly engaged in dancing near caravanserais, where they could entice spectators and travelers.[48] Yet some of the male gypsy musicians who were associated with courtesan salons in the sixteenth century, such as Ostād Zaytun and probably

Ostād Āhu, were outstanding *sāzanda*s in their own right, and a few of the prominent instrumentalists in the succeeding generation of musicians even claimed to be their students.[49]

Female performers have always been the predominant exponents of various forms of urban and rural folk dances. De Mans relates that they would engage in thousands of dances before men with their faces unveiled, and that their services were very costly.[50] Chardin declares that dancing in public was mostly performed by prostitutes and public women, and that from a religious perspective it was considered more dishonorable and reproachable than performing with musical instruments.[51] It seems that men did not dance, except for Georgian and Armenian boys who were also involved in male prostitution.[52] In this respect Thomas Herbert's description of dancing boys in 1629 is worth quoting in full:

> The Ganymedes with incanting voices and distorted bodies sympathizing, and poesy, mirth, and wine raising the sport commonly to admiration. But were this all, 'twere excusable; for though persons of quality here have their several seraglios, these dancers seldom go without their wages; and in a higher degree of baseness, the pederasts affect those painted antic-robed youths or catamites, a vice so detestable, so damnable, so unnatural as forces Hell to show its ugliness before its season.[53]

There is evidence that professional upper-class courtesans continued to be patronized by the court and the nobility almost until the end of the reign of Shah Solaymān in 1694. When Shah Solṭān-Ḥosayn acceded to the throne, courtesan districts were still active in the capital and other cities as the centers of musical activity, but under the influence of his conservative advisors, especially Moḥammad Bāqer Majlesi (1627–1699), the shah issued a decree banning the activities of public entertainers, fighting animal owners, gamblers, and courtesans throughout the capital.[54] A historian in the early years of the reign of Shah Solṭān-Ḥosayn writes:

> Musā Beg, the chief justice of the common law criminal court (*divān-begi*), and the chief of police of Isfahan (*dārugha*) spent some time implementing the issued command. They began to arrest *ma'rekagirs* (entertainers who would attract an audience), *moqalleds* (mimics and jesters), *koshtigirs* (wrestlers), *ḥoqqabāzs*

> (con artists), *quchbāzs* (fighting ram owners), and *moqāmers* (gamblers) who were in public spaces; and [also] they arrested dealers of *chars* (condensed hemp juice), *bang* (cannabis), *bāda* (alcohol) and *kabutarbāzs* (bettors on pigeon races). They also sent the *fāheshas* (prostitutes) and *qavvāls* (courtesans) to the top cleric [of Isfahan] to repent from their disgusting deeds and abominable acts and to be contrite for them and to leave such deeds behind. They subsequently arranged for most of them to marry religious men. Those who did not receive an offer of marriage were entrusted to the heads of communities and white-bearded elders of the neighborhoods—who were apprised of their states—to oversee them. Whenever a respectable candidate for a husband arrived, they conveyed both parties to the *sharī'a* court (*dār al-shar'*); and, in accord with religious law, they complied with the marital bond.[55]

However, this does not seem to have affected the activity of courtesans much, either in the court milieu or in urban centers in general (Figure 2.5). Shah Solṭān-Ḥosayn appears to have shown strong interest in music during his reign. Gemelli Careri also mentions attending some of the official banquets of the shah at which musicians were present.[56]

Figure 2.5 Detail of a pen-box showing a courtesan making love with a member of the gentry, Isfahan, dated 1712. From the Nasser D. Khalili Collection of Islamic Art, London, LAQ 361.

Courtesans in the Eighteenth Century

The Afghan invasion in 1722 and the downfall of the Safavid Empire truncated Isfahan's prominence as a cultural center and eventually culminated in the transformation of the intellectual, political, and artistic life of the entire country. Already in the late seventeenth century, the nobility and wealthy families who had supported the fine arts, and especially music, had come to ruin, and the prosperity of upper-class courtesans in Isfahan was at a low point. However, soon after the Afghan invasion, Nāder began to gain power and established a massive military camp that eventually comprised 200,000 soldiers and 20,000 women. During his campaigns, he gradually recruited a large number of urban and rural courtesans as well as village girls to serve in his encampments. Historical sources of the Afsharid period attest to the activity of numerous female musicians, dancing girls, and acrobats who were employed at the camp of Nāder along with male instrumentalists, comedians, tightrope walkers, and firework technicians. The male and female entertainers and dancers, who were broadly referred to as *bāzigars*, accompanied Nāder and his army during their campaigns while providing music, dance, and acrobatics at various festivities and ceremonial occasions.[57] Père Louis Bazin, the French physician in the camp of Nāder between 1741 and 1747, sketched a map of the camp where five tents are marked as the housing of courtesans and musicians. He also depicts a large circular area containing two other tents and marks them as the residential area of special courtesans associated with the harem (Figure 2.6).[58]

In addition to the courtesans from urban and rural backgrounds that Nāder himself accumulated or received from chieftains and regional governors, he had a number of Ottoman and European female performers and dancers in his camp that he likely obtained as gifts from other rulers.[59] It also seems to have been common among the feudal rulers, governors, and chieftains who were fond of music and dance to recruit attractive girls from various sources and train them in their harems. Nāder's chronicler, Moḥammad Kāẓem Marvi, mentions, for instance, Yusof Khān, the feudal ruler of Kunduz, who retained 600 beautiful girls trained in playing musical instruments, singing, rope-dancing, juggling, and various aspects of music.[60]

Nāder invaded India in 1739 and, after defeating the Mughals at the battle of Karnal, his army eventually captured Delhi. According to ʻAbd al-Karim Kashmiri, while staying in Delhi, Nāder frequently spent his time in the

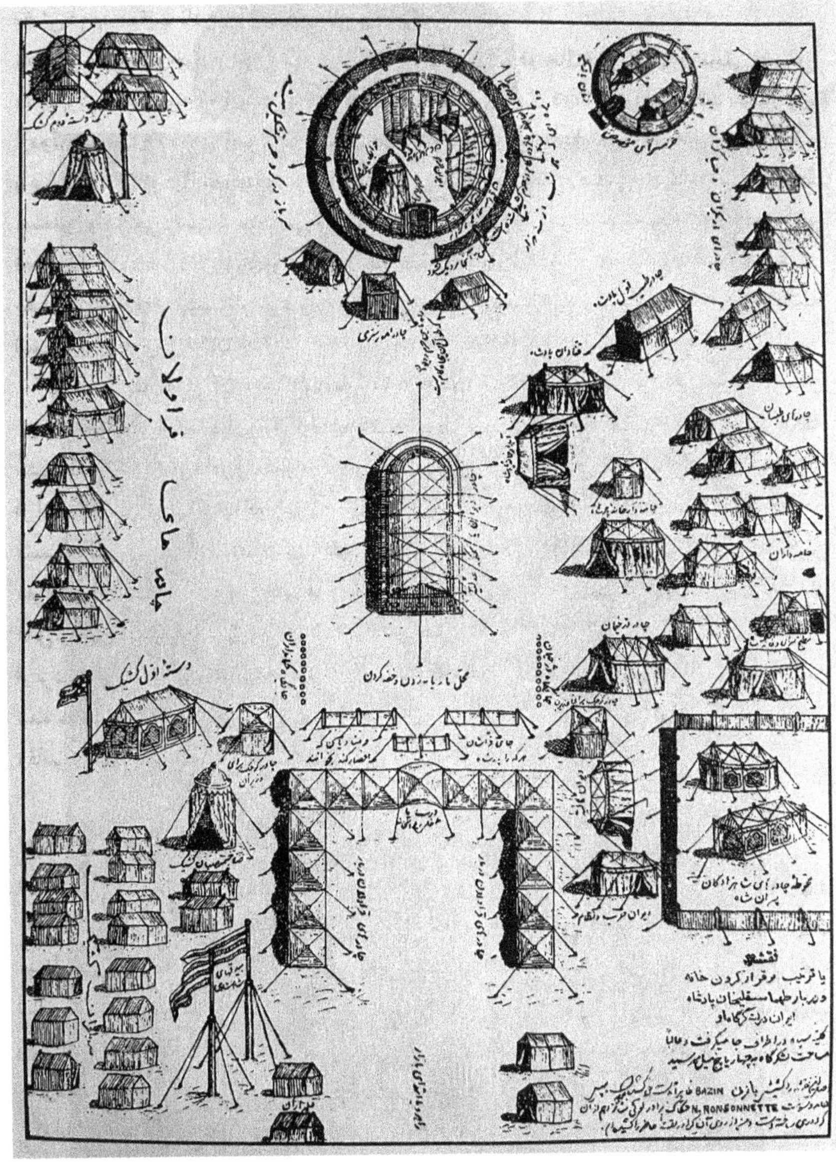

Figure 2.6 Map of Nāder's camp (1741–1747) as originally drawn by Père Louis Bazin.

company of Indian courtesans. Among them he became infatuated with Nur Bay, who was a talented singer and accomplished reciter of Persian poetry. Upon Nāder's departure, Nur Bay sang an amatory poem that affected the shah so much that he ordered his servants to give the girl 3,000 rupees. When Nāder returned to Iran, he brought back several courtesans and dancers from

Delhi. Astarābādi writes that those courtesans stayed in the camp of Nāder for four years and transmitted their artistic knowledge and expertise to their Iranian counterparts.[61]

Meanwhile, in Shiraz, Karim Khān Zand (r. 1751–1779), displayed great fondness for the fine arts, and, in particular, for the courtesan community and courtesan culture (discussed briefly at the end of Chapter 1). He was well aware of the fact that taxes collected from courtesans and prostitutes were a source of prodigious revenue for the state and, unlike his Safavid predecessors, he felt no constraints in exhibiting his interest in supporting female musicians and dancers in the new capital. He soon established a courtesan district called *khayl* in the *kharābāt* quarter of Shiraz where he gathered and even imported 5,000–6,000 urban and rural courtesans and dancing boys catering to the tastes of the nobility and of his military officials.[62] The intention of Karim Khān in creating the *khayl* district was to distract the assorted gentry and dignitaries of Shiraz with lavish entertainment and delectations so as to avert their interference with the administration of the state and thus prevent conspiracies and political attempts against him. He also maintained a large number of courtesans, especially a group of gypsies (*foyuj*), in his military camp. Aside from making music, dancing, and other forms of entertainment, these performers provided members of the army with a channeled outlet for their sexual energy.[63]

Among the female performers in the *khayl* district, there was a small but prominent group of upper-class urban courtesans. These women were notable for their beauty (*zibā'i*), seductive manners (*delrobā'i*), polished etiquette (*adab* and *kamāl*), knowledge (*ma'refat*), banter, witty conversation (*nokta-pardāzi*), and companionship (*mu'nes-e jān*). Above all, they were accomplished singers (*khosh-āvāz*), dancers (*raqqāṣ*), and professional performers (*bāzigar*s) capable of entertaining both the elite and common people.[64] The historian and literary figure of the late eighteenth century, Rostam al-Ḥokamā', names seventy courtesans of Shiraz in this period and further narrates several stories about two celebrated ones, Mollā Fāṭema and Moraṣṣa', that yield valuable insights into the basic nature of the courtesan culture of that period. Mollā Fāṭema was a famous singer and dancer renowned for her collection of memorized poetry. Her repertoire included some 20,000 verses from both classical and contemporary poets that she performed in a manner commensurate with the various moods, emotional states, and dispositions of her patrons, a technique known among singers and courtesans as *monāseb-khᵛāni* (selecting relevant verses for singing in various contexts).[65] At a purely aesthetic level, she sought to please by her talent and poetry, so that she would receive generous honoraria or tips, and be asked to perform again. Moraṣṣaʿ, by contrast, was a performer who attended private gatherings of connoisseurs in Shiraz and would be escorted by a few subsidiary courtesans (*golrokhān-e zirdastash*) who accompanied her mostly with dancing and musical instruments as she entertained her patrons.[66]

In the last eighteen years of his reign in Shiraz, Karim Khān enthusiastically invited male and female musicians to his court almost every evening for *maḥfel*s and official banquets.[67] Among the courtesans of *khayl* district, Shākha Nabāt was a distinguished *setār* player and singer in her own right who became Karim Khān's mistress for many years. Edward Scott Waring, the British traveler who visited Shiraz shortly after Shākha Nabāt's death, includes her image in his book, *A Tour to Sheeraz* (Figure 2.7), and writes: "She is said to have possessed a wonderful influence over the mind of the Vakeel, obliging him, upon every occasion, to submit to her wishes. The king was sensibly affected at her death and paid her memory the same attention as he would have shewn if she had been legally married to him."[68]

Figure 2.7 "Shākha Nabāt," a courtesan of Shiraz who became Karim Khan's mistress. Bodleian Portraits Collection, University of Oxford, LP 843.

Upper-class courtesans, though considered to be prostitutes by the general public, were prominent exponents of the fine arts and custodians of refined culture in Shiraz in the second half of the eighteenth century (Figure 2.8). Pictorial sources such as lacquer works and paintings show that these performers were sometimes accompanied by subsidiary or lower-ranking female performers who were responsible for playing musical instruments and dancing during a *bazm* session (Figure 2.9). Likewise, one can presume that male *sāzanda*s of the city came to be in charge of training and accompanying courtesans as well as performing independently in various public venues.

Courtesans, along with those in charge of courtesan salons, paid large amounts of tax and were under the close scrutiny and control of the *dārugha*. Waring writes:

> . . . people who pay the heaviest tax to government, are the female dancer, and the votaries of pleasure. They exercise their profession under the immediate patronage of the governor; their names, ages, &c. are carefully registered, and if one should die or marry, another instantly supplies her place. They are divided into classes, agreeably to their merits, and the estimation they are held in; each class inhabit separate streets, so that you may descend from the *doo Toomunees* [= 2 *tumāns*] to the Pooli Seeahs [= copper coins], without the chance of making mistakes.[69]

However, neither the courtesan community nor the gentry of Shiraz were homogeneous by any means in this period. Innumerable artists, poets, and musicians had migrated from Isfahan and other places to Shiraz largely after the collapse of the Safavids to enjoy the patronage of the new aristocracy, and Karim Khān forced the migration of many tribes to the new capital.

While Shiraz was the most important hub of upper-class courtesans in this period, Isfahan still hosted a significant courtesan community. Unfortunately, there are no substantial accounts of courtesan art and culture in Isfahan for much of the eighteenth century, but some of the courtesans who were brought to Tehran after the demise of the Zands and the accession of the Qajars were reportedly from Isfahan.

Figure 2.8 A pasteboard showing courtesans entertaining a patron, Shiraz, dated 1775. Housed at Victoria and Albert Museum, London, 763-1888.

Figure 2.9 Mirror case with shutter showing courtesans entertaining a patron, Tehran, c. 1840. From the Nasser D. Khalili Collection of Islamic Art, London, LAQ. 152.

The Resurgence and Decline of Upper-class Courtesans in Tehran

When Āqā Moḥammad Khān (r. 1786–1797), the founder of the Qajar dynasty, rose to power, he captured Isfahan and Shiraz in a series of campaigns against the Zands. Soon he began to consolidate his authority and administration in Tehran, while at the same time he sent his nephew and crown prince, Bābā Khān (later known as Fatḥ-ʿAli Shah), to Shiraz as prince-regent of Fars. During his stay in Shiraz (1793–1797), Bābā Khān became exposed to courtesan art and culture and seized the opportunity to acquire a refined taste for courtly life.

Fatḥ-ʿAli Shah (r. 1797–1834) married more than 160 wives and concubines of various ethnic origins during his thirty-seven-year reign. Upon his arrival in Tehran, he summoned to the city many courtesans and female entertainers who seem to have transmitted the musical traditions of the Zands and many other urban and regional folk cultures to the new capital. Fatḥ-ʿAli Shah soon established an institution called *dastgāh-e bāzigar-khāna* (chamber of entertainers), and housed two troupes of twenty-five accomplished female instrumentalists, singers, dancers, and acrobats at his court. These troupes were organized and managed both offstage and on by two reputable senior courtesans of Isfahan, Ostād Zohra and Ostād Minā.[70] In the mornings, members of each troupe were trained by two non-Muslim male music and dance instructors: Sohrāb, an Armenian musician of Isfahan, and Rostam, a Jewish musician of Shiraz (Figures 2.10, 2.11 and 2.12).[71]

During the reign of Fatḥ-ʿAli Shah, several male instrumentalists were also associated with the *dastgāh-e bāzigar-khāna*, among whom Rajab-ʿAli Khān Kermāni (d. 1835) was the chief of musicians and courtesans at the court. As a multi-instrumentalist, he taught the *kamāncha*, *tār*, *setār*, *santur*, and dancing to the female musicians of the harem. When he left the court for the province of Gilān, his position was delegated to a certain Chālānchi Khān (d. 1836), a Jewish convert to Islam who played *kamāncha* and *santur*. Equally prominent during this period was Āqā Moḥammad-Reżā, an accomplished *tār* and *setār* player who, together with his daughter Shāhverdi Khānom, played a central role in the training and educating of female musicians in the harem.[72] Shāhverdi Khānom, who was a prominent performer in her own right, later became one of the concubines of the shah.[73]

Figure 2.10 An acrobat of *dastgāh-e bāzigar-khāna*, Tehran, c.1820. Victoria and Albert Museum, London, 719-1876.

Figure 2.11 A courtesan playing the *kamāncha* associated with the *dastgāh-e bāzigar-khāna*, Tehran, *c.* 1820. Present whereabouts unknown.

Figure 2.12 A courtesan playing the *santur* associated with the *dastgāh-e bāzigar-khāna*. Courtesy of Honolulu Museum of Art, Hawaii.

The harem of Fatḥ-'Ali Shah was a multicultural environment in which the women, including the shah's wives, concubines, and ladies-in-waiting, came from various ethnic groups. Some of the female musicians came to be concubines of the shah and his close relatives. These musicians performed only inside the harem and were not allowed to play for anyone but the shah and his relatives. Likewise, a group of upper-class courtesans associated with the *dastgāh-e bāzigar-khāna* were active as professional performers across the capital, moving around the palace courtyard on horseback, often with a maid in attendance.[74] These courtesans do not seem to have been among the concubines of the shah, and probably served the gentry and other clients outside the court (Figures 2.13 and 2.14).[75]

Following a series of wars with Russia that culminated in the loss of the Caucasus, the Imperial Treasury was all but depleted during the reign of Moḥammad Shah (r. 1834–1848), and the Qajar court could no longer afford frivolous expenditures. Unlike his tolerant forebears, Moḥammad Shah was also an orthodox monarch who attempted to curb epicurean activities like the patronage of courtesans and drinking, which offended his puritanical

Figure 2.13 A courtesan playing the *setār*, Tehran, *c.* 1820. Courtesy of Honolulu Museum of Art, Hawaii.

Figure 2.14 Two courtesans associated with the *dastgāh-e bāzigar-khāna*, Tehran, *c.* 1811–1814. Royal Asiatic Society of Great Britain and Ireland, 01 002.

temperament and that of his conservative grand vizier, Ḥāji Mirzā Āqāsi. Accordingly, the *dastgāh-e bāzigar-khāna* as a court institution ceased to receive royal patronage, and by the middle of the nineteenth century, the music of the court gradually became dominated by professional male musicians. In the second half of the nineteenth century, urban and rural courtesans were enormously active outside the court, but largely in the form of small ensembles comprising three to six performers. Professional and talented female performers including singers, instrumentalists, and dancers, often performed at the court and in the homes of nobles. The term *qavvāl* continued to refer to courtesans throughout the nineteenth century. An official decree from 1882 shows that a certain Luṭi Ṣāleḥ was appointed as the chief of *qavvālān* and *arbāb-e ṭarab* in Shāhrud and Basṭām.[76]

Summary

Before the seventeenth century, female court performers were regarded by the ruling nobility as having great value and were often sold or presented as gifts to other rulers. For instance, Solṭān-Ḥosayn Bāyqarā sent a group of female performers as a tribute to Shah Esmā'il to prevent him from invading Herat, and in 1566, Shah Ṭahmāsb dispatched four courtesans to his Ottoman counterpart, Salim II. Even during the eighteenth century, Nāder received several courtesans and female performers from regional governors. These courtesans constituted a major conduit for the transmission and exchange of musical ideas and stylistic features between courts.

Beginning in the seventeenth century, three broad groups of female performers can be identified based on their physical appearance, musical training, and knowledge, their relationship with their patrons, and, finally, the space in which they performed.[77] The first group consisted of twenty to thirty upper-class, well-dressed, educated courtesans (*qavvāls*) who dwelled in the capital and probably in a few main urban centers. While these courtesans were active in their own salons, often serving the gentry, young nobility, and high-ranking military officers with their lavish entertainments, they were also asked to perform occasionally at court ceremonial and formal gatherings. When invited to perform at the court or the house of a noble, they traveled in town without veils on horseback with an entourage of two or three maids and male servants. These courtesans belonged to the highest tax bracket and possessed substantial property, wealth, and cultural prestige. They received training in music, dance, and acrobatics as well as knowledge of poetry from master musicians and poets of the time, and sometimes went through several years of apprenticeship, working closely with celebrated courtesans as assistants or supporting performers. In the eighteenth century, the most celebrated of these performers were singers who had a vast repertoire of memorized poems and often performed verses responding to the various emotional feelings and dispositions of their patrons.

The second group were less esteemed urban and gypsy courtesans who often performed in *qavvāl-khānas*, taverns, brothels, and caravansaries, and commonly had male accompanists. The number of these women was quite large in the Safavid period, for according to some accounts, 12,000 courtesans and prostitutes were registered in the capital alone. A substantial number of courtesans in Isfahan during the seventeenth century seem to have been of Georgian, Armenian, and Indian background.

While the first and second groups of female performers provided sexual services for multiple patrons, the third group consisted of concubines who were related to potentates, princes, or governors through temporary marriage and were permitted to perform only in the harem or in the houses of the nobility when there were all-female gatherings. In many cases, talented and beautiful maidens were selected first, and were trained by male and female senior performers of the court for a few years. In the Qajar period, both upper-class courtesans and concubines were trained in music and dance by master court musicians, and they were considered to be the major exponents of *taṣnifs* and *rengs*.[78]

Between the seventeenth and nineteenth centuries, the influence of non-Muslim (Georgian and subsequently Jewish) dancing boys was prominent in the music of the capital and main urban centers. In general, one can presume that the main reason music and dance were stigmatized and frequently proclaimed as *ḥarām* was the association of musicians with other illicit activities such as male and female prostitution and drinking alcohol—behaviors that were considered evidence of moral decay in Muslim society.

Notes

1. Rudi Matthee, "The Safavids under Western Eyes: Seventeenth-Century European Travelers to Iran," *Journal of Early Modern History* 13 (2009): 170–171.
2. For an account of Safavid music discussed in travel accounts, see Owen Wright, "Persian Perspectives: Chardin, De la Borde, Kaempfer," *Rast Musicology Journal* 7(2) (2019): 2050–2083.
3. Alexander Borejko Chodźko, the nineteenth-century Polish scholar, clearly states that his collected song–texts were performed by the female court performers. See *Specimens of the Popular Poetry of Persia* (London, 1842), 417.
4. Zayn al-Din Vāṣefi, *Badāyi' al-waqāyi'*, 1: 493.
5. Dāneshpazhuh, *Nemuna'i az fehrest-e āthār-e*, 6.
6. For further information, see Abolala Soudavar, *Art of the Persian Courts* (New York: Metropolitan Museum of Art, 1992), 90.
7. *Travels to Tana and Persia*, 1: 61; Matthee, "Prostitutes, Courtesans, and Dancing Girls," 141.
8. *Travels to Tana and Persia*, 2: 52, 2: 191.
9. Możṭar, *Tārikh-e jahāngoshā-ye khāqān*, 222.
10. See *Travels to Tana and Persia*, 2: 202.
11. Charles Grey, trans. and ed., *Narrative of Italian Travels in Persia in the Fifteenth and Sixteenth Centuries* (London, 1873), 172.
12. Ḥasan Rumlu, *Aḥsan al-tawārīkh*, 323.
13. *Tārikh-e 'ālamārā-ye 'Abbāsi*, 1: 190. For the original translation, see *History of Shah 'Abbas*, 1: 280–281.
14. Ibid., 513.

15. Kaempfer, *Exotic Attractions in Persia, 1684–1688*, 108.
16. Engelbert Kaempfer, *Album of Persian Costomes and Animals with some Drawings*, British Museum, London, 1974, 0617,0.1.21.
17. Cf. Feraydun Nurzād, *Nāmahā-ye Khān Aḥmad*, 112–113, 154–155.
18. Ibid., 112–113, 154–155.
19. Ibid., 113.
20. Ibid., 155.
21. Ibid., 156.
22. Ibid., 68, 321–322.
23. Ibid., 117.
24. Navā'i, *Shāh Ṭahmāsb-e Ṣafavi*, 457.
25. Matthee, "Prostitutes, Courtesans, and Dancing Girls," 143.
26. Le Diacre Zakaria, "Mémoires historiques sur les sofis," in *Collection d'historiens arméniens*, ed. and trans. M. Brosset, 2 vols. (St. Petersburg: l'Académie imperiale des sciences, 1876), 2: 24–26.
27. Don Garcia de Silva y Figueroa, *Comentarios de d. Garcia de Silva y Figueroa de la embajada que de parte del rey de España don Felipe III hizo al rey xa Abas de Persia*, 2 vols. (Madrid: 1903), 2: 35–51; Pietro Della Valle, *Viaggi di Pietro della Valle*, 2: 7–10; Rudi Matthee, "From the Battlefield to the Harem: Did Women's Seclusion Increase from Early to Late Safavid Times," in *New Perspectives on Safavid Iran*, ed. Colin P. Mitchell (New York: Routledge, 2011), 102.
28. Pietro Della Valle, *Viaggi di Pietro della Valle*, 2: 17–18.
29. Antonio de Gouvea, *Relation des grandes guerres et victoires obtenues par le roy de Perse Chah Abbas contre les empereurs de Turquie* (Rouen: Nicholas Loyelet, 1646), 149.
30. De Silva y Figueroa, *Comentarios*, 2: 210–211.
31. Pietro Della Valle, *Les Fameux Voyages*, 3: 22–23, 3: 104–105, 3: 567; also see Ya'qub Āzhand, *Namāyesh dar dawra-ye Ṣafavi* (Tehran: Farhangestān-e Honar, 2009), 126.
32. Pourjavady, "The Musical Codex of Amir Khān Gorji," 252.
33. See L. Leupe (ed.), "Beschrijvinge van de coninclijcke stadt Spahan," in *Kronijk van het Historisch Genootschap gevestigd te Utrecht* 2e serie, 10 (1854): 205.
34. Nicholas Sanson, *The Present State of Persia* (London, 1695), 70–71.
35. Kaempfer, *Exotic Attractions in Persia, 1684–1688*, 108.
36. Olearius, *Vermehrte newe Beschreibung*, 532, 592.
37. J. J. Struys, *Drie aanmerkelijke en seer rampspoedige reysen door Italie, Griekenlandt, Lijflandt, Moscovien, Tartarijen, Meden, Persien, Oast-Indien, Japan, en verscheyden andere gewesten* (Amsterdam, 1676), 303–304.

38. Monsieur de Thevenot, *The Travels of Monsieur de Thevenot into the Levant in Three Parts* (London, 1686), 2: 100.
39. Chardin, *Voyages*, 2: 205–217.
40. Ibid., 2: 205–211.
41. Ibid., 2: 211–212.
42. de Gouvea, *Jornada do arcebispo de Goa Dom Frey Aleixo de Meneses*, 145b.
43. Chardin, *Voyages*, 7: 413–414.
44. Father Belchior dos Anjos, "Relation des motifs du Châh pour faire guerre au Turc, et des événements qui s'ensuivirent dès le 14 septembre 603 jusqu'à septembre 604," in *L'ambassade en Perse de Luis Pereira de Lacerda et des Pères Portugais de l'Ordre de Saint-Augustin, Belchior dos Anjos et Guilherme de Santo Agostinho 1604–1605*, ed. Robert Gulbenkian (Lisbon: Foudation Calouste Gulbenkian, 1972), 100; as cited in Matthee, "Prostitutes, Courtesans, and Dancing Girls," 142, n. 93.
45. Sanson, *Voyage ou relation de l'estat present du royaume de Perse*, 88.
46. Olearius, *Vermehrte newe Beschreibung*, 531; as cited in Matthee, "Prostitutes, Courtesans, and Dancing Girls," 141.
47. Chardin, *Voyages*, 8: 61.
48. Ibid., 7: 478–480.
49. Zaytun and Āhu are not traditional Muslim names. For further information about Ostād Āhu, see Mollā Jalāl Monajjem, *Tārikh-e 'Abbāsi*, 156; Sayyed Ḥosayn Maythami, *Musiqi-ye 'aṣr-e Ṣafavi*, 71, 178.
50. Francis Richard, *Raphaël du Mans missionnaire en Perse au XVIIe s.*, 2 vols. (Paris: L'Harmattan, 1995), 2: 90.
51. Chardin, *Voyages*, 4: 309.
52. Matthee, "Prostitutes, Courtesans, and Dancing Girls," 139; Floor, *A Social History of Sexual Relations in Iran*, 207.
53. Thomas Herbert, *Travels in Persia 1627–1629*, ed. Sir William Foster (New York: Routledge, 1929), 248.
54. Floor, *A Social History of Sexual Relations in Iran*, 227.
55. Moḥammad Ebrāhim b. Zayn al-'Ābedin Naṣiri, *Dastur-e Shahriyārān*, ed. Moḥammad Nāder Naṣiri (Tehran: Bonyād-e Mawqufāt-e Maḥmud Afshār, 1994), 51–52.
56. Sāsān Fātemi, *Jashn va musiqi dar farhanghā-ye shahri-ye Irān* (Tehran: Māhur, 2014), 54.
57. For the musical life in the Afsharid period, see Pourjavady, "Negāhi be ḥayāt-e musiqā'i-ye dawra-ye afshāri," 44.
58. Bāzan, *Nāmahā-ye ṭabib-e Nāder Shāh*, trans. 'Ali-Asghar Ḥariri (Tehran: Anjoman-e Āthār-e Melli, 1961), 40.

59. Cf. Pourjavady, "Negāhi be ḥayāt-e musiqā'i-ye dawra-ye Afshāri," 43–47.
60. Marvi, *'Ālamārā-ye Nāderi*, 609.
61. Astarābādi, *Tārikh-e jahāngoshā-ye Nāderi*, 430, 487–488; Pourjavady, "Negāhi be ḥayāt-e musiqā'i-ye dawra-ye Afshāri," 53–54.
62. Rostam al-Ḥokamā', *Rustam al-tawārīkh*, 340.
63. Ibid., 329–331.
64. Ibid., 340. Dwight Reynolds also mention that in the Abbasid period "the most famous *qiyan* had a reputation for being able to best the men who listened to them not only in the spontaneous composition of poetry and music, but also in banter, wordplay and witty comebacks." See "The *Qiyan* of al-Andalus," in *Concubines and Courtesans: Women and Slavery in Islamic History*, ed. Matthew S. Gordon and Kathryn A. Hain (Oxford: Oxford University Press, 2017), 103.
65. Rostam al-Ḥokamā', *Rustam al-tawārīkh*, 341–342.
66. Ibid., 348–348.
67. Abu al-Ḥasan Ghaffāri-Kāshāni, *Golshan-e morād*, ed. Gholām-Reżā Ṭabāṭabā'i Majd (Tehran: Zarrin, 1990), 420.
68. Waring, *A Tour to Sheeraz*, 61.
69. Ibid., 80.
70. 'Ażod al-Dawla (Solṭān-Aḥmad Mirzā), *Tārikh-e 'Ażodi*, ed. Abd al-Ḥosayn Navā'i (Tehran: Nashr-e 'Elm, 1997), 46–47; Sayyed Ḥosayn Maythami, "Nokāti darbāra-ye musiqidānān-e Qājār az 1210 tā 1264 H," *Māhur* 61 (2013): 97–101.
71. 'Ażod al-Dawla, *Tārikh-e 'Ażodi*, 46–49; Maythami, "Nokāti darbāra-ye musiqidānān-e Qājār," 97–101.
72. Moḥsen Moḥammadi, "Resāla-ye davāzdah dastgāh," *Māhur* 59 (2013): 140–141; 'Ażod al-Dawla, *Tārikh-e 'Ażodi*, 49.
73. Shāhverdi Khānom is mentioned in *Nāsikh al-tawārīkh* as the daughter of Āqā Moḥammad-Reżā. For further discussion, see 'Ażod al-Dawla, *Tārikh-e 'Ażodi*, 344.
74. 'Ażod al-Dawla, *Tārikh-e 'Ażodi*, 47–49.
75. Fāṭemi (*Jashn va musiqi dar farhanghā-ye shahri-ye Irāni*, 56–58) opines that, by the beginning of the nineteenth century, through an effort that he calls "culture rehabilitation," the upper-class courtesans ceased to be active in the capital and all the *bāzigars* or female performers at the Qajar court—especially those recruited to the ensembles of Minā and Zohra—were married to Fatḥ-'Ali Shah or his courtiers. It is evident that some of the female court performers were concubines of the shah, however, many were still upper-class courtesans who were specifically recruited to perform at certain court occasions. 'Ażod al-Dawla, *Tārikh-e 'Ażodi*, 46–47, refers to a group of female performers who had maids and rode horses in the palace courtyard, characteristics of courtesans in the seventeenth century. Likewise, paintings

of courtly life display a clear differentiation between the outfits of concubines and courtesans. While concubines are often depicted as wearing *shalitas* (trousers with a short skirt) and *rusaris* (head scarf), courtesans are portrayed as wearing transparent shirts with trousers made of luxurious fabrics. Courtesans' performance attire consisted of jeweled dresses decorated with pearls, gems, and embroidery as well as elaborate aigrettes.

76. *Farmān-e riyāsat-e Luṭi Ṣāleḥ be moṭrebān va qavvālān*, University of Tehran (Tehran) MS 3935.
77. For a comparison with female performing communities in Mughal India, see Katherine Butler Schofield, "The Courtesan Tale: Female Musicians and Dancers in Mughal Historical Chronicles, c. 1556–1748," *Gender and History* 24(1) (2012): 152–158.
78. The exponents of the *radif*, especially Nur'ali Borumand, mostly believed that singing *taṣnif* was primarily the specialty of female musicians. Personal communication from Ḥātam 'Askari and Moḥammad-Reżā Loṭfi.

3

MUSICAL LIFE IN THE NINETEENTH CENTURY

The nineteenth century was a period of upheaval in Iran in which many aspects of society and culture underwent dramatic changes. Before the turn of the century, the Qajars (r. 1789–1925) came to power and made Tehran their capital. At the turn of the nineteenth century, the court had reasserted its control over its former territories, but by 1813, as a result of the imperial power struggles between Britain and Russia, Iran ultimately lost its control over the Caucasus. The same decades witnessed increased contacts with the West and the beginning of intense European diplomatic rivalries in the region. In the second half of the nineteenth century, military modernization, the introduction of the printing press and telegraph, an intellectual reawakening through Western-style education, and the rise of nationalism and an increasing desire for the establishment of a nation-state eventually culminated in the transformation of Iran's political, intellectual, and artistic life.

For a long time, musical life in nineteenth-century Iran received little scholarly attention due in large part to the paucity or inaccessibility of source materials. Initial attempts to gather information from both oral and written sources were made by the two eminent Persian scholars Ruḥollāh Khāleqi and Ḥasan Mashḥun, who mainly focused on the biographies of musicians rather than on the social and cultural context of music and musical life.

Over the past thirty years, however, many new nineteenth-century sources have become available to scholars of Iranian music that have opened up rich areas of investigation, such as the role of state patronage, the social organization of musicians, including *maktab*s (stylistic schools), hereditary lineages, and performance contexts, and the impact of Western influence and contacts with other musical cultures.

The diary of Nāṣer al-Din Shah (r. 1848–1896) and several journals composed by nineteenth-century princes and noblemen have been edited and published; numerous photography albums including images of male and female musicians and entertainers have been analyzed and made available; a number of musical treatises containing information on hitherto unknown musical figures have been discovered; and, finally, 78 rpm records made by the Gramophone Company between 1899 and 1933 have been digitized and released as albums. All these documents can help us to formulate a more fine-grained picture of Iranian musical life in the nineteenth and early twentieth centuries.

This chapter focuses on musicians associated with the Qajar court in Tehran and also addresses urban musical life outside the court, including the impact of social modernization. The rationale for the focus on court music is that the Qajar court was the hub for the most celebrated musicians in the country—musicians whose musical ideas, repertoire, performance practice, and approach to teaching established the core tradition of Persian classical music—not to mention that both written and oral sources for court music are more abundant than for musical life outside the court.

It is also safe to say that no history of nineteenth-century Persian music can do justice to its subject while remaining strictly within the bounds of the years 1800 and 1900. Scholars of Iranian history have long felt a need to release the nineteenth century from those arbitrary calendrical moorings. Some have posited a "long" nineteenth century, bounded by two seminal events: the rise and fall of the Qajar court. For reasons that will become clear throughout this chapter, I adopt the same span of time as the chronological beginning and end of my survey.

Early Qajar Court Music

Āqā Moḥammad Khān (r. 1789–1797), the founder of the Qajar dynasty, belonged to the Qajar Turkmen clans that had vanquished the Afshārs and taken control of the northern provinces. Guillaume Olivier, a French traveler who visited his court in 1796, reports on a banquet at which musicians and jesters entertained the guests before dinner, but he expresses his surprise that unlike what he was accustomed to in Europe, none of the courtiers and guests participated in the performance of music and dance over the course of the night.[1] No prominent musician is mentioned specifically as associated with the court in this period. Yet Āqā Moḥammad Khān's grandson refers to the shah's own musical talent and further declares that whenever the potentate was in a good disposition and felt exuberant, he played the *dōtār*, an instrument widely used among the Turkmen.[2]

The Dastgāh-e Bāzigar-khāna

In the preceding chapter, I described the roots of Qajar court music in the courtly life of Shiraz, the capital of Karim Khan Zand, and how elements of this courtly life were brought to Tehran by Āqā Moḥammad Khān's nephew, the prince-regent Bābā Khān, later known as Fatḥ-'Ali Shah. Upon his arrival in Tehran, Fatḥ-'Ali Shah (r. 1797–1834) established a chamber of entertainers or *dastgāh-e bāzigar-khāna* at his court and hosted a large number of female performers who were either upper-class courtesans brought from Isfahan and Shiraz or his own concubines trained in music, dance, and acrobatics by male master musicians of the court. These women were organized in two groups of twenty-five performers—referred to as *bāzigar*s—directed by two former master courtesans, Minā and Zohra. In the mornings, members of each group received training from Sohrāb, an Armenian instructor from Isfahan, and Rostam, a Jewish instructor from Shiraz.

Around the same time, a few male instrumentalists, singers, and dance instructors found their way to the Qajar court and were placed in charge of training promising female performers while performing themselves at many court celebrations and gatherings. Little is known about the background of these musicians, and it is not clear whether they came from families of hereditary musicians. We may presume, however that most of them, like Sohrāb and Rostam, were experienced instrumentalists and dance instructors, and accordingly, would have been previously engaged in the training of performing artists and likely came to Tehran with their own small troupes of performers (*dasta*s).

The most respected musician at the court of Fatḥ-'Ali Shah was Āqā Bābā Makhmur (d. *c.* 1820), a singer from Isfahan who was held to be superior to all of his contemporaries. He was the favored singer in the shah's service, with his broad knowledge of both music theory and performance. Two musical texts refer to him as the most influential figure in the development of the *dastgāh* system and as an active mentor who trained a number of disciples. He is specifically credited as the first person to combine a vast collection of melody types into the twelve ordered structures known as *dastgāhs*.[3]

The principal instrumentalist and chief of musicians and entertainers (*moṭreb-bāshi*) at the court was Rajab-ʿAli Khān Kermāni (d. 1835), who performed on a number of instruments. In Tehran, he was the pupil of Āqā Bābā Makhmur, whose tutelage he followed closely.[4] The Polish orientalist Alexander Chodźko (1804–1891), who met Rajab-ʿAli Khān during his stay in Tehran, describes him as a superior *kamāncha* player and the dance instructor of courtesans, and as one of his own informants regarding the collection of *taṣnifs* that he gathered in his book.[5] As a highly paid musician, Rajab-ʿAli Khān enjoyed great renown during his lifetime and never played in other contexts outside the court milieu except for a close circle of princes and nobility.[6] For a while, he was the director of the *dastgāh-e bāzigar-khāna* and toward the end of the reign of Fatḥ-ʿAli Shah, he migrated to Gilan, where he served as court musician to Manuchehr Khān Gorji (d. 1846), the Georgian de facto ruler of that region. In 1834, he moved with Manuchehr Khān from Gilan to Shiraz and died there a year later.[7]

Three other instrumentalists, Chālānchi Khān (d. 1836), Āqā Moḥammad-Reżā, and Āqā Ebrāhim, were also associated with the *dastgāh-e bāzigar-khāna*, with each teaching specific instruments under the supervision of Rajab-ʿAli Khān.[8] Chālānchi Khān was an adolescent Jewish boy who, upon entering the court, became a Muslim. Chālānchi Khān received his vocal training at the court and soon came to be the favorite singer of Fatḥ-ʿAli Shah. However, post-puberty his voice deteriorated and subsequently, he began to play the *santur*. Eventually, the shah ordered him to play the *kamāncha* and he ended up becoming an eminent virtuoso on that instrument. After Rajab-ʿAli Khān, Chālānchi was appointed as the *moṭreb-bāshi*, and this is also probably when he became known as Chālānchi Khān.[9]

The second instrumentalist, Āqā Moḥammad-Reżā, was commonly recognized as the most celebrated *tār* and *setār* teacher at the court and was also renowned for his broad and systematic approach to the twelve *dastgāh*s and their structures. He knew a large number of melody types by name and sought to include them all in his arrangements of *dastgāh*s.[10] Moḥammad-Reżā's daughter, Shāhverdi Khānom, was also a musician and was responsible for training performers in the female quarter at the court.[11] Āqā Ebrāhim was the *santur* teacher. According to a contemporary writer, while he lacked a particularly striking style, the consensus was that he was the best *santur* player of his day.[12]

In addition to Āqā Bābā Makhmur, other singers were also active at the court. Chodźko mentions a certain Mollā Karim as a proficient singer and trainer of courtesans who assisted Chodźko when he was making a collection of vocal compositions performed by the female performers.[13] Another contemporary account confirms that Mollā Karim was a musical authority who, besides writing *taṣnif*s and playing the *tār*, was particularly adept at singing the *mathnavi*.[14]

According to the author of *Tārikh-e ʿAżodi*, every morning the male masters (*ostād-e mardāna*s), including Āqā Moḥammad-Reżā, Rajab-ʿAli Khān, and Chālānchi Khān, came to the *moʿallem-khāna* or 'chamber of instruction' to teach the female performers. Female performers—both courtesans and concubines—were collectively known as *bāzigar*s, but the word *bāzigar* more specifically referred to dancers and acrobats. The shah's concubines dressed in such a way that their entire bodies except for their faces were covered. Nonetheless, eunuchs sat in the room while *the bāzigar*s took their lessons (*mashq*) from male instructors (Figure 3.1).[15]

By the beginning of the reign of Moḥammad Shah (r. 1834–1848), Fatḥ-ʿAli Shah's successor, the *dastgāh-e bāzigar-khāna* was still active and young girls were still being recruited, but the organization of courtesans into two groups of twenty-five professional female performers was no longer maintained. Moḥammad Shah did not pursue an extravagant lifestyle and was reportedly under the influence of his advisors—specifically, his puritanical grand vizier Ḥāji Mirzā Āqāsi (*c.* 1783–1848), who was known to be a dervish. By the middle of his reign, the shah had ceased to support professional courtesans in his court while at the same time dancing boys, also known as *bāzigar*s, had become more prominent.

Figure 3.1(a–d) "Court *bāzigars*," three courtesans dancing and one concubine holding a frame drum.

The custom of having troupes of female instrumentalists, singers, and dancers in the harem does not seem to have been confined to the royal court in Tehran. During the first half of the nineteenth century, several princes and dignitaries who were appointed as governors in various urban centers retained female performers at their local courts. The number and quality of female performers in a court was a vital part of the atmosphere of court life and a measure of its ruler's prestige. In some cases, these female performers were hired courtesans, especially in big cities such as Isfahan and Shiraz, where a long tradition of courtesan culture can be traced back to the Safavid period or even earlier. In other cases, female performers were concubines of princes or nobles and rarely performed for any male spectator outside the harem.

The French painter and archaeologist Eugène Flandin (1809–1889) was once invited to the harem of Malek Qāsem Mirzā (d. 1860), a son of Fatḥ-'Ali Shah, in Urmia. Flandin reports that his host had some twenty female performers at his court. Over the course of the dinner, a group of performers, including two instrumentalists, two accompanists, and two dancers, entertained the guests with music and dance. Among the female performers, Flandin mentions that a blind male musician who performed on the *kamāncha* was also present.[16] It is not clear, however, whether the male musician was visually impaired or just blindfolded, a tradition in situations where a male instrumentalist was brought to perform before a harem or all-female gathering. More often than not, such a male instrumentalist was the trainer of female performers and attended the gathering with his own ensemble.

Princes were among the leisure class that had a serious involvement with music. While lavishly patronizing all forms of entertainment and competing with one another for musical renown, several princes were also adept at playing musical instruments. There is no doubt that some of them had direct access to the *mo'allem-khāna* at the court and thus may have studied with the most accomplished master musicians of their time. Nonetheless, the extent of musical knowledge they acquired essentially depended on their own personal motivations and does not seem to have been part of the general training a prince was required to receive.[17]

Smaller Troupes of Performers

Apart from the *dastgāh-e bāzigar-khāna* and the female performers who were primary sources of musical entertainment in courts and houses of the nobility, there were smaller *dasta*s (troupes) consisting of professional male musicians and dancing boys who were either patronized by the gentry or were independently active in urban and rural centers. These *dasta*s usually consisted of half a dozen or so entertainers who mostly performed at celebrations or public gatherings. A typical professional male ensemble seems to have included one *tār* player, one *kamāncha* player, one or two singer-accompanists playing *daf* (frame drum) or *dombak* (goblet drum), and two to four dancing boys. According to some accounts, these musicians as a general category were called *moṭrebs*. Dancing boys were also known as *bāzigars*. They danced in women's clothes with their long hair let down, and besides dance movements, they also performed acrobatic gestures.

Amateur Musicians, Music Theorists, and Poets

Throughout the nineteenth century groups of amateur musicians and singers were associated with the royal court in Tehran and other provincial courts—most notably in Shiraz, Isfahan, Tabriz, Kāshān, and Gilan—whose primary occupation was not music making. These nonprofessional and nonhereditary musicians were among the court literati, a group of classical poets, calligraphers, painters, and storytellers. They were often invited to the literary and artistic gatherings of the nobility where they performed for a small number of patrons. Several of these individuals were also poet-composers who achieved some renown in their lives and are remembered even today through written and oral traditions. Likewise, a few of them had some knowledge of music theory, and it is safe to assume that some of the music treatises compiled in this period and even earlier were written by such individuals.

During the reign of Fatḥ-'Ali Shah one such amateur court musician was 'Ali Moḥammad Khᵛānsāri, a noble of Khᵛānsār and boon companion (*lala-ye ḥożur*) of the shah who also wrote poetry under the pen name Qerqi. With a gruff, low-pitched voice, 'Ali Moḥammad Khᵛānsāri had an excellent working knowledge of music theory and performance but was reluctant to be recognized as a musician in public and only performed privately for the shah, and then only on certain occasions.[18]

In the same period, those who were studying theology and philosophy at less conservative seminaries, particularly in Tehran and Isfahan, still studied mathematics from Ibn Sinā's *Kitāb al-shifā'* (*Book of Remedies*) or similar texts, and in some cases medieval music theory was included in their curriculum. Thus, it is no surprise to find that some of the religious scholars at that time were major exponents of music theory, although they often frowned upon music performance. Gobineau reports that Mollā 'Abd al-Javād Khorāsāni, the outstanding mathematician of Isfahan, had a large circle of students and disciples at the time and was renowned as a music theorist with some knowledge of playing the *tār*. Yet since the performance of music was not held in high esteem, nobody had ever seen him playing the instrument.[19] Another such religious scholar was

Ākhund Mollā 'Ali, who had a reputation as a mathematician and music theorist but had no knowledge of playing musical instruments.[20]

Among the literati, poets were notably familiar with music, more so than any other group, and they often had close connections to court musicians. Sometimes poets were either songwriters themselves or their poems were set to vocal compositions by contemporary *taṣnif* and *āvāz* singers. During the reign of Moḥammad Shah, the most eminent poet, Forughi Basṭāmi (1798–1857), was reportedly educated in music as well. He wrote a poem in praise of the shah in which he names three *tār* players, Zāghi, Rayḥān, and the Jewish musician Melikhāy, as well as three accompanists (*żarbgir*s), Akbari, Aḥmadi, and Bābā'i.[21] Another member of the literati and a prominent patron of music in this period was Moḥammad Shah's grand vizier Ḥāji Mirzā Āqāsi, a respected aristocrat initiated into the Ne'matollāhi Sufi order who composed poetry and vocal compositions.[22] He is credited with the composition of a *taṣnif* that was later transformed into an instrumental composition known as *reng-e faraḥ*.[23]

The Court of Nāṣer-al-Din Shah

The long reign of Nāṣer-al-Din Shah (r. 1848–1896) was the period of great flourishing for Persian music, mostly due to lavish patronage by the shah and his princes. In the second half of the nineteenth century, the musicians sustained by the court were divided into two broad groups of male and female professionals. Female musicians and entertainers—mostly the shah's concubines—performed exclusively in the *andarun* (harem) and were preeminent exponents of *taṣnif*s and *reng*s. Professional male musicians and entertainers, on the other hand, formed a community known as the *'amala-ye ṭarab* (servants in the office of entertainment) or *ahl-e ṭarab-e mardāna* (community of male entertainers), two titles that were alternatively employed by the shah and his courtiers. They performed mostly in the *khalvat* (male intimate domain) at various social gatherings of the court and fell into three different categories in descending order of rank: (1) *'amala-ye ṭarab-e khāṣṣa*, (2) *'amala-ye ṭarab*, and (3) *moṭreb*.

'Amala-ye Ṭarab-e Khāṣṣa

The first category, *'amala-ye ṭarab-e khāṣṣa*, or the "special musicians of the royal court," consisted of solo specialists, including both instrumentalists and singers, who enjoyed the highest esteem at the court.[24] They were allowed to sit and perform in the presence of the shah and also received monthly stipends.[25]

The majority of these professionals belonged to musical families that were active in the nineteenth century for at least two or three generations. During the reign of Nāṣer-al-Din Shah, there were two outstanding families (*khāndān*) and some five minor families among the *'amala-ye ṭarab-e khāṣṣa*. While in many cases a given family emerged as dominant in their specialization on one particular instrument, there were also families that comprised an ensemble, and thus their members were trained in various musical instruments. The leading figures of these musical families and their prominent subsequent members were:

Āqā 'Ali-Akbar Farāhāni (d. 1862):
Supposedly from Farāhān, specialized in playing the *tār*. After him, his nephew Āqā Gholām-Ḥosayn and his three sons Mirzā Ḥasan, Mirzā 'Abdollāh, and Āqā Ḥosayn-Qoli were all members of *'amala-ye ṭarab-e khāṣṣa* as *tār* players:

Āqā Moṭalleb (d. 1872):
From Shiraz, specialized in playing the *kamāncha*. His first son, Moḥammad Ṣādeq Khān, a master *santur* player at the court, was a musical prodigy who far surpassed his father in renown to the point where it is commonly held that he founded the musical family. Āqā Moṭalleb's second son, Mirzā Shafi', was a *tār* player.

Khoshnavāz Khān:
Khoshnavāz Khān and his son were both *kamāncha* players.

Esmā'il Khān (d. 1885):
Esmā'il Khān, his brother Qoli Khān, and his son Ḥosayn Khān were all *kamāncha* players.

Moḥammad Ḥasan Khān (d. 1879):
A *santur* player. His daughter Sakina was a pupil of Āqā 'Ali-Akbar and became a famous musician in the female quarter.

Āqā Ḥasan:
A singer and *tār* player. His son was a singer and *dombak* player.

Āqā Gholām-Ḥosayn:
A *kamāncha* player. His son, Ḥabibollāh Samā'-Ḥożur, was a renowned *taṣnif* singer and *santur* player. His daughter, Zivar al-Solṭān, was the most celebrated *taṣnif* singer in the *andarun*.

Āqā 'Ali-Akbar Farāhāni, renowned for his superb instrumental technique and remarkable repertoire of Persian and adopted foreign tunes, was the most celebrated *tār* player of the Qajar period and established an instrumental *maktab* (stylistic school) for the *tār* and *setār*.[26] He developed a distinct repertoire for these instruments, incorporating a highly efficient plucking system that was perpetuated and further refined in the hands of his descendants—in particular, his sons, Mirzā 'Abdollāh and Āqā Ḥosayn-Qoli. Āqā 'Ali-Akbar's background and musical education served as the bedrock on which the subsequent generation of musicians established the authenticity of the court repertoire. Āqā 'Ali-Akbar could have been the pupil of Āqā Moḥammad-Reżā, the distinguished *tār* and *setār* player at the court of Moḥammad Shah. Āqā Moḥammad-Reżā had an older brother named Moḥammad-Reżā who was also a *tār* player, and some researchers have argued that these two Moḥammad-Reżās could have been one and the same person.[27] Furthermore, it is hard to imagine that Āqā 'Ali-Akbar received his primary musical education in Farāhān, his alleged birthplace, for Farāhān was not a center of cultural or political significance at the beginning of the nineteenth century. Presumably he was born in Farāhān and later came to the Qajar court, where he probably studied with master musicians, including Āqā Moḥammad-Reżā, who was renowned for his broad knowledge of melody types.[28]

During his professional career, Āqā 'Ali-Akbar was involved in training male and female singers and instrumentalists as well as *bāzigars*. Abu al-Ḥasan Ghaffāri, better known as Ṣani' al-Molk (1814–1866), who was the eminent court painter in the middle of the nineteenth century, depicted Āqā 'Ali-Akbar with a group of young musicians and performers (Figure 3.2). Musical artists in the picture are identified as Kawkab Khānom, Mirzā 'Abdollāh Khān 'Alā' al-Molk, 'Ali-Akbar Bāzigar, Ḥasan Khān, Mas'ud Mirzā, Solṭān Khānom,

Figure 3.2 Painting by the prominent court painter Ṣaniʿ al-Molk (1814–1866) depicting, from left to right: Masʿud Mirzā, Solṭan Khānom, Mirzā Haydar-ʿAli Sarhang, Āqā ʿAli-Akbar, Ḥasan Khān, ʿAli-Akbar Bāzigar, Mirzā ʿAbdollāh Khān ʿAlā'-al-Molk, and Kowkab Khānom. Present whereabouts unknown.

and Mirzā Haydar-ʿAli Sarhang. Among these musicians, biographical details are available only for Solṭān Khānom, who came to be a celebrated singer and composer at the seraglio during the second half of the nineteenth century.[29]

In 1863, a few photographs were taken of professional male musicians of the court. Nāṣer-al-Din Shah, who himself took a particular interest in photography and in documenting various aspects of court life, later added the names and titles of the musicians at the bottom of the pictures. In one picture the entire group of male professionals were captured in a long shot (Figure 3.3). In this picture, musicians appear to have been seated from left to right in descending order of rank, as dictated by their authority and age. The first group of musicians includes three instrumentalists: Moḥammad Ḥasan Khān (head of the court musicians and *santur* player); Āqā Moṭalleb (*kamāncha* player); and Āqā Gholām-Ḥosayn (*tār* player). The second group consists of five singers of *āvāz* and *taṣnif*: Āqā ʿAli Kāshi (singer); Āqā Ḥasan (singer and *tār* player);

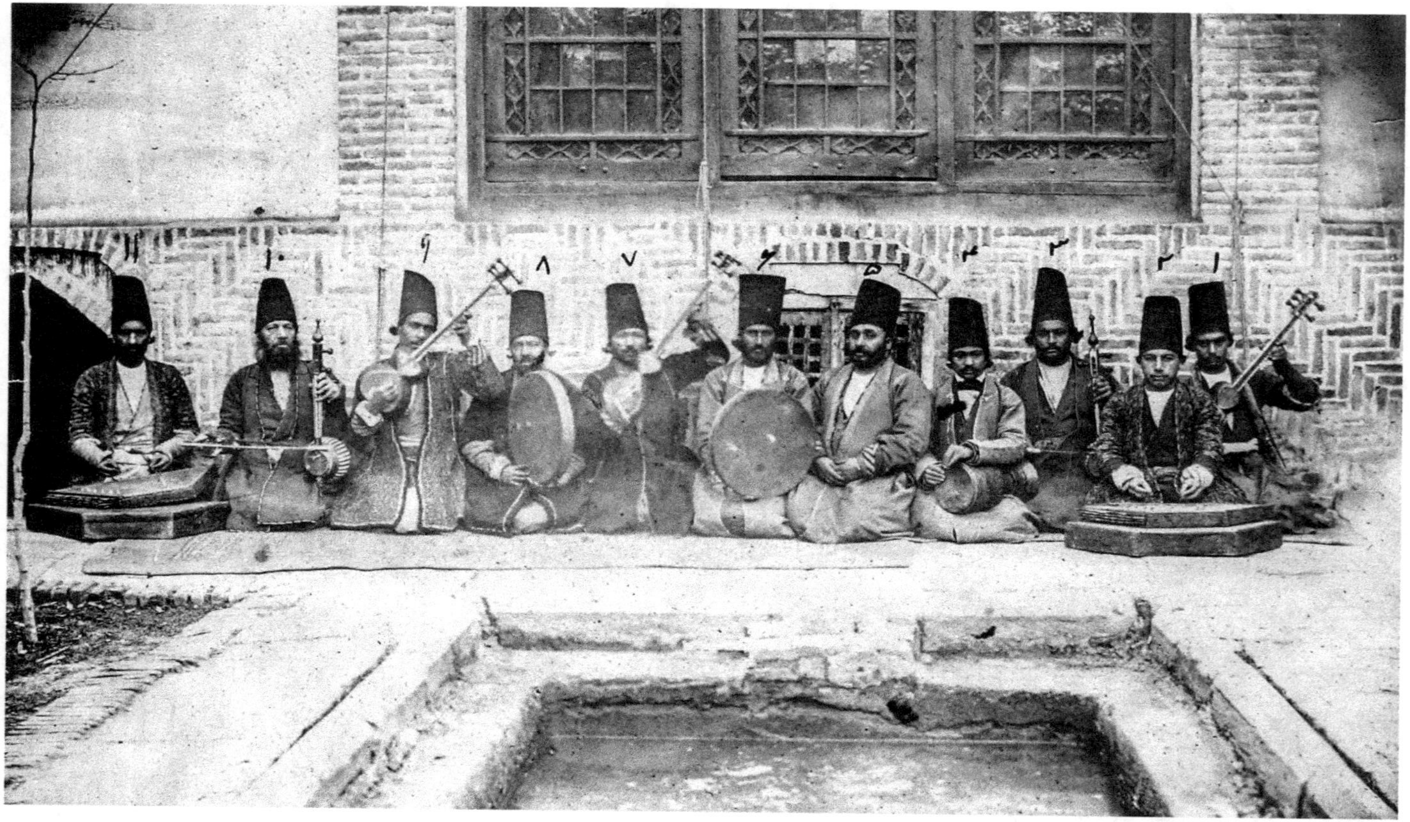

Figure 3.3 Court male musicians in 1863, who appear to have been seated from left to right in descending order of rank: Moḥammad Ḥasan Khān (the head of court musicians and *santur*); Āqā Moṭalleb (*kamāncheh*); Āqā Gholām-Ḥosayn (*tār*); Āqā ʿAli Kāshi (singer); Āqā Ḥasan (singer and *tār*); Reżā-Qoli (singer-accompanist); Sayyed Qorāb (singer); Āqā Ḥasan's son (*dombak*); Khoshnavāz Khān's son (*kamāncheh*); Moḥammad Ṣādeq (*santur*); and the son of Āqā ʿAli-akbar (*tār*). Courtesy of the Golestān Palace Museum, Tehran, Album 281, No. 2.

Reżā-Qoli (singer-accompanist); Sayyed Ghorāb (singer); and Āqā Ḥasan's son (*dombak* player). The last group consists of three younger instrumentalists: Khoshnavāz Khān's son (*kamāncha* player); Moḥammad Ṣādeq (*santur* player); and a son of the deceased Āqā 'Ali-Akbar.[30]

By 1880, the number of *'amala-ye ṭarab-e khāṣṣa* had rapidly and dramatically decreased, and all at once the instrumentalists who were recognized as such included only Moḥammad Ṣādeq Khān, Āqā Gholām-Ḥosayn, Esmā'il Khān, and Ḥāji Ḥakim (singer) (Figure 3.4). Toward the end of the reign of Nāṣer al-Din Shah, four other musicians, Mirzā 'Abdollāh, Āqā Ḥosayn Qoli, Ḥabibollāh Samā'-Ḥożur, and Abu al-Qāsem Khāldār (singer-accompanist) gradually attained that position. While these musicians were primarily soloists, they also performed together in a variety of ensembles and were occasionally accompanied by dancing boys.

Figure 3.4 Court male musicians in 1863. From right to left, first row: Moḥammad Ṣādeq (*santur*), Mirzā Ḥasan (*tār*), Khoshnavāz Khān's son (*kamāncha*), Āqā Gholām- Ḥosayn (*tār*), Āqā Ḥasan (singer and *tār*), Āqā Moṭalleb (*kamāncha*), Moḥammad Ḥasan Khān (*santur*); second row: Sayyed Qorāb (singer), Reżā-Qoli (singer-accompanist), Āqā Ḥasan's son (*dombak*), Āqā 'Ali Kāshi (singer). Courtesy of the Golestān Palace Museum, Tehran, Album 189, No. 59.

The *ʿamala-ye ṭarab-e khāṣṣa* were not only active as performers at the court but were also involved in training disciples. At times they received orders from the court to train a particular person, either a member of the royal family or a promising girl for the *andarun*. They had an exclusive chamber and more often than not some of their members were present at the court, whether or not music was to be performed. In most cases, musicians were scheduled to be present at the court for certain evenings of the week, but sometimes they were specifically summoned to perform at a special gathering or banquet. Nonetheless, respected musicians were allowed to reject these orders under certain conditions.

An enthusiastic patron of all forms of music and entertainment, Nāṣer-al-Din Shah had a particular interest in listening to *dastgāh-e homāyun* (a modal structure). He often had male musicians and *moqalleds* performing for him in the *khalvat*, except during the months of Muḥarram and Ṣafar in which mourning ceremonies were held to commemorate the martyrdom of Ḥosayn, the third Imam of Shiʿite Muslims. Throughout the year, he held weekly performances of music and dance for his wives and concubines at the Golestān Palace, and during the month of Muḥarram he held performances of *rawża*, *taʿziya*, and *shabih-khᵛāni* (Shiʿite ritual ceremonies) (Figure 3.5).[31] He also

Figure 3.5 A performance of *rawża* for the wives and concubines of the shah at the Golestān Palace in 1885. Courtesy of the Golestān Palace Museum, Tehran.

participated actively in the female musical gatherings (*bazm-e zanāna*) that his wives and concubines arranged regularly to entertain themselves and attract the attention of the shah, enticing him to spend time with them in the *andarun*. Many of the professional female performers at these gatherings were concubines of the shah (*ṣighas*) at one point or another.

The shah used to make short trips to the suburbs of Tehran, usually at the beginning of fall, and was always accompanied by a number of *'amala-ye ṭarab*, including at least a few professional male and female musicians, *moqalleds* (jesters), *maskharas* (buffoons), and *bāzigars*. The trips mostly lasted between two and ten days and were primarily centered around a cooking ceremony called *āshpazān* (making soup) that was held inside a large tent. According to several accounts, during the ceremony the entire entourage was involved in the preparation of ingredients for the soup, while the shah would sit on his throne smoking a water pipe (*qalyān*) and the *'amale-ye ṭarab* would perform music and dance for people off to the sides in the tent (Figure 3.6).[32]

In the second half of the nineteenth century, the social status of the *'amala-ye ṭarab-e khāṣṣa* was certainly higher than that of any other members of the

عمله جات اهل طرب و بازیگران که جمع شده اند در روز آش پزان در سرخه حصار

Figure 3.6 The ceremony of *āshpazān* (making soup), October 9, 1894. *Bāzigars* are sitting in the front row and professional musicians such as Mirzā 'Abdollāh are sitting in the back. Courtesy of the Golestān Palace Museum, Tehran, Album 121, No. 17.

'amala-ye ṭarab, but the status of musicians in general was lower than that of most of the *'amala-ye khalvat* (servants of intimate gatherings at the court). Unlike the Safavid court musicians, musicians at the Qajar court, especially in the second half of the nineteenth century, were considered to be recruited servants of the potentate and the royal family, hence they never bore the honorific title *ostād*.[33]

A typical ensemble at the court included *santur*, *tār*, and *kamāncha* flanked by two or three *taṣnifkhᵛān-żarbgir*s (singer-accompanists). *Tār* and *kamāncha* could be doubled in an ensemble, but rarely would two *santur*s play together. A hierarchy among the soloists and instrumentalists in the court ensemble and elsewhere was also related to the performing technique and repertoire cultivated on each instrument. In general, *santur* players were few in number and enjoyed the highest status among both musicians and the public at large. The textures and virtuosic patterns that characterized solo performances of *santur* were particularly mesmerizing for listeners. *Tār* players were second in rank and in the absence of a *santur*, a *tār* player would lead the ensemble. Finally, *kamāncha* and *dombak* players were lowest in status and rank among the *sāzanda*s, mostly recognized as lower-class *moṭreb*s.

Court ensembles in particular included separate *āvāz* and *taṣnif* singers, as their functions, roles, and repertoires were different. In some cases, an ensemble had more than one *taṣnif* singer and each one accompanied himself and the entire ensemble on the *dombak* or *daf*. It was common for two *taṣnif* singers in an ensemble to sing a composition entirely in unison or to alternate various sections.[34] Control of the repertoire and the number of *taṣnif*s they could perform were among the merits of singers. Celebrated soloists such as Moḥammad Ṣādeq Khān, Āqā Gholām-Ḥosayn, and later, Āqā Ḥosayn-Qoli, had their own singer-accompanists. In general, the social status of featured instrumentalists was significantly higher than that of singers, in contrast to much of the twentieth century, where the opposite was true.

Musicians were called by various social tags. In the context of court music, instrumentalists were referred to by the name of the instrument they played followed by the Turkish suffix *-chi*, for example, *santurchi*, *tārchi*, *kamānchachi*, *sornāchi*, *dombakchi*, *naqqārachi*. Outside the court, where the instrumentalists were no longer servants, these social tags were not employed, and using them was even considered derogatory. Average instrumentalists were referred to as *santurzan*, *tārzan*, *kamānchakesh*, *sornāzan*, *dombakzan*, and so on. Only one musician within the court, Moḥammad Ḥasan Khān, who was highly respected and the head of court musicians, is known to have received the title *santurkhān*.[35]

Sometimes musicians, like many other servants of the court, received titles (*laqabs*) from shahs. Moḥammad Ṣādeq Khān, for example, received the honorific title *Sorur al-Molk* (euphoria of the kingdom), and Zivar al-Solṭān, the celebrated female singer of the *andarun*, received the title *'Andalib al-Salṭana* (Nightingale of the Empire). Her brother, Ḥabibollāh, was a dignified and respected singer-accompanist and *santur* player who received the title *Samā'-Ḥożur* (evoking ecstasy through his presence). Another singer was Qoli Khān, who received the title *Shāhpasand* (pleasing to the king) toward the end of the nineteenth century. Although one or two instrumentalists were also awarded titles, most titles seem to have been given to singers who came to be favored by the shahs.[36]

Professional male musicians who were recruited at the royal court were always Muslims. In cases where a non-Muslim musician sought to enter court service, he had to convert to Islam. Jewish musicians, however, were prominently active throughout the capital and other urban centers. Being recognized as lower-class *moṭrebs*, Jewish musicians were major exponents of dance tunes.

Chief of Court Musicians

The *naqqāra-khāna*, described in Chapter 1 as the ceremonial and military institution of the court, consisted of three categories of musicians. Professional male and female instrumentalists, singers, and dancers constituted the first category; the second category was the *naqqārachis*—members of military and ceremonial bands; the third category consisted of less esteemed entertainers such as jesters and buffoons. Within the office of the *chālchi-bāshi*, who oversaw a city's entire community of musicians, and, more specifically, the *naqqāra-khāna*, various classes of musicians and entertainers seem to have had their own heads. In his enumeration of 137 *bāshis*, or assorted offices, at the court of the last Safavid ruler, Shah Solṭān-Ḥosayn, Rostam al-Ḥokamā' mentions five ancillary offices pertaining to music and entertainment: *moghanni-bāshi*, *moṭreb-bāshi*, *moqalled-bāshi*, *maskhara-bāshi*, and *luṭi-bāshi*.[37] During the eighteenth century, mostly due to a lack of sufficient documentation, the situation is a little vague. Nonetheless, in his travel accounts, Harutin, the Ottoman-Armenian *ṭanbur* player at the camp of Nāder, refers specifically to the tent of the *sāzanda-bāshi*, indicating that *sāzanda*s still possessed a head.

At the beginning of the Qajar period, the entire office of music at the court was still called *naqqāra-khāna*, and the chief of court musicians who supervised both male and female musicians of the *dastgāh-e bāzigar-khāna* as well as the *naqqārahchi*s was known as *moṭreb-bāshi*. During the reign of Fatḥ-ʿAli Shah, Rajab-ʿAli Khān Kermāni initially held this position, but, as I explained earlier in this chapter, a musician of Jewish background who converted to Islam replaced him and became known as Chālānchi Khan. Subsequently, *chālānchi* became an official tag employed interchangeably with *moṭreb-bāshi*. According to Ruḥollāh Khāleqi, Moḥammad Ḥasan Khān, the prominent *santur* player at the courts of Moḥammad Shah and Nāṣer-al-Din Shah, was a *chālānchi* at some point.[38] Moreover, in the photograph of court musicians taken in 1863 (Figure 3.3), Nāṣer-al-Din Shah labels Moḥammad Ḥasan Khān as the *naqqārachi-bāshi*. This label not only demonstrates that Moḥammad Ḥasan Khān was the chief of court musicians at that time, but also confirms that the entire office of court music was still known as *naqqāra-khāna* and that the *moṭreb-bāshi* was alternatively referred to as *naqqārahchi-bāshi*. Accounts of *chālānchi*s in this period are very rare and, in most cases, ambiguous. Nonetheless, a later courtier, Eʿtemād al-Salṭana, notes that after the first *chālānchi*, two other instrumentalists, Āqā ʿAli-Akbar and Āqā Moṭalleb, were also appointed as the chief of court musicians during the first half of the reign of Nāṣer-al-Din Shah.[39]

By the second half of the reign of Nāṣer-al-Din Shah, *moṭreb-bāshi*, *chālānchi*, and *naqqārahchi-bāshi* were no longer used to denote the chief of court musicians. In this period, the position of chief of court musicians was awarded to the celebrated *santur* player Moḥammad Ṣādeq Khān, who came to be known as the *ra'is*, or chief, of the *ʿamala-ye ṭarab*.[40] While he seems to have been mainly in charge of professional court musicians, his *nāyeb*, or deputy, Karim Shira'i, was responsible for arranging performances of *moṭreb*s and *moqalled*s at the court. Karim Shira'i was an outstanding court comedian who had a troupe of jesters and buffoons and performed with them frequently in the presence of the shah. He established connections with various officials, courtiers, and musical artists, both inside and outside the court, and became a renowned figure in the capital. ʿAbdollāh Mostawfi offers the following description of Karim Shira'i's character and his activities:

Karim Shira'i was the second in command (*nāyeb*) of the *naqqāra-khāna*. Appointed by the chief of this office as his deputy, he came to be overseeing the musicians at the *naqqāra-khāna* while supervising mainly the second- and third-rate troupes of *moṭreb*s who were dispersed and active throughout the capital independently from the court. He usually asked a certain amount of money unofficially to provide a business license for these *moṭreb*s and also resolved their fiscal and legal disputes when needed.[41]

In the second half of the Qajar period, a *ra'is* evidently had a *nāyeb* who was technically responsible for overseeing the activities of troupes of *moṭreb*s throughout the capital. Nonetheless, the precise roles and responsibilities of a *ra'is* and his *nāyeb* cannot be delineated clearly from the surviving accounts, especially after the reign of Nāṣer al-Din Shah. Eugène Aubin, the French ambassador during the reign of Moẓaffar al-Din Shah (r. 1896–1907), reported that the person in charge of the entire community of musicians and dancers was a courtier called Ṣamad Khān E'teṣām Khalvat, who was also responsible for selecting the chief of *naqqāra-khāna*s in other cities. Aubin named a certain Kāẓem Khān Bāshi, who came to supervise urban troupes of entertainers in Tehran, a position that, according to Aubin, was previously held by Kāzem Khān's father.[42] At the beginning of the twentieth century, Āqā Ḥosayn-Qoli, and subsequently, Ḥosayn Khān Esmā'ilzāda, the distinguished *kamāncha* player of the court, were appointed successively as the *ra'is*, and groups of court musicians and entertainers, including *naqqārachi*s and *'amala-ye ṭarab*s, were under their supervision.[43]

Moḥammad Ṣādeq Khān

The most celebrated musician in the second half of the nineteenth century in the Qajar court was Moḥammad Ṣādeq Khān (*c*. 1847–1903), an esteemed soloist with a dazzling technique and beautifully articulated style of *santur* playing. According to oral accounts, his repertoire and technique were extraordinary in and of themselves, but his greatest virtue was his brilliant sense of melody and nuance.[44]

He received his initial training from his father, Āqā Moṭalleb, a court *kamāncha* player who came from Shiraz to the capital with his three sons.[45] Later he continued to learn, whether formally or informally, from various court musicians, including the most eminent *santur* player, Moḥammad Ḥasan Khān. Moḥammad Ṣādeq Khān's musical talents were quickly recognized among his colleagues and soon he was an accomplished *santur* player at the court, far surpassing all other musicians in renown. In the late 1870s, he was appointed as the *ra'is* of the entire community of musicians and entertainers and subsequently received the honorific title *Sorur al-Molk*. As the *ra'is* of *'amala-ye ṭarab*, he arranged for different groups of male musicians to perform at various court gatherings while also taking charge of their salaries and financial demands.

He reportedly assembled distinct versions of melody types and compositions into an order and nomenclature notably distinguishable from those of his contemporaries, such as Mirzā 'Abdollāh and Āqā Ḥosayn-Qoli.[46] Mirzā 'Abdollāh was said to be particularly keen to incorporate pieces played by Moḥammad Ṣādeq Khān into his own *radif*. However, Moḥammad Ṣādeq Khān was very secretive and protective of his own repertoire to the extent that he hardly taught it to his own sons.[47]

Moḥammad Ṣādeq Khān played a number of instruments, notably *santur*, *setār*, and *kamāncha*, as well as some less common instruments. When a piano was first brought to the court, no one was able to play the instrument. Moḥammad Ṣādeq Khān managed to adapt the piano to Persian music by modifying it and introducing a new tuning system. This tuning system, which contained quarter tones, was further developed by the following generation of musicians and came to be known as *kuk-e shur* (the tuning of *shur*).[48] Another instrument that seems to have been common in Iran for several centuries and was still played at the Qajar court, mainly by Moḥammad Ṣādeq Khān, was the *chini* (a set of sounding bowls beaten with mallets). The *chini* was known throughout the seventeenth and eighteenth centuries as *anutak* or *nutak*, though it is not exactly clear that it was still recognized by these same names during the nineteenth century.[49] Moḥammad Ṣādeq Khān is mentioned as having played this instrument for Nāṣer al-Din Shah, entertaining him mostly on certain occasions when Nāṣer al-Din went to bathe.[50]

Perhaps the most disappointing aspect of Moḥammad Ṣādeq Khān's life was that he seldom taught students, and hence his complete repertoire has not been transmitted to musicians alive today. His most prominent student, Ḥabibollāh Samā'-Ḥożur (d. 1921), who acted as his singer-accompanist for many years, also studied the *santur* with him. Ḥabibollāh once declared that it was extremely challenging and difficult to learn anything from his teacher.[51] Nonetheless, according to general opinion, Moḥammad Ṣādeq Khān's style and repertoire of *santur* playing were later perpetuated only via Ḥabibollāh, who also imparted the art to his son, Ḥabib Samā'i (d. 1946). Two other students of Moḥammad Ṣādeq Khān were Mehdi Ṣolḥi, better known as Montaẓam al-Ḥokamā' (d. 1931), and Ḥabibollāh Shahrdār, known as Moshir-Homāyun (1885–1970).[52] Montaẓam al-Ḥokamā' was a court physician and a renowned *setār* player who later developed a *radif* incorporating elements of the repertoire of Moḥammad Ṣādeq Khān as well as that of his other *setār* teacher, Mirzā 'Abdollāh. In his *radif*, he marked the versions of melody types (later called *gusha*s) that he adopted from the repertoire of Moḥammad Ṣādeq Khān as *sorur al-molki* or *moḥammad ṣādeq-khāni*.[53] Moshir-Homāyun is said to have been the piano student of Moḥammad Ṣādeq Khān and also studied with other master musicians, including Āqā Ḥosayn-Qoli and Ḥosayn Khān Esmā'ilzāda. As the mayor of Shiraz and Isfahan and the music director of Iran Radio for many years, he was one of the first Iranian pianists to be recorded by the Gramophone Company in London in 1909.[54]

Moḥammad Ṣādeq Khān had two sons, Moṭalleb and 'Abdollāh, who both received initial training from their father. While Moṭalleb served as a *santur* player at the court for a while, he died when he was still young. 'Abdollāh came to be known as a mediocre musician and never pursued the *santur* in a professional capacity (Figure 3.7).[55]

Figure 3.7 Moḥammad Ṣādeq Khān with his two sons, Moṭalleb and 'Abdollāh, and his brother, Mirzā Shafi'. Courtesy of the Golestān Palace Museum, Tehran, Album 295, No. 54.

Moḥammad Ṣādeq Khān was recorded on phonograph or wax cylinders in the late nineteenth century, and some of his recordings are now available in private collections.[56]

The Farāhāni Family

It is fair to say that during the Qajar period, playing the *tār* at the court was primarily the monopoly of the Farāhāni family, and almost all *tār* players were either members or disciples of this family. When Āqā ʻAli-Akbar died in 1862, his nephew, Āqā Gholām-Ḥosayn, immediately came to be his *jāneshin* (successor) as the leading *tār* player among the *ʻamala-ye ṭarab-e khāṣṣa*. He came to be the foremost *tār* player at the court for more than two decades, from the beginning of the 1860s through the middle of the 1880s, at which point he mostly accompanied Moḥammad Ṣādeq Khān, Esmāʻil Khān, and Ḥāji Ḥakim in various ensembles. At the same time, he also married his uncle's widow and began training his cousins Mirzā Ḥasan, Mirzā ʻAbdollāh, and Āqā Ḥosayn-Qoli as well as his own son, Āqā Reżā. He also trained certain disciples outside the family circle.[57] Nonetheless, like many master musicians of this period, he was known for being very secretive and protective of his repertoire and musical technique, to the extent that he was almost hesitant to teach advanced and intelligent students. From the middle of the 1880s, Āqā Gholām-Ḥosayn was no longer active at the court, and his cousins Mirzā ʻAbdollāh (d. 1917) and Āqā Ḥosayn-Qoli (d. 1915), the two sons of Āqā ʻAli-Akbar, replaced him as the preeminent *tār* players in court ensembles.

Mirzā ʻAbdollāh and Āqā Ḥosayn-Qoli first began to study with their father and older brother, and later enhanced their studies with Āqā Gholām-Ḥosayn. Throughout their careers, these two brothers worked closely with each other and, while maintaining their shared stylistic *maktab*, supplemented their family repertoire and instruction with further training from various court musicians. Mirzā ʻAbdollāh is mentioned as having studied with a respected vocalist called Sayyed Ḥasan or Sayyed Aḥmad. According to Montaẓam al-Ḥokamā', "Mirzā ʻAbdollāh only incorporated those materials into his repertoire of *dastgāh*s whose authenticity he had already verified with Sayyed Ḥasan."[58] Āqā Ḥosayn-Qoli married Sakina, a former student of his father and one of the most celebrated female musicians of the court, and therefore came to be exposed to the whole range of female repertoire that was being performed in the *andarun*, including various *taṣnif*s and *reng*s (dance tunes).[59]

From the very beginning of the nineteenth century, the *tār* and *setār* masters of the court cultivated a meticulous and systematic approach to the nomenclature, grouping, and sequencing of materials in their performances of *dastgāhs*. The manner in which they arranged their repertoire was not as strictly observed, or, perhaps, considered impractical among performers of other instruments at that time.

Mirzā 'Abdollāh was not a high caliber soloist, and he was allegedly most proficient on the *setār*, an instrument that was rarely played in the context of court music by male musicians. However, Āqā Ḥosayn-Qoli was a prodigy on the *tār* and according to both oral and written accounts, all the *tār* players of his generation were fascinated by his dazzling technique.[60] While both brothers were enormously active in training disciples, Mirzā 'Abdollāh was primarily a pedagogue and, in order to teach his students, he sought to establish a fixed version of his repertoire, which gradually came to be known as the *radif* (Figure 3.8). Indeed, *radif* as a musical term and concept was likely coined by Mirzā 'Abdollāh, since the first references to this term appear to have been recorded in connection with his teaching. At the same time, the idea of *radif* was also adopted by Āqā Ḥosayn-Qoli, who synthesized the repertoires of his brother, Mirzā 'Abdollāh, and cousin, Āqā Gholām-Ḥosayn, with his own

Figure 3.8 Mirzā 'Abdollāh and his disciples.

creative input. Toward the end of the nineteenth century, Mirzā ʻAbdollāh's *radif* was transmitted through his students and subsequently recorded and transcribed, thereby bringing a substantial degree of standardization and canonization to twentieth-century Persian music.

ʻAmala-ye Ṭarab and Moṭreb

Apart from the *ʻamala-ye ṭarab-e khāṣṣa*, a number of lesser instrumentalists, singers, accompanists, dancing boys, and *moqalled*s were associated with the court who were collectively referred to as *ʻamala-ye ṭarab*. All these musicians and entertainers received monthly salaries from the court. Instrumentalists and singers in this category were neither as educated and accomplished as *ʻamala-ye ṭarab-e khāṣṣa* nor permitted to sit in the presence (*ḥożur*) of the shah at a private *majles*.

Finally, the last category, *moṭreb*s, were hereditary professional musicians who were not recruited to the court; they were brought in to perform only occasionally when referred to the shah by courtiers and the nobility, or at times when special celebrations or public gatherings were taking place. These musicians were usually active in the form of small *dasta*s in the capital and in most cases their troupes included dancing boys or girls. The other characteristic feature of *moṭreb*s concerned their repertoire for professional purposes, which mostly consisted of lighter songs and dance-oriented pieces.

Instrumentalists, Singers, and Accompanists

A hereditary professional instrumentalist in both urban and rural circles was called a *sāzanda*, a term frequently employed in the context of court music as well. In the second half of the nineteenth century, the term *sāzanda* came to be gradually replaced by *navāzanda* and subsequently, *sāzanda* continued to be employed only in the context of regional folk music.[61]

In keeping with a tradition established during the Safavid period or even earlier, two types of male vocalist can be identified in Persian court music during the Qajar period: (1) singers of the free rhythmic *āvāz* (mostly *ghazal* and *dōbayti*); and (2) performers of *taṣnif*. While the first type often had an initial training in religious genres, the second type was more of an entertainer whose principal skill was in performing various types of metric song. The repertoire of these entertainers consisted of light vocal compositions accompanied on the *daf* or *dombak*. The distinction between the two types of vocalists, however, was not always sharp. An *āvāz* singer would sometimes perform metrical songs, especially those set to classical poems, when there was no *taṣnif* singer, and likewise a professional *taṣnif* singer usually incorporated one or two lines of *āvāz* in the course of his performance.

In urban musical culture of the sixteenth and seventeenth centuries the performer of *āvāz* was usually a male singer called a *ḥāfeẓ* or *khᵛānanda* and the performer of *taṣnif* was known as a *guyanda*.[62] However, the terms *ḥāfeẓ* and *guyanda* were no longer common throughout the nineteenth century in Iran and both types of vocalists were either called *khᵛānanda*s or *āvāz-khᵛān*s. While a singer of *āvāz* often possessed a wider vocal range and was more proficient in performing subtleties of melody type and modulation, a *taṣnif* singer typically had a narrow vocal range, and his ability was judged by the number and variety of vocal compositions he knew from memory. If the performer of *taṣnif* was a professional *dombak* player who also accompanied *sāzanda*s in rendering instrumental compositions, he was referred to as a *żarbgir* ("the keeper of the time") as well. Nonetheless, on rare occasions, especially in the context of court music, a *żarbgir* was merely expert in playing the *dombak* and not adept in performing *taṣnif*s.

In the course of the nineteenth century, adolescent boy singers were widely popular and sometimes highly respected in urban centers. Most of these boys had their own *dasta*s and were often maintained by a prince or nobleman. Evidence shows that they were brought to perform occasionally at the royal court, including in the *andarun* and *khalvat*. Around 1866, the most celebrated adolescent boy singer was ʿAbdollāh, who is mentioned in Nāṣer al-Din Shah's diaries.[63]

Raqqāṣ and Bāzigar

Dancing boys continued to be known as *raqqāṣ* or *bāzigar* throughout the eighteenth and nineteenth centuries and they were integral parts of ensembles in Tehran and other cities. They used to dance either in long colorfully embroidered coats and pants or in women's clothes with their long hair let down. A dancing boy performed various tumbling acts, typically handsprings and somersaults in the air, while he also danced mainly in a feminine and seductive manner (Figure 3.9).

Some of the courtiers and noblemen of this period were particularly fond of dancing boys and invited them to court celebrations and to their private gatherings. It also seems that most of the musicians performing at the court,

Figure 3.9 A troupe of rural musicians and *bāzigars*. Institute for Iranian Contemporary Historical Studies, Harvard University.

including the *'amala-ye ṭarab-e khāṣṣa*, employed one or two dancing boys in their ensembles or at least accompanied them on some occasions. Several dancing boys were quite well-known and respected in their time and remained legendary throughout the Qajar period. They were first recruited and trained by a professional musician who was the proprietor of a troupe (*sardasta*), but as they became famous, they were able to claim their independence and secure their own positions of authority within the business. Nonetheless, the period of their activity as a dancer was short, typically from age ten to seventeen. Some of the dancing boys, however, still performed even in their early twenties and many of them remained in the field as professional entertainers. Unlike the seventeenth and eighteenth centuries, when non-Muslim boys (mostly Georgian and Jewish) dominated the roles of *raqqāṣ* and *bāzigar*, toward the end of the nineteenth century the majority of dancing boys, at least in Tehran, were Muslim. Qahramān Mirzā Sālur, a late Qajar prince, reports on a wedding ceremony in 1907 in which, in addition to twenty Muslim dancing boys, five Jewish dancing boys accompanied the music of *moṭrebs* after the lunch. He further states that the tradition of dancing boys was beginning to decline at that time and dancing girls and courtesans were more venerated throughout the capital.[64]

Moqalled

The other group of entertainers associated with the office of *naqqāra-khāna* was the *moqalleds* or *taqlidchis*. These were buffoons who performed various forms of stand-up comedy and comic skits collectively known as *taqlid* (lit. "mimicry"). The practice of *taqlid* was to ridicule various classes and ethnic groups through burlesque imitation, especially those who were considered to be outside social norms or who had been disobedient to the shah. The *moqalleds* did not work alone, as the nature of *taqlid* required the interaction of a small number of performers. Often a *taqlid* ensemble included one or two musicians (usually a *kamāncha* player and a *dombak* player) and dancing boys. Likewise, an ensemble of *moṭrebs* could include one or two *moqalleds*, in which case they usually performed short comic skits interspersed with two sections of dance or music.

Moqalleds in the court of Nāṣer al-Din Shah often made critical remarks about courtiers in their acts and, as long as the shah did not take offence, they would have felt safe in their position. Among the *moqalleds* in the court, Karim Shira'i and Esmā'il Bazzāz were prominent figures who both had their own *dastas*, with each appointed as the *nāyeb* or deputy of the *naqqāra-khāna* for a certain period (Figures 3.10 and 3.11).[65] Chorki, Shaykh Shaypur and

Figure 3.10 Karim Shira'i and his troupe of *moqalleds*. Courtesy of the University of Tehran.

Figure 3.11 Esma'il Bazzāz and his troupe of *moqalled*s and musicians. Courtesy of the University of Tehran.

Shaykh Karnā (d. *c* 1931) were also three *moqalled*s who performed solo *taqlid* in different periods at the court; their performances were characterized by the recitation and singing of humorous poems.[66]

Female Court Performers and Concubines

During the second half of the nineteenth century, the wives, concubines, and daughters of the shah maintained among their ladies-in-waiting mostly female entertainers especially trained in music and dance. These women performed frequently at the court as well as at the homes of the nobles, providing music for auspicious occasions like bridal showers (*ḥenā bandān*s), weddings (*'arusis* or *ṭoy*s), circumcision ceremonies (*khatna surān*s), and religious festivities such as the birth of the Prophet or of his daughter (*mawlud*s). Mahd-'oliyā (d. 1873), the queen mother of Nāṣer al-Din Shah, was one of the ardent patrons of female musicians and dancers in the *andarun*. She assigned Solṭān Khānom, one of her ladies-in-waiting to study the *tār* with Āqā 'Ali-Akbar. Solṭān Khānom later became the preeminent exponent of *taṣnif* in the *andarun* and was also credited with the composition of many songs, some of which have survived down to the present.[67] Another hereditary musical figure who later found her way into the *andarun* was Zivar al-Solṭān, the daughter of the court *kamāncha* player, Gholām-Ḥosayn. Zivar al-Solṭān was an eminent *taṣnif* singer and *santur* player who received the title of 'Andalib al-Salṭana from the shah and, together with her brother, Ḥabibollāh Samā'-Ḥożur, served as the major conduit for the transmission of the female court repertoire to the following generation of singers in the twentieth century.[68] Finally, Akram al-Salṭana was another celebrated singer who became renowned in the *andarun* and is credited with the composition of one or two *taṣnifs*.[69] During the reign of Nāṣer al-Din Shah, *'amala-ye ṭarab-e khāṣṣa* were responsible for training female court musicians and dancers, among whom Āqā 'Ali-Akbar, Āqā Gholām-Ḥosayn, Moḥammad Ṣādeq Khān, Esmā'il Khān, and Mirzā 'Abdollāh probably played the most significant roles. Zaynab and Gol'edhār were two female musicians reportedly trained by Moḥammad Ṣādeq Khān to play the *santur* in the *andarun*.[70]

Mo'ayyer al-Mamālek mentions that at some point during his reign, Nāṣer al-Din Shah ordered Māhnesā' Khānom (the harem supervisor and Mo'ayyer al-Mamālek's paternal grandmother) to find a number of talented and beautiful maidens and have them trained in various types of musical instrument, singing, and dance. After a long period of audition, twelve promising girls were finally selected for this purpose, and they were trained by male master musicians of the court for two years. Upon their first performance, the shah became so excited that he showered Māhnesā' Khānom and the master male musicians with gifts. The female performers were sent to the *andarun*, and several of them were chosen by the shah to become his concubines. Among those female performers were Delbar Khānom, Delpasand Khānom, 'Āliya Khānom, Fāṭema Solṭān Khānom, Khāvar Solṭān Khānom, and Zinat Khānom (Figure 3.12).[71] Musical education suddenly became common among female members of the nobility in this period. Several princesses were reportedly engaged in receiving musical training, often directly from *'amala-ye ṭarab-e khāṣṣa* and sometimes through the female performers in the *andarun* (Figure 3.13). Mo'ayyer al-Mamālek, the grandson of Nāṣer al-Din Shah, relates the following story about his mother's musical training:

> There was an old piano in the attic of Anis al-Dawla [one of the shah's wives] that nobody knew how to play. At that time, only five to six pianos were in Tehran and hardly anyone knew how to play them.

Figure 3.12 Female musicians at the *andarun* of Nāṣer al-Din Shah. From right to left, first row: Farangis, Jamāl, Fāṭema Solṭān Ṭārchi, Ṣāḥeb Solṭān, and Bāqeri; second row: Kurdish *dāyera*-player, ?, Neẓāra and Delbar. Courtesy of the Golestān Palace Museum, Tehran, Album 682, No. 10.

Figure 3.13 Anis al-Dawla, the favorite wife of Nāṣer al-Din Shah.

> Moḥammad Ṣādeq Khān, the master of *santur* who received the title of "Sorur-al-Molk" toward the end of his career, could play the piano beautifully. Thus, my mother sent Tabassom, one of her maids, to the aforementioned musician to study the piano and then teach my mother whatever she learned. This became a common practice among the women of the *andarun* and the shah was also pleased with what was happening. Later on, my mother was ordered to play the piano for the shah almost every night. More often than not, after a free rhythmic *āvāz* session [on the piano], one of the women who was capable of singing *taṣnif*s would have started to sing.[72]

Female performers of the *andarun* were the preeminent exponents of instrumental and vocal dance tunes as well as of dance proper. According to oral accounts, the repertoire of these performers was largely unknown to outsiders, and often male musicians were particularly keen to learn the *taṣnif*s and instrumental compositions that were performed at all-female gatherings—as, for example, was the case with *tār* player Āqā Ḥosayn-Qoli, whose style and repertoire were to a great extent shaped by his wife, Sakina, as I described above in the section *The Farāhāni Family*.

Patrons of Music

In the second half of the nineteenth century, Tehran, as the large and prosperous capital of the Qajar kings, was the hub for all forms of music. While the Qajar court was undoubtedly the most visible center of musical patronage, a substantial amount of musical activity still took place in the homes of princes, ministers, and merchants.

The third son of Nāṣer al-Din Shah, Kāmrān Mirzā Nāyeb-al-Salṭana (1856–1929), the minister of war and commander of the armed forces, was the foremost patron of music in the last decade of the nineteenth century. He hosted musicians in his house and arranged many musical activities—especially performances by military bands—at the royal court. One of the most celebrated and accomplished singers in his service was a certain ʿAli Khān, who later became known as ʿAli Khān-e Nāyeb al-Salṭana.[73]

In Isfahan, Masʿud Mirzā Ẓell al-Solṭān (1849–1918), the oldest son of Nāṣer al-Din Shah and the governor of the city, and his sister, Bānu ʿOẓmā', were both fond of music and sustained a number of musicians in their service. Ebrāhim Āghābāshi, a eunuch at the court of Ẓell al-Solṭān, is mentioned as the doyen of *nay* players and singers and as having trained many musicians, including the renowned *nay* player Nāyeb Asadollāh and the singer Sayyed Rahim.[74] Musā Kāshi (d. 1931), a Jewish *kamāncha* player, and his disciple Bāqer Khān Rāmeshgar were other active musicians at the court of Isfahan. Later they both came to Tehran to study and further their own careers.[75]

The two brothers Nāyeb al-Salṭana and Ẓell al-Solṭān seem to have competed for musical renown. This is evident from the account of ʿAli-Akbar Shāhi, who was primarily a musician in the service of Nāyeb al-Salṭana. Ẓell al-Solṭān, who lacked a *santur* player, ordered him to move to Isfahan and join his own court musicians. ʿAli-Akbar was on his way to Isfahan when he learned that Nāyeb-al-Salṭana resented his transfer. He stayed in Qom for a few days and finally moved back to Tehran, where he took refuge in the royal court's kitchen (*ābdār-khāna*). Later, he came to be known as ʿAli-Akbar-e Ābdār-khāna and became a musician in the service of Moẓaffar al-Din Shah.[76]

Among statesmen and ministers there were also a few enthusiastic patrons of music who supported musicians. Examples include two prime ministers, Mirzā ʿAli-Aṣghar Khān Atābak (1858–1907), and ʿAyn al-Dawla (1845–1926), as well as the minister of foreign affairs, Yaḥyā Khān Moshir al-Dawla (1831–1891), all of whom supported a few musicians in their own service.[77]

Urban Musical Life

Numerous urban musical ensembles were active throughout the capital in the second half of the nineteenth century and the early twentieth century. These ensembles were generally known as *dasta-ye moṭreb* and consisted of various numbers of instrumentalists, singers, dancers, and, sometimes, *moqalled*s. While celebrated *dasta*s would mostly be hired to perform at the court or the homes of princes, noblemen, and wealthy merchants, less prominent *dasta*s also performed at the homes of middle-class citizens. Families with religious and conservative backgrounds rarely hosted *moṭreb*s at their homes. Instead, on auspicious occasions like a wedding ceremony they invited a *maddāḥ* (singer of religious poems) for the male *majles*. In the female *majles*, a *mawludi khᵛān* (singer of religious poems celebrating the birth of the Prophet) could be invited, but in most cases, music was provided by the women of the family.[78]

Eugène Aubin reported that in the late Qajar period, about fourteen male ensembles and more than forty female ensembles were registered in Tehran, all of whom paid monthly taxes to Eʿteṣām Khalvat.[79] The activities of these *dasta*s were closely supervised and sometimes documented by the police department (*naẓmiya*), and one can glean much information from the reports of *naẓmiya* in the accounts of those ensembles.[80] The *dastas* of this period were made up of female performers, male performers, or both.

Ensembles of female performers (*dasta-ye zanāna*) usually performed for all-female gatherings. There was no typical size or special instrumentation associated with a female troupe. Typically, they included two or three dancers, one or two singers, one or two *dombaks* and *dafs*, and at least two melodic instruments such as *tār*, *kamāncha*, *santur*, or harmonium. Some of the ensembles also had *moqalleds*. Dancing girls usually wore different costumes, and they were trained in various folk and urban dances (Figure 3.14).

The ensembles of male performers (*dasta-ye mardāna*) were fewer in number throughout the capital and performed at all-male gatherings. The size and instrumentation of male ensembles was similar to that of female ensembles except that harmonium does not seem to have been played by men; instead, this type of ensemble may have included the *nay*. A male ensemble sometimes had one or two *moqalleds*, but in general a *taqlid* ensemble proper was larger in size and certainly would have included *kamāncha* and *dombak* players. A *dasta-ye mardāna* usually contained one to four dancing boys who joined the musicians throughout the performance. Those boys who were more talented and had naturally sweet voices would often receive vocal training as well, and some of them even became celebrated singers of this period (Figure 3.15).

Finally, two major types of mixed ensemble included both male and female performers. The first type was led by a male proprietor (*sardasta*) who was himself a musician and dance instructor and who, in most cases, would train performing artists, including female musicians and dancers. He was often related to the female performers either through familial or pedagogical ties. The second category was led by a female proprietor and was dominated by female performers. In this case, one or two male musicians were employed partly to carry musical instruments and partly to protect the women of the *dasta* from physical abuse. While both types of ensembles seem to have existed throughout the capital and probably in other major cities, both were known simply as a *dasta-ye moṭreb*. These ensembles varied significantly in terms of their numbers and other factors, such as the type of performer, instrumentation, and inclusion of male and/or female singers and dancers. The most significant characteristic

Figure 3.14(a–b) Two photographs of the troupe of ʿAziz and ʿAṭā. Courtesy of the Kimia Foundation.

Figure 3.15 A postcard showing a troupe of male musicians and a dancing boy, including Dāvud Kalimi Shirāzi (*tār*) and Aqā Jān (*dombak*).

feature of a mixed *dasta* was the inclusion of at least one female singer. Dancers were usually female, but sometimes dancing boys were employed as well. These ensembles were often invited to perform at female gatherings or gatherings where women were accompanied by close male relatives. In these circumstances, male performers were either blind or isolated in such a way so as not to be able to view the female audience.[81]

Members of these urban ensembles were mostly hereditary professional performers who could be either Muslim or Jewish. Jews, however, dominated the performance of dance, and many Jewish dancing boys and girls were reportedly active throughout major cities. Some of the sources also claim that urban ensembles were predominantly composed of Jewish musicians, but there is insufficient evidence to substantiate such a claim.[82]

Most urban and often rural ensembles maintained at least one *kamāncha* and one *dombak*, these being the stereotypical instruments associated with *moṭreb*s in the Qajar period. The second most popular musical instrument among them was the *tār*. The *santur* was less common in general, but it was still played occasionally by both male and female musicians. The harmonium was primarily played by women, while the *nay* was an instrument that belonged exclusively to the domain of men. By the late nineteenth century, some Western musical instruments such as the violin, flute, and even mandolin had also been introduced, and were adopted by some *dastas*.[83]

Moṭrebs were the major exponents of light and rhapsodic forms of Persian music. They never performed *dastgāhs* with sequences of *gushas* in an ordered structure, a performance format that was practiced by master musicians at the court. Although *moṭrebs* performed short segments of *āvāz*, most pieces in their repertoires included *żarbis*, that is, metrical vocal and instrumental compositions (*taṣnif* and *reng*), and among these, dance tunes constituted the larger part of their repertoire.

During the reign of Nāṣer al-Din Shah, the most distinguished urban ensembles in Tehran were directed by two blind male musicians, Mo'men and Karim. Mo'men and his troupe were frequently called upon to perform in the *andarun*, where, besides the shah's wives, concubines, and daughters, a few courtiers and wives of the gentry were also present.[84]

Several female *dastas*, including Bāji Qadamshād, Māshā'allāh, Gol Rashti, Monavvar, Zahrā Qomi, Zaʿfarān Bāji, ʿAziz-o ʿAṭā, and Galin, consisted principally of singers or dancers. The proprietors of two ensembles were women of African descent who had close connections with the women of the *andarun*. Most of these *dastas* were frequently invited to perform at the court.[85]

Among the female performers, two or three sisters sometimes formed a small *dasta* and performed at all-female gatherings. Two famous sisters, Marāl and Ghazāl, were celebrated dancers in the capital. The latter used to dance often in men's dress (Figure 3.16). Likewise, some of the dancers, such as Qamar Sāleki, were *taṣnif* singers as well. Some dancers were particularly skilled at playing finger cymbals while dancing, among them, Akhtar Zangi, Zahrā, and Ḥeshmat. Ḥeshmat was also proficient in candelabra dances, a tradition previously common among celebrated court *bāzigars* throughout the eighteenth and early nineteenth centuries.[86]

Court albums show that folk ensembles of both male and female musicians sometimes performed Turkmen, Kurdish, Azeri, and Lori music in the capital and, more specifically, at the Qajar court. In his 1865 diary, Nāṣer-al-Din Shah

Figure 3.16 Ghazāl (dancer), 'Aziz Shashlulband (*tār*), and Marāl (dancer).

refers to two Turkman musicians who played and sang a famous urban *taṣnif* on the *dōtār* and *kamāncha*.[87]

Musical contact with India, Kashmir, and, in particular, with Afghanistan, also increased significantly during the nineteenth century. An Indian *santur* player is mentioned to have been at the court of Moḥammad Shah and to have trained a court servant named Amir Khān.[88] An ensemble of Kashmiri musicians performing on *santur*, *sitār*, *sārangi*, *kamāncha*, and *tablā* also arrived in the Qajar court around 1865, accompanied by a larger group of entertainers.[89] During the reign of Nāṣer al-Din Shah, Ḥosām al-Salṭana, who by then had received the title "the Conqueror of Herat," brought a group of Herāti musicians including Gholām-Ḥosayn Khān Herāti, Rasul Khān Herāti, and Ja'far Khān, the son of Rasul Khān, to Tehran (Figure 3.17). These musicians later made a significant contribution to the development of the performance practice of music at the Qajar court. The complete repertoire of Afghan music has not survived; nonetheless, it is evident from song-text collections of the early twentieth century that several *taṣnif*s and a few *reng*s were still known among the court musicians as *afghāni* or *kāboli*.[90]

Figure 3.17 Herati musicians at the Qajar court. From left to right: Rasul Khān Herāti (*robāb*), Gholām-Ḥosayn Khān Herāti (*sārangi*), son of Rasul Khān (*dokra*). Courtesy of the Golestān Palace Museum, Tehran, Album 201, No. 72.

Music of Sufi Lodges

During the nineteenth century, the Dhahabiya and Neʿmatollāhi Sufi orders were active in the capital and in major cities such as Isfahan, Shiraz, and Mashhad. However, the performance practice of music in Sufi lodges (*khāneqāh*s) was almost entirely confined to the recitation of poetry and the Qur'an. In other words, instrumental music—even the performances of *nay* and *daf*—was entirely absent from their gatherings. This was mostly due to the fact that Persian Sufi orders were still following the rules of the *shariʿa* and some of the shaykhs had previous religious training or were personally related to the *ʿulamāʾ*. Vocal genres that developed closely with the performance of music in Sufi lodges were *sāqi-nāme* and *mathnavi*, both of which later crept into the repertoire of the *radif* and were recognized as *gusha*s.

Luthiers

The nineteenth century was the age of Armenian families of luthiers. These families mostly fabricated *tār*s and *setār*s, and included the well-known luthiers, Zādur and Mārkār, and the three brothers Khāchik, Hambartsum,

Figure 3.18 Āqā Ḥosayn-Qoli and his students in the house of the luthier Yaḥyā.

and Megerditch. All of these luthiers began as professional carpenters in the New Jolfā quarter of Isfahan, and turned to making instruments at the request of customers. Later, Khachik's son, Hovānes Abkāriān, better known as Yaḥyā (1876–1932), moved to Tehran and developed the art of *tār*-making to a peak that has never been surpassed (Figure 3.18). He standardized the basic form, shape, size, materials, and method of construction for the *tār*.[91] A small group of Armenian instrument makers also lived at the same time in Marāgha, a city in Azerbaijan, and were famous as makers of both *setār*s and *chogur*s.[92]

Around 1890, a craft workshop-bazaar called Dār al-Ṣanāye' (the house of crafts) was founded in southern Tehran. There Ḥājj Ṭāher, a master *setār* maker, and Ostād Farajollāh, a *tār*, *setār*, and *kamāncha* maker from Isfahan, also established instrument-making workshops and soon afterwards, emerged as well-known luthiers in the capital. Ḥājj Ṭāher and Ostād Farajollāh, who seem to have been strongly influenced by the construction of the mandolin, began at that time to make the belly of *setār*s from strips of wood, in contrast to the traditional belly carved out of a single block of wood.[93] Likewise, it is generally believed that the second Yaḥyā in fact modeled his *tār*s on Ostād Farajollāh's superior construction design.

Equally famous in the second half of the nineteenth century was Ḥājj Moḥammad Karim Khān, who made major developments in the construction of the *kamāncha* with fully decorated bone inlay work.[94]

Late Qajar Court Music

Moẓaffar al-Din Shah (r. 1896–1907), the son of Nāṣer al-Din Shah, was named crown prince in 1861 and sent as governor to the northern province of Azerbaijan. He spent thirty-five years in Tabriz in the pursuit of pleasure, where he was frequently in the company of performing artists and musicians. We are informed that Javād Khān Qazvini, the eminent *kamāncha* player of the court of Nāṣer al-Din Shah, and Āqā Ḥosayn-Qoli were often sent to Tabriz to perform at the court of the crown prince.[95]

When Moẓaffar al-Din Shah came to Tehran in 1896, he did not display much interest in court music, certainly not in the same manner that his father did. During his reign, he gradually changed the patterns of musical patronage, and, subsequently, musicians retained little presence at the royal court. Toward the end of the nineteenth century, Moḥammad Ṣādeq Khān developed gout and gradually receded from his responsibilities. Likewise, Mirzā ʿAbdollāh, Āqā Ḥosayn-Qolī, and Ḥabibollāh Samāʿ-Ḥożur were only asked to perform occasionally for banquets. At the same time, the shah allegedly sought to patronize performers of wind instruments, a new development that had been uncommon during the reign of his predecessors.[96]

During the reign of Moẓaffar al-Din Shah, the two categories of musician established earlier as *ʿamala-ye ṭarab-e khāṣṣa* and *ʿamala-ye ṭarab* were no longer differentiated at the court. Instead, renowned musicians both inside and outside the court came to be grouped and identified with the names of the individuals who patronized them, including the shah, princes, and ministers.

Some of the celebrated court musicians in this period received the title of "Shāhi" suffixed to their names, producing, for example ʿAli-Akbar Shāhi, Qorbān Khān Shāhi, and Qoli Khān Shāhi, while the various court ensembles to which they belonged were typically known as *dasta-ye shāhi*. Among the court musicians, ʿAli-Akbar Shāhi (d. 1923) was the most important figure. He played both *santur* and *tār*, while also directing the main court ensemble. ʿAli-Akbar received his initial training on the *santur* from his father, Amir Khān, who was himself supposedly trained by an Indian *santur* player in the middle of the nineteenth century.[97] Other court musicians in this period included Morād Khān, a *tār* player; Ṣafdar Khān, a *kamāncha* player; Qorbān Khān Shāhi, a singer; Qoli Khān Shāhi, a *nay* player and singer; and Gholām and Ḥabib, *dombak* players.[98] Mashḥun mentions that Qoli Khān was the *nay* player favored by the shah, and hence was given the title "Shāhpasand."[99] Likewise, Morād Khān was a privileged musician who accompanied Moẓaffar al-Din Shah on his second trip to Europe in 1903.[100]

Dancing boys still played a significant role in courtly and urban ensembles, and they seem to have been largely accepted and tolerated by people throughout the capital. It appears that besides dancing, some of these boys were celebrated singers as well. According to Eugène Aubin, the activities of dancing boys were closely supervised by the deputy of the *naqqāra-khāna*. Through a contract signed in the presence of E'teṣām Khalvat, the proprietors of troupes (*sardastas*) were committed to providing food, shelter, clothing, and health care for the boys.[101] A photograph of the *dasta-ye shāhi* shows that at least two dancing boys—probably around fourteen or fifteen years old—were part of that ensemble (Figure 3.19). Surviving photographs also indicate that several adolescent boy singers and dancing boys, such as Taymur Raqqāṣ and Ḥosayn

Figure 3.19 The *dasta-ye shāhi*, the royal court ensemble. Courtesy of the Golestān Palace Museum, Tehran.

Figure 3.20 Ḥosayn Bālā Raqqāṣ and Qorbān-'Ali Beg Jalawdār. Institute for Iranian Contemporary Historical Studies, Harvard University.

Bālā Raqqāṣ, were respected and sought after by some of the courtiers and the gentry in this period (Figure 3.20).

The patrons of these boys, in the words of John Baily, "were 'dancing boy fanciers', just as they might be pigeon fanciers or dog fanciers."[102] Baily is not implying, however, that patrons had sexual relations with the boys. Eugène Aubin observed that Iranian men in this period appreciated the seductive manners of dancing boys with no beard more than dancing girls, and hence the relation between patrons and dancing boys has been stigmatized and viewed with suspicion.[103] Some of the dancing boys were reportedly objects of adoration even into their twenties. Moẓaffar al-Din Shah's sister, Tāj al-Salṭana, refers, for example, to a twenty-year-old male dancer named Tihu, and further declares that her husband was madly in love with him.[104]

Another category of entertainers who frequently performed for Moẓaffar al-Din Shah consisted of courtesan troupes engaged in music and dance, who emerged in great numbers across the capital and other major cities in the last quarter of the nineteenth century.[105] Tāj al-Salṭana, the shah's sister is on record as having been particularly disturbed by the fact that "the King frequently hosted courtesans instead of 'real musicians' in his court."[106]

Introduction of Western Music

The influence of Western music on Iran began with the adaptation of the European military band. It is clear that Fatḥ-'Ali Shah and his crown prince, 'Abbās Mirzā, made significant attempts to modernize the Persian army. Aided by the French and the British, 'Abbās Mirzā formed a military unit that relied primarily on a fife and drum corps for musical support. Sir William Ouseley, the secretary of the British envoy who visited the provincial court of Tabriz in 1812, describes the crown prince's band as including a group of young Persian fifers and drummers who performed the tunes of English marches, country dances, and the national anthem "God save the King," exceedingly well.[107] In 1817, Moritz von Kotzebue reported on the same military band performing the British national anthem in Yerevan.[108]

The establishment of a large ensemble in the first half of the nineteenth century seems unlikely, but a painting made by the Russian traveler Alexey Saltykov (1806–1859) shows that in the 1830s the bugle horn had also been introduced to the court military band (Figure 3.21).[109]

When Moḥammad Shah came to power in Tabriz in 1834, he marched to capture Tehran with Henry Lindsay-Bethune, a British officer who was the commander of his army. In 1836, the same officer was given £400 to purchase

Figure 3.21 The court military band, as drawn by Alexey Saltykov in the 1830s.

musical instruments. Later, an Italian musician named Marco Brambilla, who was previously active in Istanbul and Tabriz, was brought to the capital to direct the court military band. Marco stayed in Iran for almost three decades and, during his tenure, he became the *muzikānchi-bāshi*, or chief of Western-style military music, at the court.[110]

In 1851, the Dār al-Fonun—Iran's first European-style institution of higher learning—was founded in Tehran. Here, upper-class Iranian youth could study medicine, engineering, military sciences, and geology. The music division of the Dār al-Fonun was established five years later, in 1856, when two French bandmasters, Messieurs Bousquet and Rouillon, were imported to form a French-style military band in the capital and train musicians for military functions. Bousquet left Iran after two years, but Rouillon continued to work there until his death in 1867, though his unstable health prohibited him from making consistent contributions throughout this period.[111] Giuseppe Anaclerio, an Italian traveler who stayed in Iran between 1862 and 1866, provides valuable information on the status of Western military music. In particular, he states that during his visit, two military bands were directed by Marco and Rouillon.[112]

In 1868, the French bandmaster and music teacher, Alfred Jean-Baptiste Lemaire (1842–1909) was sent to the Qajar court in response to a request from the court to France's defense minister, Adolphe Niel. Soon Lemaire became the director of the music department at the Dār al-Fonun and also received the title of *muzikānchi-bāshi* at the court. Since he knew no Persian, 'Ali-Akbar Mozayyen al-Dawla (1847–1932), the French-educated painting instructor at the Dār al-Fonun, was appointed as interpreter to assist him in teaching. Together they translated a treatise on music theory by G. Kuhn, of the Paris Academy of Music, into Persian.[113] A few years later, Victor Advielle published a treatise titled *La Musique chez les Persans en 1885* in which he detailed the curriculum of the music program at the Dār al-Fonun. From the curriculum it can be inferred that the duration of the program was eight years. In the first three years, students studied solmization and music theory, and focused on playing their first wind instrument. From the fourth year onward, they were required to study harmony, orchestration, a second wind instrument, and piano. In the final year, composition and conducting were also added to the program. Likewise, all students had to study French language, Persian literature, mathematics, history, and geography.[114] Lemaire was assigned to teach ten to twelve students every year; by 1885, he had trained approximately two hundred students and formed eighteen military bands.[115] By the end of the nineteenth century, Western-style bands known as *muzikānchi* had grown in diversity and number. Moreover, in 1918 the music department of the Dār al-Fonun finally became an independent institution and continued to function as the Madrasa-ye Musiqi (music school) under the supervision of the Ministry of Culture (Figure 3.22).

Lemaire spent the rest of his life in Iran, where he contributed enormously to the dissemination of Western music both within and beyond the court. He arranged concerts for royal banquets at the court and at the houses of princes as well as in the music department of the Dār al-Fonun, where he performed periodically with his talented students. He was also commissioned by the court to compose several pieces. Among them were the Iranian national anthem and a coronation march.[116] In 1883, he was sent to Paris to purchase musical instruments, sheet music, and equipment for the music department of the Dār al-Fonun and the court.[117]

Figure 3.22 Alfred Jean-Baptiste Lemaire and ʿAli-Akbar Mozayyen al-Dawla surrounded by their students at the Dār al-Fonun.

During the reign of Moẓaffar al-Din Shah, Western-style music evolved significantly in Iran. The shah was enormously influenced by the musical taste and advice of his special servant, Arslān Nāṣer Homāyun (d. 1920), a former student of Lemaire who served as the chief of military music and the shah's piano teacher. Nāṣer Homāyun accompanied Moẓaffar al-Din Shah on all his trips to Europe and was also responsible for purchasing Western musical instruments for the court.[118]

The first piano, with a range of five octaves, was sent to the court of Fatḥ-'Ali Shah by Napoleon in 1806.[119] However, no evidence has survived to suggest that the piano was ever played in the first half of the nineteenth century. In the mid-nineteenth century, a few pianos were presumably imported to Tehran, since early European instructors at the Dār al-Fonun used the instrument for teaching music theory and solmization. A German musician named Julius Heise (d. 1870) is mentioned as the pianist of Nāṣer al-Din Shah. He was reportedly active between 1866 and 1870.[120] Subsequently, on his third trip to Europe in 1883, Nāṣer al-Din Shah brought back more pianos for the court and princes.[121] As mentioned previously, a more widely accepted account credits Moḥammad Ṣādeq Khān as being the first musician to adapt the piano to Persian music. While he managed to modify the piano's system of tuning in order to play *āvāz*s (modes) on the instrument, he also trained some disciples, including princes and members of the gentry. There were some students at the Dār al-Fonun who never altered the piano's tuning and mainly used the instrument for teaching music theory, harmony, and solmization, and to perform simple versions of Western pieces or their own compositions.

It seems likely that the violin was introduced to Persian music around 1880. Before his first trip to Europe (1873), Nāṣer al-Din Shah had never seen a violin; in one travel account he refers to the instrument as *kamāncha-ye farangi* (European *kamāncha*). Early students of the violin in the late nineteenth century are mentioned as having studied with *kamāncha* players, for the violin was never taught at the Dār al-Fonun.[122] Toward the end of the reign of Nāṣer al-Din Shah, the French violinist Alexandre Duval spent two years in the Qajar court, where he trained a few students and formed a string orchestra.[123] In the first half of the twentieth century, the violin developed a prodigious following among the elite of Tehran, gradually taking the place of the *kamāncha*. While the violin was considered a chic and trendy instrument, the *kamāncha* was mostly associated with lower-class *moṭrebs*. The early style of violin playing consisted of certain techniques and idiosyncrasies adopted from the *kamāncha*, but Western idiomatic techniques were gradually assimilated, and the instrument attained a distinct character and flavor of its own in Persian music.

Flute, clarinet, trumpet, and saxophone were taught at the Dār al-Fonun as early as the 1850s. A few students at the Dār al-Fonun, who also had parallel training in Persian music, developed new techniques through which they could perform modified versions of *āvāzs* on the flute and clarinet (called *qaranay*). The trumpet and saxophone were less agile or adaptable to Persian music, but were frequently played along with other winds in the performance of *ta'ziya*.

Music and Socio-political Developments

Among the important social and cultural developments that occurred toward the end of the nineteenth century was the emergence of an elite upper middle class consisting largely of ministers, lawyers, doctors, literary figures, and merchants who came to be the new source of patronage for Persian classical music.

A fraternity known as the Anjoman-e Okhovvat (lit. "society of brotherhood") was founded in 1899 by Nāṣer al-Din Shah's son-in-law, Ẓahir al-Dawla (1864–1924) to promote the ideals of equity and brotherhood. Modeled in part after the Masonic lodges, the Anjoman also had its roots in the order established by the Sufi master Ṣafi-'Alishāh (1835–1898), which had among its members many princes, members of the nobility, and court officials. The fraternity at first professed a nonpolitical philosophy, but many of its members, including Ẓahir al-Dawla himself, came to be politically active during the constitutional movement. The official meetings of the Anjoman were held at Ẓahir al-Dawla's residence with 110 members, all carefully selected by Ẓahir al-Dawla, in attendance. Every year, on the 13th day of the Muslim lunar month of *Rajab*, the Anjoman celebrated the birth of Imam 'Ali in a garden capable of holding a large number of people who attended without any distinction in wealth, birth, rank, or office. The celebration usually went on for several hours, commencing with the Anjoman's anthem followed by a series of performances by master musicians.

The Anjoman recruited and supported a number of renowned musicians who included Darvish Khān (*tār* and *setār*), Montaẓam-al-Ḥokamā' (*setār*), Ḥosayn Hangāfarin (violin and *setār*), Moshir-Homāyun (piano), Ḥosayn Khān Esmā'ilzāda (*kamāncha*), Yusof Khān Ṣafā'i (*tār*), Ḥosayn Ṭāherzāda (singer), and Reżā-Qoli Nawruzi (singer and *dombak*) among their members.[124] During the constitutional period (1906–1911) several concerts were arranged by Darvish Khān in the form of garden parties.[125] The aforementioned musicians, together with others who were not permanent members of the Anjoman, also held monthly concerts and wrote both vocal and instrumental compositions for special events (Figure 3.23). Among the most important compositions associated with the Anjoman were a *taṣnif* in *segāh* composed by 'Ali-Akbar Shaydā (d. 1906) to commemorate the birth of the Prophet (*mawlud-e nabi*), and another piece known as the *sorud-e Anjoman-e Okhovvat* (fraternity's anthem), which was an instrumental composition in *dashti*.[126]

The majority of *taṣnifs* composed throughout the nineteenth century were amatory, describing either the pangs of separation or the playful antics of a vexatious yet ideal lover. Around the time of the constitutional revolution, a few poet-composers began to compose *taṣnifs* with critical themes in response

Figure 3.23 "Garden party at the Anjoman-e Okhovvat." The musician playing the *kamāncha* is Ḥosayn Khān Esmā'ilzāda.

to the current economic, social, and political situations. The most celebrated among them was Abu al-Qāsem 'Āref Qazvini (1882–1934), who wrote many vocal compositions to express his nationalist and reformist ideas as well as to mobilize pro-revolutionary sentiment. 'Āref Qazvini became an advocate of constitutional revolution and later, with some of his reformist friends, left Tehran first for Baghdad and subsequently for Istanbul, where he stayed from 1914 until 1918. In the early 1920s, he frequently performed his *taṣnif*s, accompanied by his favorite *tār* player, Shokri, at the Grand Hotel. Another renowned composer was Darvish Khān, who collaborated closely with the celebrated poet Malek al-Sho'arā' Bahār (1886–1951) to compose many *taṣnif*s with patriotic national themes.[127]

Recording Technology

The rise of recording technologies was another development that brought remarkable changes to Iran's musical life. A phonograph cylinder was first brought to Nāṣer al-Din Shah's court in 1888.[128] However, it was in the reign of Moẓaffar al-Din Shah that numerous phonographs were imported to the country for the court and the nobility thanks to the enterprise of a prominent businessman who later became the vice-president of the first parliament, Ḥājj Moḥammad-Ḥosayn Amin al-Żarb (1872–1932).[129] There are many references to phonographs in memoirs by princes from that period. Moẓaffar al-Din Shah, for example, mentions that he carried his own phonograph around on his visits to other cities. Among the princes who enjoyed the phonograph during this period was Dust-'Ali Mo'ayyer al-Mamālek, who also recorded a number of celebrated court musicians on wax cylinders between 1899 and 1904, including Moḥammad Ṣādeq Khān, Nāyeb Asadollāh, and Āqā Ḥosayn-Qoli.[130]

In 1906, Maxim Pick, a sales representative of the British-owned Gramophone Company (GC), arrived in Tehran with two sound technicians and began recording sessions with the permission of Moẓaffar al-Din Shah (Figure 3.24). The arrangements were made by Alfred Jean-Baptiste Lemaire, who was commissioned to select some of the best court musicians for the occasion. The recording sessions produced an assortment of music performed by master court instrumentalists and singers, *moqalled*s, *muzikānchi*s, the royal military band (*orkes-e shāhi*), and other military bands associated with the court and princes. Probably the most important project among these recordings was

Figure 3.24 The Multiplex Grand Phonograph technicians beginning to record with permission from Moẓaffar al-Din Shah.

an attempt to produce a set of seven *dastgāhs* performed by two groups of court musicians as multiple disc sets. In these recordings, Āqā Ḥosayn-Qoli and his disciples performed *chahārgāh*, *māhur*, *homāyun*, and *rāst-panjgāh*, and the *dasta-ye shāhi* directed by ʿAli-Akbar Shāhi performed *shur*, *segāh*, and *navā*.[131] The recordings were mostly pressed on single-sided 10-inch discs that could not exceed three minutes of music. Evidence suggests that the musicians sought to follow a standard format on most of the discs. Opening with an *āvāz* (set to one or two couplets and accompanied by a single instrument) they subsequently performed a short *taṣnif* and a *reng*. In some cases, even the closing *reng* is not completely recorded due to the time constraints of the disc. In the same year, the GC established a headquarters in Tehran and hired a local agent, Hambartsum Hairapetian, to arrange and market recordings featuring Persian musicians.[132]

A year later, in 1907, a group of court musicians, including Āqā Ḥosayn-Qoli, Sayyed Aḥmad Khān, Bāqer Khān, Asadollāh Khān, and Moḥammad Bāqer, signed a contract with Hambartsum Hairapetian to travel to Paris to record. It seems that most of the recordings were made by Āqā Ḥosayn-Qoli either playing solo *tār* or accompanying the voice of Sayyed Aḥmad Khān.

A few recordings were also of instrumental compositions performed by the entire ensemble. Among the remainder of the recordings, there is one in which all musicians sing and play a *taṣnif* together and another one in which the ensemble performs a metrical composition accompanied by the *dombak*, on top of which the singer sings an *āvāz*.[133] Generally speaking, the musicians do not follow the typical format of *gusha*, *taṣnif*, and *reng* on these recordings and perform more freely, often performing an entirely *āvāz* section or *taṣnif* on one side of a disc. On their way back from Paris, the musicians stayed in Turkey for one month and held a concert in support of the Iranian School of Istanbul.[134] Upon their return to Tehran, complications arose between musicians and the agent of the GC. As a result, save for a few copies, the discs remained incomplete productions and never reached Tehran.[135]

Two years later, in 1909, another group of eight musicians went to London and recorded more than 260 titles. On these recordings, Ḥosayn Ṭāherzāda mostly performed the *āvāz* sections while Reżā-Qoli Nawruzi, whose name appears as the *taṣnif-khᵛān* and *żarbgir* on more than 120 discs, rendered the *taṣnifs*. The instrumentalists were divided into two groups: Darvish Khān, Bāqer Khān, and Asadollāh Khān played the Persian *tār*, *kamāncha*, and *santur*, while Ḥabibollāh Moshir-Homāyun, Akbar Khān, and Ḥosayn Khān Hangāfarin played the piano (and organ), flute, and violin, respectively. The majority of recordings included vocals, but a few were of solo instrumental pieces.[136]

In 1912, the same Gramophone Company that had failed to sell out the 10,000 discs produced in 1906 resumed recording sessions in Tehran with a new target audience. Instead of focusing solely on male court musicians whose music mostly catered to the tastes of the elite upper classes, the GC began to record select courtesans, who not only performed a lighter repertoire of music but also incorporated among their songs the national liberation-themed *taṣnifs* of ʿĀref Qazvini. Three female singers, Amjad, Eftekhār, and Zari, performed a repertoire of *āvāzs* and *taṣnifs* that amounted to more than seventy-five discs.[137] Likewise, the celebrated male singer Jenāb Damāvandi recorded copiously accompanied by Ḥosayn Khān Esmāʿilzāda on the *kamāncha* and Āqā Ḥosayn-Qoli on the *tār*. These two musicians also recorded a few solo instrumental discs. Of particular significance that year was the recording of *monājāt* (religious chants) and *adhān* (call to prayer) sung by Jenāb Damāvandi and some *taqlids* performed by ʿAli-Akbar Nafti.[138]

In 1914, the German-owned Monarch Records arranged for another group of musicians to go to Tbilisi. Two prominent *āvāz* singers, Ḥosayn Ṭāherzāda and Abu al-Ḥasan Eqbāl al-Solṭān along with the young ʿAbdollāh Davāmi, who was featured as the *taṣnif-khᵛān* and *żarbgir*, were accompanied by Darvish Khān and Bāqer Khān on the *tār* and *kamāncha*, respectively. The choice and arrangement of repertoire recorded on this trip seem to have been entirely based on the musicians' predilection. The recordings made in Tbilisi were later sent to Germany for pressing, but unfortunately their arrival coincided with the advent of the First World War and, with the exception of a small number of discs, the recordings were never pressed nor were they sent back to Tehran.[139]

After a twelve-year gap, the GC sent recording technicians to Tehran in 1926, 1928, and 1929 and mostly recorded female singers during this period. In 1926, the two celebrated female singers Qamar al-Moluk Vaziri (1905–1959) and Moluk Żarrābi (d. 1999), accompanied by the well-known Jewish *tār* player Morteżā Naydāvud, recorded fifty and thirty titles, respectively. Likewise, in the same year and subsequently in 1928, Pari Āqābāyev, Irān Khānom, Parvāna Khānom, Akhtar Khānom, and Nayyera ʿAẓam Rumi recorded a wide array of classical, light classical, and Western-influenced music.[140] Such music performed by female singers was more appealing to the urban middle class than the sober classical music previously or concurrently recorded by the majority of male singers, and middle-class listeners became part of the market for recorded music. Before 1926, turntables cost around 100 *tumāns* and 78 rpm records retailed at 3 *tumāns* apiece, hence the purchasing audience was largely confined to the urban upper class. After 1926, cheaper turntables were produced and imported by rival companies, and 78 and 45 rpm records were sold for around 1.5 or 2 *tumāns*, thus abetting the expansion of the market for recordings.

The Impact of Western Music on Traditional Practices

Western music exerted considerable influence on traditional practices in the first few decades of the twentieth century. This influence is most evident in the choice of performance venues, musical instruments (especially piano and violin), rhythmic structures, scales and intervals, performance format, and instrumental and vocal idioms.

In his first trip to Europe in 1873, Nāṣer al-Din Shah attended performances at the Royal Opera House and Royal Albert Hall in London as well as the Verona Arena in Italy. Impressed by these structures and encouraged by the advice of his courtiers, he ordered a comparable venue to be built adjacent to the Golestān Palace for public performances. The building was named Takiya Dawlat, and it remained the most prominent place for the performance of Shi'ite mourning rituals for many decades. While this large audience hall was not suitable for the performance of Persian music, Western-style military bands occasionally performed there, especially preceding and following the performance of a *ta'ziya*.[141] Moreover, at the beginning of the twentieth century, the luxurious Grand Hotel was built in Tehran with a concert hall that frequently hosted performances of European-derived plays and Persian music. The concerts of Persian music held at the Grand Hotel were mostly attended by members of a growing middle-class elite. Among the musicians who performed there were 'Āref Qazvini and later, the two prominent female singers Qamar al-Moluk Vaziri and Moluk Żarrābi.[142]

After the introduction of European military music, Persian musicians began to adopt the Western duple, triple, and quadruple meters and impose them on various genres of composition, especially *taṣnif*s and *pishdarāmad*s. The stress patterns of Western meters subsequently changed the dynamics and rhythmic structure of compositions that were originally set to cycles of two, three, four, five, six, and seven beats.

Western influence was also evident in the alteration of intervals in some *āvāz*s (modes). For example, in older versions of *bayāt-e esfahān* the second below the tonic was larger than a semitone (minor second) and smaller than a wholetone (major second). In the twentieth century, there was a tendency to alter this interval to conform to a minor second, creating the impression of a leading tone and making *bayāt-e esfahān* resemble the harmonic minor scale. Likewise, 'Ali-Naqi Vaziri (1886–1979), the first student of Persian music to receive musical training in Europe, proposed a twenty-four-quarter-tone scale. Vaziri soon became the director of Madrasa-ye Musiqi in Tehran and his twenty-four-quarter-tone scale, which was derived from further division of the Western equidistant twelve-note chromatic scale, was put into practice by his disciples.[143] Beginning in the 1920s, Vaziri emerged as the most prominent musical figure in Iran for more than three decades. He taught Western musical instruments (mainly piano and violin), solfège, and music theory, and also wrote instruction manuals introducing new playing techniques and various exercises for the *tār* and violin.[144]

The performance format of Persian music also evolved noticeably at the beginning of the twentieth century. As will be discussed in Chapter 6, an overture-like genre called *pishdarāmad* was first introduced by Āqā Ḥosayn-Qoli and later cultivated by two outstanding composers, Rokn al-Din Mokhtāri (d. 1971) and Darvish Khān. The genre largely developed thorough the public performances of music held at the Anjoman-e Okhovvat. Moreover, Darvish Khān and Vaziri presented new instrumental compositions (not in traditional genres) that came to be commonly known as *qeṭ'a* (lit. "piece").[145] While Darvish Khān wrote a few Persian instrumental compositions, titled "Polka" and "March," Vaziri also changed the typical structure and performance format of vocal compositions. Ruḥollāh Khāleqi states:

> In the performance of old *taṣnifs*, each *jomla* (melodic phrase or section) was rendered twice: the first time was introduced by the singer and the second time was repeated by an instrument. Vaziri changed the convention. In his compositions, following the vocal phrase, the orchestra rendered a distinctive melody [as an interlude]. Likewise, in some of his more serious compositions marked as program music, he sought to dramatize the meaning of texts through music. Furthermore, old *taṣnifs* always commenced with the singer without an instrumental introduction, but Vaziri wrote orchestral overtures for vocal sections. All these developments were first in contradiction with the established tradition and were criticized by the knowledgeable listeners, but today they sound completely standard and part of the conventional practice.[146]

Western harmony was another element that permeated some compositions by Vaziri and his disciples. Harmonic accompaniment became particularly prevalent in modes resembling the Western minor scale and, especially, major scales. Chordal progressions, however, tended to be simple, generally consisting of primary major and minor triads built on the scalar tones of the melody. In some Persian modes, simple harmony was occasionally employed more as a superfluous ornament that did not alter the fundamentally modal character of the music. In 1935, Vaziri compiled a treatise on harmonizing Persian music in which he delineated his theory of harmony within a quarter-tone system.[147] Of particular significance was the conspicuous use of arpeggios, previously an unlikely occurrence in Persian music but later incorporated as a performance technique in both Western-adopted and Persian instruments, notably the piano, violin, *santur*, *nay*, and *tār*.

Summary

In the first half of the nineteenth century, the performance of music at the court was dominated by upper-class courtesans and the shah's concubines, who were organized into two groups of twenty-five performers. At the same time, a number of male instrumentalists, singers, and dance instructors were hired to train female performers. These male musicians also performed individually and as members of ensembles at courtly occasions. Beginning in the 1840s, the tradition of upper-class courtesans declined, and subsequently more male instrumentalists were recruited to the court. In the second half of the nineteenth century, male musicians and entertainers associated with the court fell into the three categories of *'amala-ye ṭarab-e khāṣṣa*, *'amala-ye ṭarab*, and *moṭreb*. While all categories of musician were servants of the court and never bore the honorific title of *ostād*, the *'amala-ye ṭarab-e khāṣṣa* (solo specialists) developed stylistic schools and repertoires, and through a defensive, secretive strategy managed to preserve their hereditary uniqueness and prestige. What came to be known as the *radif* was the ordered repertoire of the Farāhāni family, who were the most eminent *tār* players at the court. Like their predecessors, *'amala-ye ṭarab-e khāṣṣa* were also responsible for training promising girls and young women, the most talented and beautiful among whom were selected to be the shah's concubines. Lesser instrumentalists, singers, accompanists, dancing boys, and *moqalled*s were also active in Tehran and other urban centers in the form of troupes or *dasta-ye moṭreb*s. They were mostly male and female professional musicians who were not recruited to the court, though the most celebrated troupes were occasionally brought to perform at the court and homes of the nobility.

As in Turkey, the influence of Western music in Iran was primarily through military music, but this process occurred in Iran at a much later date and at a slower pace than in Turkey. Western influence was apparent mostly in the assimilation of musical instruments, intervals, harmony, some aspects of musical form, and orchestration. More important, Persian musicians barely showed interest in Western music repertoire before the second half of the twentieth century. The role of Alfred Jean-Baptiste Lemaire in modernizing the Persian military band and in disseminating Western music at the court, beginning in 1858, can be compared with the role of the Italian bandmaster Giuseppe Donizetti (1788–1856), who had arrived at the Ottoman court for the same purpose thirty years earlier, in 1828. Above all, the *naqqāra-khāna* in Iran continued to be operational for much of the first half of the twentieth century, whereas the music of the Janissary Corps (*mehterkhâne*) was abolished in 1826, following the radical and European-looking reforms of the Ottoman Sultan Mahmut II (r. 1808–1839).[148]

At its outset, the recording industry and its market did not have much impact on improving the economic situation or social status of musicians, nor did it create a mass audience for Persian music. Many of the recordings of Persian musicians made during the first two decades of the twentieth century never reached Tehran, and even when they did arrive, they were prohibitively expensive for all but a few members of the upper class. It was during the Pahlavi period (1925–1979) and mostly through commercial recordings of female singers that the recording industry experienced a rapid growth among the emerging middle class.

Notes

1. Guillaume Antoine Olivier, *Voyage dans l'empire Othoman, l'Égypte et la Perse*, 3 vols. (Paris: 1801/7); trans. Moḥammad-Ṭāher Mirzā, as *Safarnāma-ye Olivie*, repr., ed. Gholām-Reżā Varahrām (Tehran: Eṭṭelā'āt, 1992), 90–99.
2. 'Ażod al-Dawla, *Tārikh-e 'Ażodi*, 168.
3. Moḥammadi, "Resāla-ye davāzdah dastgāh," 125–146; Żiā' al-Din Yusof, *Resāla-ye musiqi mowsum be kolliyāt-e Yusofi*, ed. Bābak Khażrā'i (Tehran: Farhangestān-e Honar, 2011), 27.
4. Moḥammadi, "Resāla-ye davāzdah dastgāh," 142.
5. Chodźko, *Specimens of the Popular Poetry of Persia*, 417.
6. Moḥammadi, "Resāla-ye davāzdah dastgāh," 142–143.
7. Ibid., 143.
8. Ibid.; 'Ażod al-Dawla, *Tārikh-e 'Ażodi*, 47.
9. Moḥammadi, "Resāla-ye davāzdah dastgāh," 143.
10. Ibid.
11. 'Ażod al-Dawla, *Tārikh-e 'Ażodi*, 26–27. At the end of his edition of *Tārikh-e 'Ażodi*, Navā'i adds a list of the shah's wives from *Nāsikh al-tawārikh* and provides additional information about Shāhverdi Khānom. See ibid., 344.
12. Moḥammadi, "Resāla-ye davāzdah dastgāh," 143.
13. Chodźko, *Specimens of the Popular Poetry of Persia*, 417.
14. Hārun Vahuman (ed.), "Safarnāma-ye Kajlor," in *Safarnāmahā-ye khaṭṭi-ye Fārsi*, 4 vols. (Tehran: Nashr-e Akhtarān, 2009), 3: 466, 480.

15. ʿAżod al-Dawla, *Tārikh-e ʿAżodi*, 26–27. Fāṭemi (*Jashn va musiqi dar farhanghā-ye shahri-ye Irāni*, 56–58) opines that, by the beginning of the nineteenth century, through an effort that he calls "culture rehabilitation," the upper-class courtesans ceased to be active in the capital and all the *bāzigar*s or female performers at the Qajar court—especially those recruited to the ensembles of Minā and Zohra—were married to Fatḥ-ʿAli Shah or his courtiers. It is evident that some of the female court performers were concubines of the shah, however, many remained still upper-class courtesans who were specifically recruited to perform at certain court occasions. ʿAżod al-Dawla, *Tārikh-e ʿAżodi*, 46–47, refers to a group of female performers who had maids and rode horses in the palace courtyard, characteristics of courtesans in the seventeenth century. Likewise, paintings of courtly life display a clear differentiation between the outfits of concubines and courtesans. While concubines are often depicted as wearing *shalita*s (trousers with a short skirt) and *rusari*s (head scarf), courtesans are portrayed as wearing transparent shirts with trousers made of luxurious fabrics. Courtesans' performance attire consisted of jeweled dresses decorated with pearls, gems, and embroidery as well as elaborate aigrettes.
16. As cited in Ruḥollāh Khāleqi, *Sargodhasht-e musiqi-ye Irān* (Tehran: Safiʿalishāh, 1983), 1: 33–38.
17. See Mehdi-Qoli Hedāyat, *Majmaʿ al-adwār*, 10; Mashḥun, *Tārikh-e musiqi-ye Irān*, 372; Reżā-Qoli Mirzā (Ḥasan ʿAbdollāh Sarābi), *Safar-nāma-ye Reżā-Qoli Mirzā Nāyeb al-Ayāla*, ed. Asghar Farmānfarmāʾi Qājār (Tehran: Asāṭir, 1994), 791–792; Maythami, "Nokāti darbāra-ye musiqidānān-e Qājār," 99.
18. ʿAżod al-Dawla, *Tārikh-e ʿAżodi*, 153–156.
19. Joseph Arthur Gobineau, *Trois ans en Asie, 1855 à 1858* (Paris, 1859), 464.
20. Ibid.
21. Khāleqi, *Sargodhasht-e musiqi-ye Irān*, 1: 18–19.
22. Mashḥun, *Tārikh-e musiqi-ye Irān*, 362–363, 446.
23. Ibid., This *taṣnif* was recorded by Reżā-Qoli Nawruzi in 1909.
24. In the royal court, *khāṣṣa* was a term referring to the sector of the administration particularly belonging and responding to the crown.
25. Mashḥun, *Tārikh-e musiqi-ye Irān*, 387 n. 40.
26. Gobineau. *Trois ans en Asie, 1855 à 1858*, 464.
27. Maythami, "Nokāti darbāra-ye musiqidānān-e Qājār," 100.
28. Cf. Moḥammadi, "Resāla-ye davāzdah dastgāh," 143.
29. Solṭān Khānom was the most prominent singer and composer of the seraglio who was in the service of Mahd-e ʿOliyāʾ (the Queen mother). For further detail, see Mashḥun, *Tārikh-e musiqi-ye Irān*, 391, 461, 563.

30. Bahman Kazemi, Mehdi Farahani, and Vahraz Puraḥmad, *Persian Music in the Past Century* (Tehran: Farhangestān-e Honar, 2012), 144–145.
31. Mashḥun, *Tārikh-e musiqi-ye Irān*, 386–390, 402–411.
32. *Marāsem-e darbār-e Nāṣeri: jashn-e āshpazān* (1868–1896), ed. Fāṭema Qāzihā (Tehran: Sāzemān-e Asnād va Ketābkhāna-ye Melli, 2012), 28, 30, 47, 71.
33. In the list of musicians provided by Eskandar Beg Monshi, the chronicler of Shah 'Abbās, some of the musicians are called "ostād." For further information, see Eskandar Beg Turkamān, *Tārikh-e 'ālamārā-ye 'Abbāsi*, 1: 190.
34. In early recordings, several *taṣnifs* were jointly performed by two singers.
35. Khāleqi, *Sargodhasht-e musiqi-ye Irān*, 1: 156–157.
36. Mashḥun, *Tārikh-e musiqi-ye Irān*, 414.
37. Rostam al-Ḥokamā', *Rustam al-tawārikh*, 100.
38. Khāleqi, *Sargodhasht-e musiqi-ye Irān*, 1: 16.
39. E'temād al-Salṭana, *Al-ma'āthir va al-āthār* (Tehran: Asāṭir, 1984), 1:48.
40. Khāleqi, *Sargodhasht-e musiqi-ye Irān*, 1: 157–162.
41. 'Abdollāh Mostawfi, *Sharḥ-e zendegāni-ye man* (Tehran: Zavvār, 1992), 1: 359–361.
42. Eugène Aubin, *Irān-e emruz 1906–1907*, Persian trans. Ali-Asghar Sa'idi (Tehran: Nashr-e 'Elm, 1983), 248; Sāsān Fāṭemi, "Tārikh-e musiqi-ye Qājār," in *Tārikh-e jāme'-e Irān*, ed. Ṣādeq Sajjādi, 20 vols. (Tehran: Bonyād-e Dā'eratolma'āref-e Bozorg-e Eslāmi, 2014), 18: 270.
43. Gholām-'Ali 'Aziz al-Solṭān, *Ruznāma-ye khāṭerāt-e Gholām-'Ali 'Aziz al-Solṭān, Malijak* (Tehran: Zaryāb, 1997), 3: 2210; Mashḥun, *Tārikh-e musiqi-ye Irān*, 428.
44. Personal communication from Dāriush Ṣafvat.
45. Mashḥun, *Tārikh-e musiqi-ye Irān*, 507.
46. See Ṭali'a Kāmrān and Shehāb Menā, *Bakhshhā'i az radif-e Ḥabib Samā'i be revāyat-e Ṭali'a Kāmrān* (Tehran: Nashr-e Musiqi-ye 'Āref, 2009), 18–21.
47. Mashḥun, *Tārikh-e musiqi-ye Irān*, 510.
48. Ibid., 509.
49. Cf. Pourjavady, "Negāhi be ḥayāt-e musiqā'i-ye dawra-ye Afshāri," 45; Mashḥun, *Tārikh-e musiqi-ye Irān*, 367.
50. Mashḥun, *Tārikh-e musiqi-ye Irān*, 510; Khāleqi, *Sargodhasht-e musiqi-ye Irān*, 1: 161–162.
51. Mashḥun, *Tārikh-e musiqi-ye Irān*, 510.
52. Khāleqi, *Sargodhasht-e musiqi-ye Irān*, 1: 161–162.
53. See Mehdi-Qoli Hedāyat, *Radif-e haft dastgāh-e musiqi-ye Irāni be revāyat-e Mehdi Ṣolhi* (Tehran: Māhur, 2014), 11, 26, 30, 79, 82, 91, 120, 121; Mashḥun, *Tārikh-e musiqi-ye Irān*, 714, 724, 725, 727.

54. Michael Kinnear, *The Gramophone Company's Persian Recordings 1899–1934* (Victoria, Australia: Bajakhana, 2000), 55–72.
55. Khāleqi, *Sargodhasht-e musiqi-ye Irān*, 1: 161; Mashḥun, *Tārikh-e musiqi-ye Irān*, 512.
56. Sāsān Sepantā, *Cheshmandāz-e musiqi-ye Irān* (Tehran: Māhur, 2003), 89–90.
57. Mashḥun, *Tārikh-e musiqi-ye Irān*, 564–565.
58. Ibid., 569.
59. Ibid., 575.
60. Ibid., 574–575.
61. Mostawfi, *Sharḥ-e zendegāni-ye man*, 1: 339–340.
62. For further information, see Chapter 5.
63. *Ruznāma-ye khāṭerāt-e Nāṣer al-Din Shah Qājār (4.1282–3.1283 H)*, ed. Majid 'Abdeamin (Tehran: Anjoman-e Āthār va Mafākher-e Farhangi, 2016), 69.
64. Qahramān Mirzā Sālur, *Ruznāma-ye khāṭerāt-e 'Ayn al-Salṭana*, 10 vols. (Tehran: Asāṭir, 1995–2001), 3: 2236.
65. Mostawfi, *Sharḥ-e zendegāni-ye man*, 1: 359–361.
66. For an account of Shaykh Shaypur, see ibid., 1: 348–349.
67. Mashḥun, *Tārikh-e musiqi-ye Irān*, 391, 563.
68. In his interview with Mohammad Reżā Lotfi, the eminent *taṣnif* singer, 'Abdollāh Davāmi mentions that he learned a substantial section of his repertoire from Ḥabibollāh Samā'-Ḥożur and his sister. For further information, see Moḥammad-Reżā Loṭfi, *Musiqi-ye āvāzi-ye Irān: dastgāh-e shur, radif-e ostād 'Abdollāh Davāmi* (Tehran, Enteshārāt-e Gutenberg, 1974), 12.
69. Khāleqi, *Sargodhasht-e musiqi-ye Irān*, 1: 467; for her compositions, see Farāmarz Pāyvar, *Radif-e āvāzi va taṣnifhā-ye qadimi be revāyat-e 'Abdollāh Davāmi* (Tehran: Māhur, 1996), 452.
70. Khāleqi, *Sargodhasht-e musiqi-ye Irān*, 1: 467.
71. Dust-'Ali Mo'ayyer al-Mamālek, *Yāddāshthā-'i az zendegāni-ye khoṣuṣi-ye Nāṣer al-Din Shah* (Tehran: Nashr-e Tārikh-e Irān, 1982), 21–22.
72. Ibid.
73. Ibid., 372; Mashḥun, *Tārikh-e musiqi-ye Irān*, 664.
74. Ibid., 675.
75. Ibid., 540–541, 545–546.
76. Khāleqi, *Sargodhasht-e musiqi-ye Irān*, 1: 162.
77. Mashḥun, *Tārikh-e musiqi-ye Irān*, 513, 540, 545, 566, 617, 676.
78. Pious people refused to keep or allow musical instruments in their houses.
79. Aubin, *Irān-e emruz 1906–1907*, 248; Fāṭemi, *Jashn va musiqi dar farhanghā-ye shahri-ye Irāni*, 88–89.

80. See Ensiya Shaykh Reżā'i and Shahlā Ādhari (ed.), *Gozāreshhā-ye naẓmiya az maḥallāt-e Tehrān: Rāport-e vaqāye'-e mokhtalef-e maḥallāt-e dār al-khelāfa (1303–1305 H)*, 2 vols. (Tehran: Sāzemān-e Asnād-e Melli-ye Irān, 1998), 1: 336.
81. For further details about the account of ensembles, see Fāṭemi, *Jashn va musiqi dar farhanghā-ye shahri-ye Irāni*, 57–80.
82. A. S. Wolfson, *Irāniān dar godhashta va ḥāl*, Persian trans. Mirzā Ḥosayn Khān Anṣāri (Tehran: Chapkhāna-ye Khāvar, 1930), 47. See also Fāṭemi, *Jashn va musiqi dar farhanghā-ye shahri-ye Irāni*, 31–35.
83. Unlike the piano, the Western instruments harmonium, flute, and mandolin were not tuned in the *dastgāh* system, hence, what was played on them was limited to two or three modes (*māhur*, *eṣfahān*, *chahārgāh*).
84. Dust-'Ali Mo'ayyer al-Mamālek, *Rejāl-e 'aṣr-e Nāṣeri* (Tehran: Nashr-e Tārikh-e Irān, 1982), 287–290; Mo'ayyer al-Mamālek, *Yāddāshthā-'i az zendegāni-ye khoṣuṣi-ye Nāṣer al-Din Shah*, 26–27, 63.
85. Khāleqi, *Sargodhasht-e musiqi-ye Irān*, 1: 471–483; Mashḥun, *Tārikh-e musiqi-ye Irān*, 394; Fāṭemi, *Jashn va musiqi dar farhanghā-ye shahri-ye Irāni*, 68–70. See also Mostawfi, *Sharḥ-e zendegāni-ye man*, 1: 214; E'temād al-Salṭana, *Ruznāma-ye khāṭerāt-e E'temād al-Salṭana*, ed. Iraj Afshār (Tehran: Amir-Kabir, 2000), 457; Sālur, *Ruznāma-ye khāṭerāt-e 'Ayn al-Salṭana*, 1: 655, 920–921; Tāj al-Salṭana, *Khāṭerāt-e Tāj al-Salṭana*, ed. Manṣura Etteḥādiya (Tehran: Nashr-e Tārikh-e Irān, 1992), 71; Mo'ayyer al-Mamālek, *Yāddāshthā-'i az zendegāni-ye khoṣuṣi-ye Nāṣer al-Din Shah*, 49, 63; Mu'nes al-Dawla, *Khāterāt-e Mu'nes al-Dawla, nadima-ye haramsarā-ye Nāṣer al-Din Shah*, ed. Syrus Sa'dvandiyān (Tehran: Zarrin, 2010), 46.
86. Khāleqi, *Sargodhasht-e musiqi-ye Irān*, 1: 480–483.
87. *Ruznāma-ye khāterāt Nāṣer al-Din Shah Qājār* (*4.1282–3.1283 H*), 188.
88. Khāleqi, *Sargodhasht-e musiqi-ye Irān*, 1: 462–463.
89. Mo'ayyer al-Mamālek, *Yāddāshthā-'i az zendegāni-ye khoṣuṣi-ye Nāṣer al-Din Shah*, 27; for their image, see Kazemi, Farahani, and Pourahmad, *Persian Music in the Past Century*, 209.
90. Cf. Pourjavady, "Negāhi be ḥayāt-e musiqā'i-ye dawra-ye Afshāri," 3–5; Mashḥun, *Tārikh-e musiqi-ye Irān*, 459; Pāyvar, *Radif-e āvāzi va taṣnifhā-ye qadimi be revāyat-e 'Abdollāh Davāmi*, 250, 283.
91. Mashḥun, *Tārikh-e musiqi-ye Irān*, 693–697.
92. Ibid., 699
93. Jay Gluck and Sumi Gluck, *A Survey of Persian Handicraft* (Tehran: The Bank Melli, 1977), 369–370.

94. Ibid.; for a further account on the subject, see Khāleqi, *Sargodhasht-e musiqi-ye Irān*, 1: 169–171; Mashhun, *Tārikh-e musiqi-ye Irān*, 693–694.
95. Ibid., 540.
96. Sālur, *Ruznāma-ye khāṭerāt-e 'Ayn al-Salṭana*, 2: 1283.
97. Khāleqi, *Sargodhasht-e musiqi-ye Irān*, 1: 462–463.
98. Mashḥun, *Tārikh-e musiqi-ye Irān*, 643.
99. Ibid., 414.
100. 'Āref Qazvini, *Divān*, ed. Mehdi Nurmoḥammadi (Tehran: Sokhan, 2002), 111.
101. Fāṭemi, *Jashn va musiqi dar farhanghā-ye shahri-ye Irāni*, 88.
102. John Baily, *Music of Afghanistan: Professional Musicians in the City of Herat* (Cambridge: Cambridge University Press, 1988), 141.
103. Fāṭemi, *Jashn va musiqi dar farhanghā-ye shahri-ye Irāni*, 75.
104. Tāj al-Salṭana, *Khāṭerāt-e Tāj al-Salṭana*, 90.
105. Aubin, *Irān-e emruz 1906–1907*, 248; Fāṭemi, "Tārikh-e musiqi-ye Qājār," 18: 266.
106. Tāj al-Salṭana, *Khāṭerāt-e Tāj al-Salṭana*, 71.
107. William Ouseley, *Travels in Various Countries of the East: More Particularly Persia* (London: Rodwell & Martin, 1823), 3: 399.
108. Moritz von Kotzebue, *Narrative of a Journey into Persia in the Suite of the Imperial Russian Embassy in the Year 1817* (Philadelphia, 1820), 107–108.
109. See Alexis Soltykoff, *Voyage en Perse* (Paris, 1851), 80.
110. Mohsen Mohammadi, "Chef de Musique or Chef de Macaroni: The Twisted History of the European Military Music in Persia," *Rivista Italiana di Musicologia* 51 (2016): 71–72.
111. Victor Advielle, *La Musique chez les Persans en 1885* (Paris, 1885), 6.
112. Giuseppe Anaclerio, *La Persia descritta. Relazione di un viaggio* (Napoli: Vincenzo Marchese, 1868), 98.
113. The treatise was published in the original French with Persian translation by the Dār al-Fonun Press as *Ta'rif-e 'elm-e musiqi (Théorie de la musique composée pour les classes du conservatoire de musique de Paris, par G. Kuhn)*, trans. Mirzā 'Ali-Akbar (Tehran: Dār al-Fonun, 1883).
114. For the curriculum of the program, see Maryam Ebtekar, "Harmony or Cacophony: Music Instruction at the Dār al-Fonūn," in *Society and Culture in Qajar Iran*, ed. Elton L. Daniel (Costa Mesa, CA: Mazda, 2002), 58.
115. Ibid., 56–57.
116. Khāleqi, *Sargodhasht-e musiqi-ye Irān*, 1: 214–215.
117. Ibid., 1: 216–217.

118. Ibid., 1: 227–230. Mashḥun, *Tārikh-e musiqi-ye Irān*, 438–439, 527.
119. Mashḥun, *Tārikh-e musiqi-ye Irān*, 508; Sepantā, *Cheshmandāz-e musiqi-ye Irān*, 113–114.
120. Tinco Martinus Lycklama a Nijeholt, *Voyage en Russie, au Caucase et en Perse, dans la Mésopotamie, le Kurdistan, la Syrie, la Palestine et la Turquie* (Paris: Arthus Bertrand, 1873), 355; Mohammadi, "Chef de Musique or Chef de Macaroni," 76.
121. Khāleqi, *Sargodhasht-e musiqi-ye Irān*, 1: 251–252.
122. Ibid., 1: 251.
123. Ibid., 1: 218.
124. Mashḥun, *Tārikh-e musiqi-ye Irān*, 543, 681; Khāleqi, *Sargodhasht-e musiqi-ye Irān*, 1: 87.
125. Ibid., 1: 83–90.
126. Ibid., 1: 87–90; Pāyvar, *Radif-e āvāzi va taṣnifhā-ye qadimi be revāyat-e 'Abdollāh Davāmi*, 348. The *sorud-e Anjoman-e Okhovvat* is included in *Żarbihā-ye qadimi be revāyat va ejrā-ye Ostād Yusof Forutan*, Tehran: Māhur, 2012 (M.CD-311).
127. For the accounts of *taṣnifs* by 'Āref Qazvini and Darvish Khān, see Mashḥun, *Tārikh-e musiqi-ye Irān*, 469–476, 482–484.
128. Moḥammad-Reżā Sharāyeli, "Muzik-e fawj-e makhṣuṣ," *Māhur* 66 (2015): 99.
129. Ibid., 100.
130. Sāsān Sepantā, *Tārikh-e taḥavvol żabṭ-e musiqi dar Irān* (Tehran: Māhur, 1998), 73–104.
131. Kinnear, *The Gramophone Company's Persian Recordings*, 49–52.
132. Ibid., 9.
133. Cf. Bahman Kāẓemi, Mehdi Farāhāni, and Vahraz Puraḥmad, *Golbāng-e sarbolandi: mabāni va barrasi-ye āvāz-e Irān* (Tehran: Farhangestān-e Honar, 2010), 104–105.
134. Khāleqi, *Sargodhasht-e musiqi-ye Irān*, 1: 134.
135. Kāẓemi, Farāhāni, and Puraḥmad, *Golbāng-e sarbolandi*, 100–103.
136. For further details, see Kinnear, *The Gramophone Company's Persian Recordings*, 55–76.
137. Ibid., 77–83.
138. Ibid., 83–88.
139. Kāẓemi, Farāhāni, and Puraḥmad, *Golbāng-e sarbolandi*, 131–139.
140. Kinnear, *The Gramophone Company's Persian Recordings*, 89–110.
141. Khāleqi, *Sargodhasht-e musiqi-ye Irān*, 1: 341–346.

142. Khāleqi declares that in the beginning, the concert hall at the Grand Hotel was considered a fancy and high-class venue where, except for Armenian women, who did not have veils, Muslim women were not allowed to attend performances. For further details, see ibid., 1: 411–413.
143. Cf. Hormoz Farhat, *The Dastgāh Concept in Persian Music* (Cambridge: Cambridge University Press, 1990), 7–10, 76–77.
144. For details about the life and contributions of ʻAli-Naqi Vaziri, see Khāleqi, *Sargodhasht-e musiqi-ye Irān*, 1: 2; ʻAli-Reżā Mirʻalinaqi and ʻAli-Naqi Vaziri, *Vaziri-nāma* (Tehran: Moʻin, 1998).
145. Darvish Khān began his musical career as a student at Dār al-Fonun. For further details, see Khāleqi, *Sargodhasht-e musiqi-ye Irān*, 1: 298–299.
146. Khāleqi, *Sargodhasht-e musiqi-ye Irān*, 2: 92–93.
147. The treatise is still in manuscript: ʻAli-Naqi Vaziri, *Armuni-ye musiqi-ye Irāni*, Majles Library (Tehran) MS 8738.
148. Sāsān Fāṭemi, "Sayr-e nofudh-e musiqi-ye gharbi be Irān dar ʻaṣr-e Qājār," *Nashriya-ye honarhā-ye zibā-honarhā-ye namāyeshi va musiqi* 19(2) (2014): 14–15.

PART II

MUSIC THEORIES AND PRACTICES

4

THE MODAL SYSTEM

From the middle of the thirteenth to the end of the fifteenth century, two approaches to the description and analysis of the modal system coexisted and were developed by two classes of music theorists in Iran. The first approach originated from the teachings of Ṣafī al-Dīn al-Urmawī, author of the *Kitāb al-adwār* (*Book of Cycles*) and *Risāla al-Sharafiyya fī al-nisab al-ta'lifiyya* (*Treatise on Musical Proportions Dedicated to Sharaf al-Dīn Hārūn*). In these texts, al-Urmawī presented a complete list of modal entities, indicating their proper names and analyzing their scales on the basis of pairings of tetrachord and pentachord species. His approach became known as the *'ilm al-adwār* (theory of cycles), and later theorists regarded his treatises as the cornerstone of modal theory and the pinnacle of its achievement. For more than two centuries, al-Urmawī's disciples and followers, who are referred to in contemporary scholarship as the Systematist music theorists, either wrote explications and commentaries (*sharḥs*) on al-Urmawī's treatises or adopted his theory as an analytical tool for describing and characterizing modal entities.

The second approach was put forward by a class of theorists who had hands-on experience with music, but were influenced neither by al-Urmawī's theory of cycles nor by earlier writings on music with a number-driven "Pythagorean" orientation, for example, by the Ikhwān al-Ṣafā (Brethren of Purity), Ibn Sīnā (980–1037), and Ibn Sīnā's student Ibn Zayla (d. 1048). Exponents of this second approach, such as Moḥammad b. Maḥmud b. Moḥammad Nayshāburi (thirteenth century) and 'Alā' al-Din Bokhāri (d. *c.*1291), not only presented a hierarchical list of modal entities and their modulatory relationships, but often discussed extra-musical associations of modes. These associations included emotional states, races, and skin colors, professions and ranks, prophets and men of wisdom, planets, times of day, and seasons of the year.

Another distinguishing feature of Systematist versus non-Systematist approaches to music is their treatment of general concepts of scale and rhythm. In the first case, while Systematist texts divide the theoretical octave scale into seventeen steps based on string lengths or ratios and employ an alphabetical (*abjadi*) notation for the representation of tones (*naghmas*), non-Systematist texts typically define a heptatonic scale in reference to the frets of the lute. In this way, modes were described on the basis of the instrument's scale degrees or frets, and names of modes were adopted from the name of the lute fret that corresponded to the mode's initial pitch.

With respect to rhythm, Systematist texts often present long, complex rhythmic cycles that were used in the composition of courtly genres, whereas non-Systematist texts mention only short meters of one, two, three, or four beats and are devoid of any indication of genre. The Systematist tradition first emerged in Baghdad and immediately expanded to the western part of Iran—principally Shiraz and Tabriz—where it continued to develop throughout the fourteenth century. It was only at the beginning of the fifteenth century that the Systematist tradition moved to Herat, the most prominent stronghold of the Timurids, though Tabriz remained an abiding center of patronage for Systematist scholars. Meanwhile, early traces of the non-Systematist approach can be discerned in the eastern part of the Persianate world, particularly in Khorasan and Central Asia. With two or three exceptions, however, non-Systematist texts are neither dated nor ascribed to a specific author.[1]

By the end of the Timurid period, the Systematist approach came almost entirely to an end. Throughout the Safavid period and the following two centuries, authors of musical treatises no longer discussed ratios between intervals or used tetrachord and pentachord species as a basis for the analysis of modes. Musical treatises that appeared after the fifteenth century were presumably direct descendants of non-Systematist texts. They often present discussions of modal entities through references to heptatonic scales while elaborating on extra-musical associations of the modes. In these treatises, ancient Greek philosophers who wrote about music, such as Euclid, Aristotle, Plato, Nicomachus, and Ptolemy are revered as "men of wisdom" (*ḥokamā'*), and medieval Arab and Persian writers on music, such as Abū Naṣr al-Fārābī, Ibn Sīnā, Ṣafī al-Dīn al-Urmawī, and 'Abd al-Qāder Marāghi are often mentioned as musical authorities of the past.

The extent to which medieval music theory was sustained beyond the fifteenth century is not clear—or at least it is not clear on the basis of surviving music treatises. In the late sixteenth century, a music theorist lamented that the manuscripts of Marāghi (d. 1435) were no longer accessible and that Marāghi was mainly known through oral tradition and the writings of a small number of scholars who allegedly had first-hand access to his manuscripts.[2] Nonetheless, manuscripts of the *Kitāb al-adwār* and *Risāla al-Sharafiyya* were evidently still being copied in Iran between the sixteenth and nineteenth centuries—as might have been expected, given that the tradition of studying the quadrivium in academic schools remained in force throughout this period—but they were not actively used by music theorists.[3]

We also know that at least one manuscript of Marāghi's *Jāmi' al-alḥān* (*Compiler of Melodies*), which is currently housed in the Bibliothèque nationale de France, was copied in Isfahan in 1656.[4] Another musical codex was copied in Isfahan in 1619 for the celebrated Iranian philosopher Sayyed Mir Abu al-Qāsem Astarābādi (1562–1640), better known as Mir Fendereski. This codex also includes Ibn Zayla's *Kitāb al-kāfī fī al-musīqī* (*The Book of Sufficiency in Music*) and the Arabic translation of the *Sectio Canonis* attributed to Euclid.[5]

Major Sources for the Persian Modal System from 1500 to 1900

Treatises on music composed in Iran after the fifteenth century are diverse and were written by a wide range of authors. Two treatises seem to have been completed in the early sixteenth century, both of which contain sections on melodic modes and rhythmic cycles but lack any discussion of compositional genres.

The first treatise, *Nasim-e ṭarab* (*Breeze of Euphoria*), was presumably written by the eponymous Nasimi for the provincial ruler of western Gilān, Moẓaffar Sultan (r. 1515–1534). Nothing is known about the author of this tract except that as a youth he obtained some knowledge of music and later studied the music section of Qoṭb al-Din Shirāzi's *Durrat al-tāj* with a mentor. *Nasim-e ṭarab* is written in verse and prose and the author attempts to approach music theory through references to the performance practice of his own time. While surveying various categories of mode, Nasimi presents a discussion of the general scale and note names followed by a list of modal entities with definitions. Of particular interest in this text are references to local terminology regarding modal theory. The author confirms that his intention was to write a self-contained music treatise, not a commentary on the texts of his predecessors, yet he pays homage to al-Urmawī and Marāghi as the two most important musical authorities of the past.

The second treatise, which has some parallels with the *Nasim-e ṭarab*, is *Taqsīm al-naghamāt wa bayān al-daraj wa al-shu'ab wa al-maqāmāt* (*Distribution of Notes and Explication of Scale Degrees,* sho'ba*s, and* maqām*s*), which, despite its Arabic title, is written in Persian. The treatise contains an account of the scales and, more specifically, the melodic contours of the twelve *maqāms*, six *āvāzs*, and twenty-four *sho'bas*. The author seems to have been a *nay* player himself and thus claims to describe the modal system through reference to the special arrangement of the finger holes of the *nay*. Making a diagram for each modal entity, he demonstrates graphically—through the shapes of the *nay*'s finger holes—the melodic contour of each mode. Nonetheless, his diagrams only seem to be symbolically representive of the *nay*'s finger holes, for the number of holes in an actual *nay* was certainly less than what is depicted in most diagrams. The sole surviving copy of this Persian-language treatise was made in Istanbul.[6]

Toward the end of the sixteenth century, two other monographs were written, one in Herat, the second most important city of Safavid Iran, to which the Safavid crown prince was sent, and one in Isfahan, the newly established capital.

In Herat, Dawra Beg Karāmi, the composer and steward (*sofrachi*) of 'Ali Qoli Khān Shāmlu (d. 1589), the governor of the city and guardian of prince 'Abbas, wrote a music treatise in the 1580s. Karāmi was presumably of Turkic origin and wrote his poetry in both Persian and Turkish.[7] No music treatise was as frequently copied as the *Resāla-ye Karāmiya* between the sixteenth and nineteenth centuries, and this text must have been considered a benchmark for treatises on music during this period.[8]

Music theory and practice in the Safavid court were described for the first time by Mir Ṣadr al-Din Moḥammad Qazvini (d. 1600), a prominent court calligrapher who was also distinguished as a music theorist, composer, and amateur singer.[9] According to the colophon of the manuscript at the Bodleian Library, Mir Ṣadr al-Din Moḥammad's treatise was completed in 1600 and was dedicated to Ḥosayn Mirzā (b. 1591), a son of Shah 'Abbās I.[10]

Seventeenth-century music theorists invariably discuss the hierarchical classification of various modal entities. Among them, ʿAbd al-Bāqi Nā'ini (d. *c.* 1658), known by his pen name Bāqiyā, was a poet-composer who spent early stages of his career in Nā'in, Isfahan, Mashhad, and Herat, and subsequently set off on a journey to India in 1614, where he compiled a music treatise titled *Zamzama-ye vaḥdat* (*Murmur of Unity*). He dwelled in Ajmer, Deccan, Patna, Benares, and Agra, and served as a court musician to Jahāngir (r. 1605–1627) and Prince Khurram (later crowned as Shāhjahān). During his stay in India, Bāqiyā Nā'ini studied Indian *rāg*s and composed many *rikhta*s and *naqsh*s in the styles of Indian and Persian composers.[11] In his music treatise, Bāqiyā Nā'ini attempts to examine Persian and Indian modal entities and compositional genres as two separate topics, but in a few cases, he makes a comparison between Persian *maqām*s and Indian *rāg*s. On the basis of the information provided in the colophon of the Tashkent manuscript, *Zamzama-ye vaḥdat* was completed in October of 1654 and dedicated to the Mughal emperor Shāhjahān (r. 1628–1658).[12]

It is safe to say that the most important musical text of the seventeenth century is the codex of Amir Khān Gorji, a Georgian *gholām* (servant) and composer at the courts of the last two Safavid potentates. Commissioned by Shah Solṭān-Ḥosayn (r. 1694–1722) in 1697, the codex encompasses three treatises and two song-text collections. The first treatise is anonymous. The second treatise was compiled by Āqā Mo'men Moṣannef, a prolific composer and chief of musicians (*chālchi-bāshi*) in Isfahan in the first half of the seventeenth century. This treatise is followed by a collection of fifty-four *taṣnif*s that Āqā Mo'men composed between 1622 and 1648 for various courtly occasions. The third treatise was written by Amir Khān Gorji in verse and prose, and is followed by a collection of Persian and Turkish *taṣnif*s by numerous seventeenth-century composers of Isfahan and other cities. The codex includes no musical notation, and while the discussions of modal entities are brief, the references to their development and to the structure of their vocal compositions are particularly significant for understanding the way that practicing musicians implemented—and experimented within—the hierarchical system of modes. Several copies of Amir Khān Gorji's codex survive, the most exquisite, complete, and reliable one of which—ostensibly the royal copy made at the court of Isfahan—is currently housed in the Bibliothèque nationale de France.[13]

Another music treatise, *Dar bayān-e 'elm-e musiqi va dānestan-e sho'abāt-e ou* (*On the Science of Music and Understanding of its Branches*), was presumably compiled at some time in the final quarter of the seventeenth century. The treatise is anonymous and undated, but is included in a voluminous codex along with other texts that were all transcribed gradually after 1698. The treatise contains the earliest references to the term *dastgāh* and is particularly noteworthy for its prescriptive representation of *maqāms* and other modal entities in a format used in performance practice.

After the collapse of the Timurid court, two musical texts appeared in Bukhara that were closely related to the tradition of Herat. The first text is an untitled treatise written by Najm al-Din Kawkabi Bokhāri (d. 1535), a prominent musician and music theorist in the service of the Shaybanid Uzbek ruler 'Ubayd Allāh Khān (r. 1530–1536). The treatise is arranged in twelve chapters and one epilogue. The chapters first define musical concepts with reference to Systematist texts and subsequently treat three topics—modal system, rhythmic cycles, and musical genres—with respect to the performance practice of Kawkabi's own time.[14] The second text, titled *Tuḥfat al-surūr* (*Gift of Rapture*), is composed by Darvish-'Ali Changi (*c.* 1547–1611), a late sixteenth-century musician who identifies himself as a descendent of the Timurid *qānun* player Shehāb al-Din 'Abdollāh Morvārid (1461–1516). The most complete copy of *Tuḥfat al-surūr*, preserved in the Rudaki Institute of Language and Literature, in Dushanbe, Tajikistan, contains two main sections. While the first is a musical tract largely based on Kawkabi's treatise, the second section is an extensive *tadhkera* that includes biographies of around seventy musical figures along with samples of their verses and vocal compositions, most of whom were active between the fifteenth and seventeenth centuries in Khorasan.[15]

A few extant musical texts seem to have been composed in the eighteenth century, but most of them are anonymous and none can be ascribed with any degree of certitude to the court of a notable ruler. It is certain, however, that in 1736, the Armenian-Turkish court musician Tanburi Harutin was sent along with the official delegation of Mustafa Paşa to the camp of Nāder Shah. After spending six years in Iran and India, he returned to Istanbul, where he recorded his observations in a music treatise as well as in a short monograph on the history of Nāder's reign. Both texts were written in Ottoman Turkish with Armenian characters and contain references to musical performance practice in Iran.[16]

The *Bahjat al-qulūb* (*Delight of Hearts*) is another music treatise from the middle of the eighteenth century. While the compiler of this text avoids revealing his identity, he indicates that his primary intention was to distill and synthesize the gist of several music treatises and present them as a single entity. In addition to being an important text on musical instruments, the *Bahjat al-qulūb* provides a fresh approach to the emergence and early development of the *dastgāhs*.[17]

An important reference to the sung *maqām* as a sequence of modal entities is made in *al-Durr al-naqī fī fann al-mūsīqī* (*A Pure Pearl in the Art of Music*), an Arabic treatise written by Aḥmad al-Rifāʿī al-Muslim b. ʿAbd al-Raḥmān al-Mawṣilī (b. 1712). The author claims that his treatise is a rough translation of a Persian text written by ʿAbd al-Mu'min al-Balkhī.[18] While the title of al-Balkhī's treatise is mentioned as *Bayān al-maqāmāt al-ʿaliyya maʿ al-furūʿ wa al-awzān al-aṣliyya* (*Explication of Primary and Secondary Maqāms and Principal Meters*), the Arabic text exhibits a close affinity with the *Bahjat al-rūḥ* (*Delight of Souls*), an enigmatic late seventeenth-century Persian treatise attributed in many extant manuscripts to ʿAbd al-Mu'min Ṣafī al-Dīn al-Balkhī.[19]

The hundred-odd years between the mid-eighteenth and mid-nineteenth century produced a series of music treatises that, with one or two exceptions, can neither be accurately dated nor ascribed to a specific author. Some of these treatises consist of compilations of various texts that include references to both *maqām* and *dastgāh*, and the interpretation of these texts must be undertaken cautiously. Two such treatises are *Resāla dar ʿelm-e musiqi* (*Treatise on the Theory of Music*) and *Resāla dar bayān-e chahār dastgāh* (*Treatise on Explication of Four* dastgāhs). In the first treatise, *dastgāh* is used with reference to compositions of *ṣawt* and *naqsh*; in the second text the sequences of four large-scale *dastgāhs* of *chahārgāh*, *navā*, *rāst*, and *rohāb-e dāvudi* are laid out in some detail.[20]

Texts including verses on religious topics, especially *nawḥa* (lamentation) and *taʿziya* (passion play), sometimes indicate sequences of modes and melody types to which the verses were set. An early nineteenth-century text of this kind is the *Ādāb-e āvāzhā va dhekr-hā'i ke dar manāber va joz ān khᵛānda mishavad* (*Instructions for Singing* āvāzas *and Chanting on the Pulpit*), a lengthy collection of prayers and lamentations in both Arabic and Persian to be performed on various occasions. In addition to a long list of *āvāzs* at the beginning of the text, the author marks the verse and prose sections with *āvāzs* he recognized as most suitable for their performance.[21] Another text is a short manuscript containing Moḥtasham Kāshāni's elegy in twelve strophes (*davāzdah-band*) on the martyrdom of Imam Ḥosayn wherein each strophe is set to a specific *dastgāh*.[22]

Two musical treatises written around 1840, *Kolliyāt-e Yusofi* and *Resāla-ye davāzdah dastgāh* (*A Treatise on Twelve* dastgāhs) have recently surfaced. In both texts, Āqā Bābā Makhmur Eṣfahāni is mentioned as the most prominent court singer in the reign of Fatḥ-'Ali Shah (r. 1797–1834) and is credited with combining *maqāms*, *sho'bas*, and *āvāzs* and arranging them into sequences of twelve *dastgāhs*. However, the account of *dastgāh* in *Kolliyāt-e Yusofi* is very brief, while the *Resāla-ye davāzdah dastgāh* contains notable lacunae. Nevertheless, these treatises provide valuable information about the formation and evolution of the *dastgāh* system and its prominent exponents in the first half of the nineteenth century.[23]

During the nineteenth century, the music of Azerbaijan's urban centers, especially Shusha, Shamākhi, Ganja, Baku, and Tabriz, shows many parallels with the music of the Persian court. While *maqām* and *sho'ba* were the major modal entities in that tradition, *dastgāh* was also characterized as a sequence of modal entities and melody types. Two musical treatises have survived that represent the characteristic features of the *maqām/dastgāh* system in Baku and Tabriz. The first treatise (in Azeri Turkish), *Vożuḥ al-arqām dar 'elm-e musiqi* (*Clarification of Numbers in the Theory of Music*) was written by Navvāb Mir Moḥsen b. Ḥāji Sayyed Aḥmad Qarabāghi in 1884 and published in Baku in 1913.[24] Qarabāghi presents sequences of six *dastgāhs*: *rāst*, *māhur*, *shahnāz*, *rahāvi*, *chahārgāh*, and *navā*. The second treatise (in Persian) was compiled by Ḥāj Ḥasan b. Ḥāji 'Ali-Naqi Ganja'i—better known as Mo'ayyad al-Tojjār—around 1900. The author was a noble merchant in the circle of Moẓaffar al-Din Shah when the latter was seated in Tabriz as the crown prince. The treatment of modal terms in this text is very brief, but references to certain *maqāms*, for example, *bayāt-e qājār*, *manṣuriya*, and *segāh-e mirzā ḥosayn*, clearly indicate connections with traditions cultivated in Shusha and Baku.[25]

The most essential text related to Persian modal theory in the early twentieth century is the *Majma' al-adwār* (*Collection of Musical Cycles*) by Mehdi-Qoli Hedāyat (d. 1955), a statesman who served at the Qajar court and, from 1927 to 1933, as prime minister. As a youth, he studied in Berlin for a short time, and on his return to Tehran, he received a broad traditional education that encompassed Arabic and Persian literature and medieval mathematics and philosophy. Hedāyat had a profound knowledge of medieval Muslim and Western music theory and studied the *setār* with Mehdi Ṣolḥi (Montaẓam al-Ḥokamā'), an outstanding physician and prominent *setār* student of Mirzā 'Abdollāh and Moḥammad Ṣādeq Khān. He also transcribed the entire *radif* of Mehdi Ṣolḥi over the course of seven years (1914–1921). Following in the footsteps of ancient Greek and medieval Muslim music theorists, he wrote the *Majma' al-adwār* in three chapters. In the first chapter, "*aḥwāl al-nagham*" ("physical nature of melodies"), he describes the science of acoustic theory, and in the second chapter, "*ta'lif al-nagham*" ("elements out of which melodies are built"), he addresses the science of harmonic theory, mostly synthesizing medieval Persian and Western modal theories. In the third chapter, "*dar taḥqiq-e vaż'iyat-e ḥāżera*" ("examination of the current situation"), which is the most original and important part of the book, he examines the structure and performance practice of the *radif*, *dastgāh*s, and a range of musical genres, encapsulating as well the verbal discourse about music prevalent among practicing musicians in the nineteenth century.[26] The *Majma' al-adwār* was published as a lithograph in 1938 in a slightly modified form that was abridged from Hedāyat's own manuscript, currently preserved at the University of Tehran.[27]

A few amateur musicians and poets also made significant contributions to the field of music, most prominent among them Forṣat al-Dawla Shirāzi (d. 1920), the author of *Buḥūr al-alḥān dar 'elm-e musiqi va nesbat-e ān bā 'aruż* (*Meters of Melodies in the Science of Music and Their Relation to the System of Poetic Meter*). Forṣat al-Dawla compiled a collection of poems that were frequently used by eminent singers and, for each poem, assigned the *dastgāh*s or *āvāz*s he recognized as most suitable for its performance. This collection is prefaced by a short treatise containing descriptions of musical terms applicable to contemporary performance practice as well as several charts that represent the sequence of constituent *āvāz*s and *gusha*s in each *dastgāh*. As Forṣat al-Dawla declares, in writing the theory of *dastgāh*s, he was advised and directed by Mehdi Ṣolḥi. The *Buḥūr al-alḥān* was first published in the form of a lithograph in 1914 in Bombay and later was regularly reprinted in Tehran.[28]

A final entry in the compendium of early twentieth-century treatises is one by Mirzā Shafi', written in Kāshān in 1912. Nothing is known about the author beyond the fact that he was a cultivated musician with a profound knowledge of court music. The treatise outlines the sequences of seven *dastgāhs* (*shur, māhur, homāyun, chahārgāh, segāh, dōgāh, rāst-panjgāh*) based on the personal repertoire of a *tār* player who was presumably the author himself. The arrangement of *dastgāhs*, the distinctive terminology concerning their constituent units, and the account of compositions and dance tunes in this treatise are particularly noteworthy and represent an exceptional approach to the *dastgāh* system.[29] Table 4.1 presents a compilation of the treatises referenced above.

Table 4.1 Musical sources written between the fifteenth and twentieth centuries

Historical Period	Date of Texts/Accounts	Author or Source
Timurid (1370–1507)		
	Early 15th century (Herat)	'Abd al-Qāder Marāghi
	1470s (Herat)	'Alishāh b. Buka Awbahi
	Late 15th century (Herat)	'Abd al-Raḥmān Jāmi
	1484 (Tabriz and Herat)	'Ali b. Moḥammad Bannā'i
	Late 15th century	*Resāla-ye musiqi-ye gomnām*
Safavid (1501–1736)		
	Early 16th century (Bukhara)	Najm al-Din Kawkabi Bokhāri
	Mid-16th century (Gilān)	*Nasim-e ṭarab*
	Mid-16th century	*Taqsīm al-naghamāt*
	1580s (Herat)	Dawra Beg Karām
	1590s (Qazvin, Isfahan)	Mir Ṣadr al-Din Moḥammad
	1650s	Bāqiyā Nā'ini
	1650s	*Bahjat al-rūḥ*
	1650s (Isfahan)	Āqā Mo'men Moṣannef
	1697 (Isfahan)	Amir Khān Gorji
	Mid-17th century (Bukhara)	Darvish-'Ali Chang
	Late 17th or early 18th century	*Dar bayān-e 'elm-e musiqi…*
	1673–1677	Jean Chardin
	1684–1685	Engelbert Kaempfer
Invasion of Afghans (1722) Nāder and his successors		
	1740	Tanburi Harutin
	Mid-18th century	*Bahjat al-qulūb*
Zand (1751–1794)		

Historical Period	Date of Texts/Accounts	Author or Source
	Late 18th century	*Resāla dar ʿelm-e musiqi*
	Late 18th century	*Resāla dar bayān-e chahār dastgāh*
	Late 18th century	*Sharḥ-e chahār dastgāh va . . .*
Qajar (1795–1925)		
	Early19th century	*Davāzdah dastgāh*
	Early19th century	*Ādāb-e āvāzhā . . .*
	c. 1840	*Resāla-ye davāzdah dastgāh*
	1840s	*Kolliyāt-e Yusofi*
	1884 (Baku)	*Vożuḥ al-arqām dar ʿelm-e musiqi*
	1899 (Tehran)	*Majmaʿ al-adwār*
	1904 (Tehran)	*Buḥūr al-alḥān . . .*
	c. 1900	Ḥājj Ḥasan b. Ḥāji ʿAli-Naqi Ganja'i
	1906	Eugène Aubin
	1912 (Kāshān)	Mirzā Shafiʿ

Early Descriptions of the Modal System in Persia

From the early Islamic period, only a few paragraphs in Arabic texts have survived that make references to Persian melodies or melodic modes. The interpretation of these texts, however, is challenging, mostly because they are vague, faulty, and Persian terms are often deciphered and transcribed inaccurately by Arab scribes.

The most important account of the early Persian modal system is provided by Ibn Khurdādhbih (d. 913), a scholar of music and musicians, who states that the performance practice of Persians contained its own melodies, rhythms, and short compositions, and that it was based on eight entities, including *bon-dastān*, *bahār*, *abarin*, *abarina*, *mādārustān* (a distortion of *māda-dastān*), *sheshom*, *qoba*, and *asperās*.[30] While all these names may be construed as melodic or modal types, *bon-dastān* (*bon*: basis, foundation; *dastān*: position of finger, fret, pitch) and *sheshom* (lit. "the sixth") are explicit references to the initial and sixth scale degrees, and *māda-dastān* (lit. "female pitch") can be an indication of the dominant—here the fifth degree of the scale.

bon-dastān	*bahār*	*abarin*	*abarina*	*māda-dastān*	*sheshum*	*qoba*	*asperās*
1	2	3	4	5	6	7	8

Thus, the above names may suggest the existence of a heptatonic scale resembling, or possibly influenced by, one of the modal systems of ancient India, Greece, or Mesopotamia. Moreover, the appearance of the suffix *dastān* in two instances might suggest the beginning of two basic scales or pitch sets, the first commencing from *bon-dastān* and the second beginning from *māda-dastān*.[31]

bon-dastān *bahār abarin abarina māda-dastān sheshom qoba asperās*
māda-dastān *sheshom qoba asperās bahār abarin abarina māda-dastān*

Each scale degree was presumably the initial or tonal center of a mode that took its name from that degree. Hence, as the celebrated polymath Muḥammad b. Aḥmad al-Khᵛārazmī (d. 997) confirms, the term *dastān* designates both a scale degree or fret and a mode that was formed based on that particular degree.[32] References to additional *dastān*s in other sources suggest that there were more than eight modal entities, and thus one may assume that *dastān*s were classified into primary and secondary categories. Eight *dastān*s, or primary modes, were associated with the scale degrees and took their names from them, while others were likely derived from the primary *dastān*s, though the nature of this derivation is not clear.

The eight *dastān*s could also have resembled or been analogous to the contemporaneous *oktoechos*, a group of eight melody types associated with the early Byzantine liturgical chant. As Byzantine music specialist Egon Wellesz stated, the eightfold system of *oktoechos* "was the ruling principle of composition in Oriental music and, with the expansion of Christian music, spread over the whole Mediterranean basin."[33] Just like the *oktoechos*, *dastān*s were characterized as modes with their own distinctive flavors and characteristic melodic behaviors. Ibn Khurdādhbih describes *bahār* as the most eloquent one; *abarin* as being largely rendered on lower strings; *abarina* as containing the most exquisite ascending and descending melodic phrases, frequently moving from one tessitura to another; *māda-dastān* as being the most suited to lower registers and having the most intense structure, progressing gradually through shifting melodic phrases; and *sheshom* as being played with propulsive agility by the fingers.[34]

The term *dastān* was not commonly used by all music theorists who wrote or commented on music in the early Islamic period. In the ninth century, for example, the Arab philosopher Abū Isḥāq al-Kindī (d. 873) mentions *sheshum*, *abaren*, *asferās*, *sabdān*, *nayruzi*, and *mehrejāni* as some of the principal modes (*uṣūl*) of Persians.[35] Likewise, the prominent Arab historian Abū al-Ḥasan 'Alī b. al-Ḥusayn al-Mas'ūdī (d. 957) refers to Ibn Khurdādhbih as an authority and presents a comparable list of mode names that includes *sakāf*, *bahār*, *amras*, *māda-dastān*, *saykād*, *shishum*, and *jubarān*.[36] Moreover, in some Arabic texts written between the eighth and eleventh centuries, the Persian *dastān*s are simply interpreted and referred to as compositions or melodic types (*alḥān* or *anghām*). In the eleventh century, Abū Manṣūr al-Ḥosayn b. Zayla refers to *dastānāt* as melodic or modal types rendered through sung poetry and particularly associated with the two geographical regions of Khorasan and Isfahan. He further mentions a few *dastān*s, including *firuzgar*, *nāqusa*, *nām-awrang* (or *nām-afrang*), and *kharawsāl*, that were frequently performed by practicing musicians.[37]

Before the thirteenth century, the establishment of certain modal entities is sometimes attributed to Bārbad, the legendary musician at the court of the last Sasanian ruler, Khosraw II (r. 590–628).[38] However, Bārbad was responsible for the composition and development of two sets of courtly repertoires, namely, seven *khosravāni*s—arranged in praise of Khosraw II and performed as corresponding to the seven days of the week—and some thirty to fifty compositions referred to in later sources as *laḥn*s or *ṣawt*s. While neither repertoire's structure is precisely clear from the surviving documents, there seem to have been elements of solo improvisation in the rendering of the seven *khosravāni*s, with each *khosravāni* containing a sequence of instrumental and vocal sections and partly set to verse. This feature corresponds to the notion of seven *al-ṭurūq al-mulūkiyya* ("ordered repertoires performed in royal courts") that Mas'ūdī ascribed to Bārbad.[39] Two thirteenth-century linguists, Moḥammad 'Awfi Bokhāri (d. 1242) and Shams al-Dīn Muḥammad b. Qays al-Rāzī later opined that *khosravāni*s were set to prose texts with no poetic meter or rhyme pattern, but this perception probably derives from the fact that *khosravāni*s were set to pre-Islamic Persian poems with qualitative meters focusing more on syllable weight than stress.[40] In the fifteenth century, *khosravāni*s were still understood to be sequences of vocal melodies with no fixed meter.[41] While no names are mentioned for the seven *khosravāni*s in Persian and Arabic sources, the thirty or more compositions of Bārbad all bore specific titles, presumably named after the occasion, emotional state, or musical context in which they were composed.[42]

Non-systematist Modal Theory

In the beginning of the eleventh century, a new modal term, *parda*, appeared first in literary sources and subsequently in musical treatises. In these treatises, *parda*, in addition to denoting the concept of "fret," "pitch," and "note," incorporates a different set of mode names. Manuchehri Dāmghāni (d. 1040), a panegyrist at the Ghaznavid court (r. 977–1186) is the first poet who refers to *dastān* and *parda* in his poems, showing that both terms were known and employed in the first half of the eleventh century. In his collection of poems, he mentions *dastān*s of *sheshum*, *ourmazd*, *qālus* and *nāqus* while he also refers to *parda*s of *rāst*, *rāhavi*, *māda*, and *'oshshāq*.[43] Likewise, the eleventh-century philosopher Ibn Sinā makes reference to *mostaqim* [= *rāst*], *esfahān*, *navā*, *salmaki*, and *saliki* [= *busalik*].[44] By the late eleventh century, 'Onṣor al-Ma'āli Kaykābus b. Voshmgir Ziyār, author of the *Qābus-nāma* (*c.* 1082), reveals that a greater number of *parda*s were recognized among practicing musicians when he mentions *rāst*, *'erāq*, *rāhavi*, *esfahān*, *māda*, *busalik*, *navā*, and *'oshshāq* in a short paragraph.[45] More references to *parda*s appear in the verses of Persian poets of the twelfth and thirteenth centuries, including Awḥad al-Din Anvari (d. 1189), Khāqāni (d. 1190), Neẓāmi Ganjavi, Farid al-Din Aṭṭār (d. 1221), and Awḥad al-Din Kermāni (d. 1298).[46]

The first musical text to include a complete list of *parda*s, however, is the treatise of Moḥammad b. Maḥmud Nayshāburi, a twelfth- or thirteenth-century musician of Khorasan, better known as *'ajab al-zamān* ("the marvel of the time"). Nayshāburi outlines the structure of a modal system comprising twelve *parda*s and six *sho'ba*s in such a way that each *sho'ba* was associated with two *parda*s.[47]

Table 4.2 The twelve *parda*s and their related *sho'ba*s in the treatise of Nayshāburi

Parda	***Sho'ba***
rāst	*sepehri*
mokhālef-e rāst	
'erāq	*ḥejāzi*
nehāvand	

Parda	***Sho'ba***
mokhālefak	*basta*
rāhavi	
ḥosayni	*zirkash*
māda	
busalik	*negārin*
esfahān	
navā	*'ozzāl*
'oshshāq	

Of particular importance in the account of Nayshāburi is the description of *mokhālef-e rāst*. He clearly shows that *mokhālef-e rāst* as a *parda* was not just an abstract scale or a single mode, but contained characteristics of a modulatory sequence of units rendered progressively through an extended tessitura of low, medium, and high registers. This indicates that each of the twelve *pardas*, such as *rāst*, *'erāq*, and *busalik*, while beginning with a main mode from which it took its name, was also a sequence of modes or a modulatory scheme. Nayshāburi defines *sho'ba* as a short modulatory sequence combining modal structure and melodic behaviors of two *pardas*.

The author further states that the total number of twelve *pardas* comprised eighteen *bāngs*, and he subsequently enumerates the constituent number of *bāngs* in each *parda* as follows:

> Know that the theory of music is eighteen *bāngs*: *rāst* is two *bāngs*; *mokhālef-e rāst* is two *bāngs*; *māda* is two *bāngs*; *'erāq* is one and a half *bāngs*; *mokhālefak* is one and a half *bāngs*; *busalik* is one and a half *bāngs*; *navā* is one *bāng*; *nehāvand* is one and a half *bāngs*; *rāhavi* is one *bāng*; *esfahān* is one *bāng*; *ḥosayni* is one *bāng*; *'oshshāq* is half a *bāng* and that arises from the upper register of the *rāst*. If one plays on a single string, *rāst* and *'oshshāq* are in the same register and the difference between *rāst* and *'oshshāq* is only half a *bāng*. The other half *bāng* [of *'oshshāq*] is produced in the lower register.

The concept of *bāng* is not explicitly delineated in the treatise of Nayshāburi or other subsequent musical treatises that adopted the same approach to music theory.[48] Nonetheless, from the above description, it seems to be synonymous with the range of an octave, and therefore "half a *bāng*" would designate the range of a tetrachord or pentachord. Consequently, *pardas* that occupy the range of two *bāngs*, such as *rāst*, *mokhālef-e rāst*, and *māda*, were characterized as extensive modulatory schemes, whereas *pardas* in the range of one *bāng*, or even half of a *bāng*, such as *rāhavi*, *esfahān*, and *'oshshāq*, were shorter modulatory schemes and thus lacked many substantial modulations. The idea of eighteen *bāngs* is perplexing, however. It could either mean eighteen "octave species," with each corresponding to one of the twelve *pardas* and six *sho'bas*, or it could more likely denote the sum of all integral *bāngs* of the twelve *pardas*.[49]

Toward the end of the thirteenth century, the author of *Ashjār va athmār*, 'Alā' al-Din Bokhāri (d. *c.* 1291), who was an astrologist, singer, and music theorist, associated the modal entities with seven stars and classified them into seven primary (*aṣl*) and seven secondary (*far'*) *pardas*.[50]

Table 4.3 The fourteen *pardas* and their cosmological affiliations in the treatise of 'Alā' al-Din Bokhāri

Stars	Primary *Pardas*	Secondary *Pardas*
zoḥal	*navā*	*ḥosayni*
moshtari	*busalik*	*gozāshta*
merrikh	*rāst*	*'oshshāq*
āftāb	*'erāq*	*eṣfahān*
zohra	*negārin*	*zirafkanda-ye bozorg*
'oṭāred	*zirafkanda-ye khord*	*nehāvand*
qamar	*rahāvi*	*basta*

The division of *pardas* into two categories—one consisting of seven primary *pardas* and the other of five secondary *pardas*—together with their affiliations with the seven stars that are emphasized by both Nayshāburi and Bokhāri, are of great significance, and may suggest the existence of a heptatonic scale similar to the *dastān* system, with its seven primary modes based on the seven scale degrees.

There is no mention of the term *sho'ba* in *Ashjār va athmār*, but the author introduces other modes, including *nawruzak*, *mokhālefak*, *ḥejāzi*, *sāzegāri*, *māda*, and *sepehri* as the *āvāzhā-ye nāzok*, or narrow-ranged *āvāz*s. Compositions could not be created in these *āvāz*s unless they were combined as an auxiliary mode with one of the fourteen *parda*s listed in Table 4.3.[51]

Non-Systematist treatises composed during the thirteenth and fourteenth centuries resemble the treatise of Nayshāburi in many ways. They all present the names of twelve *parda*s and six secondary modal entities called *sho'ba*, *āvāz*, or *āvāza*. These treatises also discuss various modulatory schemes (*tarkib*s) and the extra-musical associations of modes, most significantly with times of day and seasons of the year.[52]

Systematist Modal Theory

In the second half of the thirteenth century, Ṣafī al-Dīn al-Urmawī introduced the modal system as consisting of twelve *shudūd* (sing. *shadd*), six *āwāzāt* (sing. *āwāz*), and a third category called *murakkabāt*s (compound modes). Offering a theoretical scheme for systemizing the scale of modal entities, al-Urmawī first specifies a seventeen-note octave gamut that adopts features from Pythagorean scales reconciled with certain indigenous Arab and Persian elements. Later, he defines seven tetrachord and twelve pentachord species from which eighty-four possible octave cycles (*adwār*) were derived by combination and permutation. He goes on to project the intervallic structure of the *shudūd*, *āwāzāt*, and *murakkabāt*s that were used in practice with the *adwār* that he calculated by the combination of tetrachords and pentachords. In so doing, he demonstrates that the twelve *shudūd* and two of the *āwāzāt* are octave species, while the rest of the *āwāzāt* are octave species with a restricted ambitus.[53]

Al-Urmawī also specifies twenty-nine species of third, fourth, and fifth, of which twenty-one were characterized by particular melodic features and were known by proper names.[54] From the category of *murakkabāt*, he mentions only one example and clarifies that in theory, the scales of these modes were formed in each case using a tetrachord and pentachord species characteristic of two distinct modes.[55] In the *Kitāb al-adwār*, the scales of twelve *shudūd* and six *āwāzāt* are delineated in two ways: first, by a simple alphabetical (*abjadī*) notation related to the seventeen notes of the octave gamut, and, second, by the old finger notation (*aṣābi'*) that dominated Arab practical theory before the eleventh century.[56] The author further divides the *shudūd* into three subgroups and associates each group with a particular emotion or set of emotions. He declares that *ʿushshāq*, *būsalīk*, and *nawā* inspire strength (*quwwa*), courage (*shajāʿa*), and pleasure (*basṭ*); *rāst*, *ʿirāq*, and *iṣfahān* induce delightful and refined gaiety (*basṭ ladhīdh laṭīf*); and *rāhawī*, *ḥijāzī*, *ḥusaynī*, *buzurg*, *zankūla*, and *zīrafkand* evoke sadness (*ḥuzn*) and languor (*futūr*).[57]

The Development of the Modal System after Ṣafī al-Dīn al-Urmawī

Al-Urmawī's books significantly changed theoretical discourse about music among subsequent generations of music theorists. For more than two centuries, the majority of Persian and Arab music theorists used Al-Urmawī's classification scheme to analyze modal entities, and many of these theorists sought to adopt it to the music and performance practice of their own times and regions.

From the beginning of the fourteenth century, Persian music theorists refer to a nomenclature of octave scale degrees that included *rāst*, *dōgāh* ("second degree"), *segāh* ("third degree"), *chahārgāh* ("fourth degree"), *panjgāh* ("fifth degree"), and so on. This nomenclature seems to have been used primarily in the everyday practice of playing and teaching musical instruments. References to this nomenclature appear in both non-Systematist and Systematist musical texts, though the Systematists tend to lay out their theoretical discussions on the basis of the seventeen-note octave gamut introduced by Ṣafī al-Dīn. A notable fact about the scale degree nomenclature is that not all degrees of the octave had degree-specific names. Only the names of the first five degrees were conventional and commonly mentioned in all sources. However, even if nonstandardized, all other notes in the same octave, as well as lower and higher octaves, were associated with and named after a mode.

Two early Systematist music theorists who refer to this scale-degree nomenclature are Qoṭb al-Din Shirāzi (d. 1311) and Ibn Kurr (d. 1357). The latter was the son of a Baghdadi musician of Persian origin who fled Baghdad and settled in Cairo in the late thirteenth century.[58] Likewise, Ḥasan Kāshāni, author of *Kanz al-tuḥaf* (*Casket of Rarities*) and Muḥammad b. ʿAbd al-Ḥamīd al-Lādhiqī (d. 1495), author of *al-Risāla al-fatḥiyya fī al-mūsīqī* (*Treatise of Victory on Music*), make references to this nomenclature, with some variations, as do a series of non-Systematist treatises.[59]

At the beginning of the fourteenth century, a new set of modal entities emerged as *sho'ba*s that were completely different in name and structure from the older set of *sho'ba*s presented in non-Systematist texts, especially in the treatise of Nayshāburi. While the *sho'ba*s introduced by Nayshāburi were short modulatory sequences classified as combinations of two *parda*s, the new concept of *sho'ba* showed characteristic features of a single mode. Qoṭb al-Din Shirāzi is the first music theorist who refers to nine *sho'ba*s as an independent category, without linking them to the twelve *parda*s. He defines *sho'ba* as a specific melodic movement centered around a particular note or scale degree.[60] The nine *sho'ba*s he mentions are:

> *dōgāh*, *segāh*, *chahārgāh*, *panjgāh*, *zavoli*, *ruy-e 'erāq*, *mobarqa'*, *māya*, and *shahnāz*.[61]

Qoṭb al-Din Shirāzi also used the term *maqām* for the first time as a general category that includes twelve *shodud*, six *āvāzāt*, nine *sho'ab*, and the miscellaneous *morakkabāt*, or, as he calls this last category, *tarkib* (combination).[62]

Later the number of *sho'ba*s increased significantly to the extent that, by the beginning of the fifteenth century, 'Abd al-Qāder Marāghi ennumerated twelve *maqām*s, six *āvāz*s, and twenty-four *sho'ba*s as the three categories of mode that were known to practicing musicians.

According to Marāghi, the twelve *maqām*s referred to as *advār-e mashhura* ("famous cycles") were all octave species, and in common practice they were also known as *parda*s and *shadds*.[63] He describes *sho'ba*s as differing from *maqām*s insofar as their ambitus did not necessarily constitute an octave species. In the case of *maqām*s and *āvāz*s, he describes them as two separate sets of entities completely detached from one another. Yet he emphasizes that in practice, every two *sho'ba*s were associated with one particular *maqām*.[64]

The other modal concept discussed in both Systematist and non-Systematist texts is *tarkib*. Qoṭb al-Din Shirāzi defined *tarkib*s as a diverse category of assorted modal entities that typically consist of elements of two modes. Nonetheless, Timurid music theorists, more specifically Marāghi and his successors 'Alishāh b. Buka Awbahi (second half of the fifteenth century) and 'Ali b. Moḥammad Bannā'i (d. 1513), make no provision for *tarkib*s in their hierarchical system of modes and only refer in passing to some modal entities as *tarkib*s or *morakkab*s.[65] Evidently, practicing musicians used both of these terms, often interchangeably, in reference to vocal modulatory schemes containing elements of multiple *maqām*s, as Marāghi explains in the following passage:

> After having an awareness of the tonic and finalis, singing can be of two types: simple (*mofrad*) and compound (*morakkab*). The simple type is when the entire singing is, for instance, in *parda-ye ḥosayni* and [in the course of performance] no *parda*, *āvāza*, *sho'ba* or any other melodic modes (*davāyer-e digar*) is added to it. The compound type is when they combine it with one, two, three or more *ajnās* and *jomu'*. They might even combine all the *davāyer* in one session of singing, and that is determined by the temperament and discretion of the performer.[66]

Finally, *gusha* is another modal term mentioned for the first time by Marāghi. It does not appear to have been a well-established concept in the fourteenth and fifteenth centuries, and Marāghi states that *gusha* was only used (perhaps loosely) by some musicians as a synonym for *maqām* or *shadd*.[67] In the second half of the fifteenth century, the *gusha* is mentioned neither by Awbahi nor by Bannā'i, and it was by no means current in the musical parlance of eastern Persia, that is, a milieu of arts and learning with its center in Herat.

Modal Entities and Concepts in Safavid Sources

In the early sixteenth century, the author of *Nasim-e ṭarab* first introduced the entire musical gamut in terms of four hierarchical octaves (*marāteb-e darajāt-e arba'a*), with each octave comprising seven basic scale degrees (*naghma*s): *rāst*, *dōgāh*, *segāh*, *chahārgāh*, *panjgāh*, *ḥosayni*, and *'ashirān*.[68] He states that the first degree in higher octaves was referred to as *methl* (lit. "duplicate" or "replacement") and other pitch levels were simply called *shabih* (similar), meaning similar to their counterpart in lower octaves. Another term, *eyvān parda* ("the outstanding note"), denotes the predominant note, or what he calls *naghma-ye chahārom az har parda* ("the fourth above each tone").[69] According to Nasimi, modal entities could be categorized as species of trichord, tetrachord, and pentachord. He calls the initial and final notes of modal entities *shāmel* (all-encompassing) and *ghāyat* (final), respectively, and mentions that the melodic contours of all modes could fall into the tripartite classification of ascending (*ṣa'udi*), descending (*nozuli*), and arched (*sa'udi-nozuli*) patterns.[70] While discussing various components of the modal system, Nasimi makes an analogy comparing a *maqām* with the stem of a white poplar tree (*derakht-e khadang*) that has two *sho'bas*, or branches: *aqrab* (nearest) and *qarib* (near).[71]

The author of *Taqsīm al-naghamāt* presents a registral span of three octaves and designates them as the lower register (*taḥt*), main register (*aṣl*), and higher register (*fawq*), respectively. His seven basic scale degrees in each octave have the same names as those offered by Nasimi except in one case: *rāst*, *dōgāh*, *segāh*, *chahārgāh*, *panjgāh*, *ḥosayni*, and *maghlub*. As Owen Wright states, the precise definitions of interval sizes, whether by ratios or fret positions, are not mentioned in the text, but based on Systematist and contemporaneous treatises, one can propose that the intervals between *rāst* and *dōgāh*, *chahārgāh* and *panjgāh*, and *panjgāh* and *ḥosayni* were whole tones, while the remainder—those between *dōgāh* and *segāh*, *segāh* and *chahārgāh*, *ḥosayni* and *maghlub*, and *maghlub* and the octave *rāst*—were neutral, that is, approximately three-quarter tones.[72] Therefore, the basic heptatonic scale beginning from *rāst* can be represented as follows:

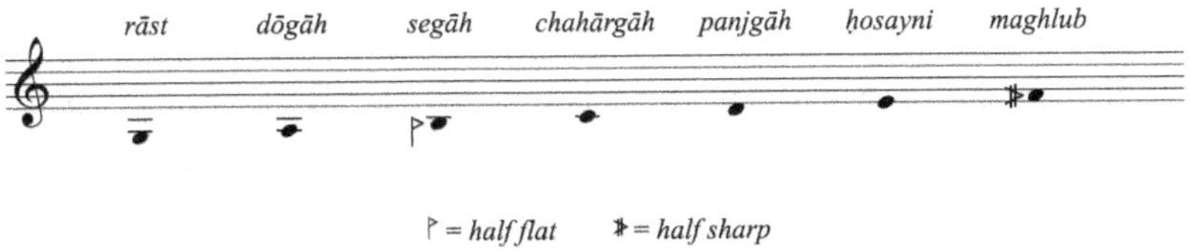

Example 4.1 The basic heptatonic scale presented in the *Taqsīm al-naghamāt*

The author of *Taqsīm al-naghamāt* declares that a *maqām* could appear either as a single mode (*mofrad*) or as a modulatory scheme (*jam'*) incorporating its two *sho'bas*. Likewise, all the *āvāzs* could appear either as a single form of a mode or as a modulatory scheme combining elements of two *maqāms*. In the end, he presents an elaborate form of modulatory scheme that integrates fifty-four modal and melody types and declares that the inner structure of melodic theory is no longer enigmatic to a person who can perform this modulatory scheme.[73] He also offers a terminology that is particularly important for understanding the way modes were conceptualized in the sixteenth century.

For instance, he uses the verb *namudan* ("to exhibit or display") with reference to the skeletal scale of each mode, which includes applicable changes for ascending and descending directions, and employs *rabṭ dādan* ("to connect") to convey modulation from one mode to another.[74] In reference to melodic elaboration on a mode, he employs the term *sayr* or *sayr kardan* ("to perambulate"), a term that in later Ottoman musical parlance came to be interpreted as "melodic progression."[75]

Later music theorists barely specified the scale type or melodic contour of modes. For the most part, they list various modal entities and their proper names while describing their interrelations. In the second half of the sixteenth century, Dawra Beg Karāmi indicated that modes in Herat were organized in the hierarchical system of twelve *maqām*s, six *āvāz*s, and twenty-four *sho'ba*s.[76] While it is clear from his account that the number of modes recognized as *sho'ba*s was more than twenty-four, Karāmi seemed determined to confine himself to the canonical number of twenty-four. He attempts to justify the existence of other *sho'ba*s as lesser variants or as instances of the relabeling of preexisting *sho'ba*s.[77]

An account of modes in the Safavid court music of Qazvin and Isfahan is offered by Mir Ṣadr al-Din Moḥammad, who privileges *ḥosayni*, in the hierarchical system of twelve *maqām*s.[78] He also emphasizes that the term *shadd* had acquired a new meaning in his own time, coming to refer to common pitch levels from which instrumentalists played a *maqām*. He states that every *maqām* was typically rendered from two or three pitch levels (*shadd*s) at the time, and further castigates contemporary practicing musicians for their lack of skill in performing *maqām*s from various scale degrees.[79]

In their treatises, music theorists often included a section on the attribution of various names of *maqām*s, and Mir Ṣadr al-Din Moḥammad was no exception. Sixteenth-century theorists typically referred to three or four regional schools, including those of Māvarā' al-nahr (Transoxiana), Khorasan (northeastern Persia), 'Erāq-e 'Ajam and Fārs (western Persia), and Rum (Anatolia), where some *maqām*s or other modal entities were known by different names.[80]

An important development in the second half of the sixteenth century is the gradual emergence of a new modal category known as *gusha*. As for the number of *gusha*s, Karāmi states that there are thirty-six, but Mir Ṣadr al-Din Moḥammad mentions them as being forty-eight, though he does not present a complete list.[81] Karāmi refers to *gusha* as the same modal entity already known as *tarkib*, and states that the term *gusha* was mainly cultivated in the western regions of Iran, more specifically, 'Erāq-e 'Ajam (that is, Isfahan, Ray, Qazvin, and Kāshān) and Fārs.[82] Mir Ṣadr al-Din Moḥammad describes the *gusha* as a short melody type that cannot serve as the basis for composition. Yet it seems that by the time of his musical treatise, no conventional set of *gusha*s had been established among practicing musicians in the capital.[83] When the capital shifted to Isfahan, the *gusha* was already an established concept incorporated into the court modal system. A complete list of forty-eight *gusha*s is provided for the first time by Bāqiyā Nā'ini (d. *c.* 1640), who also asserts that the entire modal system was recognized as a hierarchical sequence of various components classified into some ninety melody types or specific tunes (*āhang*), including six *āvāz*s, twelve *maqām*s, twenty-four *sho'ba*s, and forty-eight *gusha*s.[84]

In the first half of the seventeenth century, Āqā Mo'men Moṣannef, the chief of court composers in Isfahan, still denied the significance of the *gusha* as an essential modal concept and rejected its inclusion in the canonical system of modes. He insisted that the twelve *maqām*s, six *āvāza*s, and twenty-four *sho'ba*s sufficiently encompassed all the modalities (*āhang-e ṣedā*) of his own time and castigated those "inexperienced musicians" who tend to incorporate a set of forty-eight *gusha*s into the core of the modal system and ascribe their introduction and further development to Marāghi.[85] By the beginning of the eighteenth century, when Amir Khān Gorji was compiling his musical treatise, the *gusha* was unquestionably an established modal entity even in the context of court music. In his discussion of modes, Amir Khān identifies the *āvāza* as the main component of the modal system and refers to it as the "mother of melodies" (*umm al-nagham*), with all other modal entities as its progeny (*farzandān*). For each *āvāza* he presents two associated *maqām*s, twenty-four *sho'ba*s, and a number of *gusha*s.[86]

The Organization of the Modal System in Safavid Persia

While music theorists attempt to describe certain aspects of modes and classify them as a coherent system, their descriptions are not always intelligible enough to reconstruct a detailed structure and the relationship of assorted modal entities. Moreover, it is not clear to what extent the treatises were rehashing accounts from earlier sources as opposed to reflecting upon the practice of their own times, not to mention that music theory in general is not always congruent with actual practice. Nonetheless, these treatises and traces of music in later periods provide us with a wide range of data that can be synthesized and interpreted in a coherent appraisal.

The first part of this chapter outlined the development of modal entities and concepts in Safavid musical texts. The next section examines in more detail the conceptual underpinnings of *maqām* and other modal entities, their function in the musical repertoire and in performance, and their organization into the modal system.

Maqām

Maqāms are always characterized as the principal set of modes in Persian musical treatises, and two separate concepts are denoted by the term *maqām*. First, a *maqām* is a modulatory scheme theoretically consisting of a few segments that include two *sho'bas*: an upper *sho'ba* and a lower *sho'ba*. Second, it signifies the original mode in this compound structure, which remains dominant throughout the performance.

The first and foremost distinguishing feature of each *maqām* seems to have been its scale. Safavid musical texts always name twelve *maqāms*, and, unlike earlier theorists who mentioned *rāst* or *'oshshāq* as the initial mode or, in their own words, "the mother of *maqāms* from which all other *maqāms* are derived," Safavid theorists mostly consider *ḥosayni* to hold that position.[87] One theorist also divides the *maqāms* into two categories: challenging (*moshkel*) and straightforward (*āsān*).[88]

As a modulatory scheme, a *maqam* stereotypically began with a free-rhythmic exposition of the first mode featuring typical characteristic phrases.[89] Indeed, the *maqām* proper consisted of this section, wherein the original mode was fully revealed and developed. The act of unfolding the melody in this section was frequently referred to as *āghāz kardan* (lit. "to initiate") or *darāmad kardan* (lit. "to enter"), depending on different practices. Once the melodic configuration of the initial mode was foregrounded, the *maqām* was further expanded by modulating to the first, or lower, *sho'ba*, in which a new mode with a distinct tonal center and characteristic phrases was introduced and elaborated. A return to the *maqām* was followed by the upper *sho'ba*, which marked the second modulation in the sequence. While the second *sho'ba* had its own melodic movements and characteristic phrases, it mostly explored an ambitus higher than that of the first *sho'ba*. After each modulation to the lower or upper *sho'ba*, the melody returned to the first mode to punctuate segments of *maqām* with some recognizable melodic phrases (*maḥaṭṭs*). At length, the performance concluded with a conspicuous cadential phrase known as the ultimate *maḥaṭṭ* (also called *forud*).[90] The following pattern seems to have been the typical scheme of modal progression in the performance practice of every *maqām*.

> exposition of *maqām*—lower *sho'ba*—return to *maqām*—upper *sho'ba*—return to *maqām*—*maḥaṭṭ*

In the middle of the sixteenth century, the structure of the *maqām* system seems to have developed through synthesizing numerous elements of both rural and urban music. The development occurred largely in the *sho'ba* segments. Each *sho'ba* was expanded and enhanced by assimilating units derived from rural music as well as by the creative input of outstanding musicians. A series of miscellaneous urban and rural melody types and songs began to acquire classical features and receive recognition in the courts. In this process, the preexisting term *gusha* was adopted to address various types of melodies rendered in *sho'ba* segments. Therefore, in keeping with the division prescribed for other entities, just as two *maqām*s were linked with every *āvāza* and two *sho'ba*s were linked with every *maqām*, music theorists began to associate two *gusha*s with every *sho'ba*. Nevertheless, it is likely that the number of *gusha*s performed within the segment of each *sho'ba* was more than two.

While today we tend to consider *maqām* as the modal system of the fifteenth–eighteenth centuries, for music theorists and musicians of that period, *maqām* was more of a standard performance format. Instructions for sequencing, selection, and omission of modes and melody types in the performance of a *maqām* were seldom prescribed or discussed by music theorists, and any arrangement of the internal structure of a *maqām* was evidently determined by a performer's repertoire of melodic ideas, temperament, and discretion. Nonetheless, there has always been a tendency to move gradually from lower to higher materials or to a climatic point, and then to return to the lower.

The term *darāmad*, as the introductory section of a musical piece or suite, was not used in the Timurid period; no reference to this term can be found in the treatises of Marāghi or in those of his immediate successors. From the mid-sixteenth century, however, some musicians began to employ *darāmad* as a reference to the opening section of both measured compositions and the free-rhythmic exposition of modes, while *āghāz* was still predominately in vogue.[91] Likewise, the Arabic term *maḥaṭṭ*, meaning "the ending of a piece," was interchangeably used with the Persian term *forud* (descent) as early as the sixteenth century.[92]

Sho'ba

In the gradual and continuous evolution of the *maqām* system, the number of *sho'ba*s ostensibly increased throughout the fourteenth century and were incorporated into the performance practice of *maqām*s. However, it is hard to assume that the twenty-four *sho'ba*s each revealed melodic characteristics that distinguished them from other modal entities and that they all fit into a single category of mode. By way of further illustration, we may look at some of the dynamics of *maqām*s and *sho'ba*s based on the account of the *Taqsīm al-naghamāt*. The following example shows the twelve *maqām*s and twenty-four *sho'ba*s listed in their conventional order, together with their octave species or typical melodic contour. By "melodic contour," I mean a series of notes that represent a *maqam* or *sho'ba*:

3. ḥejāz

segāh (lower *sho'ba*)

ḥeṣār (upper *sho'ba*)

4. 'erāq

maghlub (lower *sho'ba*)

ruy-e 'erāq (upper *sho'ba*)

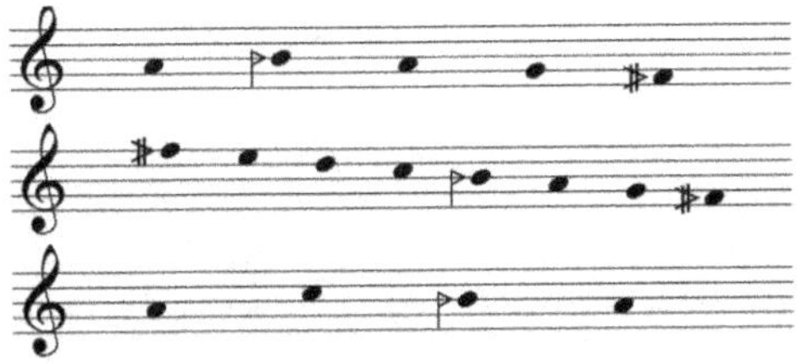

5. rahāvi

nawruz-e 'arab (lower *sho'ba*)

nawruz-e 'ajam (upper *sho'ba*)

6. zangula

chahārgāh (lower *sho'ba*)

'ozzāl (upper *sho'ba*)

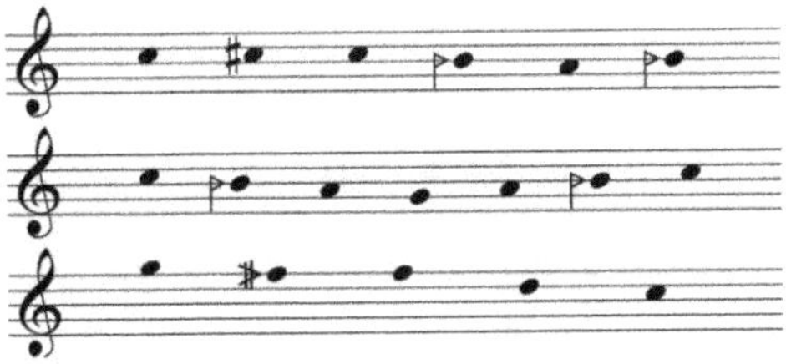

7. 'oshshāq

zāvol (lower *sho'ba*)

awj (upper *sho'ba*)

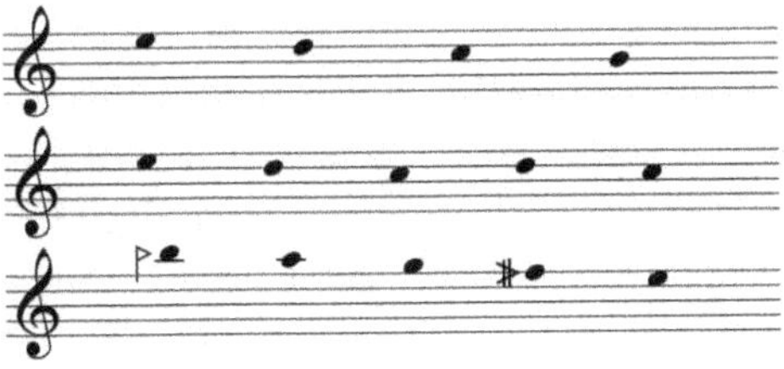

8. navā

nawruz-e khārā (lower *sho'ba*)

māhur (upper *sho'ba*)

Example 4.2 Melodic contours of *maqām*s and *sho'ba*s in the *Taqsīm al-naghamāt*

It is clear that *maqām*s and *sho'ba*s can be divided into two major groups: those using only basic scale degrees (*parda-ye moṭlaq*) and those using secondary scale degrees (*parda-ye moqayyad*), that is, all scale degrees that are not basic scale degrees. *Rāst*, *dōgāh*, *segāh*, *chahārgāh*, *panjgāh*, *ḥosayni*, and *maghlub* used only basic scale degrees, commencing and ending on their eponymous scale degree:

Example 4.3 The seven modes using basic scale degrees

In his article on "Mode" in the *New Grove Dictionary of Music and Musicians*, Harold Powers described mode as a term applied to a spectrum of entities that lie between what he called a "generalized tune" and a "particularized scale." Modal entities in different cultures, or even within one and the same modally organized system, could vary on the scale–tune continuum.[93] On the scale–tune continuum proposed by Powers, the twelve *maqāms* and twenty-four *sho'bas* exhibit more affinity with "scale" than with "tune," especially if one considers the directional changes in representations of scale. In all likelihood, *sho'bas* were self-sufficient modes that were either rendered in isolation or in conjunction with the *maqāms* to which they were related. Moreover, they were used as models for solo improvisation and bases for composition. A composition could be entirely or partly within the melodic confines of a *sho'ba*. Among the fifty-four vocal compositions in Āqā Mo'men Moṣannef's song-text collection, only seventeen compositions are in *maqāms*, while thirty-two compositions are exclusively written in *sho'bas*.[94] Nonetheless, it is evident that *sho'bas* were not rendered as modulatory schemes comparable with *maqāms* and *āvāzas*.

While the names of the twelve *maqāms* were generally consistent in Safavid musical texts, only a semi-conventional set of *sho'bas* was affiliated with them. In other words, the *sho'bas* rendered in a *maqām* differed among practicing musicians and in various regional schools. Hence, music theorists often mention differences of opinion among musicians regarding the selection of *sho'bas* and their association with *maqāms*. They also refer to frequent discrepancies in what was mentioned in the theoretical treatises of their predecessors and what was common in the performance practice of their own time.[95]

Another significant issue was the number of *sho'ba*s associated with each *maqām*. Najm al-Din Kawkabi Bokhāri, who tended to codify a living performance practice, informs us that according to practicing musicians, *sho'ba*s of each *maqām* varied in number, and the exact association of two *sho'ba*s with every *maqām* was intended mainly to present a rational and balanced system that abetted its preservation (*moḥāfeẓat*). He further states that in practice a *maqām* could contain from one to four *sho'ba*s. As examples, he mentions *rāst*, which, with more melodic richness, contained four *sho'ba*s, and *navā*, perhaps a less prominent *maqām*, which was associated with only one *sho'ba*.[96]

However, the association of more than two *sho'ba*s with a *maqām* is sometimes even more complicated than it seems. Evidence suggests that, at least during the sixteenth century, in the actual performance of a *maqām*, performers were at liberty to deviate from the standard format and modulate to other *sho'ba*s that were extraneous to the original *maqām*. The author of *Taqsīm al-naghamāt* provides aesthetic guidelines and formulas for such modulations. For instance, he writes:

> Connecting (*rabṭ dādan*) two *sho'ba*s of *rāst*, performers must commence with *mobarqa'* and after that elaborate (*sayr konand*) on *rāst* and from there modulate to *panjgāh*. This is the sequence (*ṭariq*) of combining them. However, it is also appropriate here to perform *eṣfahān*, *nayriz*, *neshāburak*, *ḥejāz-e tork*, *salmak*, *gardāniya*, and *māhur*. It is better to return in conclusion (*forud āvarand*) to *rāst*.[97]

As the above passage shows, modulations that conformed to the standard format of the *maqām* were not only accepted practice, but sometimes even encouraged by musical authorities.

Āvāza

In general, the concept of *āvāza* appears in all Safavid musical texts as a set of six separate entities consisting of *gardāniya*, *salmak*, *gavasht*, *māya*, *nawruz* (or *nawruz-e aṣl*), and *shahnāz*. In some sixteenth- and seventeenth-century texts, *āvāza* is described as a type of mixed or hybrid mode, containing melodic elements of two *maqāms*. The anonymous author of *Dar bayān-e 'elm-e musiqi va dānestan-e sho'abāt-e ou*, for instance, states that "an *āvāza* was formed when two *maqāms* meet at a certain point and display the same [melodic] features."[98] He emphasizes that "if the *āvāza* was rendered before the initiation of the *maqām*, the performance was improper and irregular."[99] Dawra Beg Karāmi, the Herati composer and steward of 'Ali Qoli Khān Shāmlu, states in the *Resāla-ye Karāmiya* that earlier music theorists initially arranged the *maqāms* and later derived one *āvāza* from every two *maqāms*. He defines the *āvāza* as a modal entity commencing with the first relevant *maqām* and making reference to a second *maqām* (*darāmad-e ān az maqāmi ast va shāhed az maqāmi*).[100] His contemporary Mir Ṣadr al-Din Moḥammad further clarified that an *āvāza* often combines melodic elements of two *maqāms* (*morakkab az dō maqām ast*), adding the caveat that distinguishing an *āvāza* from the two principal *maqāms* as well as describing its relation to them is a difficult task that requires careful analysis.[101] The description of Mir Ṣadr al-Din Moḥammad suggests two different hypotheses about how *āvāzas* were used in practice. The first is that *āvāza* represented a modulatory scheme typically capable of moving between two specific *maqāms* that were related to one another. Accordingly, from one *maqām* a performer could only modulate to one other specific *maqām*. The author of *Taqsīm al-naghamāt*, who confirms this quality of *āvāza*, provides a guideline for modulation between two *maqāms* through the associated *āvāza*.[102]

A second hypothesis is that *āvāzas* comprised a set of independent modes, each traditionally incorporated into, and rendered in conjunction with, more than one *maqām*. In the performance practice of a *maqam*, incorporating the associated *āvāza* was of course common, but modulation to other neighboring *āvāzas* could also occur. This is further confirmed in the *Taqsīm al-naghamāt* where the author gives aesthetic guidelines for modulations.[103] Āqā Mo'men's association of six *āvāzas* with the twelve *maqāms* is somewhat different from those of other music theorists. While discussing the relationships between *āvāzas* and *maqāms*, he connects each *āvāza* with a different pair of *maqāms*. For example, he associates *gavasht* with *ḥejāz* and *zangula*, and *gardāniya* with *eṣfahān* and *rāst*, whereas in other Safavid sources *gavasht* is predominantly associated with *navā* and *ḥejāz*, and *gardāniya* with *rāst* and '*oshshāq*.[104]

Characteristic Melodic Phrases

For practicing musicians, characteristic melodic phrases, no less than scales, served as an important distinctive feature of mode. Safavid music theorists were interested in the proper exposition of modes and refer to this topic frequently. As mentioned earlier, Bāqiyā Nā'ini states that each entity with a proper name, including *maqām*s, *āvāza*s, *sho'ba*s, and *gusha*s, was mainly recognized through its *āhang*, a term that in a technical sense can be understood to mean characteristic motives or specific melodic phrases.[105] Mir Ṣadr al-Din Moḥammad also employs the same term and, for example, in the case of *bayāti* mentions that "it has a heavily ornamented (*shekofta*) and delightful (*maṭbu'*) *āhang*."[106]

Bāqiyā Nā'ini and Mir Ṣadr al-Din Moḥammad do not provide further information on this issue, but there are other sources that allude to significant points. The author of *Dar bayān-e 'elm-e musiqi va dānestan-e sho'abāt-e ou* states that the cadential phrase of *mobarqa'*, one of the *sho'ba*s of *rāst*, contained four passages of *maḥaṭṭ*s (in spoken language spelled out as *maḥad*s), and if a musician was unaware of their proper rendition, the *āhang* of *mobarqa'* would be unconventional and anomalous.[107] The same author, while mentioning various *gusha*s, claims that some of them retained characteristic ascending phrases (*awj*) and some contained characteristic descents (*maḥaṭṭ*s).[108]

In the same period, the term *sayr*, which was frequently used by Ottoman Turkish musicians, was also employed by Persian music theorists, though apparently in reference to both melodic progression and elaboration.[109]

Since the Timurid period, melodic configuration has also been determined by the concept of *taḥrir*, which in recent literature on music is sometimes merely interpreted as "melismatic vocalization" or a "particular technique involving glottal closure."[110] Yet musicians viewed *taḥrir* as the most essential feature of a modal entity. Indeed, every modal entity was usually considered to have specific and distinguishing characteristic phrases that were often expressed and outlined in its opening, middle, and concluding *taḥrir* passages.[111] Moreover, *taḥrir* was not confined to vocal music; it was possible to render instrumentally, and it served as a basis for interpretive melodic improvisation.[112]

Tarkib and Gusha

By the sixteenth century, the terms *morakkab* and *tarkib* had come to be widely used by both music theorists and practicing musicians in Central Asia,

Anatolia, and, probably, some parts of Persia. Najm al-Din Kawkabi defines *morakkabāt* as a category containing elements of either two *maqāms*, two *sho'bas*, or one *maqām* and one *sho'ba*. Kawkabi enumerates twenty-four *morakkabs* and assigns for each one an opening mode or *bonyād* (lit. "foundation," "nucleus") and a closing mode or *qarār* (lit. "settling onto the ground").[113]

In the same period, the Ottoman music theorist Seydi (*c.* 1500) indicates that *tarkib* was a significant modal structure in the early emergence of the Ottoman musical tradition. His description is similar to that of Kawkabi. He mentions the concepts of *bonyād* and *qarār* in relation to *tarkibs* and shows that, in addition to the compound structures provided by Kawkabi, a *tarkib* may also emerge through the combination of two *āvāzas*, a *maqām*, and an *āvāza*, or a *sho'ba* and an *āvāza*. He names fifty-eight *tarkibs* that were common in the musical practice of his own time, sixteen of which appear in Kawkabi's musical treatise as well. However, rather than listing the two constituent modal entities, Seydi presents a loose melodic contour for each *tarkib*.[114]

During the seventeenth century, *tarkib* came to be the second most important modal category in Ottoman Turkish music. In his musical treatise, Demetrius Cantemir (d. 1723), who, like Qoṭb al-Din Shirāzi, takes the term *maqām* as the superordinate category for mode, divides *maqāms* into the two subsets of *mofrad* (single) and *morakkab* (compound).[115] According to Feldman, Cantemir makes a distinction between the categories of compound *maqām* (*mürekkeb makam*) and combination (*terkîb*). While the former contained only five members, the latter group could have infinite variations. Throughout his musical treatise, Cantemir usually names twenty standard *terkîbs*, and he notates *peşrevs* in some of them.[116] In the sixth chapter of his treatise, he introduces *terkîbs* as follows: "In the third chapter, it was mentioned that the terkîbs were twenty in number but there is no doubt that there is no end to the terkîbs of music. Nevertheless, due to the fact that a number of terkîbs are more prominent than others, among the musicians it is a widespread error that they are named 'makam.' Due to the exaggeration of the vocalists, they claim that since *bestes* and *nakş* were composed of them, they have given them the name 'makam.' Nevertheless, it cannot be denied that every terkîb is subordinate to a major makam" (*c.* 1700: VI: 50).[117]

Between the seventeenth and nineteenth centuries in Iran the term *tarkib* continued to refer to a "vocal modulatory scheme."[118] Likewise, a competent singer capable of making extended modulations to multiple *maqām*s was commonly known as a *tarkib-band*.[119] This concept of the Safavid *tarkib*, however, is closely related to what is mentioned in Cantemir's treatise, particularly when the latter states that "there is no end to the *terkib*s of music." Here he is simply referring to the modulatory character of *tarkib*s in the performance of music, rather than to *tarkib*s as compound or hybrid modes.[120]

While in post-Timurid Persia the term *tarkib* was not employed as a distinct category in the same way as it probably was in Transoxiana and Anatolia, the category of *gusha* gradually came to be integrated into the canonical *maqām* system. As noted previously, Karāmi claims that the term *gusha* was frequently used in the western regions of Persia, more specifically in 'Erāq-e 'Ajam and Fārs, and that it was to some extent synonymous with *tarkib*.[121] Further evidence also indicates that the standard number of *gusha*s in Persian treatises and of *tarkib*s in Ottoman sources was often forty-eight. Moreover, several mode names that were listed in the Ottoman sources as *tarkib* were recognized among Persian musicians as *gusha*.[122]

Nevertheless, claiming that *tarkib* and *gusha* were practically the same contributes nothing but further confusion to our understanding of each concept. Evidently there were some parallels between miscellaneous Persian *gusha*s and Ottoman-Transoxanian *tarkib*s in the sixteenth and seventeenth centuries. Yet, just like *tarkib*s, *gusha*s were not one type of modal entity. As the names of *gusha*s imply, some of them were probably *tarkib*s containing elements of more than one mode, such as *ḥejāzi-ye mokhālef* or *ḥejāzi-ye 'erāq*. Some, such as *bayāt-e kord*, *bayāt-e tork*, and *ṭabari*, were recognized as folk-derived vocal genres.[123] A few *gusha*s were modal types or compositions borrowed from neighboring traditions, such as *nehāvand-e rumi*, *qarachaqā-ye rumi*, and *sepehr-e hendi*.[124] And, of course, a number of *gusha*s could have been short compositions or aggregates of particular phrases developed from idiosyncratic styles of prominent musicians, as this was the typical characteristic feature of some *gusha*s in the nineteenth-century Persian repertoire.

Insufficient evidence, in particular a lack of notated melodies and modal descriptions, prevents us from being able to delineate thoroughly the structure and typology of *gusha*s in the Safavid period. At the same time, the Safavid and modern concepts of *gusha* cannot be considered as entirely the same thing. During the sixteenth and seventeenth centuries, *gusha*s were regarded as certain melody or modal types integrated within the performance formats of *maqām*, *āvāza*, and *sho'ba*, whereas, in the twentieth century, the generic term *gusha* was indiscriminately applied to all modal entities within the *dastgāh* system. Yet, as discussed later, the Safavid concept of *gusha* might have been closer to its nineteenth-century counterpart.

It is fair to say that throughout the sixteenth century, the hierarchical *maqām*, *āvāza*, and *sho'ba* were considered the established modal components. At the same time, the modal system was continuously being influenced by numerous urban and rural elements, including the creative inputs of musicians, folk-derived song types and genres, and borrowed modal and melody types from neighboring traditions. The *maqām* system subsequently began expanding through the assimilation of some of these elements that had come to be conceptualized as assorted vocal and instrumental melody types and were labeled by that point as *gusha*s. Accordingly, by the middle of the seventeenth century, a number of *gusha*s began to acquire classical features and came gradually to be integrated into the *maqām* system as subsets of *sho'ba*s. In general, the integration of *gusha*s was not considered anomalous if this integration was executed with taste, and if the image of the original *maqām* was not totally obscured.

Therefore, it seems that any melody or modal types in urban music that could not be situated within the well-defined modal categories of *maqām*, *āvāza*, and *sho'ba*, were recognized and labeled by musicians—and subsequently by music theorists—as *gusha*. The choice and interpolation of *gusha*s within the repertoire was primarily determined by the performers' melodic ideas, ethnic background, and discretion. Performers or stylistic schools associated with particular urban centers presumably had developed and selected their own collections of *gusha*s. This is evident from the multiple assortment of *gusha*s in musical treatises of the seventeenth and eighteenth centuries. The nomenclature of *gusha*s in the treatise of Amir Khān is quite different from the list of *gusha*s in the treatise of Baqiyā Nā'ini and the anonymous *Dar bayān-e 'elm-e musiqi va dānestan-e sho'abāt-e ou*. Several other music treatises, for example, *Bahjat al-rūḥ*, also present a rather different set of names for *gusha*s.[125] Nonetheless, the author of *Bahjat al-qulūb* mentions that the arrangement of forty-eight *gusha*s received a strong impetus from the contribution of Serāj al-Din Moḥammad Ghavvāṣ (probably a seventeenth-century musician).[126]

To a large extent, instrumentalists and, sometimes, vocalists, were more responsible than composers for the introduction of *gusha*s into the urban music repertoire and their cultivation within it. Sixteenth- and seventeenth-century court composers still wrote their compositions within the melodic confines of the twelve *maqām*s, six *āvāza*s, and twenty-four *sho'ba*s, and there was a substantial amount of dispute among musicians regarding the adoption of *gusha*s in that period. Mir Ṣadr al-Din Moḥammad, for example, opined that a *gusha* could not be used as the basis for composition. Likewise, Āqā Mo'men claimed that the canonical *maqām*s, *āvāza*s, and *sho'ba*s contained all the modal entities of the time and criticized those musicians who incorporated *gusha*s into their repertoire.[127]

All in all, the incorporation of *gusha*s into the modal system and court repertoire indicates that while in theory *maqām* was discussed as a rational construction devised and revised by music theorists, in practice it was more a traditional assemblage of musical entities employed and retained by practicing musicians. At a broader level, the accretion of *gusha*s certainly enriched the performance palette of Persian music from many perspectives and rendered it distinct from the performance practice of neighboring traditions, particularly in Central Asia and Ottoman regions.

Shadd

Writers discussing the modal system in the thirteenth and fourteenth centuries generally acknowledge that what Persians called *parda* was predominantly referred to as *shadd* by Arabs, and that the two terms were almost synonymous.[128] But during the fourteenth century, *shadd* appears in Persian musical texts referring to another modal structure. The first reference to this new concept is mentioned in the epilogue of *Jāmi' al-alḥān*, where Marāghi identifies a few *shadd*s as modulatory schemes (*tarkib-e naghamāt-e davāyer*), each performed through an unusual tuning on the *'ud*. Labeling three of them as *shadd*s of *ruḥ* (soul), *ṣabā* (caressing breeze, stirring yet soothing), and *khᵛāb* (sleep), he makes clear that the main purpose of rendering these modulatory schemes was to generate certain emotions in the audience and ultimately move the listeners to tears, make them laugh, or put them to sleep. According to Marāghi, the emotions and feelings associated with these *shadd*s could be intensified if the performer set the melodies to appropriate poems. He further specifies that *shadd*s were performed mostly for a refined audience (*sāme'ān-e ṣāḥeb dhawq*) and made prodigious demands upon the listener.[129]

During the sixteenth and seventeenth centuries, four modulatory schemes known as *shadd*s are also occasionally mentioned in musical treatises, and their performances seem to have been common in both Iran and Central Asia. In Safavid musical texts, the four *shadd*s are mostly identified as *rāst*, *dogāh*, *mokhālef*, and *chahārgāh* (*ruḥ*).[130] While one *shadd* is referred to as *shadd-e ruḥ*, it is not clear that the effects or actions attributed to them earlier were still retained and were part of their characteristics in this period.

The Eighteenth Century

There is no doubt that the eighteenth century is the murkiest period for Persian music. Many music treatises show that the hierarchical system of twelve *maqām*s was in decline from many perspectives while a number of modal entities coexisted in this period.

As discussed earlier, the twelve *maqām*s, six *āvāza*s, twenty-four *sho'ba*s and, finally, forty-eight *gusha*s formed a system of modes that was used, upheld, and venerated by music theorists and court musicians for more than three centuries. In the first quarter of the eighteenth century, with Isfahan under siege by Afghan invaders, the city was repeatedly sacked and the Safavid court ultimately collapsed in 1736. As a result, the political, economic, and cultural glory of the capital began to decline and court musicians who were once serious practitioners of art music abandoned the profession or moved to other cities.[131] The exodus of court musicians had repercussions for many long-established elements of Persian music, including the modal system, rhythmic cycles, and compositional genres.

The Turkish-Armenian musician Tanburi Harutin, who arrived in Iran around 1736, reported that Persian musicians had specific terms for scale degrees, and Harutin compared these names with the names for scale degrees used concurrently in Ottoman music.[132] Table 4.4 displays the Persian and Ottoman names for scale degrees provided by Harutin (also known as Tanburi Küçük Artin) in the mid-eighteenth century together with their equivalents in the mid-sixteenth-century *Nasim-e ṭarab*, by Nasimi, and *Taqsīm al-naghamāt.*

Table 4.4 Names of scale degrees in Persian and Ottoman musical sources between the sixteenth and eighteenth centuries

Nasim-e ṭarab	*Taqsīm al-naghamāt*	Harutin	Ottoman Music
rāst	*rāst*	*yegāh*	*rāst*
dōgāh	*dōgāh*	*dōgāh*	*dōgāh*
segāh	*segāh*	*segāh*	*segāh*
chahārgāh	*chahārgāh*	*chahārgāh*	*chārgāh*
panjgāh	*panjgāh*	*panjgāh*	*nevā*
ḥosayni	*ḥosayni*	*sheshgāh*	*ḥosayni*
ʿashirān	*maghlub*	*haftgāh*	*eviç*
		hashtgāh	*gerdāniye*

After the collapse of Isfahan, it appears that lay musicians and courtesans who continued to perform in urban centers were not extensively trained in court music and therefore did not strictly adhere to the standards of *maqām* tradition.[133] These musicians, known as major exponents of *taṣnif*s and dance tunes, were insensitive and even careless about the meticulously correct exposition and elaboration of *maqām* and its submodes. Moreover, they did not employ the same nomenclature that prevailed among theorists and court musicians with respect to different categories of mode.

From the beginning of the eighteenth century, if not earlier, the modal categories of *maqām* and *shoʿba* were presumably referred to in noncourtly contexts as *āvāz*, whereas *gusha* as a separate category still retained its name. Thus, a parallel modal system comprising the two categories of *āvāz* and *gusha* coexisted with the older system. In this parallel system, *āvāzs*, just like *maqāms*, were performed in sequences of units integrated with various *gusha*s and, at the same time, their melodic material was used as a basis for both improvisation and composition.

While surviving music treatises from the Safavid period largely address the *maqām* and its submodes, it is hard to establish how far back the term *āvāz* had been used in a sense synonymous with *maqam* (as opposed to its use as a modulatory sequence of modes, similar to *āvāza*). The situation seems even more perplexing in light of the fact that *āvāz* has often had multiple connotations in Persian culture. Nonetheless, *āvāz* as a category of mode appears in musical texts at least as early as the thirteenth century.[134]

In the first half of the eighteenth century, authors of music treatises still followed the long-established practice of introducing the principal elements of the modal system as *maqām*, *āvāza*, and *sho'ba*. References to *maqām*s and *sho'ba*s can be found in nonmusical literature as well.[135] Yet it is not clear whether the compilers of these texts were reporting on the performance practice of their own time or repeating information from earlier sources. It seems that the idea of *maqām*s and *sho'ba*s as austere, classic, and timeless sets of modes was still current among music cognoscenti and scholars while lay musicians simply referred to modes as *āvāz*. Clear evidence of this approach is provided by Harutin who, as a short-term resident of Iran in the first half of the eighteenth century, used the term *āvāz* or *āvāza* as a synonym for *maqām*.[136]

In the second half the eighteenth century, when the capital was transferred to Shiraz, the repertoire of *āvāz* continued to develop by assimilating various urban and folk melodic elements, including modal and melody types, as well as vocal and instrumental genres. It is conceivable that some of the folk-based and semi-classical modes that later came to be included in the nineteenth-century repertoire of *radif*, for example, *dastān-e 'arab*, *afshāri*, *dashti*, *shushtari*, *bakhtiyāri*, *dashtestāni*, *ḥājiāni*, and *ḥejāz-e baghdādi*, none of which are mentioned in Safavid musical texts, were introduced into the urban music repertoire in this period. In the early eighteenth century, what was recognized as *āvāz* was probably a loose and informal version of the Safavid *maqām*s and *sho'ba*s as well as some vernacular and folk-derived modes and vocal genres. However, by the early nineteenth century the urban repertoire had already developed, and certain modes such as *shur*, *rohāb*, *shushtari*, and *mansuri* evolved into mature *āvāz*s with clearly defined characteristics.

The Emergence of *Dastgāh*

Musicians and ethnomusicologists today usually define *dastgāh* as a system comprising seven or twelve modal complexes, or multimodal cycles.[137] Hormoz Farhat proposed the following definition of *dastgāh* in the modern practice of Persian music:

> Two separate ideas are addressed by the *dastgāh* concept. It identifies a set of pieces, traditionally grouped together, most of which have their own individual modes. It also stands for the modal identity of the initial piece in the group. This

> mode has a position of dominance as it is brought back frequently, throughout the performance of the group of pieces, in the guise of cadential melodic patterns.
> Accordingly, a *dastgāh* signifies both the title of a grouping of modes, of which there are twelve, and the initial mode presented in each group.[138]

A closer examination indicates that the modern *dastgāh* resembles the seventeenth-century *maqām* in many ways. Both *maqām* and *dastgāh* are modulatory schemes that follow the same form of melodic progression. Both begin with an exposition of the first mode, called *darāmad*, followed by a series of *sho'ba/āvāz* and *gusha*. Throughout the performance of both *maqām* and *dastgāh*, the first mode recurs at the conclusion of every *sho'ba/āvāz* and various sequences are punctuated with a cadential melodic phrase, called *forud*. While the number of *maqām*s was always twelve, there was also a tendency to maintain this symbolic number within the arrangement of *dastgāh*s and their associated modes (*mota'aleqāt*).

Be that as it may, *maqām*, *sho'ba*, *shadd*, *āvāz*, and *dastgāh* coexisted during the eighteenth century, and *dastgāh* emerged mainly out of a musical system whose principal modal entities were still referred to as *maqām* and *sho'ba*. To understand the origin and evolution of *dastgāh* as the term was understood at the beginning of the twentieth century—an understanding that remains current today—I have looked backward at musical sources of the eighteenth and nineteenth centuries. Accounts furnished by these sources are at times ambiguous in the way they use the terms *maqām* and *dastgāh*, yet provide significant information that illuminates the trajectory of these musical concepts.

Explicit references to *dastgāh* first appear in some late Safavid musical treatises. The *Dar bayān-e 'elm-e musiqi va dānestan-e sho'abāt-e ou* seems to be the earliest musical text to mention this term. While describing the sequences of *sho'ba*s and *gusha*s within the twelve *maqām*s, the author makes a distinction between modal entities that display the character of *dastgāh* (*ṣāḥeb-e dastgāh*) and those in which *dastgāh* is absent (*bi dastgāh*) or that lack substantial characteristics of *dastgāh* (*dastgāh chandāni*). The shows that by *dastgāh* he means the free-rhythmic exposition of a modal entity followed by one or two metric compositions based on the same melodic characteristics.[139] As examples of two such modal entities, he mentions *'erāq-e moshāba*, a *gusha* in which composers made delightful vocal compositions, and *moḥseni*, another *gusha* employed by Turkic composers in creating charming *varsāqi*s. Additionally, in the case of *maqām-e kuchak*, he directly states that the entire *maqām* lacked *dastgāh* throughout.[140]

The author of another early eighteenth-century musical treatise, *Resāla dar 'elm-e musiqi*, also employs the term *dastgāh* with reference to *maqām*s and *sho'ba*s. After a series of short amatory texts identified as *ṣawt* and *naqsh* in *maqām*s *ḥosayni*, *rāst*, *'oshshāq*, *'erāq*, and *ḥejāz*, he emphasizes that because the melodic range of six other *maqām*s constitutes only a brief sequence of units (*nim parda*), one cannot arrange *ṣawt* and *naqsh* in them and, hence, they lack the status of *dastgāh*. Similarly, following another collection of short song-texts labeled as *naqsh*s in *sho'ba*s of *dōgāh*, *panjgāh*, *mokhālef*, *chahārgāh*, *segāh*, *nayriz*, *nayshāburak*, and *bayāt*, he adds that there were other *sho'ba*s comprising *nim parda* and therefore they cannot be used as a basis for metrical compositions.[141]

These two early references to the incipient *dastgāh* evidently suggest that the term was employed when a sequence of modal entities—whether a *maqām*, *sho'ba*, or even a *gusha*—was followed by compositional genres. In other words, a modal entity was recognized as having the character of *dastgāh* when certain vocal (and probably instrumental) metrical compositions were commonly associated with it. While the author of the *Resāla dar 'elm-e musiqi* identifies some *maqām*s and *sho'ba*s as acquiring the status of *dastgāh*, the account of *Dar bayān-e 'elm-e musiqi va dānestan-e sho'abāt-e ou* shows that, at least according to some practices, prominent *gusha*s were rendered in the form of *dastgāh* as well.

Historical sources suggest that *dastgāh* did not develop primarily in the context of Safavid court music. For one thing, it does not appear in the codex of Amir Khān Gorji, yet it evidently flourished in urban musical centers or provincial courts, where it fostered the performance practice of *maqām* and *sho'ba*.

In the first half of the eighteenth century, *dastgāh* emerged as a more extensive sequence of modal entities or as a compound form, displaying closer affinities with the four *shadd*s but still embracing metrical compositions. In the *Resāla dar bayān-e chahār dastgāh-e a'ẓam*, four large-scale *dastgāh*s (*dastgāh-e a'ẓam*) are introduced as (1) *chahārgāh*, (2) *navā*, (3) *rāst*, and (4) *rohāb-e dāvudi*.[142] The author of this treatise clearly refers to the affinity of *dastgāh* and *shadd* at one point and further identifies *maqām*, *gusha*, and *parda* as the main modal entities in the performance of *dastgāh*. From this description, it is clear that *dastgāh* was a scheme of modulation containing sequences of modal entities and concluding with metrical compositions of *kār-o-ʿamal* (a modulatory vocal genre) and *taṣnif*s. The sequences of units had more or less the same type of progression as was found in the Safavid *shoʿba* and *āvāza*. For example, in *dastgāh rohāb-e dāvudi*, the sequence was: *rohāb-e dāvudi*, *ḥosayni*, *dōgāh*, *nahoft*, *busalik*, and *rohāb-e dāvudi*. The author also indicates that in some less extensive sequences, the instrumental opening unit was called *moqaddama*.[143] Subsequent units were designated by proper names, yet they were generically referred to as *motaʿalleqāt* (component entities or units) of a particular sequence as well. Some units, such as *zangula* and *bozorg*, were probably recognized as rhythmic motifs or specific poetic meters (just like *zangula* and *kereshma* in today's Persian *radif*), since the author claims that they could be performed in many sequences and "often manifested themselves in the guise (*lebās*) of a different entity."[144]

Each *dastgāh* was by no means a fixed grouping of free-rhythmic units and metric compositions, since a performer was able to exercise considerable latitude with regard to the selection of units, modulation, and length. As the author of the anonymous treatise suggested, *navā* could be performed in three conventional arrangements, with different groupings of units. Likewise, from the middle of *rāst* a performer had the option to take the progression of *navā* in two different directions. *Dastgāh*s allowed for metrical vocal compositions of *kār-o-ʿamal* to appear in the middle of sequences as well. Finally, numerous references to *khᵛāndan* (singing) in the performance of various segments, together with the existence of vocal compositional genres indicate that *dastgāh* was essentially a vocal structure accompanied by musical instruments, though probably not rendered entirely on instruments.

Some affinities between Safavid *maqām*s and eighteenth-century *dastgāh*s could be suggested from the account of this anonymous treatise. For instance, if we assume that *maqām-e ḥosayni* and its lower *shoʿba*, *dōgāh*, retained their modal characteristics, then they were certainly performed within a new *tarkib*, or modulatory scheme, in the eighteenth century. Likewise, when *rāst* was performed in this period, we may presume that there were two conventional approaches to its performance practice. In a certain practice, which was likely the result of Indian or Afghan influence, a sequence of *rāk*s (adaptations of Indian *rāg*s) was performed, whereas in a more indigenous practice *rāst* still retained its *sho'ba*s of *panjgāh* and *mobarqa'*. But these are only hypotheses and, in many cases, Safavid modal entities seem to have evolved by the late eighteenth century. For instance, *bozorg*—a prominent *maqām* throughout the Safavid period—was characterized by the anonymous author of the *Resāla dar bayān-e chahār dastgāh-e a'ẓam* only as a rhythmic motif.

The terminology used by the author also directs us toward a set of distinctions that is fundamental for understanding the way in which musicians conceptualized *dastgāh* and its melodic progression. For the beginning of a new modal entity or melody type, he uses the verbs *āghāz nemudan* ("to initiate") and *dākhel shodan* ("to enter"); for the exposition and unfolding of a modal contrast, he uses the verbs *nemudār kardan* ("to display") and *ẓāher nemudan* ("to make manifest"). When elaborating melodic material through a sequence of units, he uses *sayr kardan* ("to make an excursion"), and for embellishing a melody type he uses *chāshni dādan* ("to add spices") or *taz'in* ("ornamentation").

The second eighteenth-century reference to *dastgāh* is in *Bahjat al-qulūb*, a music treatise compiled by 'Abd al-Ḥosayn b. Mehdi al-Shirāzi. The text is a compilation of more than one treatise and contains some curious anomalies. *Dastgāh* is again referred to as a sequence of units followed by a few *taṣnif*s and *kar-o-'amal*s. The author specifies four *dastgāh*s, but all are characterized as containing elements of two principal modes. The *dastgāh*s are (1) *rāst-panjgāh*, (2) *chahārgāh-mokhālef*, (3) *ḥosayni-segāh*, and (4) *homāyun-dōgāh*. The account of *dastgāh*s is represented in a round diagram or circle (*dāyera*) in which a hierarchical set of modal entities together with their appropriate rhythmic cycles are listed (Figure 4.1).[145]

Besides the four *dastgāh*s, the author of *Bahjat al-qulūb* includes a separate discussion on *tarkib-e parda* in which he provides guidelines for musicians to acquaint themselves with sixteen sequences of units, or *tarkib*s, that he alternatively calls *maqām*s.[146] The fact that the author refers to these sequences as *tarkib* and *maqām* is an important point, and suggests that perhaps other eighteenth-century music theorists who mention *maqām* in their treatises may have used the term with the same implication. In other words, by using the term *maqam*, they did not necessarily mean the Safavid system of twelve *maqām*s and twenty-four *sho'ba*s. This assumption is further supported by the account

Figure 4.1 Four *dastgāhs* as represented in a hierarchical set of modal entities together with their appropriate rhythmic cycles. *Bahjat al- qulūb*, Majles Library (Tehran) MS 2242, f. 60.

of another musical text titled *Davāzdah dastgāh*, written around the turn of the nineteenth century. In this text the twelve strophes (*davāzdah-band*) of the famous elegy composed by Moḥtasham Kāshāni are set to sequences of twelve *maqāms* that differ significantly from the Safavid modal system. These twelve *maqāms* display more affinities, at least nominally, with the *maqāms* mentioned in *Bahjat al-qulūb*. The *maqāms* in *Davāzdah dastgāh* are:

> 1. *rāvandi*, 2. *nawruz-e ʿarab*, 3. *dōgāh-denāṣori*, 4. *bayāt-e ʿajam*, 5. *navā-neyshābur*, 6. *rohāb*, 7. *chahārgāh*, 8. *homāyun*, 9. *nayriz-navā*, 10. *ʿashirān*, 11. *ʿoshshāq-navā*, 12. *rāst*.[147]

The text of *Davāzdah dastgāh* also shows that *maqām* in this period was conceived as a form of *tarkib*. While in the case of each *maqām* the author mentions the concepts of *tarkibāt* and *shoʿbajāt*—probably referring to its associated modal entities—he does not specify what, exactly, they were. Finally, a conspicuous list of miscellaneous *āvāzs* is given at the end of the text, which, in many cases, is the earliest reference to *āvāzs* that later appear in the repertoire of the *radif*, such as *abu'atā*, *afshār*, *mollānāzi*, *qaṭar-e tork*, and *layli-o majnun*.[148]

References to assorted *āvāz*s and their performance practice in various musical contexts also appear in another anonymous treatise known as *Ādāb-e āvāzhā*. The author presents guidelines and the text of *āvāz*s performed in numerous settings, including mosques, Sufi lodges, and convivial gatherings. Following a few lines of a didactic poem on *maqām*s, the author presents a list of more than one hundred modal entities under the broad title of "*gusha*s, *āvāz*s, *rang*s, *sho'ba*s, *parda*s, and *naghma*s."[149] The *āvāz*s in this text in fact show traces of both urban and rural music. A large number of names are those of seventeenth-century *maqām*s, *sho'ba*s, *āvāza*s, and *gusha*s, though their structure may have varied in practice and changed over the eighteenth century. A few names, especially at the bottom of the list, seem to be folk-derived vocal or instrumental melody types or genres and composed songs and dance tunes of diverse provenance.

The author does not assign any of the items specifically to the categories of *maqām*s, *sho'ba*s, *gusha*s, or *naghma*s, but he labels a number of them as *āvāz* and shows that each constitutes a short sequence of units. He also gives the names of certain *āvāz*s and mentions the unit at the higher end of their ambitus (*awj*). One may notice that while the names of *āvāz*s were largely derived from classic *maqām*s and *sho'ba*s, their component units could include regional melodies as well.[150]

Another group of modal entities described by the author of *Ādāb-e āvāzhā* is the *rāk*s. In a separate chapter he explains the affinity of *rāk*s and certain *āvāz*s.[151] As mentioned previously, after Nāder Shah's invasion of India in 1739, several Indian musicians and dancers joined his camp and were brought to Iran, where they stayed apparently for less than a decade. Evidence shows that during this period, several Indian *rāg*s were adopted and later came to be incorporated into the Persian music repertoire of the eighteenth and nineteenth centuries.[152]

In general, we may assume that after the collapse of the Safavid court and dispersal of the musicians from urban centers throughout Iran, *maqām* continued an attenuated existence in urban centers. In the later part of the eighteenth century, musicians still recognized a series of *terkib*s or sequences of units as *maqām*s. Yet the hierarchical set of twelve *maqām*s, twenty-four *sho'ba*s, six *āvāza*s, and forty-eight *gusha*s described in Safavid musical sources was entirely forsaken. Instead, *āvāz* came to be used first in semi-classical and gradually, in court music, to refer both to sequences of modal and melodic units, and also to vocal genres.

The Qajar Court

By the end of the eighteenth century when the capital was moved from Shiraz to Tehran, two significant developments took place within the modal system that jointly enhanced the concept of *dastgāh* while simultaneously contributing to the eventual dissolution and disappearance of *maqām* and *sho'ba* as prominent structural concepts.

First, a number of vernacular and semi-classical modes used in eighteenth-century *taṣnif*s, dance tunes, and religious genres that were not clearly definable and recognizable modal entities in the *maqām* and *sho'ba* system were refined into a set of individual *āvāz*s with relatively clear distinguishing phrases, scales, and characters. Examples include *shul* (later called *shur*), *qaracha*, *abu'aṭā*, *sāranj*, *afshāri*, *dashti*, *hājiyāni*, *gilaki*, *shushtari*, *bakhtiyāri*, and *fayli*. These modal entities, which in the eighteenth century existed merely as melodic possibilities latent in extant regional and semi-classical modes and vocal genres, had become crystalized into distinct *āvāz*s by the beginning of the nineteenth century. Most of these *āvāz*s are not mentioned in treatises predating 1750.[153]

Second, the establishment of the Qajar court in Tehran attracted a number of talented musicians, some of whom contributed effectively to the arrangement of the court music repertoire and the cultivation of new modulatory schemes. In the *Kolliyāt-e Yusofi* and *Resāla-ye davāzdah dastgāh*, Āqā Bābā Makhmur Eṣfahāni, the most celebrated singer at the court of Fatḥ-'Ali Shāh (r. 1797–1834), is credited with refining and shaping twelve ordered repertoires or extensive sequences of *dastgāh*s. As the author of *Resāla-ye davāzdah dastgāh* states:

> What has been common practice among the singers and instrumentalists in the past and present is based on the system (*qānun*) established by Āqā Bābā. This master musician combined all the *āvāz*s, *maqām*s, *sho'ba*s, and *gusha*s together and arranged a set of twelve *dastgāh*s in the following order:
>
> 1. *rāst-panjgāh*, 2. *navā-nayshābur*, 3. *homāyun*, 4. *māhur*, 5. *rohāb*, 6. *shul-shahnāz*, 7. *chahārgāh-mokhālef*, 8. *segāh*, 9. *dōgāh*, 10. *zābol*, 11. *'ashirān*, 12. *nayriz*.[154]

While *Kolliyāt-e Yusofi* only refers to the names of *dastgāh*s arranged by Āqā Bābā Makhmur, *Resāla-ye davāzdah dastgāh* details the sequences of three *dastgāh*s of *rāst-o panjgāh*, *navā-o nayshābur*, and *homāyun*.[155]

Evidently court musicians in the early Qajar period synthesized urban and regional modes and melody types with a new, classicized sophistication and sobriety. Āqā Bābā's achievement was to present aesthetic guidelines for twelve modulatory schemes, each comprising an ordered sequence of *āvāz*s interpolated with vocal and instrumental metric compositions.

All these developments took place in the capital and, more specifically, within the musical milieu of the court. But what was cultivated in Tehran was not necessarily practiced in provincial towns and other urban centers. In all other musical contexts, less extensive sequences of melody types were mostly recognized as *āvāz*s. Only in the early decades of the twentieth century did musicians in major Iranian cities—particularly Isfahan and Shiraz—gradually begin to conform to the musical norms of the capital while continuing at the same time to retain established local characteristics in their music making.[156]

The Second Half of the Nineteenth Century

By the second half of the nineteenth century, the *dastgāh* was widely recognized as the most prestigious modulatory scheme and performance format at the Qajar court. The two celebrated court musical families directed by Moḥammad Ṣādeq Khān and Mirzā 'Abdollāh, respectively, developed two separate groupings and repertoires of *dastgāh*s that differed significantly from one another with respect to classification, inclusion of *āvāz*s, titles, terminology, and melodic progression. These two groupings can be roughly illustrated as follows:

Moḥammad Ṣādeq Khān's arrangement of *dastgāh*s and *boyutāt*:

1. *shur*
2. *māhur*
3. *homāyun*
4. *segāh*
5. *chahārgāh*
6. *rāst-panjgāh*
7. *navā*

8. *rohāb*
9. *dōgāh*
10. *suz-o godāz*
11. *ṭarz-e tajnis*, and a series of sequences called *boyutāt*.[157]

Mirzā 'Abdollāh's arrangement of *dastgāh*s and *āvāz*s:

1. *shur*
2. *māhur*
3. *homāyun*
4. *segāh*
5. *chahārgāh*
6. *rāst-panjgāh*
7. *navā* and five *āvāz*s, including *abu'aṭā*, *bayāt-e tork*, *afshāri*, *dashti*, *bayāt-e eṣfahān*.

As mentioned in the previous chapter, Moḥammad Ṣādeq Khān was celebrated for his innovative style of *santur* playing and repertoire, which in his own time came to be known as the Moḥammad Ṣādeq Khāni *revāyat* (line of transmission). As the chief of court musicians, he was also exposed to and well acquainted with the entire court repertoire. While his *maktab* (school) showed more affinities with the early Qajar court tradition, his entire repertoire has not survived to the same extent as Mirzā 'Abdollāh's repertoire, which is widely available today. Nonetheless, segments of his repertoire, including his compositions and melody types, have come down to us through oral tradition and the early transcriptions made by Mehdi-Qoli Hedāyat (1863–1955).[158]

In addition to the seven *dastgāhs*, *shur*, *māhur*, *homāyun*, *segāh*, *chahārgāh*, *rāst-panjgāh*, and *navā* shared by Moḥammad Ṣādeq Khān and Mirzā 'Abdollāh, Moḥammad Ṣādeq Khān incorporated four additional *dastgāh*s into his repertoire: *rohāb*, *dōgāh*, *suz-o godāz* and *ṭarz-e tajnis*. While *rohāb* and *dōgāh* can be traced back to the performance practice of the late eighteenth century, the other two *dastgāhs*, *suz-o godāz* and *ṭarz-e tajnis*, may have represented his own innovations. Furthermore, evidence suggests that Moḥammad Ṣādeq Khān had arranged distinctive sequences of units that he referred to as *boyutāt*.

It is clear that Mirzā 'Abdollāh arranged his repertoire into seven *dastgāh*s and five *āvāzs*, but currently available evidence cannot support a determination as to whether this classification was one he took from his father or one he developed himself, or with his disciples. Surviving sources reveal some discrepancies. First, it is unclear why Mirzā ʿAbdollāh eliminated *dōgāh* from the core of *dastgāh*s while many other contemporaneous sources attest to the prevalence of this *dastgāh* in the second half of the nineteenth century. Second, *rohāb* in Mirzā ʿAbdollāh's surviving versions of the *radif* is represented as a sequence of units often affixed as a supplement to the end of *dastgāh*s *segāh* or *navā*. Again, it is not clear whether the addition of *rohāb* to another *dastgāh* was Mirzā ʿAbdollāh's own innovation or whether it was introduced by his disciples and subsequent musicians.[159]

Beside the group of five *āvāz*s consisting of *abu ʿaṭā*, *bayāt-e tork*, *afshāri*, *dashti*, and *bayāt-e esfahān*, there were other less extensive sequences of units, such as *bayāt-e kord*, *qaṭār*, *gerayli*, and *ḥejāz*. But it was the group of five that were granted the space to develop into independent *āvāz*s, most likely because of the desire to keep the total number of *dastgāh*s and *āvāz*s at twelve. Table 4.5 presents a comparative list of *dastgāh*s in six central eighteenth- and nineteenth-century sources.[160]

Table 4.5 Lists of *dastgāh*s in six eighteenth- and nineteenth-century musical sources

Chahār dastgāh-e aʿẓam	***Bahjat al-qulūb***	***Davāzdah dastgāh* MS. Neubauer**	**Āqā Bābā Makhmur**	**Moḥammad Ṣādeq Khān**	**Mirzā ʿAbdollāh**
rāst	*rāst-panjgāh*	*rāst-panjgāh*	*rāst-panjgāh*	*rāst-panjgāh*	*rāst-panjgāh*
navā		*navā-nayshābur*	*navā-nayshābur*	*navā*	*navā*
	homāyun-dōgāh	*homāyun*	*homāyun*	*homāyun*	*homāyun*
		rāvandi	*māhur*	*māhur*	*māhur*
rohāb-e dāvudi		*rohāb*	*rohāb*	*rohāb*	
		nawruz-e ʿarab	*shul-shahnāz*	*shur*	*shur*
chahārgāh	*chahārgāh-mokhālef*	*chahārgāh*	*chahārgāh-mokhālef*	*chahārgāh*	*chahārgāh*
	ḥosayni-segāh	*bayāt-e ʿajam*	*segāh*	*segāh*	*segāh*
		dōgāh-denāṣori	*dōgāh*	*dōgāh*	
		ʿoshshāq-navā	*zābol*	*suz-o godāz*	
		ʿashirān	*ʿashirān*	*ṭarz-e tajnis*	
		nayriz-navā	*nayriz*		

Dastgāhs *in the Nāṣeri Period*

The four large-scale modal schemes *rāst-panjgāh*, *navā*, *homāyun*, and *chahārgāh* were characterized as traditional *dastgāhs* during the reign of Nāṣer-al-Din Shāh (r. 1848–1896), and their formation could be traced back to the late eighteenth century, if not earlier.

In the second half of the nineteenth century, *rāst-panjgāh* was only performed by a small number of hereditary court instrumentalists who mostly played *tār* and *santur*, and was seldom performed by singers, or by *kamāncha* or *nay* players. In other words, there seems to have been no vocal counterpart to the instrumental version.[161] Nor was *rāst-panjgāh* known to musicians in Isfahan, Shiraz, and other cities apart from Tehran. It was only in the middle of the twentieth century that ʿAbdollāh Davāmi organized a vocal sequence of *rāst-panjgāh*, mostly adopting the names and structure of melodic units and their progressions from the instrumental *radif*.[162]

Navā as an extensive sequence of units was also performed exclusively by court instrumentalists, and only a loose and less extensive *āvāz* of *navā* was common among the court singers, though some of the components and characteristic phrases of the vocal version were conspicuously different from their instrumental counterparts.[163] *Navā* does not appear to have been widely performed outside the capital.[164]

Homāyun and *chahārgāh* were common as *āvāz*s in most urban centers, but as *dastgāh*s developed and were performed within the courtly musical setting. As *dastgāhs*, they came to include an assortment of *āvāz*s and melodic units that were typically more elaborate and extensive.

No other *dastgāh*s or *āvāz*s in Persian music have been so abundantly rich in stereotypical phrases and phrase sequences as *shur* and *segāh*. While *dastgāh-e shur* was customarily rendered in the form of *shur-shahnāz* (*shahnāz* was known as the second *shur*, commencing on the fourth above the tonic), two prominent versions of this *dastgāh* were developed by Moḥammad Ṣādeq Khān and Mirzā ʿAbdollāh, respectively. Moḥammad Ṣādeq Khān's version seems to have been marked as foregrounding a vocal idiom, and often incorporated more metric compositions of *taṣnif* and *reng*, whereas Mirzā ʿAbdollāh's version was based on an instrumental idiom with a complex plucking system. The titles of *āvāz*s and units were also sometimes different in the two versions. For example, what was called *shahnāz* in Moḥammad Ṣādeq Khān's *shur* was referred to as *salmak* in Mirzā 'Abdollāh's *radif*. This is an example of a divergence that resulted in confusion later on among the subsequent generation of musicians regarding the title of some *āvāz*s and their units.

While *segāh* was less sober and more popular than *chahārgāh*, they shared a number of *āvāz*s and followed more or less the same melodic progression throughout a *dastgāh* performance. However, certain stereotypical phrases were often exclusively rendered in *segāh* and were inadmissible in the sequence of *chahārgāh*.[165]

The scales of *māhur* and *rāst-panjgāh* were almost the same in the *darāmad* section, but the subsequent *āvāz*s and units in the two *dastgāh*s were significantly different. *Rāst-panjgāh* was more sober and contained stereotypical melodic phrases, such as *parvāna*, that were considered a hallmark of this *dastgāh*. In *māhur*, melodic elaboration was more rhapsodic and, in contrast to *rāst-panjgāh*, modulations to dramatically different *āvāz*s were restricted and, in many cases, inadmissible.[166]

A few sources, for example, *Resāla-ye davāzdah dastgāh*, also indicate that *rohāb* and *dōgāh* were arranged and performed as *dastgāh*s by court musicians, but surprisingly, they were omitted from the classification of Mirzā 'Abdollāh.[167]

Before 1900, when *māhur*, *shur*, *homāyun*, *segāh*, *chahārgāh*, and *navā* were performed outside courtly musical settings, especially when taking the form of less extensive sequences, they were referred to as *āvāz*. The only exception was *rāst-panjgāh*, which was only performed in the form of a large-scale modulatory scheme or *dastgāh*, and in practice its performance was mostly confined to the circle of solo specialists at the court.

Āvāzs

At the turn of the twentieth century, Mehdi-Qoli Hedāyat described a *dastgāh* as an ordered structure consisting of several juxtaposed *āvāz*s based on the musical taste of talented musicians with no "theoretical necessity" behind it.[168] He further specified an *āvāz* as a sequence of modal entities comprising a *darāmad* and a *qesmat-e āvāzi* (a free-rhythmic segment) followed by a *taṣnif* and *reng*.

According to Hedāyat, *āvāz*s varied in their internal structure, with most of them consisting of either a free-rhythmic segment devoid of any sense of metrical composition, or a small segment of free-rhythmic pieces interspersed with vocal and instrumental compositions. In any event, the core of *āvāz* was free-rhythmic, beginning with a *darāmad* and followed by a series of units, each having specific characteristic motives that functioned as melodic elaboration.

The units through which an *āvāz* unfolded and developed were known by proper names such as *kereshma*, *zangula*, *naghma*, *basta-negār*, and *mathnavi*. Some short units that were not performed with poems were categorized as *taḥrir* (for example, *dōtā-yeki*, *parastu*, *sārebānak*, *panja-muya*, *basta-negār*). All of these units had distinctive modal, melodic and, sometimes, rhythmic features and did not fall into one category of modal entity, nor were they designated by a single all-encompassing term. Only later, in the early twentieth century, were they referred to as *gusha*.

Hedāyat states that during the nineteenth century, the term *gusha* was only used in reference to a contrasting melody type that was interpolated in the sequence of a *dastgāh* mostly as a temporary modulation or to display the taste of a different *āvāz*.[169] In other words, *gusha* was nearly synonymous with the concept of *namud* in the *shashmaqom* music of Central Asia. For instance, right after the *darāmad* in *dastgāh*-e *homāyun*, a performer could play the *gusha chahārgāh*, or in the middle of *dastgāh*-e *shur* one could perform the *gusha abu'aṭā*. Likewise, *shekasta* and *delkash* in *dastgāh*-e *māhur* were both considered as *gusha* with the provision in both cases that it was inadmissible for an artist to move on to new modes, that is, that the presence of the *gusha* had to be temporally limited.[170]

In the mid-twentieth century, *āvāz*s could be classified into two major categories. The first consisted of short *āvāz*s that were the fundamental sequences of a *dastgāh*, with the *dastgāh* itself named after the first *āvāz*. The *āvāz*s in the seven *dastgāh*s could roughly be illustrated as follows:

1. ***dastgāh*-e *shur***: *darāmad*, *shahnāz* (*salmak*), *qaracha*, *rażavi*, and *ḥosayni*.
2. ***dastgāh*-e *māhur***: *darāmad*, *dād*, *khāvarān*, *fayli*, *ḥeṣār-e māhur*, *'erāq*, and *rāk*.

3. ***dastgāh*-e *segāh***: *darāmad*, *zābol*, *muya*, *ḥeṣār*, *mokhālef*, *mo'arbad*, and *ḥodi*.
4. ***dastgāh*-e *chahārgāh***: *darāmad*, *zābol*, *muya*, *ḥeṣār*, *mokhālef*, and *manṣuri*.
5. ***dastgāh*-e *homāyun***: *darāmad*, *chakāvak*, *bidād*, *shushtari*, and *bakhtiyāri*.
6. ***dastgāh*-e *navā***: *darāmad*, *bayāt-e rāje'*, *nahoft*, *neyshāburak*, *'erāq*, *ḥosayni*, and *rohāb*.
7. ***dastgāh*-e *rāst-panjgāh***: *darāmad*-e *rāst*, *nayriz*, *panjgāh*, *qaracha*, *shushtari*, *'erāq*, and *rāk*.

The sequence of *āvāz*s in a *dastgāh* was distinct, mostly based on their scales, melodic characteristics, emphasis, and contour. Sometimes two *āvāz*s shared the same scale and even a tonal center, but their characteristic phrases were conspicuously different. A typical *āvāz* usually commenced with an introductory section (a short *darāmad* or *moqaddama*) representing principal characteristic melodic or rhythmic phrases of the *āvāz*, and was further elaborated through a *kereshma*, *naghma*, *basta-negār*, or other melodic units. Within an *āvāz*, characteristic phrases were also marked as *taḥrir*s and brief contrasting melody types relative to another *āvāz* were called *gusha*s. While *forud* referred to the ending phrases of the constituent units within an *āvāz*, the ending of each *āvāz*, called *forud-e motammam* (finalizing *forud*), was the vehicle through which the melody always returned to the first mode of the *dastgāh*, that is, the mode of the *darāmad*.[171]

In the middle of the twentieth century, this type of *āvāz* gradually came to be called *shāh-gusha* or *gushahā-ye aṣli* (principal *gusha*s) and their constituent units, including *kereshma*, *zangula*, *naghma*, *basta-negār*, *mathnavi*, and *taḥrir*s, were all indiscriminately referred to as *gusha*. While in classical music the melodic elaboration of an *āvāz* was based on its constituent units and stereotypical phrases, in semi-classical music this elaboration was more subject to far-flung and loose improvisation. In both practices, however, an *āvāz* in a higher register was commonly marked as *awj* in the sequence of *āvāz*s, which corresponded with the concept of upper *sho'ba* in the Safavid *maqām* tradition. For instance, in *segāh* and *chahārgāh*, *mokhālef* was considered as *awj*. In *shur*, *ḥosayni* and in *homāyun*, *bidād* were *awj*s. *'Erāq* in *māhur* and *rāst-panjgāh* could be taken as *awj*, and in *navā* certainly *nahoft* played this role.

The second category of *āvāz*s had an independent and more extensive character and were seldom performed within the sequence of the aforementioned *dastgāh*s, yet they were not called *dastgāh* in their own right. Toward the end of the nineteenth century, these *āvāz*s were recognized as *dastān-e ʿarab* (*abuʿaṭā*), *bayāt-e tork*, *afshāri*, *dashti*, and *bayāt-e esfahān*.

Abuʿaṭā is a relatively new name, and the sequence of *abuʿaṭā* in its present form was known in Tehran in part as *dastān-e ʿarab* and in part as *sārnaj*. Its *awj* was called *ḥejāz-e baghdādi*. *Abuʿaṭā* seems to have been the alternative name of this *āvāz* in Isfahan.[172] However, toward the end of the nineteenth century the Isfahani *abuʿaṭā* with fairly defined characteristics became more prevalent and gradually eclipsed the name *dastān-e ʿarab* in Tehran. As musicologist Ruḥollāh Khāleqi explained in his 1937 work *Naẓari be musiqi*, *abuʿaṭā* was a light *āvāz* used in the composition of many popular songs or *taṣnif*s in the late nineteenth century.[173]

The names *bayāt-e tork* and *bayāt-e kord* can be traced back to the seventeenth century, when they both appeared as *gusha*s in Bāqiyā Nā'ini's *Zamzama-ye vaḥdat*. Both are also mentioned in early nineteenth-century texts as *āvāz*s.[174] Yet it seems that when the practice of *dastgāh-e dōgāh* gradually fell into decline, some of its *āvāz*s and units, including *āvāz-e dōgāh* itself, were already incorporated into a grouping labeled as *bayāt-e tork*.

The names, melodic character, and use of *motaghayyer*s (tones appearing in two slightly different pitches) in *afshāri* and *dashti* suggest that they were folk-based, informal modes. Evidence also suggests that their sequences evolved into mature *āvāz*s in the last few decades of the nineteenth century. During the Nāṣeri period, *afshāri* was commonly use in religious vocal genres, and the *mathnavi* in *afshāri* was commonly performed in Sufi lodges. The sequence of *dashti* was also formed as an aggregate of melodic units derived from folk *āvāz*s and genres developed in southern Iran (*hājiyāni*, *dashtestāni*, *bidegāni*, and *chupāni*) and on the southern coast of the Caspian Sea (*gilaki*, *ghamangiz*, and *amiri*).

In general, modulation to distant modes—the nineteenth-century concept of *gusha*—was not common in the sequences of *dastān-e ʿarab* (*abuʿaṭā*), *bayāt-e tork*, *afshāri*, and *dashti*. In other words, these *āvāz*s were not modulatory schemes in the same sense as *dastgāh*s. At the same time, the sequences of these *āvāz*s were not clearly delineated and hence many melodic units could be performed jointly in sequences of *abu'aṭā* and *dashti*, or *bayāt-e tork* and *afshāri*.

Radif

Unlike Moḥammad Ṣādeq Khān, a master improviser who mostly refused to train students, Mirzā 'Abdollāh was primarily a pedagogue and later achieved his prodigious influence largely through his disciples. In order to convey his knowledge and teach students systematically, he began to establish a fixed and unchanging version of his repertoire that came to be known as the *radif*. *Radif* as a musical concept was likely coined by Mirzā 'Abdollāh, as no references to this term appear to have been recorded before him. Toward the end of the nineteenth century, Mirzā 'Abdollāh's *radif* was transmitted through his disciples and subsequently recorded and transcribed, thereby bringing a substantial degree of standardization and canonization to nineteenth-century Persian music.

At the same time, Mirzā 'Abdollāh's younger brother, Āqā Ḥosayn Qoli, added his own creative input to the family repertoire and made a slightly different version of the *radif* that was to some extent more elaborate and technically complex than that of his brother. The third and last version of the *radif* in the nineteenth century was compiled by Montaẓam-al-Ḥokamā', a court physician and *setār* player who studied with both Moḥammad Ṣādeq Khan and Mirzā 'Abdollāh. His *radif* also represents an assortment of pieces he adopted from his two teachers. The *radif* of Montaẓam-al-Ḥokamā' was later transcribed by Mehdi-Qoli Hedāyat and some of the melody types were conspicuously marked as "Moḥammad Ṣādeq Khāni *revāyat*."

Radif was originally a concept in instrumental music that evolved through the practice of *tār* and *setār*, the two musical instruments on which Mirzā 'Abdollāh was a master.[175] While adhering to a predominantly instrumental idiom throughout, the genius of Mirzā 'Abdollāh's *radif* was the incorporation of a hereditary, sophisticated, and complex system of plucking that had matured in his family (*khāndān*) over the course of successive generations.[176] It is also safe to say that in the nineteenth century, the *radif* was only known among the Farāhāni family and their immediate disciples. It was practiced neither outside the court nor in any other urban centers. Moreover, the concept of a vocal *radif*—an extensive repertoire of units with specific names used for teaching purposes—did not exist at that time. Classical singers performed *āvāz*s and their units, but probably not in such extensive sequences. More significantly, they never referred to their own repertoire as *radif*. In the 1940s, 'Abdollāh Davāmi, a celebrated *taṣnif* singer of the late Qajar and Pahlavi periods, sought to construct a vocal *radif* version based on the training he had received from a few master singers including Ḥosayn Ṭaherzāda, and the overall groupings of *āvāz*s and *gusha*s he adopted from the current instrumental *radif*s. In some cases, he created new vocal units just by using instrumental units as a model and setting *taḥrir* and words to them.[177] Hence, the vocal *radif* evolved as a product of, on the one hand, the repertoire and judicious use of phrases developed by prominent singers, and, on the other hand, the underlying structure of the instrumental *radif*. Davāmi trained several students, among them Maḥmud Karimi, who later came up with another version of the vocal *radif*, and hence they both Karimi and Davāmi attempted to standardize and canonize the vocal repertoire of Persian music as well.[178]

Summary

The earliest modal entities in Iran were known as *dastān*s and were classified into primary and secondary categories. While eight primary *dastān*s were associated with scale degrees and took their names from them, the secondary *dastān*s were presumably derived from the primary ones. The eight *dastān*s could have been associated with, or analogous to, the early Byzantine *oktoechos*. Subsequent concepts of *parda*, *maqām*, *āvāz*, and *dastgāh* were always modulatory schemes, normally commencing with the exposition of the first mode followed by a series of secondary modes and contrasting melody types—*sho'ba*, *āvāz*, or *gusha*—in which distinct tonal centers and characteristic phrases were introduced and elaborated.

Between the thirteenth and seventeenth centuries the modal system was defined as twelve *maqām*s, six *āvāza*s, and twenty-four *sho'ba*s. While *maqām*s and *āvāza*s were modulatory schemes, *sho'ba*s were single modes that were either rendered in isolation or in conjunction with related *maqām*s. A *maqam* began with a free-rhythmic exposition of the original mode (from which the name of the *maqām* was taken) and was further expanded by modulating to lower and upper *sho'ba*s in which new modes with distinct tonal centers and characteristic phrases were introduced and elaborated.

From the middle of the eighteenth century, the terms *maqām* and *sho'ba* were no longer in use, and modulatory schemes and modes were referred to only as *āvāz*s. In the performance format of court music, some *āvāz*s were arranged in extended modulatory sequences interpolated with vocal and instrumental compositions. These sequences gradually attained standard forms and came to be called *dastgāh*s.

In the second half of the nineteenth century, Mirzā 'Abdollāh, a prominent court musician, began to establish a fixed version of his repertoire of *dastgāh*s that became known as the *radif*. His *radif* was later transmitted through his students and subsequently brought about a remarkable degree of standardization and canonization in Persian music.

Notes

1. For a list of Systematist and non-Systematist treatises, see Appendix 1 and Appendix 2.
2. See Mir Ṣadr al-Din Moḥammad, "Resāla-ye 'elm-e musiqi," 90.
3. See Dāneshpazhuh, *Nemuna'i az fehrest-e āthār-e dāneshmandān-e Irāni*, 84–88.
4. Cf. Massoudieh, *Manuscrits persans concernant la musique*, 124–125.
5. Melli Library (Tehran) MS 1651. For further information on this manuscript and the edition of the Arabic translation of *Sectio Canonis*, see Eckhard Neubauer, "Die Euklid zugeschrieben 'Teilung des Kanon' in Arabischer Übersetzung," *Zeitschrift für Geschichte der Arabisch-Islamischen Wissenschaften* 16 (2004/5): 309–385.
6. The treatise was also edited and extensively interpreted by Owen Wright in *Music Theory in the Safavid Era: The taqsīm al-naġamāt* (London: Routledge, 2018).
7. For the biography of Dawra Beg Karāmi, see Ṣādeghi Ketābdār, *Majma' al-khawāṣṣ*, 122–123; *Resāla-ye Karāmiya* was published first by Yaḥyā Dhokā' as "Ma'refat-e 'elm-e musiqi," in *Nāma-ye minovi*, ed. Ḥabib Yaghmā'i and Iraj Afshār (Tehran, 1971), 189–198. Subsequently, it was edited and translated into English by Mehrdad Fallahzadeh, *Two Treatises–Two Streams*, 76–177. The most reliable and complete manuscript of *Resāla-ye Karāmiya* is the Russian Academy of Sciences MS B1844. I sometimes refer to this manuscript as well.
8. See Massoudieh, *Manuscrits persans concernant la musique*, 54–59.
9. Mir Ṣadr al-Din Moḥammad, "Resāla-ye 'elm-e musiqi," 81–96.
10. Cf. Mir Ṣadr al-Din Moḥammad, "Resāla-ye 'elm-e musiqi," 95.
11. Mollā 'Abd al-Nabi Fakhr al-Zamāni Qazvini, *Tadhkera-ye maykhāna*, 873.

12. Bāqiyā Nā'ini, *Zamzama-ye vaḥdat*, Biruni Institute of Oriental Studies (Tashkent) MS 10226.
13. Pourjavady, "The Musical Codex of Amir Khān Gorji."
14. Kawkabi's treatise was first published in the form of facsimile by Askar-'Ali Rajabov as *Resāla-ye musiqi dar bayān-e davāzdah maqām* (Dushanbe: Nashriyāt-e Erfān, 1983) and for the second time was edited by Manṣura Thābetzāda as "Resāla-ye musiqi-ye Najm al-Din Kawkabi Bokhārā'i," in *Sa Resāla-ye musiqi-ye qadim-e Irān* (Tehran: Anjoman-e Āthār va Mafākher-e Farhangi, 2012).
15. Darvish-'Ali Changi. *Toḥfat al-surūr*.
16. Popescu-Judetz, *Tanburî Küçük Artin*.
17. A complete edition of *Bahjat al-qulūb* is not available yet, but the treatise is introduced in Bābak Khażrā'i, "Sharh-e chahār dastgāh va taṣāvir-e chand sāz," *Māhur* 59 (2013): 147–158.
18. Aḥmad al-Rifā'ī al-Muslim b. 'Abd al-Raḥmān al-Mawṣilī, *al-Durr al-naqī fī fann al-mūsīqī*, ed. Jalāl Ḥanafī (Baghdad: Wizārat al-Thaqāfah wa al-Irshād, 1964), 11, 18, 27.
19. See Mashḥun, *Tārikh-e musiqi-ye Irān*, 249–252.
20. See Amir Hosein Pourjavady, "Resāla dar 'elm-e musiqi," *Māhur* 14 (2002): 101–114; Amir Hosein Pourjavady, "Resāla dar bayān-e chahār dastgāh-e a'ẓam," *Māhur* 12 (2001): 81–92.
21. *Ādāb-e āvāzhā va dhekrhā'i ke dar manāber va joz ān khᵛānda mishavad*, Malek Library (Tehran) MS 2830.
22. Eckhard Neubauer, "Zwölf Dastgāh. Eine persische Handschrift aus dem 19. Jahrhundert mit Angaben zum musikalischen Vortrag der Elegie auf den Tod des Märtyrers Ḥosein b. 'Ali b. Abi Ṭāleb von Moḥtašam Kāšāni," *Zeitschrift für Geschichte der Arabisch-Islamischen Wissenschaften* 17 (2006/7): 301–372.
23. See Żiā' al-Din Yusof, *Resāla-ye musiqi mawsum be kolliyāt-e Yusofi*; Moḥammadi, "Resāla-ye davāzdah dastgāh," 125–146.
24. Navvāb Mir Moḥsen b. Ḥāji Sayyed Aḥmad Qarabāghi, *Vożuḥ al-arqām dar 'elm-e musiqi* (Baku, 1st ed. 1884; 2nd ed. with Russian translation 1913).
25. See Amir Hosein Pourjavady, "Athari musiqā'i az dawra-ye Qājār: Ḥājj Ḥasan b. Ḥāji 'Ali-Naqi Ganja'i," *Māhur* 28 (2005): 71–81.
26. Mehdi-Qoli Hedāyat, *Majma' al-adwār*, University of Tehran (Tehran) MS Ḥoquq 120.2.
27. Mehdi-Qoli Hedāyat, *Majma' al-adwār* (lithograph), Tehran, 1938.
28. Forṣat al-Dawla Shirāzi, *Boḥur al-alḥān*, 2nd ed. (Tehran: Forughi, 1996).
29. Mirzā Shafi', *The Treatise on the Seven Dastgah of Iranian Music*, ed. Moḥsen Moḥammadi (Tehran: Mirāth-e Maktub, 2018).

30. Ibn Khurdādhbih, *Mukhtār min kitāb al-lahw wa al-malāhī*, ed. Ighnāṭiūs 'Abduh Khalīfa (Beirut: Dār al-Mashriq, 1961), 15. I belive that *māda-dastān* has not been properly deciphered by the editor.
31. These two scales could be comparable with the two old Indian basic scales of *Sa-grāma* and *Ma-grāma*. For further information, see Richard Widdess, *The Rāgas of Early Indian Music: Modes, Melodies and Musical Notations from the Gupta Period to c. 1250* (Oxford: Clarendon, 1995), 5.
32. Cf. Abū 'Abdallāh Muḥammad b. Aḥmad b. Yūsif al-Kātib al-Khᵛārazmi, *Mafātīḥ al-'ulūm*, ed. 'Abd al-Amīr al-A'sim (Beirut: Dār al-Manāhil, 2008), 210.
33. See Harold Powers, "Mode," *New Grove Dictionary of Music and Musicians*, 6th ed. (1981), 830. It has also been argued that the modal codification of early Abbasid court music ascribed to Isḥāq al-Mawṣilī (d. 850) may have been derived conceptually from the model of already established Byzantine *oktoechos*. For further details see Owen Wright, "Ibn Munajjim and the Early Arabian Modes," *Galpin Society Journal* 19 (1966): 27–48; Eckhard Neubauer, "Die acht 'Wege' der Musiklehre und der Oktoechos," *Zeitschrift für Geschichte der Arabisch-Islamischen Wissenschaften* 6 (1994): 373–414.
34. Ibn Khurdādhbih, *Mukhtār min kitāb al-lahw wa al-malāhī*, 15.
35. Abū Isḥāq al-Kindī, "Al-risālat al-kubrā fī ta'līf," in *Mu'alifat al-Kindī al-mūsīqiyya*, ed. Zakariyyā Yusuf (Baghdad: Maṭba'at Shafīq, 1962), 137; Henry George Farmer, "The Old Persian Musical Modes," *Journal of the Royal Asiatic Society* (1926): 94–95.
36. Ibid., 94; Henry George Farmer, "The Old Arabian Melodic Modes," *Journal of the Royal Asiatic Society* (1965): 99.
37. Ibn Zayla. *Kitāb al-kāfī fī al-musīqī*, ed. Zakariyā Yusef (Cairo: Dār al-Qalam, 1964), 66–67.
38. For further detail on Bārbad, see Aḥmad Tafażżoli, "Bārbad," in *Encyclopædia Iranica*, online edition, 1988.
39. Abū al-Ḥasan 'Alī b. al-Mas'ūdī, *Murūj al-dhahab wa ma'ādin al-jawhar*, ed. Charles Pellat (Paris: Société asiatique, 1962), 5: 127–128.
40. Cf. Moḥammad 'Awfi, *Lubāb al-albāb*, ed. Edward G. Browne (Leiden: Brill, 1903), 1: 20; Shams al-Dīn Muḥammad b. Qays al-Rāzī, *Al-mu'jam fī ma'ā'īr ash'ār al-'ajam*, ed. Moḥammad b. 'Abd al-Vahhāb Qazvini (Tehran: Dāneshgāh-e Tehrān, 1957), 1: 200–201. Likewise, Moḥammad Ḥosayn b. Khalaf Tabrizi, the author of the Persian dictionary *Borhān-e qāṭe'*, mentions that *khosravānis* were set to rhymed prose.
41. See Mir Ṣadr al-Din Moḥammad, "Resāla-ye 'elm-e musiqi," 92–93.

42. The renowned Persian poet Neẓāmi Ganjavi (d. 1209) lists these compositions in his *Khosraw va Shirin*, ed. Ḥasan Vaḥid Dastgerdi (Tehran, Mo'assasa-ye Maṭbu'āti-ye 'Elmi, 1934), 190–194.
43. Manuchehri Dāmghāni, *Divān*, ed. Moḥammad Dabirsiyāqi (Tehran: Zavvār, 1968), 1, 4, 80, 127–128, 138, 172, 182, 186, 195, 231. *Māda* has been read and transcribed inaccurately by the editor as *bāda*.
44. See Owen Wright, "Die melodischen Modi bei Ibn Sīnā und die Entwicklung der Modalpraxis von Ibn al-Munaǧǧim bis zu Ṣafī al-Dīn al-Urmawī," *Zeitschrift für Geschichte der Arabisch-Islamischen Wissenschaften* 16 (2004/5): 283–284.
45. 'Onṣor al-Ma'āli Kaykābus b. Voshmgir Ziyār, *Qābus-nāma*, ed. Gholām-Ḥosayn Yusofi (Tehran: Bongāh-e Tarjoma va Nashr-e Ketāb, 1973), 196.
46. For the account of Persian poets of the twelfth and thirteenth centuries referring to *parda*s, see Amir Hosein Pourjavady, "Resāla-ye musiqi-ye Moḥammad b. Maḥmud b. Moḥammad Nayshāburi," *Ma'āref* 34/35 (1995): 44–57.
47. Ibid., 62–63.
48. *Bāng zadan* in Persian means to shout or to raise one's voice to a higher register.
49. See Appendix 2. For further discussion on *bāng*, see Eckhard Neubauer, "Music History II. ca. 650 to 1370 CE," *Encyclopædia Iranica*, online edition, 2009. Neubauer, however, suggests that *bāng* conveys the concept of a whole tone and it must have been used by practicing musicians in pre-Islamic times.
50. Sajjād Nikfahm Khubravān and Sa'id Kordmāfi, "Musiqi dar ashjār va athmār-e 'Alā' al-Din Bokhāri," *Māhur* 70 (2016): 76.
51. Ibid.
52. See Appendix 2.
53. Ṣafī al-Dīn al-Urmawī, *Kitāb al-adwār*, ed. Ghaṭṭās 'Abd al-Malik Khashabah and Maḥmūd Aḥmad al-Hifnī (Cairo, 1986), 235–246; Owen Wright, *The Modal System of Arab and Persian Music, A.D. 1250–1300* (Oxford: Oxford University Press, 1978), 79–94.
54. Wright, *The Modal System of Arab and Persian Music*, 79–80.
55. Ibid., 90–91.
56. Ṣafī al-Dīn al-Urmawī, *Kitāb al-adwār*, 235–246.
57. Ibid., 309–310; Wright, *The Modal System of Arab and Persian Music*, 81–82.
58. See Qoṭb al-Din Shirāzi, *Durrat al-tāj li ghurrat al-dubbāj*, ed. Moḥammad Meshkāt, 5 vols. (Tehran, 1939–1945), 4: 118–119; Owen Wright, *Music Theory in Mamluk Cairo: The ġāyat al-maṭlūb fī 'ilm al-adwār wa-'l-ḍurūb by Ibn Kurr* (Farnham: Ashgate, 2014), 329–338, 114–120.

59. Ḥasan Kāshāni, *Kanz al-tuḥaf*, ed. Taqi Binesh (Tehran: Markaz-e Nashr-e Dāneshgāhi, 1992), 105–106; Muḥammad b. ʻAbd al-Ḥamīd al-Lādhiqī, *Al-risāla al-fatḥiyya*, ed. Hāshim Muḥammad al-Rajab (Kuwait, 1976), 157–172. Most of these texts refer to *rāst* (*yekgāh*), *dōgāh*, *segāh*, *chahārgāh*, etc. not as note names or scale degrees, but as modes which took their names from those scale degrees.
60. Wright, *The Modal System of Arab and Persian Music*, 172.
61. Ibid., 172–180. In the Ottoman tradition, there were four *sho'ba*s known as *yekgāh*, *dōgāh*, *segāh*, and *chahārgāh*. For further detail, see *The Science of Music in Islam, vol. 6: Seydī's Book on Music*, trans. and ed. Eugenia Popescu-Judetz in collaboration with Eckhard Neubauer (Frankfurt: Publications of the Institute for the History of Arabic-Islamic Science, 2004), xiv, 43–45.
62. Wright, *The Modal System of Arab and Persian Music*, 192, 292.
63. ʻAbd al-Qāder Marāghi, *Maqāṣid al-alḥān*, 56.
64. ʻAbd al-Qāder Marāghi, *Sharḥ-e advār*, ed. Taqi Binesh (Tehran: Markaz-e Nashr-e Dāneshgāhi, 1991), 303–310.
65. ʻAlishāh b. Buka Awbahi, *Muqaddimat al-uṣūl*, 147–148; ʻAli b. Moḥammad Bannā'i, *Resāla dar musiqi* (Tehran: Markaz-e Nashr-e Dāneshgāhi, 1989), 93, 96, 98.
66. ʻAbd al-Qāder Marāghi, *Maqāṣid al-alḥān*, 119.
67. ʻAbd al-Qāder Marāghi, *Jāmiʻ al-alḥān*, ed. Taqi Binesh (Tehran: Mo'assasa-ye Moṭāleʻāt va Taḥqiqāt-e Farhangi, 1987), 127; *Sharḥ-e advār*, 208.
68. Nasimi, *Nasim-e ṭarab*, 71–72.
69. Ibid.
70. Ibid., 83–84.
71. Ibid., 72–73.
72. Wright, *Music Theory in the Safavid Era: The taqsīm al-naġamāt*, 360. For Wright's commentary on this issue, see ibid., 37–44.
73. Ibid., 421.
74. Ibid., 403–414.
75. Ibid. The concept of *sayr* was also used in the Timurid period. For instance, see ʻAbd al-Qāder Marāghi, *Maqāṣid al-alḥān*, 108.
76. Fallahzadeh, *Two Treatises–Two Streams*, 105–114.
77. Ibid., 110–111. I refer to the pages of the Persian text edited by Fallahzadeh (see n. 6), but I use my own English translation.
78. Mir Ṣadr al-Din Moḥammad, "Resāla-ye ʻelm-e musiqi," 87–90.
79. Ibid., 87–88.
80. Ibid., 88.

81. Fallahzadeh, *Two Treatises–Two Streams*, 124; Moḥammad, "Resāla-ye 'elm-e musiqi," 90.
82. *Resāla-ye Karāmiya*, Russian Academy of Sciences MS B1844, 27a.
83. Mir Ṣadr al-Din Moḥammad, "Resāla-ye 'elm-e musiqi," 90.
84. Bāqiyā Nā'ini, *Zamzama-ye vaḥdat*, Biruni Institute of Oriental Studies (Tashkent) MS 10226, 11–12.
85. Pourjavady, "The Musical Codex of Amir Khān Gorji," 195–196.
86. Ibid., 257–258.
87. During the thirteenth century, some music theorists, including Moḥammad Nayshāburi and 'Alā' al-Din Bokhāri, introduce *rāst* as the ruler (*shāh*) or the mother (*umm*) of all modes, whereas both Nasimi and Mir Ṣadr al-Din Moḥammad mention *ḥosayni* as the most prominent *maqām*. Cf. Amir Hosein Pourjavady, "Resāla-ye musiqi-ye Moḥammad b. Maḥmud b. Moḥammad Nayshāburi," *Ma'aref* 34-35 (1995); Khubravān and Kordmāfi, "Musiqi dar ashjār va athmār-e 'Alā' al-Din Bokhāri," 76; Nasimi, *Nasim-e ṭarab*, 73; Mir Ṣadr al-Din Moḥammad, "Resāla-ye 'elm-e musiqi," 89.
88. See Pourjavady, "The Musical Codex of Amir Khān Gorji," 197.
89. By "free-rhythmic" I mean the section that is not typically accompanied by a percussion instrument, otherwise free-rhythmic is a problematic concept and can hardly be used in reference to the sections of a *maqām*. A number of sections may follow a rhythmic cycle or poetic meter, for instance, and should not be categorized as free-rhythmic.
90. This scheme is somewhat described in Amir Hosein Pourjavady, "Dar bayān-e 'elm-e musiqi va dānestan-e sho'abāt-e ou," *Māhur* 15 (2003): 64–68.
91. *Darāmad* has been used as early as the mid-sixteenth century and Dawra Beg Karāmi is one of the first music theorists who employs this term. Cf. Fallahzadeh, *Two Treatises–Two Streams*, 119. *Āghāz* is mentioned in a few musical texts including H. L. Rabino de Borgomale (ed.), *Bahjat al-ruḥ* (Tehran: Bonyād-e Farhang, 1965), 54–56.
92. The term *forud* is frequently mentioned in the *Taqsīm al-naghamāt*.
93. Powers, "Mode."
94. For further discussion of this subject, see Pourjavady, "The Musical Codex of Amir Khān Gorji," 128–129.
95. For instance, see Mir Ṣadr al-Din Moḥammad, "Resāla-ye 'elm-e musiqi," 89.
96. Kawkabi Bokhārā'i, "Resāla-ye musiqi-ye Najm al-Din Kawkabi Bokhārā'i," 52.
97. Wright, *Theory in the Safavid Era: The taqsīm al-naġamāt*, 403–404.
98. Pourjavady, "Dar bayān-e 'elm-e musiqi va dānestan-e sho'abāt-e ou," 64.
99. Ibid.

100. Fallahzadeh, *Two Treatises–Two Streams*, 113
101. Mir Ṣadr al-Din Moḥammad, "Resāla-ye 'elm-e musiqi," 89.
102. Wright, *Theory in the Safavid Era: The taqsīm al-naġamāt*, 415–420.
103. Ibid.
104. Pourjavady, "The Musical Codex of Amir Khān Gorji," 196.
105. Bāqiyā Nā'ini, *Zamzama-ye vaḥdat*, Biruni Institute of Oriental Studies (Tashkent) MS 10226, 8.
106. Mir Ṣadr al-Din Moḥammad, "Resāla-ye 'elm-e musiqi," 90.
107. Pourjavady, "Dar bayān-e 'elm-e musiqi va dānestan-e sho'abāt-e ou," 64–65.
108. Ibid., 64–68.
109. For the discussion of the Ottoman concept of *seyir*, see Feldman, *Music of the Ottoman Court*, 255–273. In Persian sources, cf. Wright, *Theory in the Safavid Era: The taqsīm al-naġamāt*, 403–414; Borgomale, *Bahjat al-ruḥ*, 55–56; Moḥammad Moḥiṭ Ṭabāṭabā'i, "Resāla-ye musiqi-ye gomnām," *Majalla-ye musiqi* 10/11 (1941): 19.
110. See Owen Wright, *Touraj Kiaras and Persian Classical Music: An Analytical Perspective* (Farnham: Ashgate, 2009), 32.
111. *Taḥrir* as the obligatory initial section of an Iraqi *maqām* performance retains its meaning as "melodic configuration" as well.
112. For a historical account of *taḥrir* as both melismatic vocal expression and melodic phrase, see 'Abd al-Qāder Marāghi, *Jāmi' al-alḥān*, 189, 240; Bāqiyā Nā'ini, *Zamzama-ye vaḥdat*, 16; Pourjavady, "Resāla dar 'elm-e musiqi va dānestan-e sho'abāt-e ou," 112; Pourjavady, "Resāla dar bayān-e chahār dastgāh-e a'ẓam," 90.
113. Kawkabi Bokhārā'i, "Resāla-ye musiqi-ye Najm al-Din Kawkabi Bokhārā'i," 52–54. See the discussion of this topic in William Sumits, "The Evolution of the maqām Tradition in Central Asia: From the Theory of 12 maqām to the Practice of Shashmaqām," Ph.D. dissertation, University of London, SOAS, 2011, 82–94.
114. Eugenia Popescu-Judetz, *Seydī's Book on Music, vol. 6*, 46–75.
115. See Feldman, *Music of the Ottoman Court*, 223.
116. Ibid., 232.
117. Ibid.
118. Cf. Borgomale, *Bahjat al-ruḥ*, 54–56.
119. Pourjavady, "Dar bayān-e 'elm-e musiqi va dānestan-e sho'abāt-e ou," 65.
120. See Feldman, *Music of the Ottoman Court*, 232.
121. *Resāla-ye Karāmiya*, Russian Academy of Sciences MS B1844, 27a.
122. The number of *tarkib*s is mentioned forty-eight—corresponding to twenty-four hours—in *Seydī's Book on Music*, 129–133.

123. *Bayāt* was originally a typical singing style or vocal genre attributed to an ethnic group (e.g., *bayāt-e tork*, *bayāt-e kord*) or inhabitants of a particular urban center (e.g., *bayāt-e eṣfahān*, *bayāt-e shirāz*).
124. *Nehāvand-e rumi* is mentioned in Pourjavady, "The Musical Codex of Amir Khān Gorji," 258. *Qarachaqā-ye rumi* and *sepehr-e hendi* are among the *gusha*s presented in the "Dar bayān-e ʿelm-e musiqi va dānestan-e shoʿabāt-e ou," 65, 67.
125. Cf. Borgomale, *Bahjat al-ruḥ*, 93.
126. *Bahjat al-qulūb*, Majles Library (Tehran) MS 2242, 56.
127. See Mir Ṣadr al-Din Moḥammad, "Resāla-ye ʿelm-e musiqi," 90; Pourjavady, *The Musical Codex of Amir Khān Gorji*, 195.
128. For instance, see ʿAbd al-Qāder Marāghi, *Maqāṣid al-alḥān*, 56.
129. ʿAbd al-Qāder Marāghi, *Jāmiʿ al-alḥān: khātima*, ed. Taqi Binesh (Tehran: Moʾassesa-ye Moṭāleʿāt va Taḥqiqāt-e Farhangi, 1993), 205–207.
130. See Pourjavady, "The Musical Codex of Amir Khān Gorji," 189–190. For further discussion of this subject, see Sumits, "The Evolution of the maqām Tradition," 115–136.
131. See Pourjavady, "Negāhi be ḥayāt-e musiqāʾi-ye dawra-ye Afshāri," 54–58.
132. *Tanburî Küçük Artin: A Musical Treatise of the Eighteenth Century*, 131; for further discussion, see Feldman, *Music of the Ottoman Court*, 199.
133. See Pourjavady, "Negāhi be ḥayāt-e musiqāʾi-ye dawra-ye Afshāri," 43–49.
134. See Khubravān and Kordmāfi, "Musiqi dar ashjār va athmār-e ʿAlāʾ al-Din Bokhāri," 76; also cf. Neubauer, "Music History II. ca. 650 to 1370 CE."
135. See Pourjavady, "Negāhi be ḥayāt-e musiqāʾi-ye dawra-ye Afshāri," 36.
136. See Feldman, *Music of the Ottoman Court*, 230.
137. Wright, *Touraj Kiaras and Persian Classical Music*, 28–29.
138. Farhat, *The Dastgāh Concept in Persian Music*, 19.
139. Pourjavady, "Dar bayān-e ʿelm-e musiqi va dānestan-e shoʿabāt-e ou," 64–68.
140. Ibid., 67.
141. Pourjavady, "Resāla dar ʿelm-e musiqi," 112–114. Among the music theorists of the Safavid period some refer to *parda* apparently as an extensive sequence of units, see, for instance, Malek Library (Tehran) MS 893, 21.
142. Pourjavady, "Resāla dar bayān-e chahār dastgāh-e aʿẓam," 90–92.
143. The term *moqaddama* was used as the opening section of short sequences or units throughout the Qajar period. For instance, in the *radif* of *dastgāh-e shur* the two sequences of *golriz* and *bozorg* both commence with a *moqaddama*. *Moqaddama* was also interchangeably used with *darāmad*, cf. Musā Maʿrufi and Mehdi Barkechli, *Radif-e haft dastgāh-e musiqi-e Irāni/Les Systèmes de la musique traditionelle iranienne (radif)* (Tehran: Vezārat-e Farhang va Honar, 1962), *alef*, *be*, *jim*, *dāl*.

144. Pourjavady, "Resāla dar bayān-e chahār dastgāh-e aʿẓam," 92.
145. *Bahjat al-qulūb*, 60.
146. Ibid., 33–34.
147. Neubauer, "Zwölf Dastgāh," 306–337, 360–372.
148. Ibid., 338–339, 358–359.
149. *Ādāb-e āvāzhā*, 2a–2b.
150. Ibid., 2b.
151. Ibid., 5a–5b.
152. For further discussion, see Pourjavady, "Negāhi be ḥayāt-e musiqā'i-ye dawra-ye Afshāri," 52–54.
153. Some *āvāz*s such as *gilaki*, *abu ʿaṭā*, and *afshāri* are not even mentioned in treatises predating 1800.
154. Moḥammadi, "Resāla-ye davāzdah dastgāh," 142; Żiā' al-Din Yusof, *Resāle-ye musiqi mawsum be kolliyāt-e Yusofi*, 27.
155. Moḥammadi, "Resāla-ye davāzdah dastgāh," 144–145.
156. The case of Azerbaijan was rather different. As mentioned in the previous chapter, Tabriz came to be the second capital in the Qajar period and some court musicians were sent to this city to be in the service of the crown prince.
157. See Kāmrān and Menā, *Bakhshhā-i az radif-e Ḥabib Samāʿi be revāyat-e Ṭaliʿa Kāmrān*, 18–19.
158. See Mehdi-Qoli Hedāyat, *Radif-e haft dastgāh-e musiqi-e irāni be revāyat-e Mehdi Ṣolḥi*, 11, 26, 30, 79, 82, 91, 120, 121.
159. In the version of *radif* collected by Musā Maʿrufi, *rohāb* is affixed to the *dastgāh*-e *navā*, whereas in Mirzā ʿAbdollāh's *radif* it comes at the end of *dastgāh*-e *segāh*. For Mirzā ʿAbdollāh's *radif*, see Jean During, *The Radif of Mirzâ Abdollâh: A Canonic Repertoire of Persian Music* (Tehran: Māhur, 2006), 116–119.
160. *Gerayli* is also mentioned by Hedāyat as an independent *āvāz*. Cf. Hedāyat, *Majmaʿ al-adwār* (manuscript), 2:116.
161. The extensive sequence of *rāst-panjgāh* was never performed by singers. A few court singers, however, performed a brief version of *rāst*. For further discussion, see Sayyed Ḥosayn Maythami, "*Āvāz-e rāst dar dawrān-e Qājār*," *Māhur* 51/52 (2011): 127–141.
162. Personal communication from Moḥammad-Reżā Loṭfi, 7/2001.
163. In an early recording of *dastgāh*-e *navā* sung by Qoli Khān and accompanied by Ṣafdar Khān on *kamāncha*, the units are *darāmad*, *shekasta-ye kuchak*, *ḥosayn*, *pahlavi-o ḥosayn*, *layli majnun*. Cf. Kinnear, *The Gramophone Company's Persian Recordings*, 49–50; the recording is reproduced in *The Early Recording of Seven Dastgâhs*, Māhur, M.CD-345, 2013.

164. Even for much of the twentieth century, *navā* was not performed in Isfahan, Shiraz, or Tabriz. It was only toward the end of the twentieth century that musicians in other cities came to be influenced by the tradition of Tehran and began to perform *navā* as well. Nonetheless, many singers believed that *navā* carried an ill-omens and refused to perform it as frequently as other *dastgāh*s.
165. Personal communication from Dāriush Ṣafvat.
166. Personal communication from Dāriush Ṣafvat.
167. *Dastgāh-e dōgāh* is mentioned in a few texts, including Neubauer, "Zwölf Dastgāh," 370; Moḥammadi, "Resāla-ye davāzdah dastgāh," 142; Eugène Aubin, *La Perse d'aujourd'hui* (Paris: Colin, 1908), 229; Mirzā Shafi', *The Treatise on the Seven Dastgah of Iranian Music*, 33–34.
168. Hedāyat, *Majma' al-adwār* (manuscript), 2: 85, 87–88.
169. Hedāyat, *Majma' al-adwār* (lithograph), 3:124.
170. Cf. *dastgāh*-e *homāyun* and *dastgāh*-e *shur* in Ma'rufi and Barkechli, *Radif-e haft dastgāh-e musiqi-e Irāni*.
171. *Forud-e motammam* was a term frequently used by Dāriush Ṣafvat and Moḥammad Irāni Mojarrad while teaching and analyzing the *radif*. It is also mentioned by Hedāyat in *Radif-e haft dastgāh-e musiqi-e Irāni*, 67–68.
172. An early nineteenth-century musical text also attributes *abu'aṭā* to Isfahan by referring to it as *abu'aṭā'i-ye esfahān*. Cf. Neubauer, "Zwölf Dastgāh," 358.
173. Ruḥollāh Khāleqi, *Naẓari be musiqi* (Tehran, 1937), 1:272.
174. Bāqiyā Nā'ini, *Zamzama-ye vaḥdat*, 11; Neubauer, "Zwölf Dastgāh," 339, 358.
175. Personal communications from Dāriush Ṣafvat, Moḥammad-Reżā Loṭfi, and Dāriush Ṭalā'i.
176. The plucking system that developed through the practice of Mirzā 'Abdollāh's *radif* in Tehran was unique and it was not common in the practice of instrumental repertoire of Isfahan, Shiraz, or Tabriz. Likewise, outside the capital, the instrumental repertoire was not often defined as something independent of the vocal repertoire.
177. Personal communication from Moḥammad-Reżā Loṭfi, 7/2001. As Dāriush Ṣafvat informed me, Davāmi's *radif* was first transcribed by Abol-Ḥasan Ṣabā in the 1950s and Farāmarz Pāyvar used Ṣabā's transcription in his *Radif-e āvāzi va taṣnifhā-ye qadimi be revāyat-e 'Abdollāh Davāmi*. In the 1970s Davāmi recorded his *radif* while some of its segments were accompanied by Moḥammad-Reżā Loṭfi on the *tār*.
178. Cf. Mahmud Karimi and Mohammad-Taghi Massoudieh, *Radif-e āvāzi-ye musiqi-ye sonnati-ye Irān be revāyat-e Maḥmud Karimi/Radif vocal de la musique iranienne* (Tehran: Sorush, 1978). Karimi was also known for creating new vocal units by using instrumental units as a model and setting *taḥrir* and words to them. Personal communication from Fāṭema Vā'eẓi (Parisā), 1/2019.

5

RHYTHM

Between the ninth and sixteenth centuries, discussions of rhythm often fall under the rubric of *ʿilm al-īqāʿ* (lit. "science of rhythm"). In essence, this topic describes elements of rhythm, including attack, duration, the analogy between poetic and musical meter, and, more significantly, the structure of rhythmic cycles that were the backbones of vocal and instrumental compositions.

While the Arabic word for "cycle" is *dawr* (pl. *adwār*), the characteristic rhythmic cycles used in practice were called *īqāʿāt* by al-Kindī and al-Fārābī, and *alḥān* (also *qawānīn*) by the Ikhwān al-Ṣafā.[1] Systematist theorists referred to rhythmic cycles as *īqāʿāt*, *adwār al-īqāʿ*, and *advār-e iqāʿi* up until the end of the Timurid period, though their contemporaries among practicing musicians began to call the rhythmic cycles *oṣul*s.[2] Subsequently, in the course of the sixteenth and seventeenth centuries, Safavid music theorists and practicing musicians, along with their Central Asian and Ottoman counterparts, all came to refer to rhythmic cycles as *oṣul*s. These three musical cultures seemingly shared a stock of common cycles, however, the *oṣul* pattern associated with a given name sometimes differed among the three traditions. At the same time, each tradition incorporated a number of rhythmic cycles from regional folk repertoires and featured its own modified versions of the common *oṣul*s.

In the tenth century, al-Fārābī employed the term *naqra* to refer to "attack," and differentiates among three types of attack on the basis of their timbre or dynamics. He also uses *zamān* to designate the length of time between two attacks.[3] Three centuries later, Ṣafi al-Dīn al-Urmawī defined rhythm based on the concept of the rhythmic cycle. He used *naqra* to designate "the total number of pulses/beats in a cycle" and distinguished those that are marked with drum strokes (*żarb*) from those that are "omitted."[4] By the beginning of the sixteenth century, the term *naqra* was no longer used by music theorists, and in theory and practice it was replaced by "*żarb*." While the basic meaning of both *naqra* and *żarb* was "attack," evidently, these two terms were also used in reference to the tactus beat in a rhythmic cycle (comparable with the concept of *mātrā* in Indian music).[5]

Al-Urmawī represented the cycles through both poetic feet and *atānin* mnemonic patterns (*ta*, *tan*, *tanna*), and his successors, including the Timurid writers, continued to employ the *atānin* patterns throughout the fourteenth and fifteenth centuries while also using a cipher notation to complement this system.[6] Safavid music theorists of the seventeenth century finally adopted a new method and represented the cycles through *dik dak* drum patterns and number of attacks—similar to the Turkish qualitative *düm tek* syllables—but without indicating durations.

Toward the second half of the eighteenth century, the term *oṣul* was still used in Central Asian and Ottoman regions, whereas in Iran it gradually became obsolete. At the same time, the concept of rhythm came to be identified only as *żarb*, while some of the Safavid and eighteenth-century *oṣul* names and structures were still prevalent among practicing musicians in the capital and other urban centers. It is fair to say that the term *żarb* in the Qajar period and later in the twentieth century had multiple meanings, just as it did during the medieval period. While it continued to mean "attack," "beat," "combination of both attack and duration," and "rhythmic pattern," it also conveyed the concept of meter.

This chapter begins with a summary account of rhythmics in the Systematist tradition drawing primarily on excellent studies by Owen Wright and Eckhard Neubauer.[7] It then provides a translation and analysis of major musical sources on rhythm throughout the Timurid and Safavid periods. Accounts of rhythmic cycles during the Safavid period have previously been analyzed in two outstanding articles by Wright, but this chapter introduces a few previously unknown musical sources. While following Wright's analytical approach, I further examine the structure of *oṣul*s in Iran and make comparisons with accounts in Ottoman sources.[8] The final part of the chapter constitutes its most original contribution: a discussion of the development of rhythm and meter in the eighteenth and nineteenth centuries, mainly through examination of sporadically occurring musical references, early recordings, and interviews with senior master performers and *dombak* players versed in traditional approaches.

Early Accounts of Rhythm in Arabic and Persian Sources

In the early Islamic period, four major *īqā'*s—*ramal, al-awwal, al thānī*, and *hazaj*—were known in urban centres, especially in Medina, Mecca, Damascus, and, later, in Baghdad, the capital of the Abbasid caliphate.[9] Three of the four meters were rendered in two different tempi, *thaqīl* (heavy) and *khafīf* (light).[10]

Thaqīl	***Khafīf***
ramal (3/2)	*khafīf al-ramal* (3/4)
thaqīl al-awwal (4/2)	*khafīf al-thaqīl al-awwal* (4/4)
thaqīl al-thānī (5/2)	*khafīf al-thaqīl al-thānī* (5/4)
hazaj (6/8)	

The earliest articulation of these meters is ascribed to the Abbasid court musician Isḥāq al-Mawṣilī (d. 850), but later it was al-Fārābī who classified and explicated them meticulously in his treatises.[11] Subsequently, Ibn Sinā outlined the same meters in the music chapter of *Kitāb al-shifā'* and his prominent student, Ibn Zayla, attested that the abovementioned rhythmic system governed the entire repertoire of Arabic, Persian (*fārsi*), and Khorasani tunes by the eleventh century.[12]

The author of the late eleventh-century Persian *Qābus-nāma* categorizes melodies largely in two types of meters: *gerān* (Persian for the Arabic *thaqīl*) and *sabok* (Persian for the Arabic *khafīf*), and subsequently urges musicians to perform melodies set to heavy meters for the potentates, nobility, and elderly; melodies set to light meters for the youth; and, finally, melodies set to more delicate and lighter meters, in the form of *tarāna*, for women and children.[13]

As Eckhard Neubauer aptly noted, these three types of meter could be correlated to al-Fārābī's system of metrics in such a way that the first type can be compared with "heavy" meters, the second to the "light" version of heavy meters, and the third to the meter *hazaj*.[14]

In the period between the eleventh and thirteenth centuries, the old metric system in Baghdad gradually underwent a substantial development. While the *īqā*ʿs mostly retained the same titles, their patterns became elaborated and increased in length. In the second half of the thirteenth century, a set of six major rhythmic cycles (*adwār al-żurūb*) was recognized by Ṣafi al-Dīn al-Urmawī, which came to be the standard set of *īqā*ʿs, discussed in subsequent Systematist musical texts written in Tabriz, Shiraz, Isfahan, and Herat for almost two centuries.

In his *Kitāb al-adwār*, al-Urmawī describes *īqā*ʿ as "a collection of attacks (*naqarāt*) with intervening durations (*azmina*) of specific length (*maḥdūdat al-maqādīr*), forming cycles (*adwār*) of equal magnitude (*mutasāwiyāt al-kammiyya*)."[15] He introduces four different lengths of notes:

1. letter *alif* or syllable ***ta***	(*sari*ʿ or *hazaj* representing the duration of 1 *naqra*)
2. letter *bā'* or syllable ***tan***	(*sabab* or *khafīf* representing the duration of 2 *naqra*s)
3. letter *jīm* or syllables ***tanan***	(*watad* or *khafīf al-thaqīl* representing the duration of 3 *naqra*s)
4. letter *dāl* or syllables ***tananan***	(*fāṣila* or *thaqīl* representing the duration of 4 *naqra*s)

For each rhythmic cycle, al-Urmawī designates the structure of cycles by means of *atānīn* mnemonic devices. Later, in the *Risāla al-Sharafiyya*, he uses the mnemonic patterns derived from the Arabic root *fa*ʿ*ala* that represent metrical feet in the *aruz* system of quantitative prosody. Therefore, the basic form of *thaqīl al-awwal* in his two texts is:

Kitāb al-adwār	*tanan* (3), *tanan* (3), *tananan* (4), *tan* (2), *tananan* (4)
Risāla al-Sharafiyya	*mafā*ʿ*ilun* (3 + 3), *fā*ʿ*ilun* (4), *mufta*ʿ*ilun* (2 + 4)[16]

The division and grouping of al-Urmawī's six cycles can be demonstrated as follows:

1.	*thaqīl al-awwal*	3 + 3 + 4 + 2 + 4 = 16 *naqras*
2.	*thaqīl al-thānī*	3 + 3 + 2 = 8
3.	*khafīf al-thaqīl*	2 + 1 + 1, or 1 + 1 + 2 = 4
4.	*thaqīl al-ramal*	4 + 4 + 2 + 2 + 2 + 2 + 2 + 2 + 4 = 24 (*Kitāb al-adwār*)
		4 + 2 + 4 + 2 + 4 + 2 + 4 + 2 = 24 (*Risāla al-Sharafiyya*)
5.	*ramal*	2 + 2 + 2 + 2 + 2 + 2 = 12
6.	*hazaj*	4 + 2 + 4 + 2 = 12

In describing the structure of a rhythmic cycle, al-Urmawī first mentions its number of *naqras* and subsequently marks them as necessarily stressed beats (*a'midat al-ḥarakāt*), variably articulated beats, and necessarily silent beats (*a'midat al-sakanāt*). He refers to the fundamental pattern (*żarb al-aṣl*) of several cycles consisting of two attacks within the cycle.[17]

While al-Urmawī states that Persian melodies were predominantly composed in *mużā'af al-ramal* (another term for *thaqīl al-ramal*), his successor, Qoṭb al-Din Shirāzi, claims that *thaqīl al-ramal*, especially the version mentioned in *Kitāb al-adwār*, was common only among Persians in earlier times.[18] They both mention *fākhti* as another rhythmic cycle favored by Persians.[19]

fākhtī (al-Urmawī)	4 + 2 + 4 + 4 + 2 + 4 = 20
fākhti (Qoṭb al-Din Shirāzi)	2 + 4 + 4 + 2 + 4 + 4 = 20
fākhti-ye zā'ed (an extended form)	2 + 4 + 4 + 4 + 2 + 4 + 4 + 4 = 28

In addition to the above cycles, Qoṭb al-Din Shirāzi also refers to the following four rhythmic cycles prevalent among practicing musicians who were his contemporaries.[20]

mokhammas	2 + 2 + 4 = 8
żarb-e rāst or *żarb-e aṣl*	2 + 2 + 2 + 2 + 4 = 12
chahār-żarb	8 + 4 + 4 + 4 + 4 = 24
torki (in theory)	3 + 3 + 4 + 4 + 3 + 3 = 20
(in practice)	2 + 2 + 2 1/3 + 2 1/3 + 2 + 2 = 12 [2/3][21]

In the same period, some urban centers from Baghdad to Bukhara seem to have developed distinctive rhythmic configurations or to have just given different names to rhythmic cycles introduced in Systematist tradition. ʿAlāʾ al-Din Bokhāri, a prominent contemporary of al-Urmawī, mentioned the term *oṣul* for the first time in reference to long and short rhythmic cycles. His typology for these cycles includes seven principal meters (*oṣul*, sing. *aṣl*) and seven spin-offs (*foruʿ*, sing. *farʿ*), the latter being introduced only as the faster (*saboktar*) versions of the same *oṣul*s: (1) *ṭavil*, (2) *ʿamud*, (3) *dō-yeki*, (4) *khafif*, (5) *thaqil*, (6) *arbāʿ*, (7) *eḥdāth*.[22]

The Timurid Period

In the first half of the fifteenth century, ʿAbd al-Qāder Marāghi treated the topic of rhythm in a more systematic way in all his treatises, dividing the chapter on *iqāʿ* into three sections: (1) rhythmic cycles that were invented in the past by his predecessors; (2) the predominant rhythmic cycles established among his contemporaries; and (3) rhythmic cycles that he invented himself.[23]

In the first section, he initially expounds upon definitions of rhythm and meter offered by his predecessors, especially al-Fārābī and al-Urmawī, while examining the six standard rhythmic cycles presented in *Kitāb al-adwār*. Marāghi mentions *varashān* as an alternative name for *thaqil al-avval* commonly used by Persian musicians.[24] He refers to *chanbar* as a subset of *hazaj* that was prevalent in Tabriz and predominantly played by *qavvālān* and *moghanniyān*. He also refers to *fākhti* as a cycle specifically used by Persians, yet he adds that, except for himself, other composers seldom wrote compositions in *fākhti*.[25]

In the second section, Marāghi introduces eight rhythmic cycles and their spin-offs that were practiced frequently in his own time in the composition of *nawbats*, *basiṭs*, *ʿamals*, *qawls*, and *ṣawts*. He clearly indicates that some of the rhythmic cycles already introduced in the Systematist tradition had been renamed by then:

1. *thaqil*: previously named *thaqil-e ramal*.
2. *khafif*: previously named *thaqil-e thāni*.
3. *chahār-żarb*[26]

24-beat cycle	4 (× 6) = 24
48-beat cycle	4 (× 12) = 48

4.	*torki-ye aṣl*	2 + 4 + 4 + 4 + 4 + 2 = 20
	far'-e torki-ye aṣl	4 + 4 + 2 = 10
	far'-e far'-e torki-ye aṣl	3 + 2 = 5
	old *torki-ye aṣl*	2 + 4 + 4 + 4 + 4 + 2 + 4 = 24
	torki-ye khafif	2 + 2 + 4 + 4 = 12
	torki-ye sari'	3 + 3 = 6
5.	*mokhammas-e kabir*	2 + 4 + 2 + 4 + 4 = 16
	mokhammas-e awsaṭ	3 + 3 + 2 = 8
	mokhammas-e ṣaghir	2 + 2 = 4
6.	*ramal*[27]	2 + 2 + 4 + 4 = 12
7.	*hazaj*[28] (old version)	4 + 2 + 4 + 2 = 12
	(in practice)	4 + 2 = 6
8.	*fākhti-ye kabir*	2 + 8 + 10 = 20
	fākhti-ye awsaṭ	2 + 4 + 4 = 10
	fākhti-ye ṣaghir	3 + 2 = 5

Finally, in the third section, Marāghi presents six rhythmic cycles that he invented himself during a long period while he was in the service of various rulers. The account of these rhythmic cycles can be summarized as follows:

1. *żarb al-fatḥ* (beats of conquest): 3 + 3 + 4 + 4 + 3 + 3 + 4 + 3 + 2 + 4 + 4 + 4 + 4 + 4 = 49
   He invented and wrote a composition in this rhythmic cycle when Ghiyāth al-Din Shahzāda conquered Baghdad in 1382.[29]
2. *dawr al-rabi'* (cycle of spring): 4 + 4 + 4 + 4 + 4 + 4 = 24
   He invented and wrote a composition in this rhythmic cycle in a courtly musical gathering held by Solṭān-Ḥosayn Jalāyer (r. 1377–1382) in the garden of the *dawlat-khāna* in Tabriz. Since it was in springtime, he named the cycle *dawr al-rabi'*.
3. *dawr-e shāh-żarb* (cycle of kingly beats): 4 + 3 + 2 + 2 + 3 + 4 + 2 + 2 + 3 + 3 + 2 = 30
   He invented and wrote a composition in this rhythmic cycle when he was in a boat in Baghdad with Solṭān-Aḥmad Jalāyer (r. 1382–1410). Marāghi arranged this rhythmic cycle in 30 beats so as to match the number of sailors who were in the boat.

4. *me'atayn* (cycle of 200 beats): 4 (× 50) = 200
   He invented and wrote a composition in this rhythmic cycle in a courtly musical gathering held by the prince Ghiyāth al-Din Moḥammad in the garden of *naqsh-e jahān* in Samarqand.
5. *dawr-e 'adl* (cycle of justice): 2 + 2 + 4 + 4 + 4 + 3 + 3 + 2 + 4 = 28
   He invented this rhythmic cycle in a courtly musical gathering of Shāhrokh (r. 1405–1447) in the garden of *zāghān* in Herat.
6. *qomriya*: 4 + 4 = 8
   He invented this rhythmic cycle based on the call of the *qomri* (European turtle dove) when he was in a courtly musical gathering in the service of Timur's grandson, Khalil Sultan (r. 1405–1411), in Khojand.[30]

Marāghi continues with the discussion of "entering a rhythmic cycle from various beats" and in doing so, he refers to durations in terms of poetic feet. These poetic feet can be described as follows:

naqra	short = 1 beat
sabab-e khafif	long = 2 beats
vatad-e majmu'	short-long = 3 beats
fāṣela-ye ṣoghrā	short-short-long = 4 beats

In the second half of the fifteenth century in Herat, Awbahi and Bannā'i both classified the rhythmic cycles into three groups: *theqāl* (*thaqil*s), *armāl* (*ramal*s), and *favākht* (*fākhti*s), and designated one cycle as the "reference" (*marja'*) for each group.[31]

Awbahi further referred to two long rhythmic cycles of *me'atayn* and *żarb al-fatḥ* invented by Marāghi and specified that *me'atayn* was a compound *oṣul* comprising three or four short cycles, including *mokhammas*, *varashān*, and others.[32] This suggests that other long *oṣul*s were presumably shaped as the result of combining rhythmic cycles of shorter length, a practice that clearly manifested itself later in an Ottoman rhythmic cycle called *zencîr* (lit. "chain"). In general, we could also assume that the invention and dissemination of long cycles largely began with Marāghi in the late fourteenth century, since other members of the Systematist school mostly expounded upon the standard set of six cycles introduced by al-Urmawī.

Another significant topic raised by both Marāghi and Awbahi is the *anāmel va kaf* (lit. "fingers and palm"), the clap pattern and hand gesture to count out a rhythmic cycle, a tradition which has long been practiced in Indian music and is discussed in technical treatises as early as Bharata's *Nāṭyaśāstra*. Marāghi describes the topic in reference to the rhythmic cycle of *chahār-żarb*, as follows:

> The *chahār-żarb* is a cycle invented by recent musicians and as we have heard, its inventor was Moḥammad-Shāh Robābi. The duration (*zamān*) of this cycle equals the duration of *thaqil-e ramal*; they are both twenty-four *naqra*s but their attack patterns (*żarb*) are different. While *thaqil-e ramal* has eight attacks, *chahār-żarb* has only four attacks. *Chahār-żarb* can be outlined as six *faṣela*s (i.e., *tananan*). The first attack is placed on the *t* of the first *faṣela*, the second attack on the *t* of the fourth *faṣela*, the third attack on the *t* of the fifth *faṣela*, and the fourth attack on the second *n* of the fifth *faṣela*. By moving fingers and palm one can exhibit *faṣela*s and further stress their attack patterns. We mark the indication of attacks as "*m*" and the indication of fingers (*anāmel*) as "*a*" in the following pattern:

tananan	*tananan*	*tananan*	*tananan*	*tananan*	*tananan*[33]
m a a	*a a*	*a a*	*m*	*m m*	*a a*

Awbahi also explains the time keeping of the twenty-four-beat *chahār-żarb* through hand gestures as follows:

> [Musicians] have derived *chahār-żarb-e ṣaghir* from *możā'af al-ramal* with some modifications. It consists of twenty-four [beats] including one *faṣela*, one *sabab*, one six-beat time unit, four *sabab*s and one more *faṣela* in the following order:

tananan	*tan*	*tanananananan*	*tan*	*tan*	*tan*	*tan*	*tanan*
4	2	6	4	*khinsir*	*binṣir*	*wusṭā*	*sabbāba*

> The last four attacks should be kept with the fifth finger (*khinṣir*), the ring finger (*binṣir*), the middle finger (*wusṭā*) and the index finger (*sabbāba*), respectively, and the first four attacks should be kept with clapping, as if they are the main four attacks (*żarb-e aṣl*s). Hence the cycle is called *chahār-żarb*.[34]

In describing *żarbayn*, the practice of combining two rhythmic cycles concurrently in a musical performance, Marāghi asserts that an adept musician should be capable of keeping the rhythm of each cycle with one hand.[35]

As early as the thirteenth century, a normative rhythmic cycle among practicing musicians and music theorists was recognized as *żarb-e aṣl* or *aṣl* (lit. "original rhythm") and its variants, spin-offs, and faster versions were considered as *żarb-e far'*s (lit. "derivative rhythms").[36] At the outset, it is likely that only the *żarb-e aṣl*s were called *oṣul*, and, indeed, the term *oṣul*, denoting rhythmic cycle(s), originated from the *żarb-e aṣl*s. Gradually, however, *oṣul* was used loosely by practicing musicians to refer to all individual rhythmic cycles including both *aṣl* or *far'*.[37]

From the thirteenth to the sixteenth century, it seems that musicians who had a notably freer approach to theoretical structures or perhaps were not involved in courtly musical practices would have used a broad and less elaborate classification of metres. In a few Persian musical treatises, *żorub* are generalized as *yek-żarb*, *dō-żarb*, and *se-żarb* as in the following remark in a fourteenth-century musical text:

> Know that metre (*żarb*) is of several types: it could be either *yek-żarb*, *dō-żarb* or *se-żarb*. In the presence of the elderly, one has to play *yek-żarb* for they enjoy it the most. In the presence of the youth, one has to play *dō-żarb*, which is more commensurate to their circumstances and states of being. As long as the musician (*moṭreb*) follows this course (*ṭariqa*), [the music] would be greatly enjoyable.[38]

Categorization of rhythmic cycles and meters continued in the fifteenth century, as, for example, in the following late fifteenth-century musical treatise, which adopts the categories of *thaqil* and *khafif*. While *thaqil* seems to have encompassed the classical rhythmic cycles used in court music, *khafif* appears to comprise some meters, such as *rāh-e kord*, that were presumably employed in semi-classical or regional contexts.[39]

> Know that from *thaqil*, which is a *żarb-e aṣl*, nine other metres are produced: *zarafshān*, *tork-żarb*, *samā'iya*, *fākhta*, *sarandāz*, *chahār-żarb*, *bokhāri*, and *hazaj*. One of the other *żarb-e aṣl*s is *khafif*, from which nine other metres are produced: *ramal-e qayṣar*, *ramal-e ṭavil*, *chahār-żarb*, *se-żarb*, *rāh-e kord*, *mokhammas-e khafifa żarb*, *chahār-żarb-e khafifa*, *żāyeni* (?).[40]

Accounts of Rhythm in Safavid Treatises

The author of *Nasim-e ṭarab* is the first music theorist in the sixteenth century to provide an inventory of the *oṣul*s probably known in the provincial court of Gilan. While he does not provide a specific classification of rhythms, he enumerates about thirty-five rhythmic cycles and attributes the invention of some *oṣul*s to celebrated musicians of the past.[41]

The early sixteenth-century *Taqsīm al-naghamāt* presents seventeen cycles of *oṣul*s and divides them into three main groups. The first group is categorized as the old set of *oṣul*s invented by the antecedent master musicians. The second group contains five cycles whose inventions are ascribed to al-Urmawī and his disciples, including 'Ali Setā'i, 'Ali Robābi, Ostād Tanparvar, Ostād Ruḥparvar, and Ḥasan 'Udi. Finally, the last group of *oṣul*s is attributed to 'Abd al-Qāder Marāghi.[42]

Dawra Beg Karāmi's account of rhythm in the second half of the sixteenth century, though similar to that of *Taqsīm al-naghamāt*, is not as thorough. He introduces Nakisā, a pre-Islamic legendary musician, as the founder of metrics (*naẓm*), while opening the chapter on rhythm with a discussion of the perception and rendition of *oṣul*s by practicing musicians. Karāmi mentions the five *oṣul*s of *hazaj*, *awfar*, *dō-yek*, *torki-żarb*, and *mokhammas* as the fundamental rhythmic cycles that had been used in core compositional genres (*madār-e taṣnif*) for a long period of time. Later on, he adds that Ṣafī al-Dīn al-Urmawī, 'Ali Ruḥparvar, Ḥasan 'Udi, and 'Abd al-Qāder Marāghi made significant contributions to the development of rhythms and the establishment of the canonical seventeen cycles of *oṣul*. Nonetheless, Karāmi only refers to sixteen cycles and fails to indicate their structures. He also specifies some rhythmic cycles that he and his contemporaries invented that were not considered part of the canonical seventeen cycles.[43]

Mir Ṣadr al-Din Moḥammad, the other late sixteenth-century music theorist, goes on to enumerate the *oṣul*s and comment on their etymology, origin, and historical development, but like Karāmi, he does not specify their number of beats and internal structures.[44] He claims that for a long time, during which various rhythmic cycles had still not been invented, the rhythmic system was based only on the *oṣul* of *varashān*. He mentions *chanbar*, *torki-żarb*, and *mokhammas* as the common rhythmic cycles and opines that *torki-żarb* was one of the strange inventions at the most advanced level of performance practice. According to him, *dō-yek* was well-matched with most of the *oṣul*s and the majority of prominent *pishraw*s were composed in it. *Awfar*, which was better known as *rāh-e bālā*, was less respected (*ḥaqirtar*) in relation to other cycles, but it is one of the uniquely pleasant and charming rhythmic cycles.

From the seventeenth century, Safavid musicians adhered to a system of representing the *oṣul*s that introduced each cycle by the pattern and number of attacks. In this system, which seems to have been adopted from Ottoman music culture, characteristic patterns of various attacks are exhibited, but their durations are not indicated, and hence the rhythmic values of the cycles cannot be identified.

An anonymous musical treatise in the codex of Amir Khān Gorji is probably the earliest text that gives the structure of seven cycles based on this system.[45] The author further introduces twenty-one cycles of *oṣul*s and also mentions the number of beats or probably attacks (*żarb*s) in each cycle. In the same codex, Āqā Mo'men Moṣannef's account of rhythm is very brief, and he names only the seventeen cycles of *oṣul*s.[46] Finally, Amir Khān Gorji reiterates that the canonical set of *oṣul*s consisted of seventeen cycles, but he emphasizes that among the singers (*ḥoffāẓ*) of his time, nineteen cycles were in common use. He further introduces the drum patterns of eighteen cycles, and while he overlooks the patterns of *samāʿi* and *farʿ* in the above nineteen *oṣul*s, he adds *nim-thaqil* as a new cycle to the list.[47]

Amir Khān offers four possible strokes for the rhythmic patterns: *dik* (1 *żarb*/attack); *dak* (1 *żarb*/ attack); *daka* (2 *żarb*s/attacks); and *dikak* (3 *żarb*s/attacks). *Dik* was obviously the low center and *dak*, was the high rim strokes—two onomatopoeic syllables that later appeared in nineteenth-century Persian music as *dom* and *bak*.[48]

The *Bahjat al-ruḥ* is another notable musical treatise of the seventeenth century that classifies the rhythmic cycles into two lists of twenty-seven *oṣul*s. In the first list, the author gives the number of attacks (*żarabāt*, sing. *żarba*) for each rhythmic cycle, and in the second list, he identifies their internal structure by using a rhythmic notation called *tahajjī al-adwār* ("articulation of cycles"), that resembles for the most part the non-textual syllables (*naqrāt*) used in some sections of Safavid vocal compositions.[49]

Two more fragments outlining the qualitative drum strokes have survived from the turn of the seventeenth century. The first fragment is appended to the end of the musical treatise of Ḥājj Ḥosayn Ẓohri, a native of Isfahan who moved to India and dedicated his musical treatise to Aurangzeb (r. 1658–1707). In this fragment (referred to henceforth as AḤẒ), the attack patterns of twenty-five *oṣul*s are represented beginning with the long rhythmic cycles and ending with short rhythmic patterns. The articulation of onomatopoeic syllables in AḤẒ resembles that of the anonymous treatise in the codex of Amir Khān Gorji and is slightly different from the articulation of syllables employed by Amir Khān himself.[50] The second fragment is included in the middle of a copy of *Resāla-ye Karāmiya* (referred to henceforth as MRK). This musical text is not dated, but judging from other treatises in the same collection, it seems to have been copied in the beginning of the eighteenth century (Figure 5.1).[51]

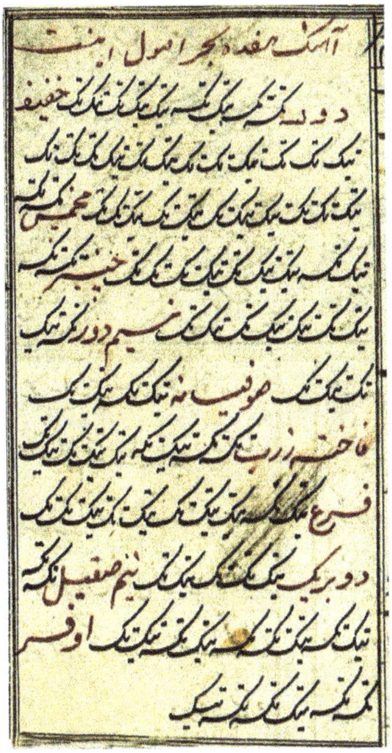

Figure 5.1 The *dik dak* drum patterns in a late Safavid musical text. University of Tehran (Tehran) MS 2591, f. 407.

In addition to the account of rhythmic cycles in musical treatises, two prominent collections of *taṣnif* have also survived from the seventeenth century that exhibit the structure of a variety of court compositions in this period. The first collection is the compositions of Āqā Mo'men Moṣannef, the leading court composer of Isfahan in the first half of the seventeenth century. The second collection contains a series of *taṣnif*s made by prominent composers of the seventeenth century and gathered together later by Amir Khān Gorji. Āqā Mo'men uses the word *taṣnif* for all his compositions and while he mentions their titles and modes, he does not indicate anything about their rhythmic structure. It is also evident that he has a distinctively loose and free approach to theoretical structures. Amir Khān is more systematic in his representation of compositions, and documents all the *taṣnif*s primarily based on their rhythmic cycles. Beginning with long *oṣul*s, he presents the compositions in two separate parts. The first part contains an anthology of respected *kār* and *'amal* compositions, including four in *żarb al-fatḥ*, eight in *thaqil*, nine in *nim-thaqil*, twelve in *mokhammas*, and ten in *khafif*. The second part, which appears only in the Bibliothèque nationale manuscript, is seemingly a lighter repertoire, marked for the most part as *taṣnif*s and including twenty-eight compositions in *dō-bar-yek*, sixteen compositions in *nim-dawr*, three compositions in *dawr*, and, finally, one composition in *ravāni*.[52] Judging from the number of vocal compositions in each rhythmic cycle, we may assume that *dō-yek* (or *dō-bar-yek*), *nim-dawr*, and *mokhammas* were the predominant *oṣul*s in the composition of *taṣnif*s throughout the seventeenth century.

Table 5.1 The rhythmic cycles mentioned by Safavid music theorists throughout the sixteenth and seventeenth centuries

Taqsīm al-naghamāt	Nasimi	Karāmi	Mir Ṣadr al-Din	Āqā Mo'men	Amir Khān Gorji
1. *żarb al-qadim*					
2. *fākhta-ye kabir*	*				
3. *shāhnāma*	*				
4. *khᵛājak*	*				
5. *awsaṭ*	*	*			
6. *hazaj*	*	*			

Taqsīm al-naghamāt	Nasimi	Karāmi	Mir Ṣadr al-Din	Āqā Mo'men	Amir Khān Gorji
7. ***me'atayn***		*	*		
8. ***chahār-żarb***	*	*	*	*	
10. *awfar*	*	*		*	1. *awfar*
11. *dō-yek*	*	*	*	*dō-bar-yek*	2. *dō-bar-yek*
12. *torki-żarb*	*	*	*	*tork-żarb*	3. *tork-żarb*
13. *mokhammas*	*	*	*	*	4. *mokhammas*
14. *thaqil*	*	*	*	*	5. *thaqil*
15. *khafif*	2 *khafif*s	*	*	*	6. *khafif*
16. *varafshān*	*varafshān*	*barafshān*	*varafshān*	*barafshān*	7. *barafshān*
17. *żarb al-fatḥ*	*	*	*	*	8. *żarb al-fatḥ*
9. *ramal*	*ramal*	*	*		9. *ramal-e ṣaghir*
	ramal-e ṭavil				10. *ramal-e kabir*
	*	*fākhta*	*	*fākhta-żarb*	**11. *fākhta-żarb***
	nim-thaqil	*		*	**12. *nim-thaqil***
		chanbar	*	*	**13. *chanbar***
	samāʿi	*	*samāʿi-ye gerān*	*	**14. *samāʿi***
				dawr	**15. *dawr***
		pir-e jamāli	*pir-e jamāli*	*nim-dawr*	**16. *nim-dawr***
	2 *ravān*s	*ravān awfar*	*dawr-e ravān*	*ravāni*	**17. *ravāni***
	ḥarbi		*		**18. *ḥarbi***
					19. *ṣufiyāna*
				farʿ	**20. *farʿ***
	2 *beshārat*s *moḥajjal ḥejāzi*				
	oṣul-e ʿamal *solṭān*	*			
	orghushtak 2 *faraḥ*s				
		żarb al-moluk	*		
		żarb al-aṣl *dawr-e hendi* *żarb al-ʿeshq*	*		
			mojammar *sarandāz* *dawr-e shāhi*		

Table 5.2 The rhythmic cycles mentioned in the Anonymous Treatise and the *Bahjat al-ruḥ* and comparing them with the accounts of the first and last Safavid musical treatises

Taqsīm al-naghamāt	Anonymous Treatise	*Bahjat al-ruḥ*	Amir Khān Gorji
1. *hazaj*	*	*	
2. *żarb al-qadim*	*	*	
3. *awsaṭ*	*	*	
4. *ramal*	*	*	
5. *shāhnāma*	*	*	
6. *khᵛājak*			
7. *chahār-żarb*		*	
8. *me'atayn*	*	*	
9. *awfar*	*	*	1. *awfar*
10. *dō-yek*	*dō-o yek*	*	2. *dō-bar-yek*
11. *torki-żarb*	*tork-żarb*	*	3. *tork-żarb*
12. *mokhammas*	*	*	4. *mokhammas*
13. *thaqil*	*	*	5. *thaqil*
14. *khafif*	*	*	6. *khafif*
15. *varafshān*	*barafshān*	*barafshān*	7. *barafshān*
16. *żarb al-fatḥ*	*	*	8. *żarb al-fatḥ*
			9. *ramal-e ṣaghir*
	kabir		**10. *ramal-e kabir***
17. *fākhta-ye kabir*	*fākhta-żarb*	*	**11. *fākhta-żarb***
	nim-thaqil	*	**12. *nim-thaqil***
	chanbar	*	**13. *chanbar***
		samā'i	**14. *samā'i***
	dawr	*	**15. *dawr***
	nim-dawr	*nim-dawr*	**16. *nim-dawr***
		dawr-e ravān	**17. *ravāni***
			18. *ḥarbi*
			19. *ṣufiyāna*
	far'	*	**20. *far'***
	żarb al-moluk	*	
		panj-żarb	
		moqaddam	
		ākel	

The Development of Rhythmic Cycles in the Safavid Period

As previously noted, Systematist music theorists introduced a standard set of six rhythmic cycles that were more elaborate than their ninth- to eleventh-century precursors and were presented through the quantitative *atānin* mnemonic patterns (that is, *tan tanan, tananan*). This set of six *iqā*ʿs, together with other cycles that were invented during the thirteenth to fifteenth centuries by practicing musicians and composers, including Marāghi, had a discernible number of beats and stress patterns in their cycles and regulated the rhythmic element of the majority of urban compositions in this period. Nonetheless, the old rhythmic system of the early Islamic period, which included three-, four-, five-, and six-beat meters was not entirely eclipsed by the new set of rhythmic cycles and continued to be employed in at least some musical contexts.

Toward the end of the fifteenth century, Awbahi mentioned twenty-four rhythmic cycles and classified them into three categories: *theqāl*, *armāl*, and *favākht*. The first category, *theqāl*, consisted of cycles of 4, 8, 16, and 32 beats; the second category, *armāl*, consisted of cycles of 6, 12, 24, 48, and 96 beats; and the third category, *favākht*, contained cycles of asymmetrical meters consisting of 5, 10, and 20 beats. Awbahi named the shortest cycle in each group the "reference cycle" (*marja*ʿ) and indicated that all of the long cycles could fit into *theqāl*, *armāl*, and *favākht*.

> It has to be known that among the above-mentioned rhythmic cycles, when a cycle is twice as long as the other cycle, either the short cycle can be regarded [as the measure,] or the long cycle. Hence a cycle of *khafif* can be measured as two cycles of *mokhammas* and vice versa; or a cycle of *torki-żarb-e aṣl* can be measured as two cycles of *torki-ye sari*ʿ and vice versa. Therefore, if the number of beats in a rhythmic cycle is divisible by four, it can be held as multiple cycles of *mokhammas-e ṣaghir* [4-beat cycle]. If the number of beats in a rhythmic cycle is divisible by three, it can be held as multiple cycles of *khafif-e ramal* or *awfar* [6-beat cycle]. If the number of beats in a rhythmic cycle is divisible by five, it can be held as multiple cycles of *fākhti-e ṣaghir* [5-beat cycle].[53]

These groupings are seemingly correlated with the three broad metrical categories of *dō-żarb*, *se-żarb*, and *lang*/*aksāk* (Persian and Turkish terms meaning "limping") that were mentioned in some non-Systematist musical treatises. While *theqāl* and *dō-żarb* were the simple duple and quadruple meters, *armāl* and *se-żarb* were the triple and compound duple meters that were typically counted in three or six, and *favākht* (*fākhti* and *torki-żarb*) was the asymmetrical or syncopated rhythmic cycle. In the late fifteenth and early sixteenth centuries, this classification appeared in a few other musical sources as well, for example, in this passage from an anonymous treatise, which calls to mind a similar passage from the fourteenth-century treatise cited earlier.

> Know that performing the *żarb* is of many types such as *yek-żarb* and *dō-żarb*. One has to play *yek-żarb* in the presence of the elderly, *dō-żarb* in the presence of the youth, and *se-żarb* in the presence of youngsters. This last group enjoy the *se-żarb*, for metres in the fast tempos (*żarb-e khafif*) are more compatible with their humors. *Żarb* is the marking of beats independent [of musical instruments] and the difference between *żarb* and *oṣul* is that the former is followed by a pause.[54]

In another late fifteenth-century musical text, the author first mentions the seventeen rhythmic cycles and subsequently adds:

> Know that following the seventeen cycles of *oṣul*, other *oṣul*s emerged to which many compositions were set. Among them were *se-żarb*, *dō-żarb* and *rajaz-e khafif*, etc. Numerous rhythmic cycles are also in India and likewise there are many rhythmic cycles known as *khᵛārazmi* but writing about all these would prolong the subject.[55]

For the most part, Safavid musical treatises mention seventeen or twenty-four cycles of *oṣul* that governed the rhythmic structure of vocal and instrumental compositions. But unlike modal entities, neither the lists of *oṣul*s nor their rhythmic patterns are consistent among the sources. This inconsistency might derive from various factors. First, in most cases, there is no reliable manuscript or scrupulous critical edition of these musical treatises, hence the outline of rhythmic cycles in these texts could contain omissions. Second, musicians of various regions may have practiced their own versions of the cycles. And, third, one should consider the possibility of musicians having had differing perceptions of how the beats should be counted, or the attacks and structure of a given rhythmic cycle discerned. The absence of an accurate system of articulating rhythmic patterns and the duration of attacks and rests adds further complications to these problems.

A few essential points can be made about the *oṣul*s in this period. First, the concepts of *żarb-e aṣl* and *far'* were no longer emphasized by Safavid music theorists, yet some less prominent *oṣul*s are mentioned as being derived from the primary ones. For example, Mir Ṣadr al-Din Moḥammad states that *ḥāvi* was similar to *żarb al-fatḥ* except that it had six fewer beats; *sarandāz* arose from *mokhammas*, and *żarb al-moluk* was identical to *fākhta-ye kabir* to the extent that there was no difference between them. Furthermore, some rhythmic cycles were associated with particular genres and forms. The long *oṣuls* of *żarb al-fatḥ*, *thaqil*, *khafif*, and *nim-thaqil* were mainly used in compositions of *kār* and *'amal*, *dō-yek* was a typical cycle for *pishraw*, and *mokhammas* was the *oṣul par excellence* for *naqsh*. Finally, from the second half of the sixteenth century, music theorists began to classify *oṣul*s into two categories of art and *naqqāra-khāna* music. This grouping further allows us to identify the *naqqāra-khāna* cycles in the preceding periods as well.

Oṣuls in Art Music

The account of rhythm in the sixteenth and seventeenth centuries is not as systematic as in the fifteenth century, hence it is rather difficult to detect a pattern of change or consistency in the development of rhythmic cycles in this period. The two early sixteenth-century musical treatises *Nasim-e ṭarab* and *Taqsīm al-naghamāt* still use the *atānin* mnemonic devices to delineate patterns of *oṣul*. Twelve cycles of *oṣul* are common to both treatises, but only five cycles share the same patterns and number of beats. In the second half of the sixteenth century, Karāmi and Mir Ṣadr al-Din Moḥammad both named certain *oṣul*s and commented on their etymology, origin, and historical development, but they did not specify their rhythmic patterns. Finally, five seventeenth-century texts, including the codex of Amir Khān Gorji, present differing listings and patterns of *oṣul*s, employing mostly variant *dik dak* qualitative drum strokes, though they all fail to indicate the time value of the cycles.

A few significant attempts have been made to examine the time value and stress patterns of the *oṣul*s in the treatise of Amir Khān Gorji by way of comparison with Ottoman sources such as 'Ali Ufuki (d. 1677) and Demetrius Cantemir (d. 1723).[56] Nevertheless, there are no conventional *dik dak* syllables for every specific *oṣul*, nor is the concept of "cycle" overly emphasized among the Safavid sources. Therefore, one might assume that standard patterns and a fixed number of beats were probably not essential features in their identifications—in contrast to the Systematist tradition. Likewise, it is not clear whether these *dik dak* syllables were commonly memorized and used by composers and instrumentalists alike or whether they were only played on a drum. To sum up, exactly how the concept of *oṣul* was perceived in this period by various types of musicians—composers, instrumentalists, and drummers—remains unclear. Nonetheless, many parallels existed between Persian and Ottoman musical traditions in the nomenclature and structure of rhythmic cycles in the second half of the seventeenth century. While many rhythmic cycles were recognized and practiced with exactly the same pattern in both traditions, some *oṣuls*, for example, *awfar*, seem to have been practiced differently. A few other *oṣuls*, for example, *dawr*, were performed exclusively in Persian music. The account of rhythm in Ottoman sources is more detailed and can elucidate some of the problems that existed in the representation of rhythmic cycles in Persian sources. The following are the major rhythmic cycles discussed in Safavid musical treatises:

1. *Ṣufiyāna*

Ṣufiyāna most likely emerged in the second half of the seventeenth century. Only the treatises of Amir Khān Gorji, AḤẒ, and MRK provide the stroke patterns of *ṣufiyāna*, and their representations are all identical to that of Cantemir's pattern of four-beat *ṣufiyān*:

düm . tek tek	Cantemir
dik Ø da ka	Amir Khān Gorji
dek Ø ka ka	AḤẒ
tik Ø ta ka | *tik Ø tak Ø*	MRK

2. *Kh*^{v}*ājak*

Kh^{v}*ājak* is a rhythmic cycle inexplicably attributed to Kh^{v}āja 'Abd al-Qāder Marāghi in both *Nasim-e ṭarab* and *Taqsīm al-naghamāt.*[57] While each treatise offers a slightly different pattern for this cycle, the number of beats in both texts is twenty-six.

2 + 4 + 2 + 4 + 3 + 3 + 2 + 4 + 2 = 26	*Nasim-e ṭarab*
2 + 4 + 2 + 4 + 2 + 4 + 4 + 4 = 26	*Taqsīm al-naghamāt*

3. *Shāhnāma*

Shāhnāma is certainly a sixteenth-century invention that was strangely attributed to Marāghi in both *Nasim-e ṭarab* and *Taqsīm al-naghamāt.*

shāhnāma 4 + 4 + 4 + 2 = 14 *Nasim-e ṭarab* and *Taqsīm al-naghamāt*

4. *Awfar*

Awbahi is the first writer who refers to *awfar* (3 + 3 = 6) as the main rhythmic cycle in the category of *ramals*. Kawkabi, Nasimi, and the author of *Taqsīm al-naghamāt* subsequently outline *awfar* as a cycle of six beats. Moreover, Awbahi, and his two Safavid successors, Karāmi and Mir Ṣadr al-Din Moḥammad, indicate that *awfar* was predominantly known among lay musicians and the public as *rāh-e bālā.*[58] Therefore, Mir Ṣadr al-Din Moḥammad's description of *rāh-e bālā* as a "fairly simple, but uniquely pleasant, charming, and highly popular and celebrated *oṣul*" may reasonably suggest that by *rāh-e bālā* they were referring to the brisk and energetic 6/8 meter which has long been the cornerstone of many dance tunes in Persia and is still known to this date in the music of Central Asia as *żarb-e awfar.*[59]

In the late seventeenth century, Amir Khān Gorji, AḤẒ, and MRK also present the stroke patterns of *awfar*, which can fit perfectly into a cycle of six beats. The pattern given by AḤẒ resembles the pattern of the six-beat cycle practiced in nineteenth-century Persian music.

dik	*daka*	*daka*	*dik*	*dik*	*dak*	Amir Khān Gorji
dek	*deka*	*deka*	*dek*	*kā*	Ø	AḤẒ
taka	*taka*	*tik*	*taka*	*taka*	*tik*	MRK

While Persian sources all indicate that *awfar* was a cycle of six beats in Persia and Central Asia, it was defined as a cycle of nine beats in the Ottoman tradition.[60]

5. *Ravāni*

At the beginning of the sixteenth century, Nasimi presents two cycles of *ravān-e kabir* (2 + 2 + 2 + 2 = 8) and *ravān-e ṣaghir* (2 + 2 + 2 = 6). Later, Āqā Mo'men Moṣannef declares that *ravāni* and *awfar* are the same rhythmic cycle, except that *ravāni* was rendered faster. Karāmi also refers to this *oṣul* as *ravān-e awfar* (smooth and fast *awfar*) and clearly indicates that it was the fast version of *awfar* that was known as *rāh-e bālā*. During the seventeenth century, *ravān-e ṣaghir* or *ravān-e awfar* began to be called *ravāni*. Amir Khān and the author of AḤẒ both present the same pattern for it.

dik	*da*	*ka*	*dik*	*dak*	*Ø*	Amir Khān Gorji
dek	*a*	*ka*	*dek*	*ā*	*Ø*	AḤẒ

6. *Dō-yek (dō-bar-yek)*

Two different rhythmic patterns for *dō-yek* are presented by *Nasim-e ṭarab* (4 + 4 = 8) and *Taqsīm al-naghamāt* (2 + 4 + 4 = 10). Karāmi and Mir Ṣadr al-Din Moḥammad also mention this *oṣul* without presenting its rhythmic pattern. Karāmi enumerates *dō-yek* among the fundamental rhythmic cycles used in the core compositional genres, and Mir Ṣadr al-Din Moḥammad refers to it as being well-matched with the majority of *oṣul*s, while emphasizing its conspicuous function in composition of *pishraws*. *Dō-yek* was the predominant rhythmic cycle of Persian *pishraws* in Cantemir's collection and *taṣnifs* in Amir Khān's codex.[61] The eight-beat *dō-yek* seems to have been the more pervasive and authentic version:

düm tek . tek düm . tek .	Cantemir
dik dak Ø dak dik Ø dak Ø	Amir Khān Gorji

7. *Mokhammas*

Marāghi mentions three cycles of *mokhammas*:

mokhammas-e ṣaghir	2 + 2 = 4
mokhammas-e awsaṭ	3 + 3 + 2 = 8
mokhammas-e kabir	2 + 4 + 2 + 4 + 4 = 16

Awbahi equates *mokhammas-e ṣaghir* with *khafif al-thaqil* and defines it as the reference cycle in the category of *thaqils*. In *Nasim-e ṭarab* and *Taqsīm al-naghamāt* the cycle of *mokhammas* emerges as a twenty-beat *oṣul* (5 + 5 + 5 + 5 = 20) with no apparent affinity with Timurid versions. Mir Ṣadr al-Din Moḥammad does not mention the structure of *mokhammas*, yet his reference to *chahār-żarb* as a derivative of *mokhammas* indicates that he is referring to the Timurid *mokhammas-e ṣaghir* (that is, a quadruple meter), not the version outlined in *Nasim-e ṭarab* and *Taqsim al-naghamāt.*

A comparison between the accounts of Amir Khān Gorji and Cantemir shows that the former is presenting a sixteen-beat cycle:

düm teke düm tek düm düm tek teke düm tek teke düm tek . teke teke Cantemir
dik daka dik dak dik dik dak daka dik daka daka dik dak Ø daka daka Amir Khān Gorji

We can conclude that the basic concept of *mokhammas* was a quadruple meter, referred to as *mokhammas-e ṣaghir*. *Mokhammas* was also known as a rhythmic cycle of sixteen beats, sometimes called *mokhammas-e kabir.*

8. *Fākhta*

Marāghi, Awbahi, and Bannā'i all offer three cycles of *fākhta-ye ṣaghir* (3 + 2 = 5), *fākhta-ye awsaṭ* (2 + 4 + 4 = 10), and *fākhta-ye kabir* (2 + 8 + 10 = 20). Fatḥ Allāh al-Shirwānī (d. 1453), a music theorist of Iranian origin, uses a slightly different labeling and calls the five-beat cycle *fākhti al-aṣghar* (3 + 2 = 5) and the seven-beat cycle *fākhti al-ṣaghir* (2 + 2 + 3 = 7). In the first half of the sixteenth century, *Nasim-e ṭarab* and *Taqsīm al-naghamāt* introduce *fākhta-ye kabir* as a seven-beat cycle (3 + 2 + 2 = 7) and ascribe its invention to Marāghi. Mir Ṣadr al-Din Moḥammad's comment that the difference between *fākhta-ye ṣaghir* (known as *fākhta żarb*) and *fākhta-ye kabir* was only two *żarb*s perhaps indicates that he recognized them as cycles of five and seven beats, respectively. He also states that *fākhta żarb* was a distinct rhythmic cycle that could not easily match with any other *oṣul*. During the seventeenth century, *fākhta żarb* appears in the codex of Amir Khān Gorji and can be compared with Cantemir's cycle of ten beats.

düm	*.*	*tek*	*.*	*.*	*düm*	*tek*	*.*	*teke*	*teke*	Cantemir
dik	*dik*	*dak*	*Ø*	*Ø*	*dik*	*dak*	*Ø*	*daka*	*daka*	Amir Khān Gorji

In summary, the basic concept of *fakhta* in the fifteenth and sixteenth centuries was the five- and seven-beat cycles, but during the seventeenth century, it was mostly rendered as a cycle of ten beats.

9. *Barafshān*

In the early fifteenth century, the term *varashān* was largely used by Persian musicians referring to *thaqil al-avval*. Toward the end of fifteenth century, Awbahi, in addition to the sixteen-beat *varashān*, mentions an eighteen-beat version called *varashān-e zā'ed*. The fourteen-beat version that is introduced in *Nasim-e ṭarab* and *Taqsīm al-naghamāt* seems to have been a sixteenth-century development. In fact, if we consider *aṣl-e varashān* (a term used by Mir Ṣadr al-Din Moḥammad) as the sixteen-beat cycle and *varashān-e zā'ed* as the eighteen-beat cycle, the fourteen-beat *varashān/barafshān* could be well-justified as the *varashān-e ṣaghir*.

varashān-e zā'ed	3 + 3 + 4 + 2 + 4 + 2 = 18	Awbahi
fifteenth-century *varashān*	3 + 3 + 4 + 2 + 4 = 16	Marāghi and Awbahi
sixteenth-century *varashān*	3 + 3 + 4 + 4 = 14	*Nasim-e ṭarab* and *Taqsim al-naghamāt*

The comparison of the accounts of Amir Khān Gorji and AḤẒ with that of Cantemir shows that the Safavid authors were outlining a cycle of fourteen beats.

düm . tek düm . tek düm . düm tek düm düm tek . teke teke	Cantemir
dik Ø dak dik Ø dak dik Ø dak Ø da ka dik Ø dak Ø	Amir Khān
dek Ø ka dek Ø ka dek Ø kā Ø de ka dek Ø kā Ø	AḤẒ

10. *Torki-żarb*

Torki-żarb is mentioned for the first time by Qoṭb al-Din Shirāzi who recognized that the cycle was defined differently in theory and practice, and in practice the duration of some beats was more extended.

3 + 3 + 4 + 4 + 3 + 3 = 20	(in theory)
2 + 2 + 2 [1/3] + 2 [1/3] + 2 + 2 = 12 [2/3]	(in practice)

Marāghi introduces the pattern of *torki* (*żarb-e aṣl*) as a twenty-beat cycle, but emphasizes that its ten-beat faster version, *far'-e torki-ye aṣl*, was also popular.

Awbahi classifies *torki-ye sariʿ* as the reference cycle in the category of *favākht*, indicating that this *oṣul* had an asymmetrical and syncopated structure.

torki (*żarb-e aṣl*)	2 + 4 + 4 + 4 + 4 + 2 = 20	Marāghi
farʿ-e torki-ye aṣl	4 + 4 + 2 = 10	Marāghi
torki (*żarb-e aṣl*)	2 + 3 + 2 + 3 + 2 + 3 + 2 + 3 = 20	Awbahi
torki-ye sariʿ	2 + 3 + 2 + 3 = 10	Awbahi

Safavid music theorists present differing rhythmic patterns for *torki-żarb*. Most theorists, however, describe its cycle as consisting of two symmetrical halves, each with asymmetrical or limping subdivisions.

3 + 3 + 4	+	4 + 3 + 3 = 20	Shirāzi
2 + 2 + 2 [1/3]	+	2 [1/3] + 2 + 2 = 12 [2/3]	Shirāzi
2 + 4 + 4	+	4 + 4 + 2 = 20	Marāghi
2 + 3	+	2 + 3 = 10	Awbahi
2 + 4	+	4 + 2 = 12	Nasimi
dik dik dak daka daka		*dik daka dik dik dak*	Amir Khān Gorji
kā ka ka dekkā Ø		*dek dekkā dek dek Ø*	AḤẒ

It seems evident that *torki-żarb* had a complex pattern and that music theorists had difficulty in delineating its cycle properly. Awbahi quotes Marāghi in saying that explaining the pattern (*adā*ʾ) of *torki-żarb* was much more difficult than explaining any other *oṣul*s and that no explanation ever did justice to the actual performing pattern (*navākht*).[62] Likewise, Mir Ṣadr al-Din Moḥammad opines that *torki-żarb* was the strangest invention at the most advanced level of musical performance.

11. *Nim-thaqil*

Awbahi is the first writer who mentions *nim-thaqil* (4 + 4 + 2 + 6 + 8 = 24) and classifies it in the category of *ramals*.[63] In the beginning of the sixteenth century, Nasimi outlines *nim-thaqil* as a cycle of ten beats (2 + 2 + 3 + 3 = 10). *Nim-thaqil* is later mentioned in the anonymous treatise included in Amir Khān's codex and the treatise of Āqā Mo'men, but it is in Amir Khān's treatise that we find its pattern and number of attacks. The pattern presented by Amir

Khān corresponds exactly with the pattern of twenty-four beats outlined by Cantemir. The patterns presented by AḤẒ and MRK also correspond with those of Amir Khān and Cantemir except that AḤẒ and MRK mark the beginning of the cycle from the seventh beat.

düm . te ke düm . te ke te ke düm . te ke düm . tek . . . te ke te ke	Cantemir
dik Ø da ka dik Ø da ka da ka dik Ø da ka dik Ø dak Ø Ø Ø da ka da ka	Amir Khān
de ka de ka dek Ø de ka dek Ø deka Ø Ø Ø de ka dek Ø de Ø ka dek kā Ø	AḤẒ
ta ka ta ka tik Ø ta ka tik Ø taka Ø Ø Ø ta ka tik Ø ta Ø ka tik tak Ø	MRK

12. *Thaqil*

Right after introducing the twenty-four beat *nim-thaqil*, Awbahi presents *możāʿaf-e nim-thaqil* as a cycle of forty-eight beats (4 + 4 + 2 + 4 + 6 + 6 + 6 + 8 + 8 = 48), which indicates that the original *oṣul* was *nim-thaqil* and the *możāʿaf-e nim-thaqil* was shaped by doubling it. Subsequently, during the sixteenth and seventeenth centuries, the forty-eight *możāʿaf-e nim-thaqil* was simply called *thaqil*. The pattern presented by Amir Khān corresponds exactly with a pattern of forty-eight beats outlined by Cantemir, but that of AḤẒ seems to have some omissions toward the end.

düm . te ke düm . te ke te ke düm . te ke düm . tek . tek.	Cantemir
dik Ø da ka dik Ø da ka da ka dik Ø da ka dik Ø dak Ø dak Ø	Amir Khān
dek Ø de ka dek Ø de ka de ka dek Ø de ka dek Ø kā Ø kā Ø	AḤẒ

düm . düm . tek . düm . tek . tek . düm . te ke düm düm tek teke	Cantemir
dik Ø dik Ø dak Ø dik Ø dak Ø dak Ø dik Ø da ka dik dik da ka	Amir Khān
dek Ø dek Ø kā Ø dek Ø kā Ø kā Ø dek Ø de ka dek kā dek ka	AḤẒ

düm tek teke düm tek . teke teke	Cantemir
dik da ka dik dak Ø daka daka	Amir Khān
Ø Ø Ø Ø Ø Ø Ø dekā	AḤẒ

13. *Khafif*

Awbahi introduces *khafif* as two cycles of *mokhammas* (2 + 4 + 2 + 4 + 4 = 16) and refers to it as *mokhammas-e możāʿaf*. In the first half of the sixteenth century, Nasimi and the author of *Taqsīm al-naghamāt* outline *khafif* as cycles of twenty-four and twenty-eight beats. Nonetheless, both cycles seem to have been quadruple metres.

4 + 4 + 4 + 2 + 4 + 6 + 8 = 32	Awbahi
4 + 4 + 2 + 4 + 2 + 4 + 4 = 24	*Nasim-e ṭarab*
4 + 4 + 5 + 3 + 5 + 3 + 4 = 28	*Taqsīm al-naghamāt*

In the late seventeenth century, Amir Khān Gorji and MRK also presented the stroke patterns of *khafif*, and their patterns may be compared with the thirty-two-beat cycle of Cantemir.

düm tek tek . düm tek tek . düm . te ke düm tek tek . düm . te ke	Cantemir
dik dak dak Ø dik dak dak Ø dik dak dik dak dik dak dak Ø dik Ø da ka	Amir Khān
tik tak tak Ø tik tak tak Ø tik tak tik tak Ø tak tak Ø tik Ø tak tak	MRK

düm düm tek teke düm tek teke düm tek . teke teke	Cantemir
dik dik Ø daka dik Ø daka dik dak Ø Ø Ø	Amir Khān
tik tik Ø tak tik Ø tak tik tak Ø tak Ø	MRK

14. *Nim-dawr*

The name of *nim-dawr* began to appear in musical texts toward the end of the sixteenth century. According to Karāmi, *nim-dawr* was alternatively called *pir-e jamāli* and Mir Ṣadr al-Din Moḥammad classifies *pir-e jamāli* as a derivative or secondary *oṣul*.

During the seventeenth century, *nim-dawr* was a common *oṣul* mentioned in almost all Safavid musical treatises. Amir Khān Gorji, AḤẒ, and MRK mention slightly different stroke patterns for this cycle.

dik daka dik dak daka daka dak	Amir Khān Gorj
dekka dekkā- kā	AḤẒ
taka tik tak tik tak	MRK

15. *Dawr*

Dawr does not emerge into historical daylight until the late sixteenth century.[64] Karāmi states that *dawr* was of many varieties, including *dawr-e qadim*, *dawr-e aṣl*, *dawr-e samāʿi*, and *dawr-e hendi*, but he does not refer to *dawr* specifically as an independent rhythmic cycle. It seems that just like *thaqil*, which was shaped by doubling *nim-thaqil*, *dawr* was also formed by doubling *nim-dawr*. *Dawr* is later mentioned in the anonymous treatise included in Amir Khān's codex and the treatise of Āqā Mo'men, and finally Amir Khān provides its stroke pattern and number of *żarb*s. MRK also gives a stroke pattern for *dawr* that is partly comparable to that of Amir Khān.

dik daka dik dak daka dik dak daka daka	Amir Khān Gorji
taka tak tik taka tik tik tak tik tak	MRK

Dawr was a Safavid development, and it was entirely absent in the preceding Timurid or contemporary Ottoman traditions.

16. *Chanbar (hazaj)*

In the Systematist texts *hazaj* is often introduced as a cycle of twelve beats (4 + 2 + 4 + 2 = 12), and according to Marāghi and al-Shirwānī this cycle was recognized in Tabriz as *chanbar*.[65] Yet Marāghi informs us that in practice it was counted as a cycle of six beats (4 + 2 = 6).[66] Toward the end of the Timurid period, Awbahi and Bannā'i introduce *hazaj-e chanbar*, and mention that while this *oṣul* was called *hazaj-e chanbar* in the west of Persia, it was known as *rāh-e samā'* in Khorasan.[67] In the first half of the sixteenth century, two different patterns for *hazaj* are presented by *Nasim-e ṭarab* (2 + 4 + 4 = 10) and *Taqsīm al-naghamāt* (2 + 4 + 2 = 8) that have no clear affinities with their Timurid precursor.

After the sixteenth century, *hazaj* was no longer known as a rhythmic cycle, but *chanbar* is mentioned frequently in seventeenth-century sources. While the pattern of *chanbar* presented by Amir Khān Gorji is congruent with Cantemir's pattern, its twelve-beat cycle suggests affinities with the *hazaj* mentioned in Systematist texts as well.

düm teke düm düm tek . . düm tek . teke teke	Cantemir
dik daka dik dik dak Ø Ø dik dak Ø daka daka	Amir Khān Gorji

17. *Awsaṭ*

Awsaṭ appears first in al-Shirwānī's *Majalla fī al-mūsīqī* in the late fifteenth century as a cycle of ten beats (5 + 5 = 10), and it was evidently the same as *fākhti-e awsaṭ* that had been mentioned by both Marāghi and Awbahi. Yet the ten-beat cycle hardly seems to have been related to the eighteen-beat *awsaṭ* (4 + 4 + 4 + 4 + 2 = 18) that is mentioned in *Nasim-e ṭarab* and *Taqsīm al-naghamāt*.

While Karāmi states that *awsaṭ* and *far'* were the same *oṣuls*, in *Bahjat al-ruḥ* and the anonymous treatise in Amir Khān Gorji's codex they are described as two different cycles. In Āqā Mo'men and Amir Khān's treatises no reference is made to *awsaṭ*, but *far'* is mentioned in both texts.

18. *Ramal-e ṣaghir and ramal-e kabir*

Between the ninth and fifteenth centuries, the quintessential concept of *ramal* was a triple meter. Yet in Systematist texts, *ramal* is predominantly introduced as a cycle of twelve beats. From the second half of the fifteenth century, some music theorists such as Awbahi and Fatḥ Allāh al-Shirwānī begin to mention two forms of *ramal* (2 + 2 + 2 + 2 + 4 = 12) and *mużā'af al-ramal* or *ramal al-ṭawīl* (4 + 4 + 2 + 2 + 2 + 2 + 2 + 2 + 4 = 24). Nasimi offers two forms of *ramal* (2 + 2 + 4 = 8) and *ramal-e ṭavil* (3 + 5 + 2 + 2 + 2 + 2 = 16), which might have been local variants of the twelve and twenty-four classical versions. Amir Khān Gorji also outlines the two forms of *ramal-e ṣaghir* and *ramal-e kabir* as twelve and twenty-eight *żarbs*, respectively.[68]

dik dak daka daka dik daka dik dik dak	*ramal-e ṣaghir*
dik dak dik dak dik dak dik daka dik dak daka daka	
daka daka dik dak dik daka dik dak	*ramal-e kabir*

19. *Samā'i*

As mentioned before, Bannā'i confirms that what was known as *hazaj-e chanbar* (4 + 2 + 4 + 2 = 12) in western Persia was called *rāh-e samā'* in Khorasan. In the second half of the fifteenth century, a rhythmic cycle called *samā'iya* was also prevalent in Persia.[69] During the Safavid period, the structure of *samā'i* is given for the first time by Nasimi as a cycle of nine beats.

2 + 3 + 4 = 9 *Nasim-e ṭarab*

In the second half of the sixteenth century, Karāmi mentions *dawr-e samā'i* and Mir Ṣadr al-Din Moḥammad makes a distinction between *samā'i-ye gerān* and *samāʿi*, while emphasizing that the former was known in Khorasan as *dawr-e shāhi*. Finally, Āqā Mo'men and Amir Khān Gorji both include *samāʿi* in the list of rhythmic cycles common in their own time, but they fail to present its structure. The rhythmic pattern of *samāʿi* is also provided by *Bahjat al-ruḥ* and AḤẒ.

tanah tanah tan tanah tanā dim (14 *żarb*s)	*Bahjat al-ruḥ*
dek dekkā- kaka dek dekkā	AḤẒ

20. *Żarb al-fatḥ*

Żarb al-fatḥ was first a rhythmic cycle of forty-nine or fifty beats invented by Marāghi after the conquest of Baghdad by Ghiyāth al-Din Shahzāda in 1382. Later, Awbahi mentions a version of *żarb al-fatḥ* with eighty-eight beats that appears to have emerged in Herat in the second half of the fifteenth century.[70]

4 + 4 + 2 + 2 + 2 + 4 + 2 + 4 + 4 + 3 + 3 + 4 + 2 + 4 + 4 + 8 + 8 + 8 + 2 + 2 + 4 + 8 = 88 Awbahi

The eighty-eight-beat *żarb al-fatḥ* was subsequently mentioned by Muḥammad b. ʿAbd al-Ḥamīd al-Lādhiqī and became prevalent in Ottoman music during the seventeenth and eighteenth centuries.[71]

During the sixteenth and seventeenth centuries, *żarb al-fatḥ* was a common *oṣul* in Persia, but its trajectory is a bit ambiguous. While the author of *Nasim-e ṭarab* presents a fifty-eight-beat cycle, for the author of *Taqsīm al-naghamāt* it was a cycle of seventy-eight beats. By the end of the seventeenth century, Amir Khān Gorji mentions mnemonic patterns of *żarb al-fatḥ* as a cycle of fifty-nine *żarb*s or attacks and further documents four *kār*s set to this cycle. The mnemonic patterns presented by Amir Khān do not correspond for the most part with the patterns given by Cantemir or any other Ottoman sources.

Rhythmic Cycles of the *Naqqāra-khāna*

The accounts in Safavid musical treatises clearly indicate that some rhythmic cycles that were mentioned earlier in Timurid musical texts developed primarily in the context of the *naqqāra-khāna*. Nevertheless, no music theorist prior to the sixteenth century includes a section specifically on this subject or even refers directly to *naqqāra-khāna* rhythms.

Toward the end of the sixteenth century, Mir Ṣadr al-Din Moḥammad mentions *jalili*, *shirāzi*, *qalandari*, *khᵛārazmi*, and *ḥarbi* as the five rhythmic cycles of the *naqqāra-khāna* and further declares that while they were identical and equal in length with some other *oṣul*s, they were simple meters insufficiently complete to constitute recognizable patterns, and thus hardly viable as the basis for compositions. The anonymous treatise in the musical codex of Amir Khān Gorji also gives the names of *shirāzi*, *ekhlāṭi*, *qalandari*, *żarb al-qadim*, *razmiyāna*, *khᵛārazmi*, and *samāʿi*, though it fails to provide their rhythmic structures.[72] And, finally, the author of *Bahjat al-ruḥ* mentions the five cycles of *qalandari* (29 *żarb*s), *shirāzi* (19 *żarb*s), *ekhlāṭi* (18 *żarb*s), *żarbi* (15 *żarb*s), and *ḥarbi* (5 *żarb*s), and subsequently ascribes their invention to one of the servants of the Saljuq potentate, Malekshāh b. Ālp Arslān (r. 1072–1092). The author of *Bahjat al-ruḥ* also declares that the rhythmic cycles of the *naqqāra-khāna* tended to be sober, unlike the *oṣul*s of art music, which were more intoxicating.[73]

Evidently the most prominent *naqqāra-khāna* rhythmic cycle played at the time of conquest, celebration, and festivity was *shādiyāna* (lit. "rejoicing"), which can be traced back to the fourteenth century, if not earlier.[74] Awbahi introduces it as a variant of *thaqil al-ramal* and outlines its pattern as follows:

shādiyāna 4 + 4 + 2 + 2 + 2 + 2 + 2 + 2 + 4 = 24

Later in the sixteenth century, Karāmi mentions *shādiyāna* in two forms: *torki* and *khafi*. Darvish-ʿAli Changi also refers to it together with *baluchi*, *ekhlāṭi*, *nayrizi*, *oṣul-e ravān*, and *olusi* as one of the *oṣul*s favored by *naqqārachi*s.[75] However, none of the Safavid musical texts describes its structure. It appears that *shādiyāna* continued to be the most prevalent *naqqāra-khāna* rhythmic pattern throughout the eighteenth century, as the two post-Safavid chroniclers, Mirzā Mehdi Astarābādi and Moḥammad Moḥsen Mostawfi, still frequently mention it in their historical accounts.[76]

Another *naqqāra-khāna* rhythmic cycle was seemingly *beshārat* (lit. "glad tidings"), whose two versions are only mentioned by the author of *Nasim-e ṭarab*:

beshārat-e kabir 2 + 4 + 2 + 2 + 4 + 2 + 2 + 4 + 2 + 4 + 4 + 2 + 2 = 36
beshārat-e ṣaghir 2 + 2 + 2 + 2 + 4 + 2 + 4 + 4 = 22

One more *naqqāra-khāna* rhythmic cycle, *rāh-e ekhlāṭi*, is also outlined by Awbahi through mnemonic devices. The same cycle is mentioned by Bannā'i as *ghuriyāna*:

rāh-e ekhlāṭi $2 + 4 + 2 = 8$

Ekhlāṭi was also mentioned in many Safavid musical treatises and, according to *Ā'in-e Akbarī*, along with *ebtedā'i*, *shirāzi*, and *qalandari*, it was a prominent rhythmic cycle in the performance of *nawbat* at the court of the Mughal emperor, Akbar (r. 1556–1605).[77]

Evidence suggests that the *oṣuls* of *naqqāra-khāna*, aside from having individual characters and functions, were also performed in the form of a sequence on various instruments. This sequence is coherently documented in *Ā'in-e Akbarī* by Abul-Fazl-'Allāmi:

> Of the musical instruments used in the *naqqāra-khāna*, I may mention the *gavorga*, commonly called *damāma*; there are eighteen pairs of them or less; and they give a deep sound.
>
> The *naqqāra*, twenty pair more or less.
>
> The *dohol*, of which four are used.
>
> The *karnā* is made of gold, silver, brass and other metals and they never blow fewer than four.
>
> The *sornā* of the Persian or Indian kinds; they blow nine together.
>
> The *nafir* of the Persian, European and Indian kinds; they blow some of each kind.
>
> The *sing* is of brass, in the form of a cow's horn; they blow two together.
>
> The *senj*, or cymbal, of which three pair are used.
>
> Formerly the band played four *gaharis* (*gahari*: twenty-four minutes) before the commencement of the night, and likewise four *gaharis* before daybreak; now they play first at midnight, when the sun commences his ascent, and the second time at dawn. One *gahari* before sunrise, the musicians commence to blow the *sornā*, and wake up those that are asleep; and one *gahari* after sun rise, they play a short prelude, when they beat the *gavorga* a little, whereupon they blow the *karnā* and the *nafir*, and the other instruments, without, however, making use of the *naqqāra*; after a little pause the *sornās* are blown again, the rhythm (*oṣul*) is being indicated by the *nafirs*. One hour later the *naqqāras* commence when all musicians raise "the auspicious stain." After this they go through the following seven sections:

1. *Morsali*; they play *morsali* and that is a conspicuous *oṣul*; and afterwards the *bardāsht*, which consists likewise of certain *oṣul*, played by the whole band. This is followed by a pianissimo, and a tendency to move from acuity to gravity.
2. The performing of four *oṣul*s, called *ekhlāṭi*, *ebtedā'i*, *shirāzi*, and *qalandari*, also known as *negar qatra* or *nokhod qatra* which occupies an hour.
3. The playing of the old and new *khᵛārazmi*s. Of these His Majesty has composed more than two hundred, which are the delight of young and old, especially *jalāl-e shāhi*, *mahāmir*, *karkut*, and *nawruzi*.
4. The swelling play of the *shādiyāna*.
5. The passing into the middle of the sequence.
6. The playing of the rhythmic cycle of *awfar* which is called *rāh-e bālā*, after which they move gradually to lower-pitched notes (*zir konnad*).
7. The playing of *morsal-e khᵛārazmi* followed by *morsali*.

At the conclusion they play the *forugozāsht* and commence the blessings on His Majesty, when the whole band strikes up a pianissimo. Then follows the reciting of beautiful sentences and poems. This also lasts for an hour. Afterwards the *sornā*-players perform for another hour, when the whole comes to a proper conclusion.

His Majesty has such a knowledge of the science of music as master musicians do not possess; and he is likewise an excellent hand in performing, especially on the *naqqāra*.[78]

The question of how the Central Asian Mughal emperors in India adopted the institution and performance of *nawbat* from the Persian royal court cannot be answered with ease. Nonetheless, there seems to have been a common practice and shared terminology of some sort among the Safavid and Mughal courts. The *nawbat*, as described by Abu al-Fażl, was a sequence of melodic and rhythmic sections opening with a *morsali*[79] and *bardāsht* and concluding with a *morsali* and *forudāsht* (or *forugozāsht*), a structure that can be traced back in Persia as early as the twelfth century.[80] These sections had certain rhythmic characters and functions. Some rhythmic cycles were played by specific instruments while some were rendered through compositions by the entire ensemble. Likewise, some sections consisted of only playing a series of *oṣul*s, such as *ekhlāṭi*, *ebtedā'i*, *shirāzi*, and *qalandari*, whereas some other sections were rhythmic compositions called *khᵛārazmi*s, new versions of which could be composed and played alternatively in various performances of the *nawbat*.[81]

In his musical treatise, Ḥāj Ḥosayn Ẓohri refers to thirty-two *khᵛārazmi*s as derivative *oṣul*s that were known to him at that time and were frequently rendered in *naqqāra-khāna*s.[82]

In summary, the repertoire of the *naqqāra-khāna* included two groups of rhythmic cycles: first, the cycles that constituted the fixed parts of the *nawbat* such as *morsali*, *ekhlāṭi*, *ebtedā'i*, *shirāzi*, and *qalandari*; and, second, those cycles or compositions that were collectively called *khᵛārazmi*s, which formed the creative part of the *nawbat* and were often improvised or composed anew by the *naqqārachi*s.

The Eighteenth Century

After the collapse of Isfahan, musicians were not strictly adhering to established musical conventions regarding the exposition of *maqām*s, rendition of *oṣul*s, and distinctions between genres. The seventeen cycles of *oṣul* that once shaped the rhythmic–metric structure of courtly compositions began to decline, and vocal genres were no longer distinguished by separate names. At the same time, a metric instrumental genre called *reng* emerged, originally as a dance tune, which was lighter, faster, and more rhapsodic than the archaic and rigid *pishraw*. Moreover, metric vocal compositions came to be labeled as *taṣnif*s, except for one particular compound form that was still recognized among court musicians as *kār-e'amal*. In a late eighteenth-century musical treatise, we find references only to *kār-e 'amal* and to fast (*khafif*) and slow (*thaqil*) *taṣnif*s.[83] Nonetheless, it is hard to insist that the exponents of early *dastgāh* music in the eighteenth century were entirely unaware of the *oṣul* cycles or patterns. For example, at the end of his musical treatise, the author of *Bahjat al-qulūb* includes a diagram representing melodic units in the sequences of *dastgāh*s in which some compound names such as *far'-e hazaj*, *far'-e aṣl*, *tork-e kabir*, *dō-yek-e navā*, and *se-yek-e khārā*, may bear indications of, or references to, rhythmic patterns.[84]

Another important development in the eighteenth century was the emergence of the *dombak* (goblet drum), which was presumably deemed too insignificant an instrument to be used in Safavid court music. The *dombak* soon became the standard instrument used by professional male musicians and courtesans for accompanying *reng* and *taṣnif*. The new technical innovations idiomatic to the *dombak* eventually influenced the rhythmic structure of many compositions to the extent that we may hypothesize that *reng*, at least, evolved very closely with the idiosyncrasies of this instrument.

The Qajar Period

It is apparent that by the beginning of the nineteenth century, long cycles were no longer recognized among Persian composers and performers, nor does the term *oṣul* seem to have existed in the vocabulary used by musicians throughout the nineteenth century.

Accordingly, while the term and concept of *oṣul* came to be antiquated, rhythmic concepts were all identified as *żarb*. It is clear that the term *żarb* in the Qajar period and later in the twentieth century had multiple meanings, just as it probably had during the Safavid period. It continued to denote attack, beat, and rhythm while it signified the concepts of *vazn* (meter) and *dawr* (cycle) as well. For example, if someone said about a piece of music, "*żarbash dorost nist*" it could either mean its stress pattern was incorrect or its meter was wrong.[85] Likewise, an instrumental or vocal segment of music that was not accompanied by a drum could either be called *be ṭarz-e āvāz* or *āvāzi*, and what was rendered to the accompaniment of a drum was called *żarbi*. Later in the twentieth century, the term *żarb* began to be used more frequently for *dombak* as well, but the title of *żarbgir* (lit. "holder of the *dombak*" or "time-keeper") referring to a *dombak* player seems to have been common as early as the eighteenth century.

The topic of rhythm is largely ignored by late nineteenth-century theoreticians such as Mehdi-Qoli Hedāyat and Forṣat al-Dawla Shirāzi, who tended to be more interested in outmoded articulations of the modal system than in contemporary vernacular rhythmic cycles performed by *żarbgirs*. However, two celebrated *taṣnif* singers, Reżā-Qoli Nawruzi and 'Abdollāh Davāmi, recorded a large number of *taṣnifs* at the beginning of the twentieth century.[86] Davāmi's repertoire of *taṣnifs*, including more than 180 compositions, was later transcribed during the 1940s and 1960s.[87] Moreover, Ḥasan Mashḥun compiled a significant body of information about the nineteenth-century *taṣnifs* with references to their rhythmic structures based on the discussions he had with the older generation of musicians.[88]

Early recordings of *taṣnif*, scattered written documents, and the recollections of elders all indicate that six basic rhythmic cycles or meters were recognized among practicing musicians during the nineteenth century and that almost every vocal or instrumental composition was set to one of these cycles.[89] These six basic rhythmic cycles are displayed below:

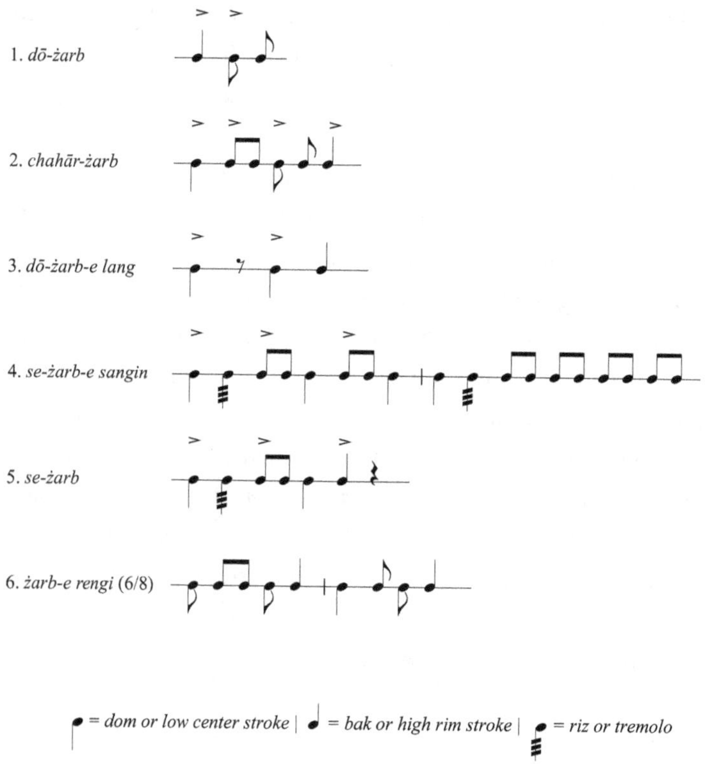

Example 5.1 The six basic rhythmic cycles in the Qajar period

In general, the majority of Qajar *taṣnifs* (almost 75 percent) were composed and performed in the *se-żarb* and *se-żarb-e sangin*, which were also identified as cycles of six beats in medium and slow tempi. Each *taṣnif* can start, depending on the meter and length of its verse, from any six beats, but in most *taṣnifs* the sixth beat serves iambically as an unvoiced pick-up note to accent the *sar-e żarb*, or first beat of the cycle. In a *taṣnif* with verses of multiple metres, the opening beat may shift when the poetic meter is changed. It is clear that the coordination of quantitative poetic meter and the number of syllables in a verse with stressed and unstressed beats of *sar-e żarb* tends to be the most intricate technique employed by *taṣnif* singers.[90]

عشق تو آتش جانا زد بر دل من   بر بـاد غم داد آخر آب و گِل من

Example 5.2 A *taṣnif* in *se-żarb-e sangin* beginning in the third beat

A small number of *taṣnif*s are also composed in *dō-żarb*, some of which could be performed alternatively in *dō-żarb-e lang* as well.[91]

Chahār-żarb was not frequently performed in classical or court music, but vocal genres associated with Sufi and Shiʿite religious contexts such as *sāqināma* and *nawḥa* were sometimes rendered in this cycle. Moreover, toward the end of the nineteenth century, a novel instrumental genre called *pishdarāmad* emerged in classical music, which was typically set to *chahār-żarb*.[92]

Finally, *żarb-e rengi*, as the name itself indicates, was widely used for the accompaniment of instrumental *reng*s and was associated with dance. The structure of *żarb-e rengi* was built around a repeated pattern of four or five drum strokes, but when a dance was accompanied by a solo *dombak*, more variations of pattern, stress, and timbre were introduced by the *żarbgir*s.

After the introduction of European military music at the Dār al-Fonun, Persian musicians adopted Western terminology and began to refer to *dō-żarb* as 2/4, *dō-żarb-e lang* as 7/8, *chahār-żarb* as 4/4, *se-żarb* as 3/4 and 6/4, *se-żarb-e sangin* as 6/4, and *żarb-e rengi* as 6/8 and 6/16. The transcription of vocal and instrumental compositions based on the stress patterns of Western meters subsequently affected the dynamics and rhythmic structure of Persian compositions that then came to be adapted to Western duple, triple, and quadruple meters.

It should also be mentioned that while the name *dombak* consists of the two contrasting strokes of *dom* and *bak* produced at the center and rim of the instrument, these strokes have never been used for didactic purposes or representations of rhythmic patterns—unlike the north Indian *tāla*'s *ṭhekā* or Turkish *düm tek*. Nevertheless, musicians sometimes used other mnemonic patterns for the demonstration of rhythms. Two mnemonic patterns widely used for didactic purposes by *żarbgirs* and other musicians in this period were "*yek ṣad-o bist-o panj*" (lit. "one hundred twenty-five") for the *chahār-żarb* and "*bala-o bala-o, ba'la diga*" (lit. "yes and yes, yes again") for *żarb-e rengi*.[93]

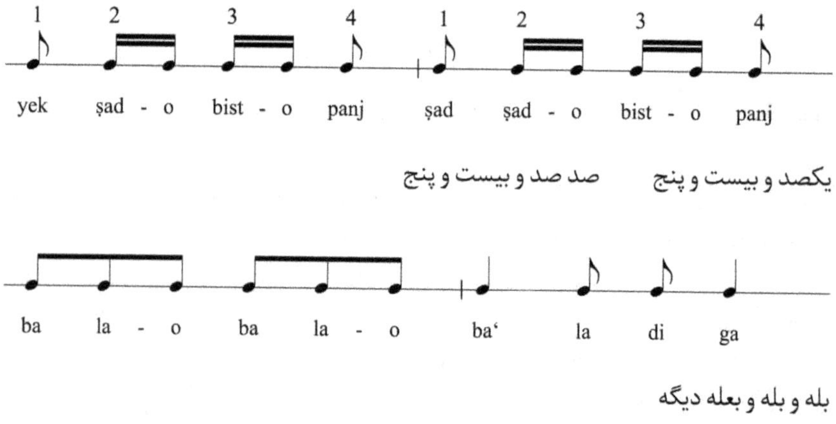

Example 5.3 Two mnemonic patterns used for didactic purposes in the late Qajar period

According to oral tradition, renowned soloists always had their own individual *żarbgirs* who were familiar with their repertoire, musical idiom, and dynamic tendencies. These talented *żarbgirs* were also known to imitate the plucking strokes (*meżrābs*) of the soloists very closely in the course of performance. Moḥammad Irāni Mojarrad (d. 1971), an authority of the Qajar music, relates:

> many *żarbgirs* like Āqā Jān were committed (*moqayyad budand*) to follow the rhythm of the melody very closely. For instance, when Ḥāji Khān played a solo *żarb* piece, one could tell that he would play that specific *pishdarāmad* in *bayāt-e tork*. In his solo performances, it was evident what [compositions] he was playing . . . In short, the old *żarbgirs* followed the plucking of soloists very closely and were committed to that style, whereas today *żarbgirs* only keep the time, and merely consider whether the piece is *dō-żarb*, *se-żarb* etc. And obviously both styles are admissible . . .
>
> The level of *żarb* had to be below the level of the melodic instruments. None of the old *żarbgirs* played louder than soloists. But today, *żarbgirs* do not follow this standard.[94]

As mentioned earlier, the repertoire of Persian music was divided into the categories of *żarbi* and *āvāzi* in the nineteenth century. The *żarbgirs* were responsible for accompanying soloists only in *żarbi* sections, which mainly included *taṣnifs* and *rengs*. Some *chahārmeżrābs*, especially when played on the *santur*, were presumably accompanied by a *dombak* or *dayera* as well. However, there were instrumental units in the *āvāz* section that, while not considered specifically as *żarbi*, were characterized as having an explicit regular pulse as the result of a recurrent poetic meter or an ostinato pattern. According to Hedāyat and Forṣat al-Dawla Shirāzi, units with such characteristics were known as *naghma* and their clear examples included *kereshma*, *pishzangula*, and *zangula*.[95] These units, though not meant to be accompanied by the *dombak*, were played in solo instrumental music to develop the melody of the associated *āvāz* or *gusha* while creating a conspicuous rhythmic contrast.

Summary

In the early Islamic period, four major *īqā'*s of *ramal* (3/2), *thaqīl al-awwal* (4/2), *thaqīl al-thānī* (5/2), and *hazaj* (6/8) were known in urban centers that were primarily rendered in two tempi, *thaqīl* (heavy) and *khafīf* (light). Toward the end of the Abbasid period, these meters gradually underwent a substantial development. While retaining the same names, their patterns became elaborated and increased in length.

Beginning with Maraghi, a few long rhythmic cycles such as *żarb al-fatḥ* and *me'atayn* were also introduced and later used in well-crafted court compositions. Long cycles were either extended or elaborated in forms of three-, four-, five-, and six-beat cycles, or they consisted of compound *oṣuls* comprising three or four various short cycles. Throughout the Safavid period, while seventeen distinct types of *osul* cycle were mentioned in theoretical treatises, in practice most compositions were in *chanbar* (*hazaj*), *dō-yek*, *torki-żarb*, *mokhammas*, *varashān*, and *awfar* (*rāh-e bālā*).

Throughout the Timurid and Safavid periods many musical sources indicate that the metric–rhythmic system of three-, four-, five-, and six-beat cycles was still widespread among musicians. This system continued to be practiced throughout the Qajar period while the performance of courtly *oṣul* cycles effectively ceased to exist after the eighteenth century.

Notes

1. Wright, *Music Theory in Mamluk Cairo*, 29.
2. This is also confirmed by Marāghi in *Jāmi' al-alḥān: khātema*, 198.
3. Cf. George Dimitri Sawa, "Theories of Rhythm and Metre in the Medieval East," in *The Garland Encyclopedia of World Music, vol. 6: The Middle East*, ed. Virginia Danielson, Scott Marcus, and Dwight Reynolds (New York: Routledge, 2002), 389.
4. Ṣafī al-Dīn al-Urmawī, *Kitāb al-adwār*, 279–307. Cf. Sawa, "Theories of Rhythm and Metre in the Medieval East,", 389.
5. In my interviews with twentieth-century Persian musicians, I found that senior master singers and instrumentalists used *żarb* referring to the internal pattern of attacks in a melody, whereas *dombak* players used the term in reference to the number of tactus beats in a cycle as well as the drum pattern.
6. The cipher notation was mostly used by the Timurid musicians of Herat especially in transcription of songs. See also 'Alishāh b. Buka Awbahi, *Moqaddamat al-uṣūl*, 164–167.
7. Wright gives a great account of al-Urmawī's rhythmics and Neubauer does the same for those of Shirāzi with some comparison with Marāghi's ideas. See Wright, *Music Theory in Mamluk Cairo*, 30–36; Eckhard Neubauer, "Quṭb al-Dīn Shīrāzī (d. 1311) on Musical Metres (īqā')," *Zeitschrift für Geschichte der Arabisch-Islamischen Wissenschaften* 18 (2008/9): 357–371.
8. Cf. Owen Wright, "The Ottoman *Usul* System and its Precursors," in *Rhythmic Cycles and Structures in the Art Music of the Middle East*, ed. Zeynep Helvacı, Jacob Olley and Rolf Martin Jaeger (Istanbul: Orient Institute, 2017); Owen Wright, "Amīr Ḫān Gurjī and Safavid-Ottoman *Usul* Parallels," in *Rhythmic Cycles and Structures in the Art Music of the Middle East*, ed. Zeynep Helvacı, Jacob Olley and Rolf Martin Jaeger (Istanbul: Orient Institute, 2017).

9. According to al-Fārābī, Isḥāq al-Mawṣilī opined that *hazaj* was just a pulse; but in a more conventional view, *hazaj* was a duple metre differentiated from *khafīf thaqīl al-awwal* by the internal pattern of attacks. For more information, see Eckhard Neubauer, "Die Theorie vom *īqāʿ*. II: Übersetzung des *Kitāb Iḥṣāʾ al-īqāʿāt* von Abū Naṣr al-Fārābī," *Oriens* 34 (1994): 162, 169; Wright, *Music Theory in Mamluk Cairo*, 29.
10. For further information, see George Dimitri Sawa, *Music Performance Practice in the Early ʿAbbāsid Era 132–320 AH/7509–32 AD* (Toronto: Pontifical Institute of Mediaeval Studies, 1989), 40–46.
11. Cf. Neubauer, "Quṭb al-Dīn Shīrāzī (d. 1311) on Musical Metres (īqāʿ)," 358–359.
12. Ibn Zayla, *Kitāb al-kāfī*, 62.
13. ʿOnṣor al-Maʿāli Kaykābus b. Voshmgir Ziyār, *Qābus-nāma*, 193–194.
14. Cf. Neubauer, "Music History II. ca. 650 to 1370 CE."
15. Wright, *Music Theory in Mamluk Cairo*, 30.
16. Ṣafī al-Dīn al-Urmawī, *Kitāb al-adwār*, 277–285; Ṣafī al-Dīn al-Urmawī, *al-Risāla al-Sharafiyya fī al-nisab al-taʾlifiyya*, ed. Hāshim Muḥammad al-Rajab (Kuwait: Dar al-Rashīd li-l-Nashr, 1982), 202–211.
17. Ṣafī al-Dīn al-Urmawī, *Kitāb al-adwār*, 288–289. Marāghi states that *żarb al-aṣl* was an expression mainly used by practicing musicians, see *Sharḥ-e advār*, 259.
18. Ṣafī al-Dīn al-Urmawī, *al-Risāla al-Sharafiyya*, 208; Shirāzi, *Durrat al-tāj*, 137.
19. Shirāzi, *Durrat al-tāj*, 137; Ṣafī al-Dīn al-Urmawī, *Kitāb al-adwār*, 306; Ṣafī al-Dīn al-Urmawī, *al-Risāla al-Sharafiyya*, 211.
20. Shirāzi, *Durrat al-tāj*, 138.
21. This is apparently the earliest known reference to an asymmetrical or syncopated meter that was later referred to as limping (Turkish *aksāk* and Persian *lang*). Cf. Neubauer, "Music History II. ca. 650 to 1370 CE." A survey on the Arabic and Persian *oṣul* from the early Islamic period to the beginning of the Timurid period is given by Neubauer in "Quṭb al-Dīn Shīrāzī (d. 1311) on Musical Metres (īqāʿ)," 357–371.
22. See Khubravān and Kordmāfi, "Musiqi dar ashjār va athmār-e," 77.
23. Marāghi, *Jāmiʿ al-alḥān*, 211–230; ʿAbd al-Qāder Marāghi, *Maqāṣid al-alḥān*, 88–100; ʿAbd al-Qāder Marāghi, *Sharḥ-e advār*, 251–276.
24. ʿAbd al-Qāder Marāghi, *Sharḥ-e advār*, 259.
25. ʿAbd al-Qāder Marāghi, *Jāmiʿ al-alḥān*, 221.
26. Marāghi ascribes the invention of *chahār-żarb* to Moḥammad-Shāh Robābi, see *Sharḥ-e advār*, 266.
27. Marāghi ascribes the invention of the group of *ramal*s to Moḥammad Tuni, see ibid., 252.

28. Marāghi mentions that the inhabitants of Azerbaijan and more specifically Tabriz called this cycle with a minor variation *chanbar* and their dances (*dastafshān*) were mostly in this cycle, see ibid., 263–264.
29. In his two other books, Marāghi mentions *żarb al-fatḥ* as a fifty-beat cycle, see *Jāmi' al-alḥān*, 227; *Maqāṣid al-alḥān*, 96.
30. *Sharḥ-e advār*, 374–379.
31. Awbahi, *Moqaddamat al-uṣūl*, 153–172; Bannā'i, *Resāla dar musiqi*, 102–121.
32. Awbahi, *Moqaddamat al-uṣūl*, 170.
33. 'Abd al-Qāder Marāghi, *Jāmi' al-alḥān*, 223.
34. Awbahi, *Moqaddamat al-uṣūl*, 164.
35. 'Abd al-Qāder Marāghi, *Jāmi' al-alḥān*, 247.
36. For *żarb-e aṣl* cf. Ṣafī al-Dīn al-Urmawī, *Kitāb al-adwār*, 289–307; Marāghi, *Sharḥ-e advār*, 259–266; see also Eckhard Neubauer, "A Historical Sketch of the Musical Metre Called Ramal," in *Rhythmic Cycles and Structures in the Art Music of the Middle East*, eds. Zeynep Helvacı, Jacob Olley and Rolf Martin Jaeger. Istanbul: Orient Institute, 2017, 21.
37. This connotation of *oṣul* is clearly suggested by *'Alā' al-Din Bokhāri* when he calls the seven primary rhythmic cycles *oṣul*s and their seven spin-offs *far'*s. For a further account, see Khubravān and Kordmāfi, "Musiqi dar ashjār va athmār-e 'Alā' al-Din Bokhāri," 77.
38. Persian Musical Treatise, Köprülü Library (Istanbul) MS 1613, 71a.
39. The rhythmic cycle of *rāh-e kord* is also mentioned by Marāghi in *Jāmi' al-alḥān*, 223, and by Moḥammad b. Muḥammad b. 'Abd al-Ḥamīd al-Lādhiqī, *Al-risāla al-fatḥiyya*, 259.
40. *Dar bayān-e paydā shodan-e 'elm-e musiqi*, Malik Library (Tehran) MS 4583, 110–111.
41. Nasimi, *Nasim-e ṭarab*, 102–112.
42. Wright, *Music Theory in the Safavid Era: The* taqsīm al-naġamāt, 425–435. For Wright's commentary on the chapter of rhythm, see ibid., 196–219.
43. Fallahzadeh, *Two Treatises – Two Streams*, 115–118.
44. Mir Ṣadr al-Din Moḥammad, "Resāla-ye 'elm-e musiqi," 90–92.
45. Pourjavady, "The Musical Codex of Amir Khān Gorji," 188.
46. Ibid., 198.
47. Amir Khān Gorji, *Resāla*, 1b–3a.
48. For the analysis of Amir Khān Gorji's patterns of rhythmic cycles and a comparison with Ottoman sources, see Wright, "Amīr Ḫān Gurjī and Safavid-Ottoman *Usul* Parallels," 49–68.

49. Borgomale, *Bahjat al-ruḥ*, 37–41.
50. Ḥāj Ḥosayn Ẓohri Eṣfahāni, *Resāla dar fann-e musiqi*, ed. Imān Ra'isi (Tehran: Solār, 2017), 106–108. I also consulted the original manuscript at the University of Edenborough, Or. MS 585, 17. The *Resāla dar fann-e musiqi* by Ẓohri Eṣfahāni has its own chapter on rhythm, and it is evident that the last section on *dik dak* patterns was a separate fragment appended to it later.
51. See *Resāla-ye Karāmiya*, University of Tehran (Tehran) MS 2591, 407.
52. Amir Khān Gorji. *Resāla*, 10a–28b.
53. Awbahi, *Moqaddamat al-uṣūl*, 171.
54. Persian Musical Treatise, University of Tehran (Tehran) MS 1974, 13a–13b.
55. Moḥammad Moḥiṭ-Ṭabāṭabā'i, "Resāla-ye musiqi-ye gomnām," 18–19.
56. Cf. Wright, "The Ottoman *Usul* System and its Precursors"; Wright, "Amīr Ḫān Gurjī and Safavid-Ottoman *Usul* Parallels"; Sa'id Kordmāfi, "Barrasi-ye barkhi janbahā-ye 'amali-ye iqā' dar resālāt-e qadim-e musiqi-ye ḥawza-ye eslāmi-ye qarn-e haftom tā davāzdahom-e hejri," *Māhur* 60 (2013): 167–198.
57. Moḥammad Moḥiṭ-Ṭabāṭabā'i, "Resāla-ye musiqi-ye gomnām," 18. In general, it is hard to declare that the representation and embodiment of *dik dak* syllables in the seventeenth-century Persian *oṣul*s was akin to the concept of *ṭhekā* in the Hindustani *tāla* system, that is, a fixed series of mnemonic syllables denoting the drum strokes within one cycle of the *tāla*.
58. Awbahi, *Moqaddamat al-uṣūl*, 162; Fallahzadeh, *Two Treatises–Two Streams*, 116; Mir Ṣadr al-Din Moḥammad, "Resāla-ye 'elm-e musiqi," 92.
59. Cf. Faizullah M. Karamatov and Ishak Radjabov, "Introduction to the Shashmaqam," trans. Theodore Levin, *Asian Music* 13(1) (1981): 111–112.
60. Wright, "Amīr Ḫān Gurjī and Safavid-Ottoman *Usul* Parallels," 59–60, adds three beats to Amir Khān's pattern of *awfar* and proposes that it could be comparable to the nine-beat Cantemir's pattern as well:

dik	*Ø*	*daka*	*daka*	*dik*	*dik*	*dak*	*Ø*	*Ø*	Amir Khān Gorji
düm	*.*	*teke*	*teke*	*düm*	*.*	*tek*	*.*	*.*	Cantemir

61. See Ārash Moḥāfeẓ, "Pishraw-ye 'ajami, qesmat-e chahārom: kolliyāt-e ritm va negāhi be āhangsāzi-ye dōyek," *Māhur* 64 (2014): 36–39.
62. Awbahi, *Moqaddamat al-uṣūl*, 168.
63. Fatḥ Allāh al-Shirwānī apparently erroneously calls this twenty-four-beat cycle *thaqīl*.
64. Awbahi only ambiguously mentions that *hazaj-e chanbar* or *rāh-e samā'* (4 + 2 + 4 + 2 = 12) was also called *dawr*, see Awbahi, *Moqaddamat al-uṣūl*, 162.
65. Marāghi, *Sharḥ-e advār*, 263–264; Fatḥ Allāh al-Shirwānī, *Codex on Music* (*Majalla fi'l mūsīqī*), 174.

66. Marāghi, *Jāmi' al-alḥān*, 226.
67. Awbahi, *Moqaddamat al-uṣūl*, 75; Bannā'i, *Resāla dar musiqi*, 113.
68. Amir Khān Gorji first mentions twenty-eight attacks for *ramal-e kabir* but the *dik dak* strokes pattern he presents has only twenty-six attacks.
69. See Persian Musical Treatise, Malek Library (Tehran) MS 893.
70. Awbahi, in *Moqaddamat al-uṣūl*, 170.
71. For the account of *żarb al-fatḥ* in the Ottoman tradition, see Yalçın Tura, "Observations on the Use of the Rhythmic Cycle *Darb-ı Fetih* ('Rhythm of Conquest') in Turkish Vocal Music of the 17th–19th Centuries," in *Rhythmic Cycles and Structures in the Art Music of the Middle East*, ed. Zeynep Helvacı, Jacob Olley, and Rolf Martin Jaeger (Istanbul: Orient Institute, 2017), 69–89.
72. Pourjavady, "The Musical Codex of Amir Khān Gorji," 185.
73. Borgomale, *Bahjat al-ruḥ*, 39.
74. Cf. 'Aliakbar Dehkhodā, "Shādiyāna," in *Loghatnāma*, ed.Moḥammad Mo'in and Ja'far Shahidi (Tehran: University of Tehran Press, 1993).
75. See Darvish-'Ali Changi, *Tuḥfat al-surūr*, 24a.
76. For instance, see Astarābādi, *Tārikh-e jahāngoshā-ye Nāderi*, 354–355; Moḥammad Moḥsen Mostawfi, *Zubdat al-tawārīkh*, 149–150.
77. Abul-Fazl-i-'Allāmi, *The Ā'in-e Akbarī*, ed. H. Blochmann, 2 vols. (Calcutta: C. B. Lewis at the Baptist Mission Press, 1872), 1: 47.
78. Ibid., 46–47. I used primarily the English translation made by Blochmann, yet I changed it according to the Persian text in certain instances where it was inaccurate. For the original translation, see Abul-Fażl-i'Allāmi, *The Ā'in-e Akbarī*, 1: 50–51.
79. Ṣafī al-Dīn al-Urmawī, *Kitāb al-adwār*, 301, mentions that *mużā'af al-ramal* in the thirteenth century was also known as *mursal*. See also Marāghi, *Sharḥ-e advār*, 263.
80. *Bardāsht* and *forudāsht* are mentioned in the poetry of Khāqāni (d. 1190) and Neẓāmi Ganjavi (d. 1209). For further information, see Mehdi Setāyeshgar, *Vāzha-nāma-ye musiqi-ye Irān*, 3 vols. (Tehran: Eṭṭelā'āt, 2002), 1: 145–156.
81. Darvish-'Ali Changi mentions a certain Sultan Manṣur who composed 360 *khᵛārazmi*s in derivative *oṣul*s that were performed by master *naqqārachi*s in their *nawbat*s. For further account see *Tuḥfat al-surūr*, 25a.
82. Ḥāj Ḥosayn Ẓohri Eṣfahāni, *Resāla dar fann-e musiqi*, 63.
83. Pourjavady, "Resāla dar bayān-e chahār dastgāh-e a'ẓam," 90–92.
84. *Baḥjat al-qulūb*, Majles Library (Tehran) MS 2242, 60.
85. Personal communications from Dāriush Ṣafvat.

86. Cf. Davāmi, *Qajar Tasnifs* [M.CD-112], liner notes by Amir Hosein Pourjavady; *Rezâ-Qoli Nowruzi, Qajari Tasnifs* [M.CD-296], liner notes by Amir Hosein Pourjavady.
87. See Pāyvar, *Radif-e āvāzi va taṣnifhā-ye qadimi be revāyat-e 'Abdollāh Davāmi.*
88. Mashḥun, *Tārikh-e musiqi-ye Irān*, 441–491.
89. See also ibid., 650–651. In personal communications I had with the two prominent *dombak* players Farid Kheradmand and Mehrdād A'rābifard, they both confirmed these cycles as the basic rhythmic patterns in the nineteenth century. Kheradmand demonstrated all the patterns to me on *dombak* and what is mentioned here is based on his notation of the cycles. A'rābifard also suggested that as a characteristic feature of traditional Persian music, the last attack in each cycle is often stressed.
90. See Davāmi, *Qajar Tasnifs* [M.CD-112], liner notes by Amir Hosein Pourjavady, 11–12.
91. For the *taṣnif*s that are in *dō-żarb* cycles, see Pāyvar, *Radif-e āvāzi va taṣnifhā-ye qadimi be revāyat-e 'Abdollāh Davāmi*, 172, 188, 197, 230, 248, 253, 265, 266, 279, 281, 290, 335, 359, 379, 389, 411.
92. *Chahār-żarb* was commonly referred to as *dō-żarb-e sangin* by *żarbgir*s as well.
93. Ḥosayn Tehrāni, interview in the radio program *Golchin-e hafta.*
94. Moḥammad Irāni Mojarrad, interview by Dāriush Ṣafvat, tape-recording, Tehran, 1969.
95. Hedāyat, *Majma' al-adwār* (manuscript) 2: 88, 104; Forṣat al-Dawla Shirāzi, *Buḥūr al-alḥān*, 21.

6

MUSICAL GENRES

To give an outline of the historical development of musical genres and forms of composition in Iran is no easy matter, especially for the first five centuries after the advent of Islam. Scattered sources of information, however, show that as early as the eighth century, many regions housed centers of musical learning and a few urban and rural areas had developed their own stylistic song types or vocal genres. According to Abū al-Faraj al-Iṣfahānī (d. 971), two singers at the Umayyad court, Ibn Misjaḥ (d. *c.* 715) and Ibn Muḥriz (d. *c.* 715), traveled to Persia and Syria to take music lessons and subsequently set Arabic verses to Persian melodies and compositions.[1] Likewise, Ibrāhīm al-Mawsilī (d. 804), the celebrated composer and *'ud* player of the Abbasid court, spent some years in Ray studying music with the master musicians of that city. He also went to al-Ubulla, a town to the northwest of the Persian Gulf, where he learned Persian songs from the Zoroastrian musician Javānuya (Arabic Jawānawayh) and his disciples.[2] Al-Kindī refers to distinct song types or melodies among the Persians, Daylamites, and Khazar communities, while prominent courts gradually began to patronize elaborate Arabic and Persian compositions.[3] The poet Rudaki (d. *c.* 941), a boon companion of the Samanid potentate Naṣr II (r. 914–943), allegedly composed songs to his own verses and accompanied himself on the lute or the harp. The same is reported of Farrokhi Sistāni (d. 1038), who was at the service of the Ghaznavid ruler, Maḥmud (r. 999–1030).[4]

No explicit account of musical genres and forms of composition in Persian culture is included in pre-Timurid or post-Safavid musical texts; only musical treatises written in the period between the fifteenth and eighteenth centuries treat this topic. In these treatises, descriptions of genres are often brief and seem to have been written in the tradition of freely copying verbal accounts from text to text, either word by word or paraphrased. Consequently, it is not surprising to see that a substantial amount of information in all treatises is similar. Yet some texts are unique in alluding to certain characteristic features of genres that are not addressed in other sources. Music theorists mostly define genres in reference to their forms, and in some cases, they mention certain obligations, prohibitions, and options attached to them. Nonetheless, each genre could also be differentiated from others based on its lyrics, poetic meters, rhythmic cycles, techniques of variation, and the rendition of verse and non-textual syllables. Music theorists often include a description and arrangement of short or extended suites in their account of musical genres. In different periods, these suites had different forms and names and typically consisted of a set of composed and improvised pieces.

The Early History of Musical Genres in Persia

Including a complete chapter on genres and outlining their formal and melodic structures in Persian musical treatises is a convention that first arose with ʿAbd al-Qāder Marāghi and continued with some of the prominent Timurid and Safavid music theorists. Sporadic references to some vocal genres, however, can be found in both literary and musical texts of the eleventh to fourteenth centuries.

Marāghi described musical genres in his three major treatises, but in *Sharḥ-e advār* he provided a more detailed account of their types and techniques of composition or rendition.[5] In chapter fifteen he writes:

> Musicians in the past (*qodamāʾ*) set the vocal compositions only to Arabic verse. Before these types of composition, there was only *nashid-e ʿarab*, and after that *basāʾeṭ* [sing. *basiṭ*], *aqvāl* [sing. *qawl*] and *navābet* [sing. *nawbat*] emerged. The names and types of vocal composition (*aṣnāf-e taṣānif*) are: *nashid-e ʿarab*, *basiṭ*, *nawbat-e morattab* (*qawl*, *ghazal*, *tarāna*, *forudāsht*, *mostazād*), *koll al-żorub*, *koll al-nagham*, *koll al-żorub va al-nagham*, *żarbayn*, *ʿamal*, *naqsh*, *ṣawt*, *havāʾi*, *pishraw*, *zakhma*, *moraṣṣaʿ*.[6]

Marāghi's statement that classical compositions were previously set to Arabic texts is of particular importance and clearly indicates that for much of the period between the ninth and twelfth centuries in Iran, stylish and elaborate sung court poetry was mainly composed in Arabic. Marāghi goes on to describe the structure of both Arabic and Persian genres, and in doing so uses a terminology for the internal divisions of compositions:

1. *ṭariqa-ye jadval* (later called *sarkhāna-ye avval*): the first section of a composition in which the first melodic line is introduced. It contained a melody of sufficient interest and attractiveness to bear frequent repetition throughout the composition;
2. *ṭariqa-ye maṭla'* (also called *jadval-e thāni* or *sarkhāna-ye dovom*): a repetition or variation of the *ṭariqa-ye jadval* set to a different text;
3. *ṣawt al-vasaṭ* (also called *miyānkhāna*): the second section of a composition in which a new theme or contrasting melodic line, often in a different mode, was introduced. The *ṣawt al-vasaṭ* was always followed by the *e'āda-ye ṭariqa*;
4. *e'āda-ye ṭariqa*: a modulatory phrase moving back to the melody of the *ṭariqa-ye jadval*;
5. *bāzgasht* or *tashyi'a* (later called *bāzguy*): the third section of a composition;
6. *naqsh-e molṣaqa*: decorating passages containing nontextual syllables connecting the *miyānkhāna* and *e'āda-ye ṭariqa*;
7. *alfāẓ-e naqarāt*: vocables or nontextual syllables in *taṣnifs*.

Arabic Genres

From the eighth or ninth century, *nashid* was the principal style of singing or chanting a *qaṣida* in an improvisatory manner in which the rhythm of the melody depended largely on a quantitative poetic meter. While Abū Naṣr al-Fārābī (d. 951) referred to *nashid* as a lengthy melodic recitation that serves as the opening sequence of a composition (*laḥn*), Abū al-Faraj al-Iṣfahānī (d. 971) indicated that it often consisted of two couplets of *qaṣida* rendered in an unmeasured fashion and normally followed by a *basiṭ*—another two couplets of *qaṣida* sung in a measured manner (that is, in conjunction with rhythmic cycles).[7]

Between the tenth and fifteenth centuries, *nashid* was frequently mentioned in *divāns* of many Persian poets, including Manuchehri Dāmghāni (d. 1040), Awḥad al-Din Anvari (d. 1189), Khāqāni (d. 1190), Farid al-Din Aṭṭār (d. 1221), and Jalāl al-Din Moḥammad Rumi (d. 1273).[8] Marāghi presented an explicit description of the genre:

> Musicians in the past set *nashid* to Arabic verses in such a way that the first two couplets rendered in *nathr-e naghamāt* are followed by another two couplets rendered in *naẓm-e naghamāt*. *Nathr-e naghamāt* is when melodizing (*talḥin*) is not done to a rhythmic cycle and thus has no *iqā'* whereas *naẓm-e naghamāt* is when it is done to a rhythmic cycle.[9]

Marāghi further stated that an entire Arabic *qaṣida* or Persian *ghazal* could have been performed in the style of *nashid* and, depending on the text, it could be called either *nashid-e 'arab* or *nashid-e 'ajam.*[10]

Along with *nashid*, as early as the ninth or tenth century, *qawl* achieved unprecedented prominence as the most popular and vital urban vocal genre, performed in various musical contexts, including Sufi *samā'* assemblies, private *maḥfels*, and courts.[11] The efflorescence of *qawl* is well documented in musical treatises as well as literary and Sufi texts. The earliest reference to *qawl* is in al-Fārābī's *Kitāb al-mūsīqī al-kabīr*, in which the author meticulously described possible variations in composing a *qawl* as a metric genre mainly in terms of its rhythmic structure, form and verse setting.[12] A few decades later 'Abd al-Raḥmān Qavvāl, a celebrated performer of *qawl*, is mentioned in *Tārikh-e Bayhaqi* as being in the service of the son of the Ghaznavid ruler Maḥmud (r. 998–1030).[13] In the eleventh century, Abū al-Karīm al-Qushayrī al-Nayshābūrī (d. 1074) related the story of an infant prince whose intelligence and acumen were assessed by his reaction to a *qawl* performed by a professional *qavvāl*.[14] Likewise, in his monumental book *Iḥyā' 'ulūm al-dīn* (*Revival of the Religious Sciences*), Abū Ḥāmid al-Ghazālī (d. 1111) frequently referred to *qawl* in reference to the assembly of *samā'*.[15] The structure of the incipient *qawl*, however, is not clearly delineated in these early sources beyond being described as a metric composition set to two to four couplets of Arabic *qaṣida*.[16] Al-Fārābī also specified that *qawl* was set to one or two rhythmic cycles and could have more than one section.[17]

Qawl was performed by a male or female singer who was called *qavvāl* in Arabic.[18] Moreover, *qavvāl* in a broad sense referred to a category of singers who performed measured songs and probably accompanied themselves on the *daf* (frame drum), in contrast to *nāshed*, the performers of free-rhythm *nashid*. Later on, when a *qawl* was set to a text combining both Arabic and Persian verses, it was known as *qawl-e moraṣṣa'*,[19] and when composed entirely in Persian, it was called *gofta*, or, probably in some practices, *pārsi*.[20] However, before the fourteenth century, *gofta* could be used to refer to any Persian measured song. The performer of *qawl* or *gofta* was referred to as *guyanda*, the exact Persian equivalent of *qavvāl*. In the eleventh century, Ghazālī mentioned both *guyanda* and *qavvāl* as performers of *qawl*.[21] Yet as explained in Chapter 1, after the fifteenth century the term *qavvāl* was used to refer specifically to a female performer who served as a courtesan in courts and public arenas, while *guyanda* was primarily reserved for a professional male performer of *taṣnif*.

A *qawl* attributed to Ṣafī al-Dīn al-Urmawī is transcribed by Qoṭb al-Din Shirāzi in the music section of *Durrat al-tāj*.[22] Even though Shirāzi does not provide a description of *qawl* or any further information about the genre, it is conceivable that *qawl* was by far the most popular form of composition in Persia up until the mid-fourteenth century. Nearly a century after Shirāzi, Marāghi outlined the structure of *qawl* as follows:

> *Qawl* is set to Arabic verse and could begin from any beat of the rhythmic cycle. *Qawl* has to have two sections (*ṭariqas*): *ṭariqa-ye jadval* and *ṭariqa-ye maṭla'*. The *ṭariqa-ye maṭla'* can be set to either a hemistich or a couplet (*bayt*). The inclusion of a *ṣawt* or *bayt al-vasaṭ* is at the discretion of the composer; he can choose to add that in the composition or not. If he sets the *ṭariqa-ye jadval* to a hemistich, he is required to set the *miyānkhāna* to a couplet; in that case the first hemistich [of *miyānkhāna*] serves to introduce a contrasting theme and the second hemistich serves to return to the first theme. Likewise, if the *ṭariqa* is set to a couplet, the *ṣawt* has to be set to two couplets—the first couplet to introduce a contrasting theme (*āhang-e motaghayyera*) and the second couplet to return to the first theme (*e'āda-ye ṭariqa*). The *e'āda-ye ṭariqa*, whether it is a couplet or hemistich, should be exactly similar to *ṭariqa-ye jadval* both in quality and quantity. If a composer desires to add decorating passages (*noqush*) it is acceptable, and if he refuses to do so, it is not defective. The passage that

comes between the *ṣawt* and *e'āda-ye ṭariqa* is called *naqsh-e molṣaqa*. It should be noted that the *miyānkhāna* and the first section can begin from the same or different beats of the rhythmic cycle.[23]

During the thirteenth century, a sequence of four *qawl*s performed in a court musical gathering was called *nawbat-e morattab*. In this sequence, the first *qawl* was set to an Arabic *qaṣida*, and the second *qawl* was set to a Persian *ghazal*; the third, called *tarāna*, was set to a quatrain; and, finally, the *forudāsht* was again set to an Arabic *qaṣida*. While *nawbat* was initially a performance format, during the thirteenth and fourteenth centuries a number of court musicians began to write compositions specifically in that form. Before Marāghi, documentation of *nawbat* is very limited. Only the texts of a few *nawbat*s ascribed to Ṣafī al-Dīn al-Urmawī and his disciples were recorded in the tenth volume of the *Masālik al-abṣār fi mamālik al-amṣār* (*Paths of Perspicacity in Sovereignty of Kingdoms*) by Ibn Fażl Allāh al-'Umarī (d. 1349).[24] A number of *nawbat*s attributed to Marāghi have been documented in both Persian and Ottoman song–text collections.[25] Moreover, Marāghi added a fifth section to the *nawbat-e morattab* and called it *mostazād*, but this seemingly did not receive much acceptance among his contemporaries or the subsequent generation of musicians.[26]

Another Arabic vocal genre, *basiṭ*, was more respected and can be traced back to as early as the ninth or tenth century through Arabic sources, specifically, the *Kitāb al-aghānī* (*Book of Songs*).[27] References to *basiṭ* appear in the fourteenth-century Persian treatise *Kanz al-tuḥaf* as well, where *basā'eṭ*, *aqvāl*, *abyāt*, and *havā'i*s are mentioned as the major vocal genres composed in various rhythmic cycles.[28] The author of *Kanz al-tuḥaf* specified that *qawl* was exclusively composed in the cycles of *thaqil-e avval* and *thaqil-e thāni*, and that *basiṭ* was in the five rhythmic cycles of *khafif-e thaqil-e avval*, *khafif-e thaqil-e thāni*, *ramal*, *khafif-e ramal*, and *hazaj*, Marāghi, however, limited the composition of *basiṭ* to three of these cycles: *thaqil-e avval*, *thaqil-e thāni*, and *ramal*. According to Marāghi, the formal structure of *basiṭ* was similar to that of *qawl*. After the two *ṭariqa*s it might include a *miyānkhāna* but invariably concluded with a *bāzgasht*. This last section could be set either to nontextual syllables or to words.[29]

Persian Genres

Between the ninth and thirteenth centuries, *nashid*, *qawl*, and *basiṭ* were the stylish Arabic vocal genres widely performed in Khorasan and Isfahan; however a few sources from this period still refer to Persian quatrains known as *fahlaviyāt* in the vernacular or regional dialects of western, central, and northern Persia. These quatrains were sung as *ōrāmanān*, *sharva*, and *bāhār*—terms that most likely indicated vocal genres.[30] The author of *Maḥāsin Iṣfahān*, an eleventh-century text, mentions a number of song types, including *qomiband*, *tājiband*, *'arusi*, *rusharmiyāt*, *shabestāniyāt*, *kākoliyāt*, and *nayruziyāt* that were ostensibly performed in dialects of their associated regions.[31] Evidently the poetic meters of *fahlaviyāt* were largely based on the principles of Middle Iranian prosody. Yet with the adoption of Arabic prosody for Persian poetry and under its influence, *fahlaviyāt* were gradually adapted to the rules of quantitative meters.[32] Shams al-Dīn Qays Rāzī, the prominent scholar of prosody in the thirteenth century, referred to *mashākil* and *hazaj* as the most popular meters of *fahlaviyāt* and further emphasized that the melodized forms of these poems were known as *ōrāmanān*.[33] Singing *fahlaviyāt* seems to have been widespread in Persia as late as the fifteenth century. Marāghi, in *Jāmi' al-alḥān*, also presents a few examples in different vernacular dialects.[34]

By the eleventh and twelve centuries, literary Persian had replaced Arabic as the dominant language in the courts of the Ghaznavids and Seljuqs for official matters as well as for poetry. Composing and singing *ghazal*s as well as classical quatrains became common alongside the Arabic *qasida*. Many poets, including Ferdawsi (d. 1020), Manuchehri Dāmghāni (d. 1040), Anvari (d. 1189), and Sa'di (d. 1291), referred to singing *ghazal*s in their *divān*s. 'Onṣor al-Ma'āli, author of the *Qābus-nāma*, also mentioned Transoxanian quatrains and *ghazal*s as appropriate forms of poetry for singing, and he urged singers to follow the poetic meters closely.[35]

When Marāghi referred to performers of vocal genres that were rendered in an improvisatory manner where the rhythm depended mostly on a quantitative poetic meter rather than on rhythmic cycles, he mentioned *nāshedān-e 'arab* (Arab performers of *nashid*) as counterparts to *motaghazzelān-e 'ajam* (Persian singers of *ghazal*),[36] adding that singing the Persian *ghazal* was modeled after the performance of the Arabic *nashid*.[37]

Marāghi also named *'amal*, *naqsh*, *ṣawt*, and *havā'i* as types of Persian *taṣnif* composed and performed in rhythmic cycles. Distinctions between them, however, went deeper than the different formal structures commonly pointed to by music theorists, and may have included differences in their social context and in the social status of the musicians who performed them. Beginning in the fourteenth century, *'amal* emerged as the most serious Persian vocal genre, typically composed by court musicians. An *'amal* in its complete and perfect structure consisted of four sections: *ṭariqa-ye jadval*, *ṭariqa-ye maṭla'*, *miyānkhāna*, and *bāzgasht*. *Miyānkhāna* could be eliminated or even doubled, and the *bāzgasht* could be set either to nontextual syllables or verse.[38] However, the formal structure of *'amal* as described in Persian treatises and reflected in song–text collections does not differ substantially from *qawl* or *basiṭ*. In other words, *'amal* was essentially a *qawl* or *basiṭ* set to a Persian text. According to Marāghi, *'amal* was predominantly composed in short rhythmic cycles such as *ramal*, *mokhammas*, and *hazaj*.[39]

Between the seventh and tenth centuries in Damascus and later in Baghdad, *ṣawt* was the most popular urban genre, and was often set to two to four couplets of Arabic *qaṣida*. The monumental *Kitāb al-aghānī* documents a great deal of information about *ṣawt*s composed in the tenth century and earlier.[40] In the early Timurid period (1370–1507), however, Marāghi categorized *ṣawt* among the Persian genres. He declared that *ṣawt* lacked nontextual syllables and that when it was composed, the verse, rhythmic cycle, and melodic phrase fit perfectly together, and all commenced and ended at the same point.[41]

At the turn of the fifteenth century, *naqsh* was a short composition set to verse and nontextual syllables. Marāghi stated that it was analogous to the *ṭariqa-ye maṭla'* of an *'amal*, stressing that there was no melodic or rhythmic modulation in *naqsh*. He indicated that in *naqsh*, only a single melodic phrase or theme was introduced, irrespective of the number of lines of poetic text.[42]

Havā'i, also called *mardomzād* (lit. "offspring of people"), was a light composition that can be traced back to the eleventh century.[43] During the fourteenth century, *havā'i* was a genre of its own, but gradually *naqsh* and *ṣawt* fell into the category of *havā'i*, especially when people performed them according to their own predilection.[44]

Another genre that seems to have emerged in the late thirteenth or early fourteenth century was *pishraw*. Ibn Fażl Allāh al-'Umarī ascribed the invention of *pishraw* to Kamāl Tawrizi, a musician at the court of the Ilkhanid ruler Abu Sa'id Bahādor Khān.[45] Kamāl Tawrizi must have been a seminal figure in the fresh infusion and development of the *pishraw*, but references to *pishraw* in early fourteenth-century texts such as the *Durrat al-tāj* of Qoṭb al-din Shirāzi and Mobārakshāh's commentary on *Kitāb al-adwār* suggest that the genre may have originated at least a few decades earlier. Shirāzi indicates that the embryonic form of *pishraw* had an accented rhythm or a regular pulse but was not in rhythmic cycles (*iqā' bāshad, bi advār*). Mobārakshāh also refers to *pishraw* as a type of melody with an explicit regular pulse.[46] In the fourteenth and fifteenth centuries, *pishraw* was described mostly as a vocal genre set to nontextual syllables. However, Marāghi made clear that *pishraw* had both vocal and instrumental versions. He stated that a *pishraw* could include up to fifteen sections (*bayt*s or *khāna*s) and a segment of the first *khāna* was often selected as the *e'āda-ye ṭariqa* that also served as a ritornello at the end of subsequent *khāna*s. In the vocal version such a ritornello was known as *tarji'band*, whereas in the instrumental version it was called *sarband*.[47] Marāghi further declared that *pishraw* had always been composed in the two rhythmic cycles of *ramal* and *mokhammas*.[48]

In addition to these vocal genres listed and described in his three treatises, Marāghi also wrote compositions in the forms of *qeṭ'a* (set to Arabic verse) and *zakhma* (set to Persian verse).[49] Samples of composition in these two forms have survived in a short song–text collection that he compiled toward the end of his life.[50]

Evidently, not all the items in Marāghi's list should be considered as vocal or instrumental genres or forms of composition. Rather, some of the items, for example, *koll al-żorub*, *koll al-nagham*, *koll al-żorub va al-nagham*, *żarbayn*, and *moraṣṣa'*, were "compositional devices" that could be employed and applied in the composition of various forms, such as *qawl*, *basiṭ*, and *'amal*.[51] While these compositional devices are not distinctly separated from genres, they were described by Marāghi as follows:

1. *koll al-żorub*: using all the rhythms in a composition;
2. *koll al-nagham*: using all the melodic modes in a composition;
3. *koll al-żorub va al-nagham*: using all the rhythms and melodic modes in a composition;
4. *żarbayn*: using two different rhythms in a composition;
5. *moraṣṣa'* (lit. "bejeweled"): using Arabic, Persian and even Turkish texts in a composition.[52]

The Late Timurid Period

Toward the end of the fifteenth century, Herati music theorists Awbahi and his disciple, Bannā'i, also described vocal genres in their treatises. The accounts of these two writers are not significantly different to that of Marāghi, but they tend to use Persian terms that were more common among practicing musicians than the complex Arabic terms employed by Systematist music theorists. For instance, instead of referring to the first two sections of a composition as *ṭariqa-ye jadval* and *ṭariqa-ye maṭla'*, they simply mention *sarkhāna-ye avval* and *sarkhāna-ye dovom*. They also state that the free exposition of modes or *āvāzs* played on musical instruments was called *navākht*, and that what was outside the category of *navākht*—primarily the parts constrained by rhythmic cycles—was categorized as *taṣnif*. Awbahi and Bannā'i both list a group of musical genres and compositional devices as "the conventional types of *taṣnif*." Their lists include the following names:

> *pishraw, ṣawt, naqsh, 'amal, basiṭ, qawl, ghazal, qawl-e moraṣṣa', koll al-nagham, koll al-żorub, kolliyāt, nawbat, tarāna, forudāsht, mostazād, rikhta, nashid-e 'arab.*[53]

Bannā'i introduced *qawl* as a bipartite vocal composition consisting of two *sarkhānas* and one *bāzguy* set to Arabic verse. Awbahi also specified that *qawl* was typically composed in a bipartite format, adding that *sarkhānas* were followed by a *bāzguy* or a *miyānkhāna*. He further stated that in a more general sense a *qawl* may consist of three sections: *sarkhānas*, *miyānkhāna*, and *bāzguy*—a broad description that exists in Marāghi's treatises as well.[54]

An important musical term that seems to have emerged in the late Timurid period is *kār*. Bannā'i used *kār* ("work") to designate different sections of *nawbat*: *qawl*, *ghazal*, *tarāna*, and *forudāsht*.[55] In his memoir, Bābur used *ish* (the Turkish equivalent of *kār*) in almost the same way to refer to various compositional genres, for example, *naqsh* and *ṣawt*.[56] While *kār* later became a specific vocal genre, any compositional genre could also be referred to as *kār*, and this remained the case even after the Timurid period.[57]

Another musical development in the fifteenth century was the likely emergence of the term *kolliyāt*. A *kolliyāt* was a composed piece in which the composer employed full sets of modes and rhythmic cycles through which he

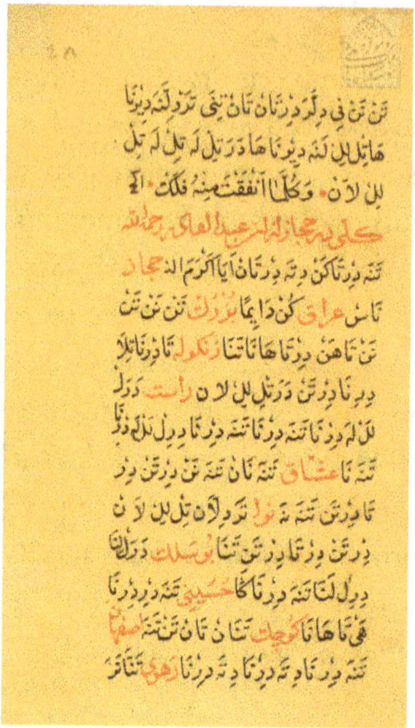

Figure 6.1 A folio with *kolliyāt* attributed to ʿAbd al-Qāder Marāghi. *Nuzhat al-arwāḥ*, Malek Library (Tehran) MS 1665, f. 48.

displayed his musical knowledge and workmanship. A *kolliyāt* further served as a reference guide that musicians used both to study and teach about the modal and rhythmic systems. Awbahi refers to the notable *kolliyāt* composed by Marāghi that represented *koll al-żorub* (all meters and rhythmic cycles) and *koll al-nagham* (all melodic modes).[58] The *kolliyāt* attributed to Marāghi was venerated among music theorists up until the end of the Safavid period and its text was occasionally documented in song–text collections and musical treatises (Figure 6.1).[59]

It is in late fifteenth-century Herat that we find early references to *faṣl* (lit. "segment," "chapter") as a sequence of pieces.[60]

Overview of Accounts of Musical Genres in Safavid Treatises

Description of genres was mostly ignored by early Safavid music theorists, who tended to be more interested in the hoary modal system and rhythmic cycles than in contemporary classical and regional genres. From the second half of the sixteenth century, however, music theorists began again to describe the genres based on their formal structures. The terminology for the internal division of compositions in the Safavid period can be recapitulated and interpreted as follows:

1. *sarkhāna-ye avval*: the first section of a composition in which the first melodic theme is introduced and set to a few verses of a poem whose length usually does not exceed two couplets;
2. *sarkhāna-ye dovom*: a repetition or variation of the *sarkhāna-ye avval* set to subsequent verses of the poem;
3. *miyānkhāna*: the second section of a composition introducing a new theme or contrasting melodic line, often in a different mode;
4. *bāzguy*: the third section of a composition, often with a contrasting poetic meter or rhythmic structure;
5. *dhayl*: a vocal ritornello containing verse and the syllables of *hay hay hā hā*;
6. *lāzema*: ritornello in both vocal and instrumental genres;
7. *naqarāt*: nontextual syllables of *dar tanā dar tanā* ;
8. *tarannom*: nontextual syllables of *ya la lā*.

Around 1580, almost a century after Awbahi and Bannā'i in Herat, Dawra Beg Karāmi, a poet-composer in the same city, outlined the compositional genres (*taṣnif*s) as follows:

> *Naqsh* is the one whose *bayti* (verse section) and *naqarāt* (nontextual syllables) are the same.
>
> *Naqshayn* is the one whose verse and nontextual syllables are different. Nontextual syllables in both [i.e., *naqsh* and *naqshayn*] are *ya la lā*; they don't contain *tan tan*.
>
> *Ṣawt* contains one section including *sarkhāna*, *miyānkhāna* and a *bāzguy* performed in the form of wailing (*nāla*).
>
> *'Amal* contains two *sarkhāna*s in the same style (*ṭarz*), a *miyānkhāna* and a *bāzguy*. Both *sarkhāna*s begin with verses. Its nontextual syllables are *tan tan* and do not include *ya la lā*.
>
> *Kār* contains a sequence of unlimited parts (*baḥri nā-motenāhi*). The *sarkhāna* begins with nontextual syllables followed by delivery of verses (*bayt khᵛāni*) and returning to nontextual syllables again. *Kār* contains two *sarkhāna*s in the above style, a *miyankhāna* and a *bāzguy*.

> *Qawl* contains two *sarkhāna*s in the same style and a *bāzguy*. It does not have the *miyānkhāna*. Its text could be either in Arabic or Persian and it is acceptable to begin either with verse or nontextual syllables. However, the majority of *qawl*s begin with nontextual syllables.
>
> *Sarghazal* is a section of verse including a *sarkhāna*, a *miyānkhāna* and a *bāzguy*.
>
> *Tarāna* contains three parts (*gusha*s), each set to a different [poetic] style (*ṭarz*). The first is a section of verse, the second a praise or blame (*madḥ ya dhamm*) and the last [the syllables] of *ya la lā* and *ta la lā*; likewise *mosajja'*.
>
> *Rikhta* is in the rhythmic cycle of *awfar* with a section of verse. Its nontextual syllables could be either *tan tan* or *ya la lā*.
>
> *Pishraw* and *sarband* are the arts of instrumentalists.
>
> *Pishraw* contains a *sarkhāna*, a *miyānkhāna* and a *bāzguy*. Every section has a *lāzema* (ritornello) or a *taqrib-e lāzema* (modified or short version of ritornello) in the same style.
>
> *Sarband* is arranged in the same rhythmic cycles as *rikhta* [i.e., light *oṣul*s such as *awfar*] and its melodic elaboration is based on improvisation (*badiha*). Whenever master musicians come together for a musical contest, they begin [their performance] by playing a *sarband* so that the ability of each can be displayed.[61]

At roughly the same time, Mir Ṣadr al-Din Moḥammad, who is discussed in Chapters 4 and 5, gives a detailed description of vocal genres that divides them into two main categories: (1) *khosh-khᵛāni be nathr* or *nathr-khᵛāni*, and (2) *khosh-khᵛāni be naẓm*.

> *Nathr-khᵛāni* does not fall into the category of *talḥin*, for using the meters (*mozun budan*) or singing based on *oṣul* (rhythmic cycles) is the main concept of the latter . . . *Khᵛānandegi* is of two types: Arabic and Persian. Singing to Arabic verse is called *nashid*, but singing to Persian verse is known by different names: *dōbayt-khᵛāni*, *ghazal-khᵛāni* and *khᵛānandegi*. This type of singing used to be called *khosravāni* in the past.
>
> *Khosh-khᵛāni be naẓm* is singing melodies that are conjoined with specific rhythmic cycles and these are of different types:
>
> 1. The one that lacks verse, but contains *sarkhāna*, *miyānkhāna* and *bāzguy* is called *pishraw*. If it only contains a *sarkhāna* without *miyānkhāna* and *bāzguy*, it is called *bi-bayti* and *sarband* which is the same.

2. The *taṣnif*s that are set to verse are of various types as follows: *kār, 'amal, qawl, ghazal, tarāna, nawbat-e morattab, rikhta, ṣawt, naqsh.*[62]

Mir Ṣadr al-Din Moḥammad subsequently states that practicing musicians use different criteria to distinguish among the genres and that there is no consensus among them. In some cases, he first mentions the prevailing opinion and subsequently gives his own verdict.

> Some have said that, if a composition contains two *sarkhāna*s, a *miyānkhāna* and a *bāzguy* and it is in any rhythmic cycles of *żarb al-fatḥ*, *chāhārżarb*, *thaqil*, and *khafif*, that composition is *kār*. And what has been composed in the rhythmic cycle of *torki żarb* is called *'amal*. And what lacks a *miyānkhāna* is *qawl*. However, this explanation is refuted for various reasons and at this time it is not tolerated.
>
> The true difference between *kār* and *'amal*, which each contain *sarkhāna*, *miyānkhāna* and *bāzguy*, is that in *kār* the composition begins with nontextual syllables, i.e., *tan dar tan* and other syllables, but in *'amal*, the beginning is from verses. In *qawl*, the beginning is often from nontextual syllables, and it happens sometimes that the beginning is from verses too.
>
> The difference between *qawl* and *kār*, when the beginning of the composition is from nontextual syllables, is that *qawl* lacks a *miyānkhāna*, whereas *kār* contains it. Likewise, the difference between *qawl* and *'amal*, when *qawl* starts with verses, is that the former lacks the *miyānkhāna*, whereas *'amal* contains it.
>
> As for the distinction between *qawl* and *ghazal*, whatever is composed on an Arabic verse without a *miyānkhāna* is *qawl*, and likewise, whatever is completed on a Persian verse without a *miyānkhāna* is *ghazal*.
>
> *Tarāna* is precisely the same as *qawl* and *ghazal*, but for the most part, its verse is nothing but *robā'i*s.
>
> *Nawbat* consists of *'amal, qawl, tarāna* and *kār*: instead of the first *sarkhāna* of *kār*, there is an *'amal* in *nawbat-e morattab*. Instead of the second *sarkhāna* of *kār*, which is akin to the first *sarkhāna* as far as the melody is concerned, there is a *qawl*—without a recurrence of melodies (*naghamat-e ghayr-e mokarrar*)—in it. Instead of a *miyānkhāna* there is a *tarāna* and instead of a *bāzguy* a *kār*. Every one of these pieces (*qeṭ'as*) included in *nawbat* should be rendered without a recurrence of verses and nontextual syllables. There is no composition more complicated than this in musical practice . . .
>
> *Rikhta*, in reality, is a form of *'amal* that is completed in light and delightful rhythmic cycles, especially *dawr-e ravān* and *awfar*. Sometimes the *sarkhāna*

and the *bāzguy* are connected with one another in such a way that they sound from the beginning to the end as a single section. And this type of composition, namely *rikhta*, is extremely charming and pleasant. This composition could only be accomplished by Khᵛāja 'Abd al-Qāder.

Ṣawt begins with verse (*she'r*) and from verse moves to nontextual syllables and comes to the second hemistich and finally a *dhayl* including *hay hay hā hā* is added to that. Sometimes *ya lā lā ya lā* are also heard in the *dhayl* of *ṣawt* which are hideous. *Ṣawt* is indeed the *sarkhāna* of an *'amal* that is lacking the *miyānkhāna* and the *bāzguy*. *Ṣawt* is not composed in long rhythmic cycles such as *khafif* and *thaqil*; its verses include conventional and established types of poems and no more than three couplets are to be sung in it, except by repetition.

Naqsh is also reminiscent of *ṣawt*, except for the fact that any verse that is fitting to the rhythm (*vazn*) of its melody is sung in *naqsh*; it doesn't have to be set to specific types of poem. What is articulated in the *bayti* section of *naqsh* is *ya la lā*, but in *ṣawt* it is *tan dar tan*. Just like *ṣawt*, it does not return to the second hemistich of the poem. Similar to *ṣawt*, *naqsh* is also a composition on light and pleasant rhythmic cycles. Strangely enough, experience has shown that by comparison a *naqsh* composed on the rhythmic cycle of *mokhammas* is more pleasant than a *ṣawt* [on the same rhythmic cycle] and the reason is not known.

At times *kār* and *'amal* are composed on two rhythmic cycles and this form is called *żarbayn*. Sometimes more than two, even up to ten or twenty, rhythmic cycles are used and this doesn't have a separate name, unless all the rhythmic cycles are combined together at once and in that case rhythmic cycles are stated throughout the composition (*āhang*) one by one and this is called *koll al-żorub*.

Another form of composition (*kār*), analogous to *nawbat-e morattab*, is *kolliyāt* in that the entire set of modes and melodies (*āhangs*), including *maqāms*, *āvāzas* and *sho'bas*, is explored in such a way that it becomes a manual for practicing musicians.[63]

As mentioned previously, Bāqiyā Nā'ini usually discusses Persian and Indian music as two separate topics. In the case of musical genres, he follows the same pattern, although here and there he makes comparisons or underlines genres commonly practiced in both traditions. In the Fourth Murmur of his musical treatise, *Zamzama-ye vaḥdat*, he introduces the Persian genres as follows:

It should be stated that a melody (*naghma*) which is sung without *oṣul* is called in Iran *dōbayti* and in India *ālāpchāri*. What is with *oṣul* is of two types; either the melody is arranged without a text or it contains a text, and the text could be either in Persian, Arabic or Turkish.

As for the one without a text, if it contains *sarkhāna*, *miyānkhāna* and *bāzguy*, it is called *peshraw*. If it only contains a *sarkhāna* without *miyānkhāna* and *bāzguy*, then it is called *bi-bayti*.

Melody set to verses is of twelve types: *kār*, *'amal*, *qawl*, *ghazal*, *tarāna*, *nawbat-e morattab*, *rikhta*, *ṣawt*, *naqsh*, *naqshayn* and *varsāqi*.

Kār contains two *sarkhāna*s, a *miyānkhāna*, and a *bāzguy*. It is composed in long rhythmic cycles such as *chāhārẓarb*, *ẓarb al-fatḥ*, *thaqil* and *khafif*. The opening section of this composition contains non-textual syllables, that is to say, *dar tanā dar tanā*.

'Amal's specifications are also the same as what was mentioned [for *kār*], except for the fact that it begins with verses, not nontextual syllables. Nonetheless, there is a difference of opinion on this issue.

Qawl is the one that contains two *sarkhāna*s and a *bāzguy*, but it lacks the *miyānkhāna*. It is set to Arabic verses just like the *qawl* of "Aḥsan Suqan", composed by Khᵛāja 'Abd al-Qāder. Amir Khosraw also composed many *qawl*s in the same category. [*Qawl*] begins sometimes with verses and sometimes with nontextual syllables.

Ghazal is also in the style of *qawl*. However, the difference between *qawl* and *ghazal* is that *qawl* is set to Arabic verses whereas *ghazal* is set to Persian verses.

Tarāna is also in the style of *qawl* and *ghazal*. However, the verses of *tarāna* are nothing but quatrains, either in Persian or Arabic.

Nawbat is a compound (*morakkab*) form consisting of *kār*, *'amal*, *qawl* and *tarāna*. At the present time nobody recalls *nawbat* or has heard its types. Only its name appears in books and treatises.

Rikhta, so-called, is an *'amal* composed in light rhythmic cycles such as *awfar* and so on. Sometimes Arabic, Turkish or Hindi words creep into Persian lines and in that case, they connect the *sarkhāna*s, *miyānkhāna*s and *bāzguy*s of *rikhta* together. By doing so, it sounds like one piece (*qeṭ'a*) from the beginning to the end and this type of composition is very delightful and pleasing.

Ṣawt begins with verses and followed by two hemistiches of nontextual syllables in the category of *dar tanā dar tanā*. A *dhayl* such as *hay hay hay* or *hā hā hay* is added after the nontextual syllables. Its verses are not more than three couplets unless they are repeated.

Naqsh can be arranged with any type of verse and with various poetic meters. Its nontextual syllables are *ya la lā* and *ta ra lā* and it is mostly composed in light rhythmic cycles.

> *Naqshayn* begins with verse and after each hemistich (*meṣra'*) a small unit of nontextual syllables such as "*ya la lā*" or "*ta ra lā*" is added and sung. It could be either one couplet (*bayt*) or more than that.
>
> *Varsāqi* is set to a Turkish text. More often than not, they perform three hemistiches of this composition and then return to the same hemistich they sang at the beginning. Subsequently, they sing three more hemistiches and then return to the hemistich they sang in the first *sarkhāna* and sing the same hemistich in the first manner. *Varsāqi* is completed either in one *sarkhāna* containing three hemistiches or more, God knows the best.[64]

Bāqiyā Nā'ini described Indian vocal genres in a separate chapter and mentioned in particular *qawl-e fārsi* and *tarāna* as two vocal genres that were cultivated by Amir Khosrow.

> *Qawl-e fārsi* and *tarāna* that are composed and sung at the present time are all styles and manners of the most accomplished of pearl-seekers of the spiritual ocean, Amir Khosraw Dehlavi. In this epoch, the Indian system of musical composition and singing is based on *khiyāl*, *dhrupad*, *vishnupad*, *qawl-e fārsi* and *tarāna*.[65]

In the first half of the seventeenth century, Āqā Mo'men Moṣannef also wrote a section on musical genres that was probably based on his own practical knowledge and experience. He was a prolific composer who created more than fifty-five compositions during his career at the court, and except in two or three cases, he labeled all his compositions as *taṣnif*. Nonetheless, in his theoretical tract, he declares:

> In the dominion of composers, a person who has composed one or two *taṣnifs* cannot be considered a *moṣannef* (composer). A fully-fledged composer should be knowledgeable of the entire melodic system and genres of composition. He is obliged to know the difference between *kār*, *qawl*, *ṣawt*, *'amal*, *nakhsh*, *nakhshayn*, and *tarāna*, so that once he is commissioned to write a particular composition, he knows how to compose it. Most of the composers whom I, Mo'men Moṣannef, have met and had discussions with on these principles, were unable to converse about this issue. What I have discovered so far are the following principles:
>
> *Kār* begins with *naqarāt* followed by verse. Verses are followed by *naqarāt* again that also include a *dhayl* (ritornello). The second *sarkhāna* is sung to the same specifications. Two *sarkhānas* are followed by a *miyānkhāna*, and it

> is up to the composer to begin and end the *miyānkhāna* with verse or *naqarāt*. Finally, the *miyānkhāna* is followed by a *bāzgu*.
>
> *Qawl* is composed in the same style as *kār* but lacks the *bāzgu*. The difference between *kār* and *qawl* is just that.
>
> *Ṣawt* is entirely in the form of *sarkhāna*. Every *sarkhāna* includes both verse and *naqarāt*. The *dhayl* section lacks *naqarāt* and always remains the same.
>
> *'Amal* is composed based on the same specifications as *kār*, that is to say, it includes two *sarkhāna*s, a *miyānkhāna* and a *bāzgu*. However, the difference between *kār* and *'amal* is that *kār* begins with *naqarāt* whereas *'amal* begins with verse.
>
> *Nakhsh* begins with verse and after that a *tarannom*, which includes *ya la lā*, is sung. No matter how many *sarkhāna*s are sung, the *tarannom* remains the same throughout.
>
> *Nakhshayn* is composed in the same style as *nakhsh*, but every hemistich is followed by a *tarannom* and at last it concludes with a *tarannom*. Since the *tarannom* appears in two sections, it is called *nakhshayn*.
>
> *Tarāna* can begin with either verse, or *naqarāt* or *tarannom*. Being set to suitable verse, it can end with any type of nontextual syllables including both *naqarāt* or *tarannom*.[66]

Unlike Āqā Mo'men Moṣannef, who was a Persian composer and always set his compositions to Persian text, Amir Khān Gorji had a Georgian background and wrote compositions in both Persian and Turkish. Throughout his short musical treatise and song–text collection, Amir Khān demonstrated that the Safavid court in the seventeenth century was bilingual and supported composition of both Persian and Turkish songs.[67] Following an outline of rhythmic cycles, he first listed Persian genres and subsequently described Turkish genres that were practiced presumably among the Qizilbāsh and Caucasian musicians:

> Now we begin with the types of vocal composition. One must know that *dōbayt-khᵛāndan* is without *oṣul*. *Taṣnif* is singing with *oṣul* and each type has a name and structure. They are distinguished from one another by their names and structures in the following order: *kār*, *'amal*, *qawl*, *ṣawt*, *naqsh*, *naqshayn*, *tarāna*, *taṣnif*, *varsāqi* and *pishraw*. In Turkish, *dōbayt* is called *ma'ni* and other types also have specific names through which they can be known. For instance, *ma'ni* is *dōbayt*, *varsāqi* is *taṣnif*, *torki* is a praise song with *oṣul*, *soy* is a song in praise of dynasties, *boy* is a prose style in praise of kings and their deeds, and finally *arasbāri* is the *pishraw* (instrumental composition) of Turks.[68]

Amir Khān Gorji further specified the structure of genres in the second part of his theoretical treatise known as *Resāla-ye mawzun*, which is entirely in verse.[69]

In addition to these Safavid sources one can find further details about the genres in two other Persian musical texts written by Transoxanian theorists, Najm al-Din Kawkabi and Darvish-ʿAli Changi.[70]

The Genres and their Structures in the Safavid Period

Musical sources reveal numerous facts about the development of vocal genres in the sixteenth and seventeenth centuries. Treatises describe the internal divisions and rhythmic structure of the genres while song–text collections mention the composer and provide details of the text setting and literary aspects of the compositions. Yet what remains more perplexing is the socio-cultural context in which these vocal genres were cultivated and performed. One may appropriately ask, who were the composers of *ʿamal*, *kār*, *qawl*, *ṣawt*, and *naqsh*—professional court composers or amateur poet-musicians? Who were their major exponents—female musicians and dancers or professional male singers and entertainers? Who were their patrons and in what musical contexts were these genres mostly performed? And, finally, what were the distinctive functions of the genres in a musical performance?

As noted above, Marāghi divided the styles of singing into *nathr-e naghamāt* and *naẓm-e naghamāt*. He and the two Herati music theorists who followed him, Awbahi and Bannā'i, also employ the term *navākht* for solo instrumental melodies not constrained by rhythmic cycles, like the later Turko-Arabic concept of *taqsim*.[71]

At the turn of the sixteenth century, Mir Ṣadr al-Din Moḥammad Qazvini indicated that the terms *nathr-e naghamāt* and *naẓm-e naghamāt* were still in use when he categorized singing into the two main styles of *nathr-khᵛāni* and *khosh-khᵛāni be naẓm*. He specified that *nathr-khᵛāni*, better known as *khᵛānandegi*, could be rendered in both Arabic and Persian. *Khᵛānandegi* in Arabic was confined to *nashid*, whereas in Persian there were two genres, *dōbayt-khᵛāni* (singing quatrains) and *ghazal-khᵛāni* (singing *ghazals*)—styles of singing formerly referred to as *khosravāni*.[72] Evidence shows that in this period the term *guyandegi* was still employed, and that it referred to singing *taṣnif*s or metric vocal genres. At the beginning of the seventeenth century, Eskandar Monshi, the prominent chronicler of the Safavid court, alluded to these two styles of singing in introducing court singers:

> Ḥāfeẓ Aḥmad Qazvini, while he excelled in *guyandegi*, was also celebrated in town for his vocal phrasing and nuances of *khᵛānandegi* . . .
>
> Ḥāfeẓ Jalājel combined both *khᵛānandegi* and *guyandegi* in the best possible way, and verily surpassed everyone else in the field. He was appointed *chālchi-bāshi* under Shah Esmāʿil II . . .
>
> It is a conventional belief that *khᵛānandegi* is the specialty of singers from Khorasan, and *guyandegi* is the specialty of singers from ʿErāq-e ʿAjam. While Ḥāfeẓ Moẓaffar Qomi was from ʿErāq-e ʿAjam, he was truly unique in ʿIrāq for performing in the style of Khorasan [i.e., *khᵛānandegi*].[73]

In general, singing *maqām*s was the responsibility of *khᵛānanda*s, who were largely male vocalists and mostly performed *dōbayt-khᵛāni* and *ghazal-khᵛāni*, whereas *taṣnif*s were sung by the male *taṣnif* singers called *guyanda*s and the female *taṣnif* singers known as *qavvāl*s. The title of *ḥāfeẓ* was also employed widely between the thirteenth and seventeenth centuries for "an esteemed male singer" who was primarily a reciter of the Qur'an and could perform both *khᵛānandegi* and *guyandegi*.[74] Other titles such as *sharva-guy*, *bāghāti-khᵛān*, and *sāqi-khᵛāni* were used to designate the singing of specific styles or subgenres, but unfortunately there are not many descriptions of them.[75] Another honorific title, *moraṣṣaʿ-khᵛān*, was also mentioned in some texts and most likely referred to a *khᵛānanda* who sang verses adorned with refined and fast passages of *taḥrir*.[76]

To sum up, the main genres that were constrained by the rhythmic cycles or *oṣul*s in the Safavid period were *kār*, *ʿamal*, *qawl*, *ṣawt*, *naqsh*, *naqshayn*, *tarāna*, *rikhta*, *varsāqi*, *pishraw*, and *arasbāri*. These are discussed below.

Kār and ʿAmal

In the late fifteenth century, *nawbat-e morattab* was still considered to be the most respected form of vocal composition, but it was gradually yielding in popularity to the large-scale forms of *kār* and *ʿamal*. The decline of the tradition-oriented Timurid court and the rise of smaller provincial courts during the sixteenth century also seems to have furthered the acceptance of *kār* and *ʿamal*, which were more virtuosic and entirely set to Persian texts.

Kār was the superordinate form of composition, and consisted of three parts: two *sarkhāna*s, a *miyānkhāna*, and a *bāzguy*. The two *sarkhāna*s were in the same mode and both commenced with nontextual syllables of *tan dar tan* followed by a few lines of a *ghazal*. *Sarkhāna*s preceded the *miyānkhāna*, which continued with subsequent lines of the opening *ghazal* while modulating to a different mode. The *miyānkhāna* could begin and end with verse or nontextual syllables, but at its conclusion it modulated back to the initial mode or theme of the composition. The last part, *bāzguy*, could also be set to nontextual syllables, verse or both, but it was apparently composed in a conspicuously different rhythmic structure, mostly set to a different verse with a distinctive poetic meter or a different *oṣul*, and it was probably rendered in a faster tempo than *sarkhāna*s and *miyānkhāna*s. While by convention a melodic modulation was to take place in the *miyānkhāna* and a rhythmic modulation in the *bāzguy*, in some cases the *miyānkhāna* was composed to a different rhythmic cycle or the *bāzguy* could be set to a different mode.[77] A *dhayl* (ritornello) was also appended to each part of *kār*. *Dhayl* was a distinct entity and usually began with the syllables *hay hay hā hā*. Syllabic material in *kār* was predominantly in the vein of *dar tanā dar tanā*, but in some cases included *ya la lā*.

The difference between *kār* and *ʿamal* is somewhat ambiguous in the Safavid period. Musical texts tend to claim that they both had the same formal division and that their only distinction was that *kār* commenced with nontextual syllables and *ʿamal* with verse. While Marāghi specified that *ʿamal* was composed in short rhythmic cycles, we know that during the sixteenth and seventeenth centuries, *kār* came to be composed in long *oṣul*s, including *żarb al-fatḥ*, *thaqil*, and *khafif*.[78] Mir Ṣadr al-Din Moḥammad stated that according to some musicians, *ʿamal* was meant to be composed in shorter rhythmic cycles, specifically, *torki żarb*, although he rejected this idea.

The respected repertoire of Safavid court music in the second half of the seventeenth century consisted of *kār*s and *ʿamal*s that were partly attributed to ʿAbd al-Qāder Marāghi and partly composed by some of the most celebrated court composers, including Amir Khān Gorji himself, Ṣāber Shirāzi, Mir Ṣawti, Kāẓem Chālchibāshi, and Morteżā-Qoli Beg Sarkār Khāṣṣa. Amir Khān Gorji documented more than twenty-two *kār*s and *ʿamal*s in his song–text collection, which represents the bulk of this material.[79]

Qawl

From the mid-fifteenth century, *qawl* was known as the bipartite vocal genre containing two *sarkhāna*s and a *bāzguy*. It largely began with nontextual syllables, and was set to Arabic texts.

During the fourteenth and probably early fifteenth century, when a *qawl* was set to a Persian text in the context of *nawbat-e morattab*, it was referred to by its poetic form, namely, *ghazal*. Yet no type of *taṣnif* under the rubric of *ghazal* ever developed as an independent genre in Iran. It seems that when a bipartite vocal composition was set to a Persian text, it was first known as *qawl-e fārsi* and only later as *qawl*. As mentioned above, Bāqiyā Nā'ini, a long-time resident of India, referred to *qawl-e fārsi* and *tarāna* as the two vocal genres that were cultivated among Muslim musicians in India and attributed their invention to Amir Khosraw. He also mentioned a kind of *ghazal* that was probably synonymous with *qawl-e fārsi* in Indian musical culture of the sixteenth century.

Āqā Mo'men and Amir Khān Gorji described *qawl* as a *kār* that lacked only the *bāzguy* section. Their descriptions may further indicate that what was primarily known as *qawl* in the Safavid period was a bipartite form containing either two *sarkhāna*s and a *bāzguy* or two *sarkhāna*s and a *miyānkhāna*. Among the *taṣnif*s composed by Āqā Mo'men there is only one composition marked as *qawl*, and it consists of two *sarkhāna*s and a *miyānkhāna* with every part followed by a *dhayl*.[80] Safavid sources do not mention anything about the rhythmic structure of *qawl*, but Darvish-'Ali Changi stated that the major difference between *qawl* and *kār* was that *qawl* was largely in short rhythmic cycles (*khafif*) while *kār* was always composed in long rhythmic cycles (*thaqil*).[81]

Female musicians and courtesans who were known as *qavvāl*s and male musicians who were linked to the same milieu seem to have been the major exponents of *qawl* in the Safavid period and earlier. The association of *qawl* with courtesan culture prevented it from being considered a respected genre that was included in Safavid song-text collections.

Ṣawt

Late Timurid music theorists defined *ṣawt* as a genre containing only one part (*khāna* or *sarkhāna*) that was repeated in a strophic style. Mir Ṣadr al-Din Moḥammad stated that *ṣawt* was similar to the *sarkhāna* of an *'amal*, and, hence, the composition characteristically lacked the *miyānkhāna* and *bāzguy*. It usually contained three couplets in a *khāna*, and every line was followed by nontextual syllables in the vein of *dar tanā dar tanā*. *Ṣawt* was usually composed in short cycles of *oṣul* and each *khāna* concluded with a *dhayl* beginning with *hay hay hā hā*. Inclusion of nontextual syllables in *ṣawt* was presumably a later development that happened in the Safavid period, for at the turn of the fifteenth century Marāghi clearly stated that *ṣawt* was devoid of *naqarāt*. Zayn al-Din Vāṣefi indicated that a *ṣawt* could also be performed in public gatherings in a call-and-response format between a lead singer and the public.[82]

Naqsh

Naqsh was primarily a novel melodic phrase or a short composition of sufficient attractiveness set to verse and nontextual syllables. Mir Ṣadr al-Din Moḥammad mentioned that *naqsh* lacked the *miyānkhāna* and *bāzguy*, but, unlike *ṣawt*, any verse that fit the rhythm of its melody could be performed in it. Bāqiyā Nā'ini also indicated that *naqsh* could be arranged with any verse and with various poetic meters. This suggests that, while *ṣawt* was invariably set to couplets containing two full hemistiches, *naqsh* could be set to verses of multiple meters or asymmetrical hemistiches. Song–text collections confirm this distinguishing feature of *ṣawt* and *naqsh*.[83] In the only example of *naqsh* documented in Amir Khān Gorji's collection, a section of the composition is marked as *saj'* (lit. "rhymed prose"), which clearly displays this particular characteristic of the genre.[84] Āqā Mo'men included a *ṣawt* among his compositions that consists of three couplets, adding that the *ṣawt* itself contained a *naqsh* that was performed as an additional section.[85] Sāsān Fāṭemi argues that *ṣawt* was perhaps distinguished from *naqsh* by syllabic declamation as well, since according to Marāghi the number of syllables in the verse fit the length of the melodic phrase. Therefore, in *ṣawt* the text was usually pronounced more distinctly and intelligibly than in *naqsh*, where the words could have been broken or rendered melismatically.[86]

A more conspicuous feature that distinguished *ṣawt* from *naqsh* concerned their syllabic materials. Safavid music theorists commonly declared that the nontextual syllables in *naqsh* were *tarannom* (*ya la lā*), whereas in *ṣawt* they were *naqarāt* (*tan dar tan*).[87] These specific characteristics of *ṣawt* and *naqsh* can be verified from the compositions in the seventeenth-century Ottoman song–text collection of Hâfız Post.[88] *Ṣawt* and *naqsh* were both composed in light rhythmic cycles. According to Mir Ṣadr al-Din Moḥammad and Darvish-'Ali Changi, *mokhammas* was a rhythmic cycle *par excellence* for *naqsh*, and a *naqsh* composed in *mokhammas* was more admired and pleasant than a *ṣawt* composed in the same rhythmic cycle.[89] Finally, Bannā'i declared that *naqsh* was less rigid than *ṣawt*, and its text was more sentimental and romantic.[90]

Naqshayn was a modified version of *naqsh* that likely emerged at the beginning of the Safavid period. While in *naqsh* the nontextual syllables were rendered at the end of each couplet (*bayt*), in *naqshayn* every hemistich (*meṣrāʿ*) was followed by nontextual syllables.

Tarāna

Mir Ṣadr al-Din Moḥammad and Bāqiyā Nā'ini introduced *tarāna* as a form of *qawl* (two *sarkhānas* and a *bāzguy/miyānkhāna*) set particularly to quatrains. Dawra Beg Karāmi described *tarāna* as having three parts, each set to a different poetic style. The first part, he stated, was a section of verse, the second part was praise or blame (*madḥ ya dhamm*) and the last part was nontextual syllables. Āqā Mo'men instead provided a very broad description of the genre, stating that it could begin with either verse or nontextual syllables but always concluded with nontextual syllables and could be set to any suitable verse.

Rikhta

The emergence of *rikhta* as a vocal genre was closely related to the *rekhta* language that was the precursor of Urdu and contained elements of both Persian and Hindi. *Rikhta* seems to have flourished in Herat probably in the first half of the fifteenth century. Bannā'i described *rikhta* as a form of vocal *pishraw* set to prose, and declared that it could be set to verses filled with humor and ridicule.[91] Mir Ṣadr al-Din Moḥammad and Bāqiyā Nā'ini both introduced *rikhta* as a form of *ʿamal* composed in light rhythmic cycles such as *dawr-e ravān* and *awfar* in which *sarkhāna*, *miyānkhāna*, and *bāzguy* were smoothly and effortlessly connected. Bāqiyā Nā'ini confirmed that the text of *rikhta* was primarily in Persian but might contain a mixture of Arabic, Turkish, or Hindi words. Dawra Beg Karāmi specifically mentioned *awfar* as the rhythmic cycle of *rikhta* and indicated that its nontextual syllables could be anything, including *tan tan* and *ya la lā*. While *rikhta* is not mentioned in the treatises of Marāghi, both Mir Ṣadr al-Din Moḥammad and Darvish-ʿAli Changi attributed the composition of highly amiable *rikhtas* to Khᵛāja ʿAbd al-Qāder.[92]

Pishraw

Dawra Beg Kerāmī is the first music theorist who directly referred to *pishraw* as an instrumental genre in the Safavid period. He described it as containing a *sarkhāna*, *miyānkhāna*, and *bāzguy*, with each part followed by a ritornello (*lāzema*) or a slightly modified version of the ritornello (*taqrib-e lāzema*). Mir Ṣadr al-Din Moḥammad stated that *pishraws* were typically composed in the rhythmic cycle of *dō-yek* and that *pishraws* not composed in that *oṣul* did not sound euphonious.[93]

Sarband

In the first half of the fifteenth century, Marāghi referred to *sarband* as the ritornello of *pishraw*. Yet almost a century later, Dawra Beg Kerāmī described *sarband* as an improvisatory (*badiha*) instrumental genre in light *oṣuls* that was played by master musicians in an interactive jam session to challenge each other's techniques. Musicians took turns improvising to display their own musical ideas and technical prowess, and as a point of reference, they all reiterated a ritornello (*sarband*) after each individual section.

Varsāqi

The most prominent Turkish vocal genre in the sixteenth and seventeenth centuries in Iran, and especially in the Safavid court, was *varsāqi*. Evidence suggests that *varsāqi* was originally a genre of sung poetry attributed to the *Varsāq* Turkmen clans.[94] In the early sixteenth century, *varsāqi* was performed by Qizilbāsh Turkish musicians known as *ozāns* at the court of Shah Esmā'il I (r. 1501–1524) in Tabriz.[95] Shah Esmā'il I, who was a poet-musician himself, wrote a number of *varsāqis* that to this date remain the earliest examples of the genre. Bāqiyā Nā'ini described *varsāqi* as three hemistiches sung strophically to a single melody. In other words, the same melody was repeated throughout the performance each time with a new set of lines.[96]

By the second half of the seventeenth century, *varsāqi* appears to have acquired some classical features, becoming the typical composition with Turkish verse in the Safavid court. In the BnF copy of Amir Khān Gorji's song–text collection, two *varsāqis* are documented, though neither is attributed to any specific composer.[97]

Arasbāri

While the instrumental counterpart of *varsāqi* is sometimes introduced as *arasbāri* in seventeenth-century musical texts, *arasbāri* was primarily a Turkish sung poetry performed by *ozāns* on the long-necked Caucasian lute, *chogur*. An early reference to *arasbāri* appears in the Chagatai *divān* of Mir 'Alishir Navā'i (1441–1501), which indicates that the genre was known in the second half of the fifteenth century at the Timurid court in Herat.[98] Amir Khān Gorji identified *arasbāri* as the *pishraw* of Turks, and the author of *Dar bayān-e 'elm-e musiqi va dānestan-e sho'abāt-e ou* referred to it and *varsāqi* as the two Turkish genres that were mostly associated with a *gusha* called *qaracheqā-ye rumi*.[99] At the beginning of the sixteenth century, Nasimi mentioned *arasbāri* as a modal entity similar to *bayāti*, but this confusion presumably derived from the association of the genre with the distinctive mode in which it was performed.[100]

The Eighteenth Century

Following the collapse of Isfahan in the eighteenth century, the performance practice of long rhythmic cycles of *oṣul* that once shaped the backbone of courtly compositions began to decline. Nonetheless, the standard vocal genres of *kār*, *'amal*, *qawl*, *ṣawt*, and *naqsh* do not seem to have disappeared altogether. By the middle of the eighteenth century, *ṣawt* and *naqsh* were still distinguished as two separate genres in some practices. It also seems that specific compositions in the forms of *ṣawt*, *naqsh*, *kār*, and *'amal* were widespread in this period, but there is no evidence to indicate that compositions in the *qawl* genre were still performed under that name. In the anonymous treatise *Resāla dar 'elm-e musiqi*, which contains early references to *dastgāh*, a few *ṣawt*s and *naqsh*s are documented as the essential compositions for musicians to learn and perform in certain *maqām*s.[101] Toward the end of the eighteenth century, single-part compositions of *naqsh* and *ṣawt* ceased to be recognized as two separate genres. Meanwhile, *kār* and *'amal* merged into one form that gradually became known as *kār-o'amal*.

The case of instrumental repertoire is more perplexing. Seventeenth- and eighteenth-century treatises do not indicate the extent to which *pishraw* and *sarband* were common among Persian instrumentalists and do not designate the relations between instrumental and vocal repertoires in general. It is conceivable that much of the existing vocal repertoire was rendered instrumentally, and also that some vocal compositions, especially in the forms of *kār* and *'amal*, were referred to as *pishraw* when played on instruments. This was probably the case with some Ottoman *peşrev*s as well.[102] For example, a few instrumental compositions that were attributed in Cantemir's collection to

Āqā Mo'men and Shāh-Morād (the two outstanding Safavid court composers) seem to have initially been vocal compositions in the Safavid court, for these two composers were primarily celebrated as *taṣnif* writers. Similarly, instrumental *varsāqi*s documented in Cantemir's collection were most likely rendered as vocal compositions in the Safavid court.[103] Hence, it seems to have been common for Ottoman and Safavid musicians to turn *taṣnif*s into instrumental compositions or vice versa.[104]

It is hard to imagine, however, that the Safavid instrumental repertoire was entirely confined to *pishraw*s, especially since in Persia this genre did not have as much recognition and popularity as it acquired in the Ottoman court. As suggested above, instrumentalists likely played all forms of vocal composition. But in most cases, instrumental renditions were more abstract than their vocal versions and, for the most part, were distinguished by their rhythmic structure rather than their form, as was mostly the case in the nineteenth century. In other words, metrically composed or improvised pieces were seemingly recognized as *dō-żarbi*, *se-żarbi*, or *chahār-żarbi*.

In discussing the Safavid compositions, I asserted that the *bāzguy* in vocal genres was mostly set to a different verse with a distinctive poetic meter or a different *oṣul*, and that it was rendered in a faster tempo than other sections. A reasonable inference is that in instrumental compositions, *bāzguy* was most likely faster as well and provided lively contrast to the leisurely-paced *sarkhāna* and *miyānkhāna* sections. *Bāzguy* could thus serve two functions. First, it provided an opportunity for a drummer to demonstrate virtuosity, and, second, its faster tempo contrasted to the preceding, slow *sarkhāna* and *miyānkhāna* sections and created an exciting, climactic interlude or finale to a performance. *Bāzguy* gradually began to be appreciated and cultivated as a composition in its own right, for some musicians seem to have been celebrated as composers of *bāzguy* at the turn of the eighteenth century.[105]

In the middle of the eighteenth century, the term *reng* came into use to refer to dance tunes of regional or foreign origin, and *reng* gradually began to serve the function of *bāzguy* as a contrasting interlude or finale in fast tempo.[106] While *bāzguy* had a purely musical function, *reng* was characterized by an affective quality that referred to a place or a people and was typically defined by charm and energetic vitality. The title of many *reng*s in the eighteenth and nineteenth centuries indicate a Caucasian origin, for example, *reng-e qafqāzi*, *reng-e armani*, *reng-e shalakhu*, *reng-e lezgi*, *reng-e nasturi*, and *reng-e ganja*. Some *reng*s bear the names of tribes or rural areas and a few were attributed to cities in neighboring regions such as *reng-e kāboli* and *reng-e baghdādi*.

Later in the nineteenth century, instrumental compositions with a similar structure, especially in 6/8 meter, were all indiscriminately recognized as *reng*.[107] One can also presume that, with the popularity of *reng* in the second half of the eighteenth century, the performance of 6/8 meter (already known as *awfar* or *rāh-e bālā*) became more prevalent than long classical *oṣul*s.

Vocal and Instrumental Genres in the Qajar Period

In the course of the nineteenth century, vocal music was classified into the major categories of *āvāz* and *taṣnif*. While *āvāz* was almost synonymous with the Timurid concept of *nathr-e naghamāt* (nonmetrical section), *taṣnif* fell into the category of *żarbi*, a musical term referring to compositions that were accompanied by percussion instruments.

Āvāz

In Chapter 4, I argued that modal categories that were closer to the "scale" end of the scale–tune continuum came to be referred to as *āvāz* in the eighteenth and nineteenth centuries. Yet when vocal music was set to verses with flexible melodies in which the rhythm depended on the meter of the poetry, typically referred to as a "free rhythm" section, it was commonly called *āvāz* as well. Thus, *āvāz* as a technical term has carried two separate meanings in the past few centuries. In this second meaning, an *āvāz* was categorized on the basis of the poetic form to which it was set and classified as belonging to one or another vocal genre, for example, *ghazal*, *dōbayti*, *mathnavi*, or *sāqi-nāma*. A performance of *āvāz* therefore consisted of either one genre or a sequence of two or three genres.

Ghazal was the most prominent *āvāz* genre, largely performed in urban musical contexts including private *maḥfel*s and courts. As a poetic form, *ghazal* consists of an indeterminate number of rhymed couplets in the scheme *aa ba ca da*, and so on. In the performance of the genre in the Qajar period, three to five couplets of a *ghazal* were usually selected and each was usually set to a different melodic or modal type. The majority of *ghazal*s performed in the Qajar period were written by Saʿdi, Ḥāfeẓ, and some nineteenth-century poets such as Qāʾāni Shirāzi (d. 1854) and Foroughi Basṭāmi (d. 1857).[108]

Ghazal was primarily a male vocal genre. When performed by female singers, the rendition contained a smaller number of couplets and shorter passages of *taḥrir*. A number of schools of *ghazal*-singing associated with different cities, including Isfahan, Tabriz, Qazvin, Kāshān, Mashhad, and Tehran, were cultivated in the nineteenth century and each one developed its own vocal characteristics.[109] In the early twentieth century, a popular form of *ghazal*-singing known as *kucha-bāghi* or *bayāt-e tehrān* also emerged in Tehran that was associated with coffeehouses, *zurkhana* (traditional gymnasium) and pigeon-flying ceremonies. The melodic variation in this subgenre was stereotypically limited and was usually associated with a distinctive melodic mode.[110]

Another *āvāz* genre was *dōbayti* (singing quatrains). Classical quatrains, mostly written by Bābā Ṭāher Hamedāni (*c.* eleventh century), and folk-regional quatrains composed by poets like Fāyez Dashtestāni were largely sung as *dōbayti* or *dōbayti-khᵛāni* in regional and folk-derived melody types such as *dashtestāni*, *hājiāni*, *gilaki*, *shushtari*, and *bakhtiyāri*.

Two unaccompanied male vocal genres, *mathnavi* and *sāqi-nāma*, were mainly sung by roaming as well as sedentary dervishes and *maddāḥ*s in Sufi *samāʿ* assemblies and Shiʿite devotional contexts such as *maddāḥi* and *rawża-khᵛāni*. As poetic forms, *mathnavi* and *sāqi-nāma* both followed meters of eleven syllables and consisted of indeterminate numbers of rhymed couplets in the scheme *aa bb cc dd*, etc. While the rhythmic structure of *mathnavi* was based on the *mathnavi* poetic meter, the *sāqi-nāma* was more melismatic and, beyond its poetic meter, was governed by a loose meter of 4/4 or 7/8. It is evident that *mathnavi* was originally rendered in vernacular and informal modes such as *afshāri*, *dashti*, *mokhālef*, and *esfahān*, whereas *sāqi-nāma-khᵛāni* was only associated with *māhur* and *esfahān*.

Following the establishment of the *radif* at the beginning of the twentieth century, all the vocal genres gradually conformed to its format, and subsequently *dōbayti*, *mathnavi*, and *sāqi-nāma* came to be identified by exponents of *radif* as *gusha*s with the same titles.

Taṣnif

At the beginning of the nineteenth century, Tehran, as the large and prosperous capital of the Qajars, became the most prominent center of court music and entertainment. Many courtesans and their associated male musicians moved to the new capital and became preeminent exponents of *taṣnif*s and the instrumental dance tunes known as *reng*s.[111] Besides urban courtesans, a group of male singers who accompanied themselves on the *dāyera* or *dombak* were also adept at performing *taṣnif*. Some of them were also active as *żarbgir*s associated with prominent instrumentalists. While the repertoires of courtesans and male singer-*żarbgir*s were slightly different, for these male and female performers, the scrupulous exposition and elaboration of the *dastgāh*s and *āvāz*s was secondary to the seductive function of *taṣnif* and *reng*.

As mentioned in Chapter 2, during the nineteenth century the term *qavvāl* was still employed in some cities to designate a female performer who was active as a public courtesan and received government protection. Likewise, the term *guyanda* was still used for a professional male *taṣnif*-singer in this period.[112]

Toward the end of the nineteenth century, there were also some master performers among male *taṣnif*-singers who supported themselves partially or entirely through teaching female musicians. These musicians stood to earn more as concubines trained in performing arts than comparable male artists could earn solely as performers. Ḥabibollāh Samāʿ-Ḥożur and Reżā-Qoli Nawruzi stand out as the two most prominent master *taṣnif*-singers who instructed female singers and regularly accompanied them in this period. The latter recorded a section of his repertoire of *taṣnif*s in London in 1909.[113]

Taṣnif in the Qajar period was a term that came to encompass all types of metric vocal compositions, regardless of their forms, internal divisions, rhythmic structures, and modes of articulation. Nonetheless, vocal compositions of this period can be classified into single-part, bipartite, and complex forms that display a certain stylistic and historical resemblance to their seventeenth-century precursors.

The Single-part Form

The collection of nineteenth-century *taṣnif*s transmitted through ʿAbdollāh Davāmi contains more than 180 compositions that can be divided into two general categories. The first of these includes *taṣnif*s set to two to four couplets of a classical *ghazal* or *robāʿi*. Compositions in this group usually have flexible melodic structures but their texts are mostly rendered distinctly and intelligibly. Each *taṣnif* could be performed with two or three typical texts—sometimes of varying poetic meters—and the melodic rendition of these texts often differs only in minor melodic details. The second category consists of *taṣnifs* set to classical poems interspersed with external words or verses of multiple meters that could be performed either according to a syllabic, easily intelligible phrasing or in a broken and melismatic fashion. Master musicians generally believed that originality and uniqueness was an essential factor in this category of *taṣnifs* and a composition was considered mediocre if it bore resemblance to a conventional or long-familiar model. Distinctions between the two categories are obviously mitigated by numerous exceptions, and a number of vocal compositions can be characterized as falling along the spectrum between these two poles of *taṣnif* convention.

The Bipartite Form

The bipartite *taṣnif* was a common vocal genre in the nineteenth century whose exponents were predominantly female musicians of the harem and urban-dwelling courtesans. A bipartite *taṣnif* was composed or performed in the form of a leisurely-paced section followed by a lively contrasting finale in fast tempo called *bargardān*.[114] Regardless of the rhythmic structure of the first section, the *bargardān* was often set to a fast duple meter and usually contrasted to the first section through the use of a different poetic meter, rhythmic structure, and tempo.

The *bargardān* as a finale or interlude could either be composed as an integral part of the composition or it could be attached to a simple *taṣnif* in the course of a performance and reiterated once or twice throughout the composition. Some *bargardāns* were just tokens of one particular mode, for instance, *segāh* or *shur* and hence were sometimes attached to more than one *taṣnif* within the same *dastgāh* or *āvāz*.

The *taṣnifs* rendered by female performers usually had a seductive function and contained texts that made them inherently appealing to listeners not steeped in the classical tradition. In such *taṣnifs*, the *bargardān* provides a bridge structure that could lead to dance finales. 'Ali-Akbar Shaydā (d. 1906) and 'Āref Qazvini (d. 1934) were two Qajar composers who wrote bipartite *taṣnifs* and most of their compositions were presumably intended to be performed by female singers. The fact that 'Āref's compositions were recorded for the first time by three renowned female singers, Amjad, Eftekhār, and Zari, supports this hypothesis.[115]

The Modulatory Form Kār-o ʿamal

After the Safavid period, the two genres of *kār* and *ʿamal* seem to have merged into one form, commonly referred to as *kār-oʿamal*. In two eighteenth-century musical treatises, *Resāla dar bayān-e chahār dastgāh-e aʿẓam* and *Bahjat al-qulūb*, the performance of each *dastgāh* is said to conclude with pertinent *kār-oʿamals* as well as fast and slow *taṣnifs*. However, neither of these treatises shows the formal structure of *kār-oʿamal*.[116]

During the nineteenth and early twentieth century, *kār-oʿamal* was known to both music theorists and male court singers in Tehran. Among the music theorists, Mehdi-Qoli Hedāyat (d. 1955) introduced *kār-oʿamal* as a complex, modulatory form of composition and described its structure with the aid of terminology used by Systematist music theorists.[117] He further mentions that *kār-oʿamal* contained *tekrār*, *eʿāda*, and *bargardān*, a definition that closely conforms to the Safavid description of the genre.[118]

ʿAbdollāh Mostawfi, a music connoisseur of the same period, also referred to *kār-oʿamal* as a metric modulatory scheme as follows:

> *Taṣnifs* are commonly composed within [the melodic confines of] a single *āvāz* (mode). Yet some *taṣnifs* composed by master musicians are primarily in one *āvāz* while they modulate to all or the major *gushas* of that particular *āvāz*. This form of all-encompassing *taṣnif* was referred to as *kār-oʿamal* by master musicians of the past. They even executed the form of *kār-oʿamal* in *rengs* (instrumental compositions). Nowadays one can recognize the *pishdarāmads* to be composed in the form of *kār-oʿamal* as well.[119]

A few prominent male singers including ʿAli Khān-e Nāyeb al-Salṭana, Qorbān Khān, and Sayyed Aḥmad Khān recorded several compositions with the title of *kār-oʿamal* in Tehran during the 1906 recording sessions of Gramophone and Typewriter, Ltd.[120] These recordings are very short and it is hard to find common elements among them. However, in one longer recording featuring an instrumental *kār-oʿamal* rendered on the *santur*, the performer modulates from the *darāmad* to two *gushas*, thus providing an example of modulatory instrumental music.[121]

In general, nineteenth-century practicing musicians, especially *żarbgirs*, classified the *taṣnifs* not on the basis of their form but on the basis of their rhythmic structures in various *āvāzs*. To these musicians, *taṣnifs* were characterized, for example, as *dō-żarb* in *shur*, *dō-żarb-e lang* in *abu'aṭā*, *se-żarb* in *segāh*, or *se-żarb-e sangin* in *homāyun*.

Composers of Taṣnifs in the Late Qajar Period

The majority of *taṣnifs* that have survived from the Qajar period are either anonymous compositions or were written by male composers ranging from poet-musicians to professional instrumentalists and master *taṣnif*-singers who were primarily based in Tehran. A few *taṣnifs* are ascribed to female singers of the court and a half dozen *taṣnifs* are also attributed to Afghan musicians who came to Tehran from Herat and Kabul.[122]

Three outstanding poet-musicians, 'Ali-Akbar Shaydā, Shurida Shirāzi (d. 1926) and 'Āref Qazvini, wrote a substantial number of *taṣnifs* in the second half of the nineteenth century. None was directly affiliated with the Qajar court, but they were patronized by the nobility and aristocrats of Tehran. Other composers such as Darvish Khān and Gholām-Reżā Sālār-Mo'azzaz were celebrated instrumentalists associated in some way with the court. Since they were not poets, they usually composed only the melodies of *taṣnifs* and subsequently set them to classical poems or asked contemporary poets to write lyrics. Some master *taṣnif*-singers, such as Ḥabibollāh Samā'-Ḥożur, who were often *żarbgirs* for prominent instrumentalists, also developed and composed a small number of *taṣnifs*.[123]

Generally speaking, *taṣnifs* written by poet-musicians are mostly composed in vernacular modes such as *afshāri*, *dashti*, *eṣfahān*, and *shur*, and are perfectly suited to the rhythms, accents, and phrasing of their poetry, whereas professional musicians and instrumentalists often used more complex text-setting techniques and wrote their compositions in both classical and vernacular modes.

Reng

Throughout the nineteenth century, instrumental metric compositions accompanied by a drum were commonly known as *rengs*. However, *reng* was more specifically a dance tune of either urban or rural origin and its name often indicated an ethnic or geographical association such as *reng-e afshār*, *reng-e qafqāzi*, *reng-e lori*, *reng-e kāboli*, *reng-e baghdādi*, and *reng-e armani*.[124] Nineteenth-century *reng*s that have survived to this date are all anonymous, but most of them have titles. Some that were known to Mirzā 'Abdollāh came to be incorporated into his *radif* and were later transcribed or recorded. Classical *reng*s that were dance tunes such as *lezgi*, *reng-e hashtari*, and *shahrāshub* were usually in compound duple meter or *żarb-e rengi*, but those that were not dance tunes such as *nastāri*, *reng-e faraḥ*, *reng-e ḥarbi*, and *reng-e oṣul* were in *se-żarb* (six-beat cycle) or *dō-żarb* (four-beat cycle).

Shahrāshub

A subgenre of *reng* known as *shahrāshub* was primarily an assortment of dance tunes in a *dastgāh*. Every *dastgāh* had a *shahrāshub*, which was in compound duple meter (6/8) throughout. Its component units were separated by short and long ritornellos called *parvāna-ye ṣaghir* and *parvāna-ye kabir*.[125] Each unit (*qesmat*) or dance tune had a proper title usually named after a corresponding dance form such as *raqs-e golrizān* ("flower-scattering dance"), *raqs-e māt* ("stop dance"), and *pā armani* ("Armenian dance step").[126] In some *dastgāh*s such as *chahārgāh*, the constituent units formed a modulatory scheme in that each *qesmat* was composed in one particular *āvāz*, for example, *darāmad*, *muya*, *ḥeṣār*, *mokhālef*, and *manṣuri*. Intimately associated with the courtesan tradition, *shahrāshub* presumably developed at the beginning of the nineteenth century in the *dastgāh-e bāzigar-khāna*, since there is no reference to it in eighteenth-century musical sources.

Chahārmeżrāb

Another instrumental genre, *chahārmeżrāb* (lit. "four-stroke plucked pattern"), distinguished by an ostinato plucking pattern (*pāya*), was predominantly played on the *tār*, *setār*, and *santur* (on which the plucking pattern was played with wooden mallets). The term *chahārmeżrāb* first appeared in *Resāla-ye davāzda dastgāh*, written around 1840, which suggests that this genre was prevalent as early as the beginning of the nineteenth century, if not earlier. *Chahārmeżrāb*s rendered on the *tār* were typically short, sober, and unaccompanied, and were usually preceded by a *darāmad* in the opening section of a *dastgāh* or a new *āvāz* within a *dastgāh*.[127] A performer usually played a *chahārmeżrāb* to display his virtuosic ability and to further establish the mood of an *āvāz* or *dastgāh* as a prelude to a vocal *darāmad*. The *chahārmeżrāb*s developed on the *santur*, and later on the *setār*, were mostly associated with Moḥammad Ṣādeq Khān and his disciples. While these *chahārmeżrāb*s were typically longer, in 3/8 or 6/16 meter, accompanied by *dombak*, and sometimes incorporating modulations to related *āvāz*s or *gusha*s, they also contained a ritornello section called *parvāna*.[128] These *chahārmeżrāb*s were independent compositions, hence they were no longer associated with a *darāmad* and could be played at any point during a performance. *Chahārmeżrāb* may have resembled *reng* in many respects, but the technique employed was to stress rhythmic complexity and intensity rather than the melodic and seductive expression that was sought in *reng*.

Pishdarāmad

One other important instrumental metrical genre that emerged at the beginning of the twentieth century is *pishdarāmad*. This genre was mostly in a slow-tempo duple meter and contained modulations to major *āvāz*s of a *dastgāh*. It was rendered by the entire ensemble as an opening piece to a musical concert, hence the name *pishdarāmad* (lit. "preceding the *darāmad*"). While a few compositions with the rhythmic structure and tempo characteristic of *pishdarāmad* were first cultivated and performed in the second half of the nineteenth century by Moḥammad Ṣādeq Khān and Āqā Ḥosayn-Qoli, they were simply regarded as the instrumental rendition of a *taṣnif*.[129] The *pishdarāmad* is said to have been invented by Rokn al-Din Mokhtāri (d. 1971), who first composed overture-like compositions to be performed as ensemble pieces in public performances. *Pishdarāmad* was further developed by Darvish Khān, who composed pieces in the same style in various *āvāz*s and taught them to his own disciples.[130] As Mehdi-Qoli Hedāyat stated, the idea of *pishdarāmad* is similar to the concept of *bardāsht*, a free-rhythm instrumental modulatory scheme played at the beginning of a performance while alluding to major *āvāz*s of a *dastgāh*.[131] He also mentioned that *pishdarāmad* as a metrical composition with multiple modulations bore stylistic resemblance to *kār-o'amal*.[132]

Table 6.1 displays the names of various formal sections of vocal and instrumental compositions that were in common use between the fifteenth and twentieth centuries.

Table 6.1 The names of various formal sections of vocal and instrumental compositions in common use between the fifteenth and twentieth centuries

Names of Various Formal Sections	Timurid	Safavid	Qajar
First section	*ṭariqa-ye jadval*	*sarkhāna-ye avval*	*band-e avval*
Repetition of the first section	*ṭariqa-ye maṭla'*	*sarkhāna-ye dovom*	*band-e dovom*
Second section	*ṣawt al-wasaṭ* *miyānkhāna*	*miyānkhāna*	–
Third section	*tashyi'a* or *bāzgasht*	*bāzguy*	*bargardān*
Refrain	*e'āda-ye ṭariqa* *tarji'band*	*lāzema/dhayl*	*tarji'band*
Instrumental ritornello	*sarband*	*lāzema/sarband*	*parvāna*
Nontextual syllables	*alfāẓ-e naqarāt*	*naqarāt/tarannom*	–

Summary

This chapter addresses the deeply socially constituted and socially embedded issues of genre formation, the relation of genre to broader questions about the social status and classification of music and musicians, the historical migration of innovation in Persian music from one city to another over the centuries under discussion, and the back-and-forth appropriations that occurred between vocal and instrumental music.

Kār, *'amal*, *qawl*, *ṣawt*, and *naqsh* were the predominant metric vocal genres in the sixteenth and seventeenth centuries. *Kār* and *'amal* were tripartite, *qawl* was bipartite, and *ṣawt* and *naqsh* were single-part genres. Additional genres included two subgenres of *tarāna* and *rikhta*, the two instrumental genres *pishraw* and *sarband*, and the two Turkish-Caucasian genres *varsāqi* and *arasbāri*, which were widely performed throughout the Safavid period.

Between fifteenth and seventeenth centuries, *kār*, *'amal*, and *qawl* were largely composed by professional court composers, whereas simpler forms of *ṣawt* and *naqsh* were mostly composed by amateur poet-musicians. After the collapse of the Safavid court, no composer of note is mentioned in the eighteenth-century musical sources.

During the Qajar period, vocal compositions were still rendered into single-part, bipartite, and complex forms, but were no longer differentiated by the erstwhile genre names (*qawl*, *ṣawt*, *naqsh*, and so on). While some of the *taṣnifs* in the Qajar period were attributed to both male and female court composers the majority of nineteenth-century vocal compositions are anonymous and cannot be ascribed to specific composers.

Notes

1. Abū al-Faraj al-Iṣfahānī, *Kitāb al-aghānī* (Cairo: Dār al-Kutub, 1927–1961), 1: 378, 3: 276.
2. Ibid., 5: 157–159; Eckhard Neubauer, "Die Urbane Kunstmusik im Islam Eine Historische Übersicht," *Zeitschrift für Geschichte der Arabisch-Islamischen Wissenschaften* 20/21 (2012/14): 333.
3. Al-Kindī, "Al-risālat al-kubrā fī ta'līf," 137.
4. Mohammad Nerchakhy, *Description topographique et historique de Boukhara*, ed. Charles Schefer (Paris: Ernest Leroux, 1892), 251, 258; 'Arużi Samarqandi, *Chahār maqāla*, ed. Moḥammad Qazvini (Tehran: Zavvār, 1910), 32, 35; Mashḥun, *Tārikh-e musiqi-ye Irān*, 156–157, 161–162; Neubauer, "Die Urbane Kunstmusik im Islam Eine Historische Übersicht," 343.
5. 'Abd al-Qāder Marāghi, *Jāmi' al-alḥān*, 241–252; 'Abd al-Qāder Marāghi, *Maqāṣid al-alḥān*, 104–107; 'Abd al-Qāder Marāghi, *Sharḥ-e advār*, 336–342.
6. 'Abd al-Qāder Marāghi, *Sharḥ-e advār*, 336.
7. See Abū Naṣr al-Fārābī, *Kitāb al-mūsīqī al-kabīr*, ed. Ghaṭṭās 'Abd al-Malik Khashabah (Cairo: Dār al-kitāb al-'Arabī, 1967), 1162; George Dimitri Sawa, *An Arabic Musical and Socio-Cultural Glossary of Kitāb al-Aghānī* (Leiden: Brill, 2015), 482–485. For further account on *nashid*, see Amnon Shiloah, "Muslim and Jewish Musical Traditions of the Middle Ages," in *Music as Concept and Practice in the Late Middle Ages*, New Oxford History of Music, ed. Reinhard Strohm and Bonnie J. Blackburn (Oxford: Oxford University Press, 2001), 3, 7.
8. Cf. 'Aliakbar Dehkhodā, "Nashid," in *Loghat-nāma*, ed. Moḥammad Mo'in and Ja'far Shahidi (Tehran: University of Tehran Press, 1993).
9. 'Abd al-Qāder Marāghi, *Sharḥ-e advār*, 336.
10. Ibid.; Marāghi, *Jāmi' al-alḥān*, 249.
11. Early sources indicate that *qawl* emerged most likely in Khorasan.
12. Abū Naṣr al-Fārābī, *Kitāb al-mūsīqī al-kabīr*, 1085–1100.
13. Abu al-Fażl Bayhaqi, *Tārikh-e Bayhaqi*, ed. Manuchehr Dāneshpazhuh, 2 vols. (Tehran: Hirmand, 2001), 1: 38, 116, 120, 122.

14. Abū al-Karīm al-Qoshayrī al-Neyshāburī, "Samā'-e she'r be āvāz-e khosh," in *Andar ghazal-e khish nahān khᵛāham gashtan: samā'-nāma-hā-ye fārsi*, ed. Najib Māyel Heravi (Tehran: Nashr-e nay, 1992), 69.
15. Abū Ḥāmid al-Ghazālī, "Vajd va samā'," in *Andar ghazal-e khish nahān khᵛāham gashtan: samā'-nāmahā-ye fārsi*, ed. Najib Māyel Heravi. Tehran: Nashr-e Nay, 1992, 99, 130, 142, 155, 158.
16. For examples of four-couplet and two-couplet *qawls*, see ibid., 142, 155.
17. Abū Naṣr al-Fārābī, *Kitāb al-musīqī al-kabīr*, 1085–1100.
18. 'Alā' al-Din Bokhāri in the thirteenth century refers to both male and female *qavvāls*. See Khubravān and Kordmāfi, "Musiqi dar ashjār va athmār-e," 79.
19. Awbahi, *Moqaddamat al-uṣūl*, 188; Bannā'i, *Resāla dar musiqi*, 127.
20. See Moḥammad-Reżā Shafi'i Kadkani, "Yek eṣṭelāḥ-e musiqā'i dar she'r-e Ḥāfeẓ," *Māhur* 15 (2002): 9–14.
21. See Abū Ḥāmid al-Ghazālī, "Vajd va samā'," 157.
22. See Wright, *The Modal System of Arab and Persian Music*, 231.
23. Marāghi, *Jāmi' al-alḥān*, 242–243.
24. Cf. Neubauer, "Music History II. ca. 650 to 1370 CE." The eminent Iranian poet Khᵛāju Kermāni (d. 1352) also refers to the four parts of *nawbat-e morattab* including *qawl*, *ghazal*, *tarāna*, and *forudāsht*, see Khᵛāju Kermāni, *Divān*, ed. Aḥmad Sohayli Khᵛānsāri (Tehran: Pāzang, 1990), 268.
25. Marāghi records the text of a *nawbat* that he composed at the court of Solṭān-Ḥosayn Jalāyer (r. 776–784) in Tabriz in 1377. See Marāghi, *Jāmi' al-alḥān*, 245–256. For compositions attributed to Marāghi in Ottoman song–text collections, see Neubauer, "Zur Bedentung der Begriffe," 326–329. For the documentation of *nawbat* in Ottoman song–text collections, see Wright, *Words without Songs*, 211–219.
26. The *mostazād* usually summarized all the lines and techniques of composition already introduced in other sections of *nawbat*. For further discussion, see ibid., 52–59.
27. See Sawa, *An Arabic Musical and Socio-Cultural Glossary of Kitāb al-Aghānī*, 25.
28. Ḥasan Kāshāni, "Kanz al-tuḥaf", 109.
29. See 'Abd al-Qāder Marāghi, *Maqāṣid al-alḥān*, 104; 'Abd al-Qāder Marāghi, *Sharḥ-e advār*, 337.
30. Cf. Aḥmad Tafażżoli, "Fahlavīyāt," in *Encyclopaedia Iranica*. online edition, 1999.
31. Mufażżal b. Sa'd al-Māfarūkhi, *Maḥasin Iṣfahān*, ed. 'Aref Aḥmad 'Abd al-Ghanī (Dār al-Kanān: Damascus, 2010), 121.
32. Cf. Tafażżoli, "Fahlavīyāt."

33. Shams al-Dīn Muḥammad b. Qays Rāzī, *Al-mu'jam fī ma'ā'īr ash'ār al-'ajam*, 114, 173.
34. 'Abd al-Qāder Marāghi, *Jāmi' al-alḥān: khātema*, 139–142.
35. 'Onṣor al-Ma'āli Kaykābus b. Voshmgir Ziyār, *Qābus-nāma*, 196.
36. 'Abd al-Qāder Marāghi, *Maqāṣid al-alḥān*, 117; 'Abd al-Qāder Marāghi, *Sharḥ-e advār*, 387.
37. 'Abd al-Qāder Marāghi, *Sharḥ-e advār*, 336–337.
38. 'Abd al-Qāder Marāghi, *Jāmi' al-alḥān*, 250; 'Abd al-Qāder Marāghi, *Maqāṣid al-alḥān*, 106; 'Abd al-Qāder Marāghi, *Sharḥ-e advār*, 342.
39. Ibid.
40. Neubauer, "Zur Bedentung der Begriffe Komponist und Komposition," 310–311.
41. Marāghi, *Sharḥ-e advār*, 342.
42. Ibid.
43. Aḥmad Jām Zhendapil (1048–1141) refers to the practice of composing and listening to a form of love song known as *samā'*-e *havā'i*. For further information, see "Samā' chist," in Abū al-Karīm al-Qushayrī al-Neyshāburī, *Andar ghazal-e khish nahān khᵛāham gashtan*, 190.
44. Marāghi, *Sharḥ-e advār*, 342.
45. Neubauer, "Musik zur Mongolenzeit in Iran und den angrenzenden Ländern," 237, 248.
46. Cf. Qoṭb al-Din Shirāzi, *Durrat al-tāj*, 128; Anvār, *Tarjoma-ye sharḥ-e Mobārakshāh Bokhāri*, 504.
47. Marāghi, *Jāmi' al-alḥān*, 251; 'Abd al-Qāder Marāghi, *Maqāṣid al-alḥān*, 107; 'Abd al-Qāder Marāghi, *Sharḥ-e advār*, 342.
48. Ibid., 252.
49. Marāghi also specifies *zakhma* as a short instrumental composition that could be analogous to a *khāna* of *pishrow*. See 'Abd al-Qāder Marāghi, *Jāmi' al-alḥān*, 251.
50. 'Abd al-Qāder Marāghi, [Song-text Collection] Rijksuniversiteit (Universiteits Bibliotheek), Leiden MS Cod. 271 Warn., 64a–66a.
51. Awbahi states that these devices could not be applied to the two simple genres of *ṣawt* and *naqsh*. For further information, see *Moqaddamat al-uṣūl*, 189. See also Sāsān Fāṭemi, "Form va musiqi-ye Irāni," *Māhur* 39 (2008): 117.
52. 'Abd al-Qāder Marāghi, *Sharḥ-e advār*, 340–342.
53. Awbahi, *Moqaddamat al-uṣūl*, 186-191; Bannā'i, *Resāla dar musiqi*, 125–128.
54. Awbahi, *Moqaddamat al-uṣūl*, 188; Bannā'i, *Resāla dar musiqi*, 127.
55. Ibid., 128.

56. Zahirüddin Muhammad Bâbur Mirzâ. *Bâbur-nâma*, ed. and trans. W. M Thackston, Jr. (Cambridge, MA: Harvard University, NELC, 1993), 375, 379.
57. Najm al-Din Kawkabi Bokhārā'i also uses *kār* as different sections of *nawbat*. Cf. "Resāla-ye musiqi-ye Najm al-Din Kawkabi Bokhārā'i," 62.
58. Awbahi, *Moqaddamat al-uṣūl*, 189.
59. See, for instance, Malek Library, Tehran MS 1665, 48–51.
60. For further discussion, see Feldman, *Music of the Ottoman Court*, 69–71.
61. *Resāla-ye Karāmiya*, Russian Academy of Sciences MS B1844, 31a.
62. Mir Ṣadr al-Din Moḥammad, "Resāla-ye 'elm-e musiqi," 92–93.
63. Ibid., 93–94.
64. Bāqiyā Nā'ini, *Zamzama-ye vaḥdat*, Biruni Institute of Oriental Studies (Tashkent) MS 10226, 23–27.
65. Ibid., 23.
66. Pourjavady, "The Musical Codex of Amir Khān Gorji," 198.
67. In addition to Persian songs, a number of Turkish *varsāqi*s are listed in the BnF copy of Amir Khān's song–text collection.
68. Ibid., 257.
69. Ibid., 257–260.
70. See "Resāla-ye musiqi-ye Najm al-Din Kawkabi Bokhārā'i," 60–63; Darvish-'Ali Changi, *Tuḥfat al-surūr*, 30a–34a.
71. For the application of *navākht* in Marāghi's work, see *Sharḥ-e advār*, 342. *Navākht* was also used as early as the thirteenth century by Mobarakshāh. For further accounts, see 'Abdollāh Anvār, *Tarjoma-ye sharḥ-e Mobārakshāh Bokhāri*, 504.
72. *Khosravāni*, as a subgenre of *khᵛānandegi*, was most likely a reference to singing *fahlaviyāt* that were in the form of quatrains in vernacular or regional dialects.
73. Eskandar Beg Turkamān, *Tārikh-e 'ālamārā 'Abbāsi*, 190.
74. As Zayn al-Din Vāṣefi suggests on many occasions (e.g., *Badāyi' al-waqāyi'*, 1: 186), during the fifteenth century in Herat, a *ḥāfeẓ* was certainly trained as a reciter of the Qur'an as well, but this does not seem to be the case in the Safavid period.
75. Mirzā Ebrāhim Yazdi, "Dibācha-ye anis al-arvāḥ," ed. Aḥmad Golchin Ma'āni, *Majala-ye adabiyāt va 'olum-e ensāni-ye Mashhad* 4 (1968): 331, 337.
76. See Pourjavady, "Dar bayān-e 'elm-e musiqi va dānestan-e sho'abāt-e ou," 65.
77. These characteristic features of *miyānkhāna* and *bāzguy* are attested in the song–text collection of Amir Khān Gorji.
78. The *kār*s documented in Amir Khān Gorji's song–text collection are mostly in long *oṣul*s of *żarb al-fatḥ*, *thaqil*, and *khafif*.
79. See Pourjavady, "The Musical Codex of Amir Khān Gorji," 262–298.

80. Ibid., 210.
81. Darvish-'Ali Changi, *Tuḥfat al-surūr*, 31a. During the Timurid period, *qawl* was predominantly composed in *możā'af-e nim-thaqil*. See Awbahi, *Moqaddamat al-uṣūl*, 163.
82. Zayn al-Din Vāṣefi reports that at a public gathering Mir Shāna Tarāsh composed a *ṣawt* in the mode *'erāq* and would perform it in the call and response format with the public. For further account, see *Badāye' al-vaqāye'*, 2: 250.
83. For instance, see specimens of *ṣawt* and *naqsh* in the song–text collection of Hâfız Post, *Güfte mecmuası*, Topkapı R. (Istanbul), MS 1724, 18b, 31b, 41b.
84. Pourjavady, "The Musical Codex of Amir Khān Gorji," 311.
85. Ibid., p. 209.
86. Sāsān Fāṭemi, "*Taṣnif-e mo'āṣer*," 89.
87. The division of nontextual syllables into two groups of *ya la lā* and *tan dar tan* is made by almost all Safavid music theorists, but Āqā Mo'men specifically refers to "*ya la lā*" as *tarannom* and to "*tan dar tan*" as *naqarāt.*
88. Cf. Hâfız Post, *Güfte mecmuası*, 18b, 31b, 41b.
89. See Darvish-'Ali Changi, *Tuḥfat al-surūr*, 32b.
90. Mir Ṣadr al-Din Moḥammad, "Resāla-ye 'elm-e musiqi," 126.
91. Bannā'i, *Resāla dar musiqi*, 128.
92. Mir Ṣadr al-Din Moḥammad, "Resāla-ye 'elm-e musiqi," 94; Darvish-'Ali Changi, *Tuḥfat al-surūr*, 33a.
93. Mir Ṣadr al-Din Moḥammad, "Resāla-ye 'elm-e musiqi," 92.
94. Cf. Faruk Sümer, *Naqsh-e torkān-e ānātoli dar tashkil-e va dolat-e safavi* (Safevî Devletinin Kuruluşu ve Gelişmesinde Anadolu Türklerinin Rolü), trans. from Turkish to Persian by Eḥsān Eshrāqi and Moḥammad-Taqi Emāmi (Tehran: Nashr-e gostara, 1992), 63.
95. Możṭar, *Tārikh-e jahāngoshā-ye khāqān*, 222.
96. Bāqiyā Nā'ini, *Zamzama-ye vaḥdat*, Biruni Institute of Oriental Studies (Tashkent) MS 10226, 26–27.
97. Amir Khān Gorji, *Resāla*, Bibliothèque nationale, 27b–28a.
98. Cf. Ali Şir Navaî, "Mizānü'l-Evzān," in *Divanlar Ile Hamse dişindaki Eserler* (Ankara: Türk Tarih Kurumu Basımevi, 1968), 117.
99. Pourjavady, "The Musical Codex of Amir Khān Gorji," 259; Pourjavady, "Dar bayān-e 'elm-e musiqi va dānestan-e sho'abāt-e ou," 65.
100. Nasimi, *Nasim-e ṭarab*, 75.
101. Pourjavady, "Resāla dar 'elm-e musiqi," 112.
102. More examples of Persian vocal compositions transformed into Turkish *pishrows* are mentioned in Neubauer, "Zur Bedentung der Begriffe Komponist und Komposition," 346.

103. Kantemiroğlu, *Kitābi ʿilmiʾl mūsīḳī ʿalā vechiʾl-ḥurūfāt: Mûsikîyi harflerle tesbît ve icrâ ilminin kitabı*, ed. Yalçın Tura, 2 vols. (Istanbul: Yapı Kredi Yayınları, 2001), 2: 298, 300.
104. Another example is a *taṣnif* documented in Amir Khān Gorji's song–text collection that according to the author was initially a *pishraw* that later was turned into a *kār*. See Pourjavady, "The Musical Codex of Amir Khān Gorji," 285.
105. In an eighteenth-century musical treatise Ostād Zaytun is introduced as a musician who composed *bāzguys*, see Pourjavady, "Dar bayān-e ʿelm-e musiqi va dānestan-e shoʿabāt-e ou," 67.
106. For further information about the *rengs*, see Bābak Khażrāʾi, "Darbāra-ye reng," *Māhur* 66 (2015): 67–87.
107. Almost all metric instrumental compositions in the *radif* are indiscriminately recognized as *rengs*.
108. This can also be attested from the collection of verses in Forṣat al-Dowla Shirāzi's *Buḥūr al-alḥān*.
109. Cf. Mashḥun, *Tārikh-e musiqi-ye Irān*, 674–687.
110. For further information, see Sāsān Fāṭemi, *Farhikhtagi dar mohiṭ-e mardomi: ghazal-khᵛāni-e Tehrāni va bastarhā-ye farhangi-ejtemāʿi-ye ān* (Tehran: Māhur, 2019).
111. Alexander Chodźko, who came to Iran in the reign of Fatḥ-ʿAli Shah, claims that he collected most of his *taṣnifs* from the courtesans and female performers of the harem and their trainers. Chodźko, *Specimens of the Popular Poetry of Persia*, 417.
112. On the label of a record (G.C.-4-12026) made by the Gramophone Company in 1906 in Tehran, the *taṣnif*-singer, Qorbān Khān Shāhi, is introduced as *guyanda*. See Kinnear, *The Gramophone Company's Persian Recordings*, 43.
113. Ibid., 55–76.
114. See Mostawfi, *Sharḥ-e zendegāni-ye man*, 1: 379–380; Hedāyat, *Majmaʿ al-adwār* (lithograph) 3: 123; Mashḥun, *Tārikh-e musiqi-ye Irān*, 446, 467.
115. For a list of recordings of Amjad, Eftekhār and Zari, see Kinnear, *The Gramophone Company's Persian Recordings*, 77–83.
116. Pourjavady, "Resāla dar bayān-e chahār dastgāh-e aʿẓam," 91–92; Khażrāʾi, "*Sharḥ-e chahār dastgāh va taṣāvir-e chand sāz dar resāla-ye Bahjat al-qulūb*," 156–157.
117. Hedāyat, *Majmaʿ al-adwār* (manuscript), 2: 157.
118. Ibid., 2: 144, 2: 157.
119. Mostawfi, *Sharḥ-e zendegāni-ye man*, 1: 297.
120. See Kinnear, *The Gramophone Company's Persian Recordings*, 34, 46, 51.
121. The recording is 19379 (Hassan Khan-Cynthour). See Kinnear, *The Gramophone Company's Persian Recordings*, 48.

122. For the *taṣnifs* ascribed to the female singers, see Pāyvar, *Radif-e āvāzi va taṣnifhā-ye qadimi be revāyat-e 'Abdollāh Davāmi*, 179, 183, 314, 452; for the *taṣnifs* attributed to the Afghan musicians who came from Herat and Kabul, see 250, 283; Mashḥun, *Tārikh-e musiqi-ye Irān*, 459.
123. For the *taṣnifs* composed by Ḥabibollāh Samā'-Ḥożur, see Pāyvar, *Radif-e āvāzi va taṣnifhā-ye qadimi be revāyat-e 'Abdollāh Davāmi*, 198, 272, 290, 293.
124. Mirzā Shafi', *The Treatise on the Seven Dastgah of Iranian Music*, 18, 23, 29, 34, 36.
125. Personal communication from Dāriush Ṣafvat.
126. Cf. Khażrā'i, "Darbāra-ye reng," 72.
127. These early *chahārmezrābs* were performed within the melodic confines of the *darāmad* in an *āvāz*. See, for instance, *chahārmeżrābs* in *dastgāhs* of *māhur*, *homāyun*, *chahārgāh*, and *navā* transcribed in Ma'rufi and Barkechli, *Radif-e haft dastgāh-e musiqi-e Irāni/Les Systèmes de la musique traditionelle iranienne (radif)*.
128. Personal communication from Dāriush Ṣafvat.
129. Personal communication from Moḥammad-Reżā Loṭfi.
130. Ḥasan Mashḥun, "Navāzandegān-e qadim-e tār va setār," *Māhur* 30 (2006): 95–96.
131. Hedāyat, *Majma' al-adwār* (lithograph), 3: 21, 82–83. For further discussion, see Hooman Asadi, "Negāhi be mafhum va sayr-e takvin-e pishdarāmad dar musiqi-ye Irāni," *Māhur* 33 (2006): 149.
132. Hedāyat, *Majma' al-adwār* (lithograph), 3: 119.

APPENDIX 1: THE SYSTEMATIST TEXTS

Arabic and Persian musical treatises that were influenced by the theories of Ṣafī al-Dīn al-Urmawī in *Kitāb al-adwār* and *Risāla al-Sharafiyya.*

Theorists	**Texts**
Baghdad:	
Ṣafī al-Dīn al-Urmawī (d. 1294)	*Kitāb al-adwār* and *Risāla al-Sharafiyya*
Tabriz:	
Qoṭb al-Din Shirāzi (1236–1311)	*Durrat al-tāj li ghurrat al-dubbāj*
Shihāb al-Dīn al-Ṣayrafī al-Tabrīzī	*Khulāṣat al-afkār fī ma'rifat al-adwār*
Isfahan:	
Ḥasan Kāshāni	*Kanz al-tuḥaf*
Shiraz:	
Shams al-Din Maḥmud Āmoli (d. 1352)	*Nafā'is al-funūn fī 'arā'is al-'uyūn*
'Emād al-Din Yaḥyā b. Aḥmad Kāshi	Commentary on the *Kitāb al-adwār*
Mobārakshāh	Commentary on the *Kitāb al-adwār*
Herat:	
'Abd al-Qāder Marāghi (d. 1435)	*Maqāṣid al-alḥān*, *Jāmi' al-alḥān*, *Sharḥ-e advār*
'Alishāh b. Buka Awbahi	*Uṣūl al-wuṣūl*, *Muqaddimat al-uṣūl*
'Ali b. Moḥammad Bannā'i (d. 1513)	*Resāla*

Samarqand:	
Loṭfollāh b. Moḥammad Samarqandi	Commentary on the *Kitāb al-adwār*
Fatḥ Allāh al-Shirwānī (d. 1453)	*Majalla fī al-mūsīqī*
Bursa and Istanbul:	
ʿAbd al-Aziz b. ʿAbd al-Qāder	*Naqāwat al-adwār*
Maḥmud b. ʿAbd al-Aziz	*Maqāṣid al-adwār*
Muḥammad b. ʿAbd al-Ḥāmid al-Lādhiqī (d. *c.* 1495)	*Risālat al-fatḥiyya fī al-mūsīqī*

APPENDIX 2: THE NON-SYSTEMATIST TEXTS

Persian musical treatises that were written before the sixteenth century and present the modal entities as *parda-sho'ba* or *parda-āvāza*.

Texts	Manuscripts
Resāla-ye musiqi by Moḥammad Nayshāburi	(1) Russian Academy of Sciences MS C.612, (2) Majles Library (Tehran) MS 14590.
Ashjār va athmār by 'Alā' al-Din al-Bokhāri (d. *c.* 1291)	Multiple copies.
Al-mukhtaṣar al-mufīd fī bayān al-musīqī wa uṣūl ahkāma	Abdul-Hamid II Library (Istanbul) MS 1447.
Anonymous 1	Köprülü Library (Istanbul) MS 1613, 70b–72b.
Anonymous 2	Majles-e Senā Library (Tehran) MS 13682, 75a–77a.
Anonymous 3	Malek Library (Tehran) MS 893, 1b–6a.
Anonymous 4	Malek Library (Tehran) MS 3326, 224a–230a.
Anonymous 5	Majles Library (Tehran) MS 5180, 499a–506a. Shahid Moṭahhari Library (Tehran) MS 2911, 104a–106a.
Anonymous 6	Shahid Moṭahhari Library (Tehran) MS 2931,119a–128a. Great Encyclopedia of Islam (Tehran) MS 1500. Tehran University (Tehran) MS 1974, 1b–30a.
Anonymous 7	Majles Library (Tehran) MS 6813, 95b–100a.

APPENDIX 3: AN ACCOUNT OF THE MODAL SYSTEM AND RHYTHMIC CYCLES IN NON-SYSTEMATIST TREATISES

The early non-Systematist treatises always introduced *rāst* as the primary *parda*, but later manuscripts including Majles 5180, Shahid Moṭahhari 2911, Shahid Moṭahhari 2931, GEI 1500, and Tehran University 1974 were more influenced by the Systematist tradition and introduced *ʿoshshāq* as the primary *parda*.

Table A3.1 The twelve *pardas* and their number of *bāngs* in non-Systematist treatises

Treatises	Nayshāburi (1)	bāng	Nayshāburi (2)	*bāng*	Köprülü 1613	*bāng*	MSI 13682	*bāng*	Malek 893	*bāng*	Malek 3326	*bāng*	SM. 2931 GEI. 1500 TU. 1974	*bāng*
1	***rāst***	2	***rāst***	2.5	***rāst***	2.5	***rāst***	2.5	***rāst***	2.5	***rāst***	2.5	***rāst***	2.5
2	*mokhālef-e rāst*	2	*mokhālef-e rāst*	2	*zirafkand*	1.5	*zirafkan-e bozorg*	1.5	*zirafkan-e bozorg*	1.5	*zirafkan-e bozorg*	1.5	*bozorg*	2.5
3	*māda*	2	*māda*	2	*māya*	2	*māya*	–	*māya*	2	*māya*	2	*ḥejāz*	2
4	*ʿerāq*	1.5	*ʿerāq*	1.5	*ʿerāq*	1.5	*ʿerāq*	1.5	*ʿerāq*	1.5	*ʿerāq*	1.5	*ʿerāq*	1.5
5	*mokhālefak*	1.5	*mokhālefak*	1.5	*mokhālefak*	2	*mokhālef*	2	*mokhālefak*	2	*mokhālef*	2	*zirafkand*	2
6	*busalik*	1.5	*busalik*	1.5	*busalik*	1	*busalik*	1.5	*busalik*	1.5	*busalik*	1.5	*busalik*	1.5
7	*navā*	1	–	–	*navā*	1	*navā*	1	*navā*	1	*navā*	1.5	*navā*	1
8	*nehāvand*	1.5	–	–	*zangola*	0.5	*zangula*	0.5	*zangula*	0.5	*zangula*	–	*zangula*	0.5
9	*rahāvi*	1	*rahāvi*	1	*rahāvi*	1	*rahāvi*	1	*rahāvi*	1	*rahāvi*	1	*rahāvi*	1
10	*esfahān*	1	*safāhān*	1	*esfāhān*	2	*esfahān*	0.5	*sepāhān*	2	*esfahān*	2	*esfahān*	2
11	*ḥosayni*	1	*ḥosayni*	1	*ḥosayni*	2	*ḥosayni*	2	*ḥosayni*	2	*ḥosayni*	2	*ḥosayni*	1
12	*ʿoshshāq*	0.5	*ʿoshshāq*	0.5	*ʿoshshāq*	0.5	*ʿoshshāq*	0.5	*ʿoshshāq*	0.5	*ʿoshshāq*	0.5	*ʿoshshāq*	0.5
Total number of *bāngs*		16.5				17.5				18				18

Table A3.2 The *sho'ba/āvāz* in non-Systematist treatises

Treatises	Nayshāburi (1)	Nayshāburi (2)	Köprülü 1613	MSI 13682	Malek 893	Malek 3326	SM. 2931 GEI. 1500 TU. 1974	MSI 6813
sho'ba/āvāz	***sho'ba***	***sho'ba***	***āvāz***	***āvāz***	***sho'ba***	***sho'ba***	***sho'ba/āvāza***	***āvāza***
1	*zirkesh*	*zirkesh*	*ashirā*	*'ashrā*	*nawruz*	*nawruz*	*nawruz*	*nawruz-e aṣl*
2	*basta*	*basta*	*basta*	*basta*	*mobarqa'*	*mobarqa'*	*salmak*	*salmak*
3	*'ozzāl*	*'ashirā*	*'ashirā*	*'ashirān*	*shahnāz*	*shahnāz*	*shahnāz*	*shahnāz*
4	*negārin*	*asirān*	*negārinak*	*negār*	*gardāniya*	*gardāniya*	*gardāniya*	*gardāniya*
5	*ḥejāz*	*ḥejāz*	*ḥejāz*	*ḥejāz*	*ḥejāz*	*ḥejāz*	*māya*	*muya*
6	*sepehri*	*sepehri*	*sepehri*	*sepehri*	*gavāsht*	*gavāsht*	*gavasht*	*gavasht*

Table A3.2 clearly shows that *sho'ba* and *āvāz* were two terms referring to a set of six modes in non-Systematist treatises. This set of six modes were known as *sho'ba*s in the treatise of Nayshāburi.

Table A3.3 The account of rhythm in non-Systematist treatises

Treatise	The Account of Rhythm
Nayshāburi	–
'Alā' al-Din al-Bokhāri	(1) *yek-żarb* (*ṭavil*), (2) *'amud*, (3) *dō-yeki*, (4) *khafif*, (5) *thaqil*, (6) *arbā'*, (7) *eḥdāth*
Al-mukhtaṣar al-mufid	–
Köprülü MS 1613	Know that *żarb* (rhythm) is of many types: *yek-żarb*, *dō-żarb*, and *se-żarb*. One has to play *yek-żarb* in the presence of the elderly as they are fond of it, and *dō-żarb* in the presence of the youth which is more suitable for them. When a musician follows this instruction (*ṭariqa*), it sounds utterly great.
Majles-e Senā MS 13682	Know that playing *żarb* is of many types: *yek-żarb*, *dō-żarb*, and *se-żarb*. One must play *yek-żarb* for the elderly, *dō-żarb* for the youth, and *se-żarb* for the youngsters.
Malek 893	*oṣul-e 'amal*, *żarb al-moluk*, *hazaj-e kabir*, *hazaj-e ṣaghir*, *thaqil*, *nim thaqil*, *khafif*, *khafif-e ṣaḥiḥ*, *thaqil-e ramal*, *ṭavil*, *mokhammas*, *samā'i*, *awsaṭ*, *sharafshān-e kabir*, *sharafshān-e ṣaghir*, *dawr-e ravān*, *chahār-żarb*
Malek 3326	*oṣul-e 'amal*, *żarb al-moluk*, *hazaj-e kabir*, *khafif-e ṣaḥiḥ*, *thaqil*, *mokhammas*, *samā'i*, *khafif-e awsaṭ*, *tarkib*, *me'atayn*, *chahār-żarb*, *zharafshān-e ṣaghir*, *dawr-e ravān*, *chanbar*, *fākhta-ye kabir*, *fākhta-ye ṣaghir*, *żarb al-qadim*, *żarb al-qadim-e far'*
Tehran University 1974 Majles 5180 Shahid Moṭahhari 2911 Shahid Moṭahhari 2931 GEI 1500	Know that famous rhythmic cycles among the Arab practitioners are six: *thaqil-e avval*, *thaqil-e dovom*, *khafif-e thaqil*, *ramal-e khafif*, *hazaj* . . . Entering with *oṣul* can be in three ways: together (*ma'a*), before (*qabl*) or after (*ba'd*).

(*Continued*)

Treatise	The Account of Rhythm
	Playing the *żarb* is of many types: *yek-żarb*, *dō-żarb*, and *se-żarb*. In the presence of the elderly, one must play *yek-żarb* since they have to calm down in their life. For the youth, one must play *dō-żarb* since they like it to be between the slow and fast tempo. For the youngsters one must play *se-żarb* since they enjoy it. The difference between *żarb* and *oṣul* is that the former is followed by a pause.
Majles 6813	Know that famous rhythms among the Arab practitioners are six: *thaqil-e thaqil*, *khafif-e thaqil*, *ramal-e khafif*, *ramal-e thaqil*, *hazaj-e khafif*, and *hazaj-e thaqil*. Know that playing *żarb* is of many types: *yek-żarb*, *dō-żarb se-żarb*, *chahār-żarb*, etc. One must play *żarb* in accordance with the nature and humor of his audience. Likewise, the drummer (*żarb giranda*) must follow the singer closely, so that his drumming would not be in opposite to the nature.

GLOSSARY

(* = see entry elsewhere in the Glossary)

adwār/advār	Plural of *dawr* "cycle." (1) The term was used in Arabic, Persian and Turkish cultures to refer to a rhythmic cycle; (2) eighty-four octave species defined by Ṣafī al-Dīn al-Urmawī that were derived by combination and permutation of seven tetrachord and twelve pentachord species.
āhang	Melody, melody-type, catch-phrase, mode in a loose sense.
ahl-e naghma	The entire community of instrumentalists, singers, courtesans, entertainers, luthiers, and storytellers in an urban center between the sixteenth and eighteenth centuries.
'amal	A tripartite modulatory vocal genre/composition consisting of two **sarkhāna*s, a **miyānkhāna*, and a **bāzguy*.
'amala-ye ṭarab	The performing artists, including instrumentalists, singers, accompanists, dancing boys, and **moqalled*s, who were at the service of the Qajar court in the second half of the nineteenth century.
'amala-ye ṭarab-e khāṣṣa	Solo specialists including both instrumentalists and singers who enjoyed the highest esteem at the Qajar court. They were allowed to sit and perform in the presence of the shah and received monthly stipends.

andarun — Harem, seraglio; the female quarter of a court or a residence that is off limits to men.

anutak/nutak — A set of sounding bowls beaten with mallets during the seventeenth and eighteenth centuries.

'arusi — The final stage in the marriage process. A wedding ceremony.

'ayd-e ażḥā/'ayd-e qorbān — A religious holiday celebrated by Muslims worldwide every year. It honors the willingness of Abraham to sacrifice his son Ishmael as an act of obedience to God's command.

'ayd-e feṭr — A religious holiday celebrated by Muslims worldwide in observance of the end of Ramadan.

'ayd-e ghadir — A Shi'ite feast held at the time when Prophet Muḥammad is said to have appointed Ali as his successor.

'ayd-e mab'ath — A religious feast held by Muslims in observance of the appointment of the Prophet Muḥammad as the messenger of God.

āvāz — Lit. "voice." (1) The Persian equivalent of Arabic **nashid*; (2) a nonmetric vocal genre; (3) a synonym for **maqam*, especially after the seventeenth century; (4) a modulatory sequence of modes.

āvāza — A type of modulatory sequence of modes. Typically, there were six *āvāza*s, each associated with two **maqām*s.

badiha — Impromptu, unrehearsed, extemporized.

bardāsht — A type of nineteenth-century instrumental modulatory scheme played at the beginning of a performance while alluding to the major **āvāz*s of a **dastgāh*. The term is still used in Azeri *mugam*.

bayt al-loṭf — Lit. "house of benevolence." Brothel.

bāzguy — A section of a composition, often with a contrasting poetic meter or rhythmic structure.

bāzigar — Dancer, acrobat-dancer.

bazm — A convivial gathering with drinking of wine, recitation of poetry, and performance of music.

chahārmeżrāb — Lit. "a four-pluck pattern." An instrumental genre, marked with an ostinato plucking pattern (*pāya*) predominantly played on the **santur* (with mallets), **setār*, and **tār*.

chahārtār — Lit. "a four-stringed lute." An instrument that seems to have been the precursor of the modern *tār*.

chālchi-bāshi — Chief of the community of male musicians, courtesans, dancers, and entertainers in urban areas and especially the capital during the Safavid period.

chālānchi — Chief of the community of musicians, courtesans, dancers, and entertainers in the capital during the Qajar period. He was also the head of court musicians.

chini — A set of sounding bowls beaten with mallets in the nineteenth century.

chogur — Long-necked fretted lute played by Turkic bards.

daf — Frame drum.

Dār al-Fonun — The first European-style institution of higher learning in Iran, founded in Tehran in 1851.

darāmad — Opening section of a **maqam*, **āvāz*, or **dastgāh* in which the primary mode is fully unfolded and developed.

dasta — Lit. "group, cluster." An ensemble of musicians or entertainers; troupe.

dasta-ye shāhi — Ensemble of court musicians in the late nineteenth century.

dastān — (1) A fret or scale degree; (2) the main category of modes forming a modal system in the Sasanian and early Islamic centuries.

dastgāh — A large-scale modulatory scheme containing sequences of units (**āvāz*s and **gusha*s) and concluding with metric compositions.

dastgāh-e bāzigar-khāna — The courtly institution of female musicians, dancers, and acrobats in the first half of the nineteenth century.

dāyera	Frame drum with jingles (iron rings) attached inside the frame, usually smaller than a **daf*.
divān	Collection of the poems of a single poet.
dōbayti	A poetic form consisting of two rhymed couplets in the scheme *aa ba*.
dohol	A large double-headed drum.
dombak/tombak	Single-headed goblet drum.
dōtār	A long-necked fretted lute with two strings.
faṣl	(1) A sequence of pieces played on musical instruments during the Timurid period; (2) cyclical concert format including both vocal and instrumental sections performed at the Ottoman court.
forud	Lit. "descent." A type of cadential phrase that punctuates each stage of a modulatory scheme or composition.
gavorga	Gigantic Mongolian drum used in the **naqqāra-khāna*.
ghazal	(1) A poetic form consisting of an indeterminate number of rhymed couplets in the scheme *aa ba ca da*, etc; (2) the third part of the **nawbat-e morattab*; (3) a light vocal genre of North Indian music.
gusha	(1) A contrasting melody type that was interpolated in the sequence of an **āvāz*, or **dastgāh* mostly as a temporary modulation or to display the taste of a different *āvāz*; (2) a term used for all the units of *dastgāh* in the twentieth century.
guyanda	(1) The Persian equivalent of Arabic **qawwāl* as the performer of **qawl*; (2) a male singer of *taṣnif*s or metric compositions who often accompanied himself on a frame drum.
ḥāfeẓ	Lit. "keeper, preserver." (1) One who has by heart the whole Qur'an; (2) a singer and reciter of religious texts who has memorized the Qur'an; (3) a title often used for respected singers and professional composers of vocal genres.
'ilm/'elm	Theory, science, knowledge.

īqāʿ/iqāʿ	Lit. "tapping of rhythm with a stick" (*qażīb*). Rhythm, meter, rhythmic cycle.
kamāncha	A type of spike fiddle.
kār	Tripartite modulatory vocal genre/composition consisting of two **sarkhāna*s, a **miyānkhāna*, and a **bāzguy*.
kār-eʿamal/kār-o ʿamal	A form of modulatory vocal composition prevalent in the eighteenth and nineteenth centuries in Iran.
kawli	Lit. "gypsy." An apparent distortion of *kāboli*, that is, coming from Kabul, now the capital of Afghanistan.
khāneqāh	A lodge where Sufis congregate to perform the ritual of the *dhikr*; the guest house of a *pir*.
kharābāt	Lit. "ruins." The run-down, dilapidated quarter in a city where taverns, brothels, and musicians' stalls could be housed.
khiyāl	A bipartite vocal genre of North Indian classical music.
*khosravāni*s	(1) Seven ordered sequences of units composed by Bārbad to be performed as corresponding to the seven days of the week in praise of the Sasanian ruler, Khosraw II; (2) a 24-beat rhythmic cycle introduced by Ibn Kurr al-Baghdādi.
khᵛānanda	A singer of the nonmetric **maqām* or **āvāz*.
*khᵛārazmi*s	Rhythmic cycles or patterns in music of the **naqqāra-khāna* that could be subject to improvisation and composition in various performances of the **nawbat*.
maddāḥ	Lit. "a person who praises someone or recites eulogies." A singer-orator in the Shiʿite tradition who primarily extols Muḥammad the Prophet of Islam, his daughter Fatimah, and the twelve Imams.
maḥaṭṭ	Lit. "the place where people deposit their baggage when alighting from a journey." A type of cadential phrase that punctuates each stage of a modulatory scheme.
maḥfel	Intimate gathering.
majles	Lit. "gathering."

maqām — (1) The twelve primary modes; (2) twelve modulatory schemes, each including two *sho'ba*s.

maskhara — Jester, clown.

mathnavi — (1) Poetic form consisting of an indeterminate number of rhymed couplets in the scheme *aa bb cc dd*, etc.; (b) an unaccompanied vocal style set to *mathnavi* verses and sung by both roaming and sedentary dervishes and **maddāḥ*s.

mawlud — Celebration in observance of the birthday of the Prophet Muḥammad.

meżrāb — Lit. "plectrum." (1) Plectrum, mallet; (2) plucking pattern.

miyānkhāna — The second section of a composition in which a new theme or contrasting melodic line, often in a different mode, is introduced.

modulatory scheme — A sequence of modulations.

moghanni — A male musician in the medieval period.

monāseb-khᵛāni — Lit. "selecting relevant verses for singing in various contexts." A skill used by trained singers and courtesans in selecting relevant verses in response to the emotional states of their patrons or spectators.

moqaddama — Lit. "introduction." Often an instrumental opening section of a **maqām*, **āvāz*, or a composition.

moqalled — A buffoon who performed various forms of stand-up comedy and comic skit collectively known as **taqlid*.

morakkab — Lit. "compound." Synonym for **tarkib*, a generic term for a modulatory scheme.

moṭreb — Lit. "someone who evokes **ṭarab*." Musician, entertainer. The term mainly referred to all urban and rural lower-class musicians and entertainers during the nineteenth century who made a living with music.

Muharram — A month in the Muslim lunar calendar respected by the Shiʿites as a period of mourning (which actually extends to the end of the succeeding month of Ṣafar).

musiqār Panpipe.

naghma (1) Tone, pitch, and note in the medieval period; (2) after the Timurid era, *naghma* typically referred to a melody type or tune; (3) it could also refer to units of an *āvāz* characterized by an explicit regular pulsation as the result of a recurrent poetic meter or an ostinato pattern such as *kereshma*, *pishzangula*, and *zangula*; (4) an instrumental piece in the music of Afghanistan.

naqqāl A storyteller.

naqqāra A pair of kettledrums.

naqqāra-khāna (1) The ensemble of drums, trumpets, and oboes playing royal, ceremonial, civic, or military music; (2) the entire office of music and entertainment at the court.

naqra Attack, beat, time unit.

naqsh A short metric composition of sufficient attractiveness set to verse and nontextual syllables. In contrast to **ṣawt*, in which the text was syllabic and pronounced distinctly and intelligibly, the words in *naqsh* were broken or rendered melismatically.

nashid Singing or chanting style of an Arabic *qaṣida* in an improvisatory manner in which the rhythm of the melody depends largely on a quantitative poetic metre.

navākht The free exposition of modes or *āvāz*s played on musical instruments during the fourteenth and fifteenth centuries similar to the later Turko-Arabia concept of *taqsim*.

navāzanda An instrumentalist.

nawbat Lit. "turn, anything done periodically." The *nawbat* was the main repertoire and performance format of the **naqqāra-khāna*. It was a sequence of melodic and rhythmic sections each containing various rhythmic characters and functions.

nawbat-e morattab The most respected form of courtly composition and performance format between the thirteenth and fifteenth centuries, consisting of four sections: *qawl*, *ghazal*, *tarāna*, and *forudāsht*.

nawḥa	Lit. "lamentation." A type of metric song in a strophic style with a religious theme performed in an antiphonal sequence and accompanied by chest beating.
nay	End-blown oblique flute.
oṣul	Plural of *aṣl* literally meaning "principle." (1) The term was used in Persian, Turkish, and Central Asian cultures to refer to a rhythmic cycle; (2) positions of the arms and figures in premodern Persian dance; (3) dance in Uzbek culture.
ozān	Bard, the precursor of *'āsheq* and *bakhshi* in the Turkic tradition.
parda	Lit. "fret." Twelve primary modes and modulatory schemes that later came to be known as **maqām*s.
pishdarāmad	Instrumental metric genre that emerged in the twentieth century. It is mostly in duple meter and a slow tempo while containing modulations to the major **āvāz*s of a **dastgāh*. It is often performed as an opening piece in a musical concert.
pishraw	Lit. "what comes first," overture. (1) Primarily a vocal genre set to nontextual syllables with an explicit regular pulsation; (2) during the fifteenth and sixteenth centuries, the *pishraw* was an instrumental genre containing a **sarkhāna*, **miyānkhāna*, and **bāzguy*, with each section followed by a ritornello. *Pishraw* was predominantly composed in the rhythmic cycle *dōyek*.
qānun	Plucked board zither. The instrument declined in Iran around the first half of the eighteenth century. It was readopted from the Iraqi musical tradition in the middle of the twentieth century.
qavvāl-khāna	Courtesan salon, brothel.
qawl	Bipartite vocal genre that largely began with nonlexical syllables. It was primarily set to Arabic text, but by the seventeenth century, it was composed in Persian.
qawwāl/qavvāl	Lit. "performer of **qawl*." (1) Male or female singers of metrical vocal compositions, especially *qawl*, who often

accompanied themselves on a frame drum. In Iran, after the fifteenth century, the term was used exclusively to refer to courtesans; (2) performer of *qawwali* style of Sufi devotional music.

rabāb/rabāba — Spike fiddle.

radif — Lit. "sequence, ordered structure." The nineteenth-century court repertoire of Persian music consisting of some 250 melody types arranged in twelve modulatory schemes called *dastgāh*s. The *radif* originally referred to a repertoire for the *tār* and *setār* that had been developed by the Farāhāni family.

raqqāṣ — Dancer.

raqṣ — Dance.

rawża — A sermon and vocal genre recounting and mourning the martyrdom of Ḥusayn b. 'Ali, the grandson of the Prophet Muhammad, in Karbalā. It is based on a collection of verses titled *Rawżat al-shuhadā'* (*Garden of the Martyrs*) composed in 1502 by Ḥosayn Vā'eẓ Kāshefi (d. 1504). The goal of the performer of *rawża* is to move the audience to tears through a dramatization of the Karbalā disaster.

reng — A dance tune, an instrumental metric composition.

rikhta — A form of vocal **pishraw* set to prose and verses filled with humor and ridicule. The text of a *rikhta* was primarily in Persian but it could contain a mixture of Arabic, Turkish, and Hindi words as well.

robāb — A generic term for a skin-bellied plucked lute. In Afghanistan, *robāb* is a short-necked double-chambered lute with three main strings, four frets, two or three long drone strings, and up to fifteen sympathetic strings.

robā'i — Lit. "quatrain." A poetic form consisting of two rhymed couplets in the scheme aa ba.

santur/sanṭur — Struck zither played with thin mallets.

sāqi-nāma — (1) A poetic genre mostly employing eleven-syllables and in an indeterminate number of rhymed couplets in the scheme *aa bb cc dd*, etc.; (2) a vocal style set to verses of *sāqi-nāma* and governed by a loose meter of 4/4 or 7/8.

sarangi — Short-necked fiddle with sympathetic strings whose resonating chamber is covered with parchment, typically used to accompany vocal music in North India and Pakistan.

sarkhāna — The first section of a composition in which the first melodic theme is introduced and set to a few verses of a poem whose length usually does not exceed two couplets.

ṣawt — (1) The most popular urban genre between the seventh and tenth centuries in Damascus and Baghdad, often set to two to four couplets of an Arabic *qaṣida*; (2) a Persian genre in the Timurid and Safavid period containing only one **sarkhāna* that was repeated in a strophic style. *Sawt* was composed in short cycles of **oṣul* with each line followed by nontextual syllables and each *sarkhāna* concluding with a ritornello. It could be performed in a call and response format between a lead singer and the public.

sayr — Lit. "itinerary, pathway, route." A term that refers to the melodic progression of a *maqām*.

sāzanda — An instrumentalist in the cultures of Iran, Afghanistan, and Central Asia. The term was no longer used in Iran after the Qajar period.

setār — Long-necked lute with three strings. A fourth string was added to the instrument in the nineteenth century.

shadd — Lit. "tightening," that is, "tuning." (1) The twelve primary modes in the Arabic tradition, synonymous with the Persian *parda*; (2) twelve modulatory schemes, each including two *sho'bas*; (3) four sequences of modal and melodic units performed in such a way as to evoke pleasure or sadness, or to put listeners to sleep.

shādiyāna — Lit. "rejoicing." A rhythmic cycle played at a time of conquest, celebration, and festivity by **naqqāra-khāna* musicians.

shetorghu/shedorghu — A Mongolian long-necked lute with a membranous resonating chamber.

sho'ba — (1) A type of modulatory scheme in the **parda* modal system; (2) in the **maqām* system, *sho'ba*s were self-sufficient modes, either rendered in isolation or in conjunction with the related *maqām*s.

sornā/surnā — Lit. "flute of celebration." A shawm, in Iran usually accompanied by a **dohol*.

Systematist theorists — Disciples and followers of Ṣafī al-Dīn al-Urmawī who either wrote commentaries (*sharḥ*s) on his treatises or adopted his modal theory (*'ilm al-adwār*) for describing and characterizing various types of modal entitities.

tadhkera — A compendium of biographical notices of poets, musicians, and Sufis, often with examples of their verses.

ṭaḥrir — Lit. "liberation." (1) Melismatic phrases; (2) characteristic phrases of a **maqām*, **āvāz*, or **gusha* that are set to vocables or to the vowels of words such as *amān*, *dād*, *yār*, *jān*, *ay khodā*.

ṭanbur/tanbur — A generic term for long-necked fretted lutes. It is sometimes referred to by its number of strings such as *dōtār*, *setār*, and *chahārtār*.

taqlid — Lit. "mimicry." A type of stand-up comedy and comic skit.

taqlidchi — A **moqalled* at the service of the court.

tār — A double-chested plucked lute used in the urban music of Iran and the Caucasus.

ṭarab — Euphoria, rapture, or pleasure induced by music.

tārchi — A *tār* player at the service of the court.

tarkib — Lit. "compound." A generic term for modulatory sequence of modes.

taṣnif — A generic term for metric vocal compositions usually accompanied by a drum. Between the fifteenth and eighteenth century, *kār*, *'amal*, *qawl*, *ṣawt*, and *naqsh* were the prominent genres of *taṣnif*.

ta'ziya — Lit. "mourning." A passion play, or a theatrical expression of religious passion based on the battle of Karbala in 680 between the army of the second Umayyad Caliph Yazīd I and a small army led by Ḥusayn b. 'Ali, the grandson of the Prophet Muḥammad.

ṭuṭak — A small wooden flute played in the Safavid period. The instrument is still common in both Khorasan and Central Asia.

'ud — A short-necked fretless lute. The instrument declined in Iran around the first half of the eighteenth century. It was readopted from the Iraqi musical tradition in the middle of the twentieth century.

'ulamā' — Religious scholars, clerics.

varsāqi — A genre of folk sung poetry attributed to the *Varsāq* Turkmen clans. *Varsāqi* became the most prominent Turkish vocal genre during the sixteenth and seventeenth centuries in Iran, and especially, at the Safavid court.

żarb — Lit. "beat, attack." (1) Beat, rhythm, rhythmic pattern; (2) *dombak*.

żarbgir — Lit. "holder of the *dombak* or timekeeper." *Dombak* player.

żarbi — A metric composition that can be accompanied by the *dombak*.

WORKS CITED

Primary Sources

'Abd al-Aziz b. 'Abd al-Qāder. *Naqāwat al-adwār*. Nuruosmaniye (Istanbul) MS 3646.

'Abd al-Qāder Marāghi. *Maqāṣid al-alḥān*, ed. Taqi Binesh. Tehran: Bongāh-e Tarjoma va Nashr-e Ketāb, 1977.

'Abd al-Qāder Marāghi. *Jāmi' al-alḥān*, ed. Taqi Binesh. Tehran: Mo'assesa-ye Moṭāle'āt va Taḥqiqāt-e Farhangi, 1987.

'Abd al-Qāder Marāghi. *Jāmi' al-alḥān: khātema*, ed. Taqi Binesh. Tehran: Mo'assesa-ye Moṭāle'āt va Taḥqiqāt-e Farhangi, 1993.

'Abd al-Qāder Marāghi. *Sharḥ-e advār*, ed. Taqi Binesh. Tehran: Markaz-e Nashr-e Dāneshgāhi, 1991.

'Abd al-Qāder Marāghi. [Song-text Collection] Rijksuniversiteit (Universiteits Bibliotheek) Leiden MS Cod. 271Warn., 64a–66a.

'Abdollāh Anvār. *Tarjoma-ye sharḥ-e Mobārakshāh Bokhāri bar advār-e Ormavi dar 'elm-e musiqi*. Tehran: Farhangestān-e Honar, 2013.

Abū al-Faraj al-Iṣfahānī, *Kitāb al-aghānī*, vols. I–XVI, Cairo: Dār al-Kutub, 1927–1961.

Abū Isḥāq al-Kindī, "Al-risālat al-kubrā fī ta'līf," *Mu'alifāt al-Kindī al-musīqiyya*, ed. Zakariyā Yusuf. Baghdad: Maṭba'at Shafīq, 1962.

Abū Naṣr al-Fārābī. *Kitāb al-mūsīqī al-kabīr*, ed. Ghaṭṭās 'Abd al-Malik Khashabah. Cairo: Dār al-Kitāb al-'Arabī, 1967.

Ādāb-e āvāz-hā va dhekrhā'i ke dar manāber va joz ān khᵛānda mishavad. Malek Library (Tehran) MS 2830/2.

ʻAli b. Moḥammad Bannāʼi. *Resāla dar musiqi* (facsimile). Tehran: Markaz-e Nashr-e Dāneshgāhi, 1989.

ʻAlishāh b. Buka Awbahi. *Moqaddamat al-uṣūl*, ed. Moḥammad-Taqi Ḥosayni. Tehran: Farhangestān-e Honar, 2011.

Amir Khān Gorji. *Resāla*. Bibliothèque nationale de France MS Suppl. persan 1087.

Bahjat al-qulūb. Majles Library (Tehran) MS 2242.

Bāqiyā Nāʼini. *Zamzama-ye vaḥdat*. Biruni Institute of Oriental Studies (Tashkent) MS 10226.

Darvish-ʻAli Changi. *Tuḥfat al-surūr*. Institute of Written Heritage (Dushanbe) MS 264.

Dawra Beg Karāmi. "Maʻrefat-e ʻelm-e musiqi," in *Nāma-ye Minovi*, ed. Ḥabib Yaghmāʼi and Iraj Afshār. Tehran, 1971, 189–198.

Dawra Beg Karāmi. *Resāla-ye Karāmiya*. Russian Academy of Sciences MS B1844.

Dawra Beg Karāmi. *Resāla-ye Karāmiya*, University of Tehran (Tehran) MS 2591, 402–413.

Farmān-e riyāsat-e Luṭi Ṣāleḥ be moṭrebān va qavvālān, University of Tehran (Tehran) MS 3935.

Fatḥ Allāh al-Shirwānī. *Codex on Music* (*Majalla fīʼl mūsīqī*), introductionckhard Neubauer, Frankfurt: Institute for the History of Arabic-Islamic Science at the Johann Wolfgang Goethe University, 1986.

Forṣat al-Dawla Shirāzi. *Boḥur al-alḥān dar ʻelm-e musiqi va nesbat-e ān bā ʻaruż*, ed. Moḥammad Qāsem Ṣāleḥ Rāmsari. Tehran: Forughi, 1988.

Hâfız Post. *Güfte mecmuası*. Topkapı R. (Istanbul) MS 1724.

Ḥājj Ḥosayn Ẓohri Eṣfahāni, *Resāla dar fann-e musiqi*, ed. Imān Raʼisi. Tehran: Solār, 2017.

Ḥasan Kāshāni. "Kanz al-tuḥaf," in *Sa resāla-ye fārsi dar musiqi*, ed. Taqi Binesh. Tehran: Markaz-e nashr-e dāneshgāhi, 1992.

Hedāyat, Mehdi-Qoli. *Majmaʻ al-adwār* (lithograph), Tehran, 1938.

Hedāyat, Mehdi-Qoli. *Majmaʻ al-adwār*. University of Tehran (Tehran) MS Ḥoquq 120.2.

Ibn Khurdādhbih, *Mukhtār min kitāb al-lahw wa al-malāhī*, ed. Ighnāṭiūs ʻAbduh Khalīfa. Beirut: Dār al-Mashriq, 1961.

Ibn Sīnā. "Musiqi-ye *Dānesh-nāma-ye ʻAlāʼi*," in *Sa resāla-ye fārsi dar musiqi*, ed. Taqi Binesh. Tehran: Markaz-e Nashr-e Dāneshgāhi, 1992.

Ibn Zayla. *Kitāb al-kāfī fī al-musīqī*, ed. Zakariyā Yusuf. Cairo: Dār al-Qalam, 1964.

Kantemiroğlu. *Kitābi ʻilmiʼl mūsīḳī ʻalā vechiʼl-ḥurūfāt: Mûsikîyi harflerle tesbît ve icrâ ilminin kitabı*, ed. Yalçın Tura, 2 vols. Istanbul: Yapı Kredi Yayınları, 2001.

Khażrāʼi, Bābak. "Sharḥ-e chahār dastgāh va taṣāvir-e chand sāz," *Māhur* 59 (2013): 147–158.

Khᵛorshāh b. Qobād Ḥosayni, *Tārikh-e ilchi-ye Neẓāmshāh*, ed. Moḥammad Reżā Naṣiri and Koichi Haneda. Tehran: Anjoman-e Āthār va Mafākher-e Farhangi, 1990.

Loṭfollāh b. Moḥammad Samarqandi. [Commentary on the] *Kitāb al-adwār*. Malek Library (Tehran) MS 1647.

Maḥmud b. ʿAbd al-Aziz. *Maqāṣid al-adwār* (*Mukhtaṣar dar ʿelm-e musiqi*). Nuruosmaniye MS 3649.1.

Mir Ṣadr al-Din Moḥammad. "Resāla-ye ʿelm-e musiqi," ed. Āriyu Rostami. *Māhur* 18 (2003): 81–96.

Mirzā Shafiʿ. *The Treatise on the Seven Dastgah of Iranian Music*, ed. Moḥsen Moḥammadi. Tehran: Mirāth-e Maktub, 2018.

Moḥammad b. ʿAbd al-Ḥamid al-Lādhiqī. *Al-risāla al-fatḥiyya*, ed. Hāshim Moḥammad al-Rajab. Kuwait, 1976.

Moḥammad Mofid Mostawfi Bāfqi, *Jāmeʿ-e Mofidi*, ed. Iraj Afshār. Tehran: Ketābforushi-ye Asadi, 1961.

Moḥammad Ṭāher Naṣrābādi, *Tadhkera-ye Naṣrābādi*, ed. A. Modaqqaq Yazdi. Yazd: Dāneshgāh-e Yazd, 1990.

Moḥammad Yusof Vāla Eṣfahāni, *Khold-e barin*, ed. Mir Hāshem Moḥaddeth. Tehran: Bonyād-e Moqufāt-e Afshār, 1993.

Moḥammadi, Moḥsen, ed. "Resāla-ye davāzdah dastgāh," *Māhur* 59 (2013): 125–146.

Moḥiṭ-Ṭabāṭabā'i, Moḥammad, "Resāla-ye musiqi-ye gomnām," *Majalla-ye musiqi* 10/11 (1941): 13–21.

Moḥsen Ta'thir Tabrizi, *Divān-e Moḥsen Ta'thir Tabrizi*, ed. Amin Pāshā Ejlāli. Tehran: Markaz-e Nashr-e Dāneshgāhi, 1994.

Najm al-Din Kawkabi Bokhārā'i. "Resāla-ye musiqi-ye Najm al-Din Kawkabi Bokhārā'i," in *Sa resāla-ye musiqi-ye qadim-e Irān*, ed. Manṣura Thābetzāda. Tehran: Anjoman-e Āthār va Mafākher-e Farhangi, 2012.

Nasimi. *Nasim-e Ṭarab (The Breeze of Euphoria): A Sixteenth-Century Persian Musical Treatise*, ed. Amir Hosein Pourjavady. Tehran: Farhangestān-e Honar, 2007.

Neẓāmi Ganjavi. *Khosraw va Shirin*, ed. Ḥasan Vaḥid Dastgerdi. Tehran, Mo'assasa-ye Maṭbuʿāti-ye ʿElmi, 1934.

Pourjavady, Amir Hosein. "Resāla-ye musiqi-ye Moḥammad b. Maḥmud b. Moḥammad Nayshāburi," *Maʿāref* 34/35 (1995): 44–57.

Pourjavady, Amir Hosein. "Resāla dar bayān-e chahār dastgāh-e aʿẓam," *Māhur* 12 (2001): 81–92.

Pourjavady, Amir Hosein. "Dar bayān-e ʿelm-e musiqi va dānestan-e shoʿabāt-e ou," *Māhur* 15 (2002): 49–70.

Pourjavady, Amir Hosein. "Resāla dar ʿelm-e musiqi," *Māhur* 14 (2002): 101–114.

Pourjavady, Amir Hosein. "Athari musiqā'i az dawra-ye Qājār, ta'lif-e Ḥaj Ḥosayn 'Ali-Naqi Ganja'i," *Māhur* 28 (2003): 70–81.

Qoṭb al-Din Shirāzi. *Durrat al-tāj li ghurrat al-dubbāj*, edi. Sayyed Ḥasan Meshkān Ṭabasi. Tehran, 1945.

Rabino de Borgomale, H. L. (ed.). *Bahjat al-rūḥ*. Tehran: Bonyād-e farhang, 1965.

Ṣafī al-Dīn al-Urmawī. *al-Risāla al-Sharafiyya fī al-nisab al-ta'līfiyya*, ed. Hāshim Moḥammad al-Rajab. Kuwait: Dar al-rashid li-l-nashr, 1982.

Ṣafī al-Dīn al-Urmawī. *Kitāb al- adwār*, ed. Ghaṭṭās 'Abd al-Malik Khashabah and Maḥmud Aḥmad al-Hefni. Cairo, 1986.

Shams al-Dīn Muḥammad b. Qays al-Rāzī, *Al-mu'jam fī ma'ā'īr ash'ār al-'ajam*, ed. Moḥammad b. 'Abd al-Vahhāb Qazvini. Tehran: Dāneshgāh-e Tehrān, 1957.

Shehāb al-Din 'Abdollāh Morvārid, *Munis al-aḥbāb: Majmu'a-ye, robā'iyāt-e Shehāb al-Din 'Abdollāh Morvārid*, ed. Sayyed 'Ali Mirafżali. Tehran: Markaz-e Asnād-e Majles-e Shorā-ye Eslāmi, 2011.

Zahiruddin Muhammad Babur, *Bâburnâma: Chaghatay Turkish Text with Abdul-Rahim Khankhanan's Persian Translation*, Turkish transcription, Persian edition and English translation W. M. Thackston, Jr. Cambridge, MA: Department of NELC, Harvard University, 1993.

Żiā' al-Din Yusof. *Resāla-ye musiqi mawsum be kolliyāt-e Yusofi*, ed. Bābak Khażrā'i. Tehran: Farhangestān-e Honar, 2011.

Travel Accounts

Bāzan. *Nāmahā-ye ṭabib-e Nāder Shāh*, trans. 'Ali-Aṣghar Ḥariri. Tehran: Anjoman-e Āthār-e Melli, 1961.

Chardin, Jean. *Voyages du chevalier Chardin, en Perse, et autres lieux de l'Orient*, ed. L. Langlès, 10 vols. Paris: Le Normant, 1811.

Daulier Deslandes, A. *Les beautez de la Perse ou la description de ce qu'il ya de plus curieux dans ce royaume*. Paris, 1673.

de Gouvea, Antonio. *Jornada do arcebispo de Goa Dom Frey Aleixo de Meneses.* Coimbra: 1606.

de Gouvea. *Relation des grandes guerres et victoires obtenues par le roy de Perse Chah Abbas contre les empereurs de Turquie*. Rouen: Nicholas Loyelet, 1646.

de Thevenot, M. *The Travels of Monsieur de Thevenot into the Levant in Three Parts.* London, 1686.

Della Valle, Pietro. *Les Fameux Voyages*, 4 vols. Paris, 1663–1664.

Della Valle, Pietro. *Viaggi di Pietro Della Valle. Il pellegrino descritti da lui medesimo in lettere familiari all-erudito suo amico Mario Schipano divisi in tre parti cioè: la Turchia, la Persia e l'India*. 2 vols. Brighton: G. Gancia, 1843.

Dunlop, Hendrik, ed. "Journal of Hubert Visnich, Nov. 1627–28 Dec.1628," in *Bronnen tot de geschiedenis der Oostindische Compagnie in Perzië 1611–1638*, 'S-Gravenhage: Nijhoff, 1930.

Father Belchior dos Anjos. "Relation des motifs du Châh pour faire guerre au Turc, et des événements qui s'ensuivirent dès le 14 septembre 603 jusqu'à septembre 604," in *L'ambassade en Perse de Luis Pereira de Lacerda et des Pères Portugais de l'Ordre de Saint-Augustin, Belchior dos Anjos et Guilherme de Santo Agostinho 1604–1605*. Lisbon: Fundacao Calouste Gulbenkian, 1972.

Gātoghikus, Abrāham. *Montakhabāti az yāddāshthā-ye Abrāhām Gātoghikus*, trans. 'Abd al-Ḥosayn Sepantā and Estiphan Hananian. Isfahan: Vaḥid, 1968.

Gobineau, Joseph Arthur, Comte de. *Trois ans en Asie, 1855 à 1858*. Paris, 1859.

Grey, Charles, trans. and ed. *Narrative of Italian Travels in Persia in the Fifteenth and Sixteenth Centuries*. London, 1873.

Herbert, Thomas. *Travels in Persia 1627–1629*, ed. Sir William Foster. New York: Routledge, 1929.

Hārutin Ṭanburi. "Tārikh-e Ṭahmāseb-Qoli Khān," in *Sefāratnāmahā-ye Irān: gozāreshhā-ye mosāferat va ma'muriyat-e safirān-e 'Othmāni dar Irān*, ed. Moḥammad Amin Riyāḥi. Tehran: Tus, 1989.

Kaempfer, Engelbert. *Exotic Attractions in Persia, 1684–1688: Travels & Observations*, trans. and annot. Willem Floor and Colette Ouahes. Washington, DC: Mage, 2018.

Leupe, L. (ed.). "Beschrijvinge van de coninclijcke stadt Spahan," *Kronijk van het Historisch Genootschap gevestigd te Utrecht*, 2e serie, 10 (1854): 191–208.

Lycklama a Nijeholt, Tinco Martinus. *Voyage en Russie, au Caucase et en Perse, dans la Mésopotamie, le Kurdistan, la Syrie, la Palestine et la Turquie*. Paris: Arthus Bertrand, 1873.

Manuchehri Dāmghāni, *Divān*, ed. Moḥammad Dabirsiyāqi. Tehran: Zavvār, 1968.

Mandelslo, Johann A. von *Beschrijvingh van de gedenckwaerdige zee-en landtreyze deur Persien naar Oost-Indien*. Amesterdam, 1658.

Moginié, Daniel. *L'illustre paisan, ou, Memoires et avantures de Daniel Moginié . . .: où se trouvent plusieurs particularités anecdotes des derniéres révolutions de la Perse & de l'Indostan & du règne de Thamas-Kouli-kan*. Lausanne: Au depens de la compagnie, 1761.

Olearius, Adam. *Vermehrte newe Beschreibung der moscowitischen und persischen Reyse*, ed. D. Lohmeier, Schleswig, 1656 (repr. Tübingen, 1971).

Olearius, Adam. *The Voyages & Travels of the Ambassadors from the Duke of Holstein, to the Great Duke of Muscovy, and the King of Persia: Begun in the Year M. DC. XXXIII, and Finish'd in M. DC. XXXIX: Containing a Compleat History of Muscovy, Tartary, Persia, and Other Adjacent Countries*, trans. John Davies. London: Thomas Dring & John Starkey, 1662.

Olivier, Guillaume Antoine. *Voyage dans l'empire Othoman, l'Égypte et la Perse*, 3 vols. Paris, 1801/7; trans. into Persian Gholāmreżā Varahrām as *Safarnāma-ye Olivia*. Tehran: Eṭṭelā'āt, 1992.

Ouseley, William. *Travels in Various Countries of the East: More Particularly Persia*. London: Rodwell & Martin, 1823.

Sanson, N. *Voyage ou relation de l'estat present du royaume de Perse*. Paris, 1694.

Sanson, Nicholas. *The Present State of Persia*. London, 1695.

Silva y Figueroa, Don Garcia de, *Comentarios de d. Garcia de Silva y Figueroa de la embajada que de parte del rey de España don Felipe III hizo al rey xa Abas de Persia*, 2 vols. Madrid, 1903.

Soltykoff, Alexis. *Voyage en Perse*. Paris, 1851.

Struys, J. J. *Drie aanmerkelijke en seer rampspoedige reysen door Italie, Griekenlandt, Lijflandt, Moscovien, Tartarijen, Meden, Persien, Oast-Indien, Japan, en verscheyden andere gewesten*. Amsterdam, 1676.

Tavernier, Jean-Baptiste. *Les six voyages de Jean-Bapt. Tavernier en Turquie, en Perse et aux Indes*, 2 vols. Utrecht, 1712.

Travels to Tana and Persia by Josafa Barbaro and Ambrogio Contarini, ed. Lord Stanley of Alderley, trans. William Thomas and S. A. Roy. London: Hakluyt Society, 1873.

Waring, Edward Scott. *A Tour to Sheeraz, by the Route of Kazroon and Feerozabad*. London: T. Cadell & W. Davies, 1807.

Zakaria, Le Diacre. "Mémoires historiques sur les sofis," in *Collection d'historiens arméniens*, ed. and trans. M Brosset, 2 vols. St. Petersburg, 1876.

Secondary Literature

Abd al-Razzāq Beg Donbali, *Tajrubat al-aḥrār wa tasliyyat al-abrār*, ed. Ḥasan Qāżi Ṭabāṭabā'i, vol. 1. Tabriz: Mo'assasa-ye Tārikh va Farhang-e Irān, 1970.

Abu al-Fażl Bayhaqi. *Tārikh-e Bayhaqi*, ed. Manuchehr Dāneshpazhuh, 2 vols. Tehran: Hirmand, 2001.

Abu al-Fażl 'Allāmi ibn Mubārak. *Akbar Nāma*, trans. H. Beveridge, 3 vols. Calcutta: Asiatic Society of Bengal, 1907–1939.

Abū al-Ḥasan 'Alī b. al-Mas'ūdī, *Murūj al-dhahab wa ma'ādin al-jawhar*, ed. Charles Pellat. Paris: Société asiatique, 1962.

Abu al-Ḥasan Ghaffāri-Kāshāni. *Golshan-e morād*, ed. Gholām-Reżā Ṭabāṭabā'i Majd. Tehran: Zarrin, 1990.

Abu al-Karim al-Qoshayri Neyshāburī. "Samā'-e she'r be āvāz-e khosh," in *Andar ghazal-e khish nahān khᵛāham gashtan: samā'-nāmahā-ye fārsi*, ed. Najib Māyel Heravi. Tehran: Nashr-e Nay, 1992.

Abū Ḥāmed Ghazālī. "Vajd va samā'," in *Andar ghazal-e khish nahān khᵛāham gashtan: samā'-nāmahā-ye fārsi*, ed. Najib Māyel Heravi. Tehran: Nashr-e Nay, 1992.

Abul-Fazl-i-'Allāmi. *The Ā'in-e Akbarī*, ed. H. Blochmann, 2 vols. Calcutta: Asiatic Society of Bengal, 1867.

Advielle, Victor. *La Musique chez les Persans en 1885*. Paris, 1885.

Aḥmad al-Rifā'ī al-Muslim b. 'Abd al-Raḥmān al-Mawṣilī, *al-Durr al-naqī fī fann al-mūsīqī*, ed. Jalāl Ḥanafī. Baghdad: Wizārat al-Thaqāfah wa al-Irshād, 1964.

Aḥmad Jām Zhendapil. "Samā' chist," in *Andar ghazal-e khish nahān khᵛāham gashtan: samā'-nāmahā-ye fārsi*, ed. Najib Māyel Heravi. Tehran: Nashr-e Nay, 1992.

Ali Şir Navaî, "Mizānü'l-Evzān," in *Divanlar Ile Hamse dişindaki Eserler*. Ankara: Türk Tarih Kurumu Basımevi, 1968.

Anaclerio, Giuseppe. *La Persia descritta. Relazione di un viaggio*. Napoli: Vincenzo Marchese, 1868.

'Āref Qazvini. *Divān*, ed. Mehdi Nurmoḥammadi. Tehran: Sokhan, 2002.

'Aružī Samarqandi. *Chahār maqāla*, ed. Moḥammad Qazvini. Tehran: Zavvār, 1910.

Asadi, Hooman. "Ḥayāt-e musiqā'i dar dawrān-e Taymuriān," *Māhur* 14 (2001): 25–52.

Asadi, Hooman. "Negāhi be mafhum va sayr-e takvin-e pishdarāmad dar musiqi-ye Irāni," *Māhur* 33 (2006) :47–152.

Asadi, Hooman. "Mafhum va sākhtār-e dastgāh dar musiqi-ye kelāsik-e Irān: barrasi-ye taṭbiqi-ye radif" ("The Concept and Structure of the Dastgāh in Persian Classical Music: Comparative Analysis of Radif"), Ph.D. dissertation, University of Tarbiyat-e Modarres, Tehran, 2006.

Aubin, Eugène, *La Perse d'aujourd'hui*. Paris: Colin, 1908.

Aubin, Eugène, *Irān-e emruz 1906–1907*, Persian trans. Ali-Asghar Sa'idi. Tehran: Nashr-e 'Elm, 1983.

Āzhand, Ya'qub, *Namāyesh dar dawra-ye Ṣafavi*. Tehran: Farhangestān-e Honar, 2009.

'Ażod al-Dawla (Solṭān-Aḥmad Mirzā). *Tārikh-e 'Ażodi*, ed. Abd al-Ḥosayn Navā'i. Tehran: Nashr-e 'Elm, 1997.

Babayan, Kathryn. "Sufis, Dervishes and Mullas: The Controversy over Spiritual and Temporal Dominion in Seventeenth-Century Iran," in *Safavid Persia: The History and Politics of an Islamic Society*. Cambridge: University of Cambridge, 1996.

Baily, John. *Music of Afghanistan: Professional Musicians in the City of Herat*. Cambridge: Cambridge University Press, 1988.

Baily, John. "The Music of the Timurids and its Legacy in Afghanistan," in *Theory and Practice in the Music of Islamic World*, ed. Rachel Harris and Martin Stokes. London: Routledge, 2018.

Browne, Edward G. *A Year Amongst the Persians*. London: Adam and Charles Black, 1893.

Caton, Margaret. "The Classical *Tasnif*: A Genre of Persian Vocal Music," Ph.D. dissertation, University of California, Los Angeles, 1983.

Caton, Margaret. *A Persian Ode: Musical Life in Safavid and Qajar Iran*. Los Angeles, CA: Margaret Caton, 2021.

Chodźko, Alexander Borejko. *Specimens of the Popular Poetry of Persia*. London, 1842.

Dāneshpazhuh, Moḥammad-Taqi. *Nemuna'i az fehrest-e āthār-e dāneshmandān-e Irāni va Eslāmi dar ghenā' va musiqi*. Tehran: Vezārat-e Farhang va Honar, 1976.

Dawlatshāh Samarqandi. *Tdhkirat al-shu'arā'*, ed. Edward Brown. Tehran: Asāṭir, 2003.

Dehkhodā, 'Aliakbar. "Nashid" and "Shādiyāna," in *Loghatnāma*, ed. Moḥammad Mo'in and Ja'far Shahidi. Tehran: University of Tehran Press, 1993.

During, Jean. *La musique iranienne: tradition et évolution*, Institut Français d'Iranologie de Téhéran: Bibliothèque iranienne, No. 29. Paris: Editions recherches sur les civilisations, 1984.

During, Jean. *The Radif of Mirzā 'Abdollāh: A Canonic Persian Repertoire, as Recorded by Nur 'Ali Borumand*, 2nd ed. Tehran: Māhur, 2006.

During, Jean. *Musiques d'Iran: La tradition en question*. Paris: Geuthner, 2010.

Dust-'Ali Mo'ayyer al-Mamālek. *Yāddāsht-hā'i az zendegāni-ye khoṣuṣi-ye Nāṣer al-Din Shāh*. Tehran: Nashr-e Tārikh-e Irān, 1982.

Dust-'Ali Mo'ayyer al-Mamālek. *Rejāl-e 'aṣr-e Nāṣeri*. Tehran: Nashr-e Tārikh-e Irān, 1982.

Ebtekar, Maryam. "Harmony or Cacophony: Music Instruction at the Dār al-Fonūn," in *Society and Culture in Qajar Iran*, ed. Elton L. Daniel. Costa Mesa, CA: Mazda, 2002.

Emsheimer, Ernst. "Earliest Reports about the Music of the Mongols," trans. Robert Carroll, *Asian Music* 18(1) (1986): 1–19.

Eskandar Beg Turkamān. *Tārikh-e 'ālamārā 'Abbāsi*, 2 vols., 2nd ed. Tehran: Amir-Kabir, 1971.

Eskandar Monshi. *History of Shah 'Abbas*, trans. Roger M. Savory, 2 vols. Boulder, CO: Westview, 1978.

E'temād al-Salṭana. *Al-ma'āthir wa al-āthār*, 2 vols. Tehran: Asāṭir, 1984.

E'temād al-Salṭana. *Ruznāma-ye khāṭerāt-e E'temād al-Salṭana*, ed. Iraj Afshār. Tehran: Amir-Kabir, 2000.

Fallahzadeh, Mehrdad. *Two Treatises–Two Streams*. Bethesda, MD: Ibex, 2009.

Fāṭemi, Sāsān. "Form va musiqi-ye Irāni," *Māhur* 39 (2008): 103–134.

Fāṭemi, Sāsān. "*Taṣnif-e mo'āṣer*," *Māhur* 40 (2008): 85–112.

Fāṭemi, Sāsān. *Jashn va musīqi dar farhanghā-ye shahri-ye Irāni*. Tehran: Māhur, 2014.

Fāṭemi, Sāsān. "Sayr-e nofudh-e musiqi-ye gharbi be Irān dar 'aṣr-e Qājār," *Nashriya-ye honarhā-ye zibā-honarhā-ye namāyeshi va musiqi* 19(2) (2014): 5–16.

Fāṭemi, Sāsān. "Tārikh-e musiqi-ye Qājār," in *Tārikh-e jāme'-e Irān*, ed. Ṣādeq Sajjādi, 20 vols. Tehran: Bonyād-e Dā'eratolma'āref-e Bozorg-e Eslāmi, 2014.

Fāṭemi, Sāsān. *Farhikhtagi dar mohiṭ-e mardomi: ghazal-khᵛāni-e Tehrāni va bastarhā-ye farhangi-ejtemā'i-ye ān*. Tehran: Māhur, 2019.

Farhat, Hormoz. *The Dastgāh Concept in Persian Music*. Cambridge: Cambridge University Press, 1990.

Farmer, Henry George. "The Old Persian Musical Modes," *Journal of the Royal Asiatic Society* (1926): 94–95.

Farmer, Henry George. "The Old Arabian Melodic Modes," *Journal of the Royal Asiatic Society* (1965): 99.

Feldman, Walter. *Music of the Ottoman Court: Makam, Composition and the Early Ottoman Instrumental Repertoire*, Intercultural Music Studies 10. Berlin: Verlag für Wissenschaft und Bildung, 1996.

Floor, Willem. *A Social History of Sexual Relations in Iran*. Washington, DC: Mage, 2008.

Gholām-'Ali 'Aziz al-Solṭān. *Ruznāma-ye khāṭerāt-e Gholām-'Ali 'Aziz al-Solṭān, Malijak*. Tehran: Zaryāb, 1997.

Gluck, Jay and Sumi Gluck. *A Survey of Persian Handicraft*. Tehran: The Bank Melli, 1977.

Gray, Basil. "The Arts in the Safavid Period," in *The Cambridge History of Iran*, ed. P. Jackson and L. Lockhart, vol. 6. Cambridge: Cambridge University Press, 1986.

Greve, Marrin, ed. *Writing the History of "Ottoman Music."* Istanbul: Orient Institut, 2015.

Hārun Vahuman (ed.), "Safarnāma-ye Kajlor," in *Safarnāma-hā-ye khaṭṭi-ye Fārsi*, 4 vols. Tehran: Nashr-e Akhtarān, 2009.

Harutiwn Ter Hovhaneants. *Tārikh-e Jolfā-ye Esfahān* [*History of New Julfa in Isfahan*], trans. Armenian to Persian by Leon Minassian and M. A. Mussavi Feraydani. Isfahan: Nashr-e Zendarud, 2000.

Ḥasan Rumlu. *Aḥsan al-tawārīkh*, ed. 'Abd al-Ḥosayn Navā'i. Tehran: Bābak, 1978.

Hedāyat, Mehdi-Qoli. *Radif-e haft dastgāh-e musiqi-e Irāni be revāyat-e Mehdi Ṣolḥi* (*Montaẓam al-Ḥokamā'*). Tehran: Māhur, 2014.

Jung, Angelika. *Quellen der traditionellen Kunstmusik der Usbeken und Tadshiken Mittelasiens: Untersuchungen zur Enstehung und Entwicklung des Shashmaqâm*. Hamburg: K. D. Wagner, 1989.

Kaempfer, Engelbert. *Album of Persian Costumes and Animals with some Drawings*, British Museum (London) 1974, 0617,0.1.21.

Kāmrān, Ṭali'a and Shehāb Menā. *Bakhsh-hā'i az radif-e Ḥabib Samā'i be revāyat-e Ṭali'a Kāmrān*. Tehran: Nashr-e Musiqi-ye 'Āref, 2009.

Karamatov, Faizullah M. and Ishak Radjabov, "Introduction to the Shashmaqam," trans. Theodore Levin, *Asian Music* 13(1) (1981): 111–112.

Karimi, Mahmud and Mohammad-Taghi Massoudieh. *Radif-e āvāzi-ye musiqi-ye sonnati-ye Irān be revāyat-e Maḥmud Karimi/Radif vocal de la musique iranienne*. Tehran: Sorush, 1978.

Kāẓemi, Bahman, Mehdi Farāhāni, and Vahraz Puraḥmad, *Golbāng-e sarbolandi: mabāni va barrasi-ye āvāz-e Irān*. Tehran: Farhangestān-e Honar, 2010.

Kazemi, Bahman, Mehdi Farahani, and Wahraz Pour Ahmad. *Persian Music in the Past Century*. Tehran: Farhangestān-e Honar, 2012.

Kinnear, Michael. *The Gramophone Company's Persian Recordings 1899–1934* (Victoria, Australia: Bajakhana, 2000.

Khāju Kermāni. *Divān*, ed. Aḥmad Sohayli Khᵛānsāri. Tehran: Pāzang, 1990.

Khāleqi, Ruḥollāh. *Sargodhasht-e musiqi-ye Iran*. Tehran: Ṣafi'alishāh, 1983.

Khażrā'i, Bābak. "Darbāra-ye reng," *Māhur* 66 (2015): 67–87.

Kordmāfi, Sa'id. "Barrasi-ye barkhi janbahā-ye 'amali-ye iqā' dar resālāt-e qadim-e musiqi-ye ḥawza-ye eslāmi-ye qarn-e haftom tā davāzdahom-e hejri," *Māhur* 60 (2013): 167–198.

Kotzebue, Moritz von. *Narrative of a Journey into Persia in the Suite of the Imperial Russian Embassy in the Year 1817*. Philadelphia, 1820.

Loṭfi, Moḥammad-Reżā. *Musiqi-ye āvāzi-ye Irān: dastgāh-e shur, radif-e ostād 'Abdollāh Davāmi*. Tehran, Gutenberg, 1974.

Lucas, Ann E. *Music of a Thousand Years: A New History of Persian Musical Traditions*. Oakland: University of California Press, 2019.

Malekshāh Ḥosayn b. Ghiyāth al-Din Moḥammad, *Iḥyā' al-mulūk*, ed. Manuchehr Sotuda. Tehran: Enteshārāt-e 'Elmi va Farhangi, 2004.

Ma'rufi, Musā and Mehdi Barkechli, *Radif-e haft dastgāh-e musiqi-e Irāni/Les Systèmes de la musique traditionelle iranienne (radif)*. Tehran: Vezārat-e Farhang va Honar, 1962.

Ma'rufi, Musā and Mehdi Barkechli. *La musique traditionelle de l'Iran* (*radif*). Tehran: Ministère de la Culture et des Arts, 1963.

Mashḥun, Ḥasan. *Tārikh-e musiqi-ye Irān*, 2 vols. Tehran: Simorgh-Fākhta, 1991.

Mashḥun, Ḥasan. "Navāzandegān-e qadim-e tār va setār," *Māhur* 30 (2006): 79–137.

Massoudieh, Mohammad-Taghi. *Manuscrits persans concernant la musique*, RISM, Band XII. Munich: G. Henle Verlag, 1996.

Matthee, Rudi. "Prostitutes, Courtesans, and Dancing Girls: Women Entertainers in Safavid Iran," in *Iran and Beyond*, ed. Rudi Matthee and Beth Baron. Costa Mesa, CA: Mazda, 2000.

Matthee, Rudi. *The Pursuit of Pleasure: Drugs and Stimulants in Iranian History, 1500–1900*. Washington, DC: Mage, 2005.

Matthee, Rudi. "The Safavids under Western Eyes: Seventeenth-Century European Travelers to Iran," *Journal of Early Modern History* 13 (2009): 137–171.

Matthee, Rudi. "From the Battlefield to the Harem: Did Women's Seclusion Increase from Early to Late Safavid Times," in *New Perspectives on Safavid Iran*, ed. Colin P. Mitchell. New York: Routledge, 2011.

Matthee, Rudi. "Safavid Iran through the Eyes of European Travelers," *Harvard Library Bulletin* 23(1/2) (2012): 10–24. not cited in text

Minorsky, Vladimir and C. E. Bosworth, "Tabriz," *EI2*, Brill online, 45.

Mir Fażlollāh Shirāzi. *Tārikh-e dholqarnayn*, ed. Nāṣer Afshārfar, 2 vols. Tehran: Vezārat-e Farhang va Ershād-e Eslāmi, 2001.

Mir'alinaqi, 'Ali-Reżā and 'Ali-Naqi Vaziri, *Vaziri-nāma*. Tehran: Mo'in, 1998.

Mirzā Ebrāhim Yazdi, "Dibācha-ye anis al-arvāḥ," ed. Aḥmad Golchin Ma'āni, *Majala-ye adabiyāt va 'olum-e ensāni-ye Mashhad* 4 (1968): 331, 337.

Mirzā Moḥammad Tonkāboni. *Qiṣaṣ al-'ulamā'*. Tehran: 'Elmiyya, 1896.

Mirzā Mehdi Astarābādi. *Tārikh-e jahāngoshāye Nāderi*. Tehran: Donyā-ye Ketāb, 1989.

Mirzā Rafi'ā. *Dastur al-Moluk*, ed. Moḥammad-Esmā'il Marcinkowski, trans. 'Ali Kordābādi. Tehran: Markaz-e Asnād va Tārikh-e Diplomāsi, 2006.

Moḥāfeẓ, Ārash. "Pishraw-ye 'ajami, qesmat-e chahārom: kolliyāt-e ritm va negāhi be āhangsāzi-ye doyek," *Māhur* 64 (2014): 33–83.

Moḥāfeẓ, Ārash. *Approche comparative des systèmes musicaux classiques persan et turc: Origines, devenirs et enjeux*. Paris: Geuthner, 2021. not cited

Moḥammad Ebrāhim b. Zayn al-'Ābedin Naṣiri, *Dastur-e Shahriyārān*, ed. Moḥammad Nāder Naṣiri. Tehran: Bonyād-e Mawqufāt-e Maḥmud Afshār, 1994.

Moḥammad Kāẓem Marvi. *'Ālamārā-ye Nāderi*, ed. Moḥammad Amin Riyāḥi. Tehran: Nashr-e 'Elm, 1990.

Moḥammad Moḥsen Mostawfi. *Zubdat al-tawārīkh*, ed. Behruz Gudarzi. Tehran: Bonyād-e Mawqufāt-e Maḥmud Afshār, 1996.

Mohammadi, Mohsen. "Chef de Musique or Chef de Macaroni: The Twisted History of the European Military Music in Persia," *Rivista Italiana di Musicologia* 51 (2016): 71–72.

Mokhtāri, Reżā and Moḥsen Ṣādeqi (ed.), *Ghenā' Musiqi*, 4 vols. Qom: Nashr-e Merṣād, 1997.

Mollā 'Abd al-Nabi Fakhr al-Zamāni Qazvini, *Tadhkera-ye maykhāna*, ed. Aḥmad Golchin Ma'āni. Tehran: Eqbāl, 1996.

Mollā Jalāl Monajjem. *Tārikh-e 'Abbāsi*, ed. Sayfollāh Vaḥidniā. Tehran: Enteshārāt-e Vahid, 1987.

Mostawfi, 'Abdollāh. *Sharḥ-e zendegāni-ye man*, 3rd ed. 2 vols. Tehran: Zavvār, 1992.

Możṭar, A. D. (ed). *Tārikh-e jahāngoshā-ye khāqān*. Islamabad: Markaz-e Taḥqiqāt-e Fārsi-ye Irān va Pākestān, 1971.

Mufażżal b. Sa'd al-Māfarūkhi. *Maḥasin Iṣfahān*, ed. 'Aref Aḥmad 'Abd al-Ghanī. Damascus: Dār al-Kanān, 2010.

Mu'nes al-Dawla. *Khāṭerāt-e Mu'nes al-Dawla, nadima-ye ḥaramsarā-ye Nāṣer al-Din Shāh*, ed. Syrus Sa'dvandiyān. Tehran: Zarrin, 2010.

Nafisi, Sa'id. *Tārikh-e naẓm va nathr dar adabiyāt va zabān-e fārsi tā pāyān-e qarn-e dahom-e hejri*, 2 vols. Tehran: Foroughi, 1984.

Navā'i, 'Abd al-Ḥosayn. *Shāh Ṭahmāsb-e Ṣafavi*. Tehran: Bonyād-e Farhang-e Irān, 1971.

Navvāb Mir Moḥsen b. Ḥāji Sayyed Aḥmad Qarabāghi, *Vożuḥ al-arqām dar 'elm-e musiqi*. Baku, 1st ed. 1884; 2nd ed. with Russian translation 1913.

Nerchakhy, Mohammad. *Description topographique et historique de Boukhara*, ed. Charles Schefer. Paris: Ernest Leroux, 1892.

Nettl, Bruno. *The Radif of Persian Music: Studies of Structure and Cultural Context*. Champaign, IL: Elephant & Cat, 1992.

Neubauer, Eckhard. "Musik zur Mongolenzeit in Iran und der angrenzenden Ländern," *Der Islam* 45 (1969): 233–260.

Neubauer, Eckhard. "Die acht 'Wege' der Musiklehre und der Oktoechos," *Zeitschrift für Geschichte der Arabisch-Islamischen Wissenschaften* 6 (1994): 373–414.

Neubauer, Eckhard. "Die Theorie vom *īqā'*. II: Übersetzung des *Kitāb Iḥṣā' al-īqā'āt* von Abū Naṣr al-Fārābī," *Oriens* 34 (1994): 162, 169.

Neubauer, Eckhard. "Zur Bedentung der Begriffe Komponist und Komposition in der Musikgeschichte der islamischen Welt," *Zeitschrift für Geschichte der Arabisch-Islamischen Wissenschaften* 11 (1997): 307–363.

Neubauer, Eckhard. "Die Euklid Zugeschrieben 'Teilung Des Kanon' in Arabischer Übersetzung," *Zeitschri für die Geschichte der Arabisch-Islamischen Wissenschaften* 16 (2004/5): 309–385.

Neubauer, Eckhard. "Zwölf Dastgāh. Eine persische Handschrift aus dem 19. Jahrhundert mit Angaben zum musikalischen Vortrag der Elegie auf den Tod des

Märtyrers Ḥosein b. ʿAli b. Abi Ṭāleb von Moḥtašam Kāšāni," *Zeitschrift für Geschichte der Arabisch-Islamischen Wissenschaften* 17(2006/7): 301–372.

Neubauer, Eckhard. "Quṭb al-Dīn Shīrāzī (d. 1311) on musical metres (īqāʿ)," *Zeitschrift für Geschichte der Arabisch-Islamischen Wissenschaften* 18 (2008/9): 357–371.

Neubauer, Eckhard. "Music History II. ca. 650 to 1370 CE," *Encyclopædia Iranica*, Online edition, 2009.

Neubauer, Eckhard. "Die Urbane Kunstmusik im Islam Eine Historische Übersicht," *Zeitschrift für Geschichte der Arabisch Islamischen Wissenschaften* 20/21(2012/2014): 303–398.

Neubauer, Eckhard. "A Historical Sketch of the Musical Meter Called Ramal," in *Rhythmic Cycles and Structures in the Art Music of the Middle East*, eds. Zeynep Helvacı, Jacob Olley and Rolf Martin Jaeger. Istanbul: Orient Institute, 2017.

Nikfahm Khubravān, Sajjād and Saʿid Kordmāfi. "Musiqi dar ashjār va athmār-e ʿAlāʾ al-Din Bokhāri," *Māhur* 70 (2016): 39–86.

Nurzād, Feraydun, ed. *Nāmahā-ye Khān Aḥmad Khān Gilāni*. Tehran: Bonyād-e Mawqufāt-e Maḥmud Afshār, 1994.

ʿOnṣor al-Maʿāli Kaykābus b. Voshmgir Ziyār. *Qābus-nāma*, ed. Gholām-Ḥosayn Yusofi. Tehran: Bongāh-e Tarjoma va Nashr-e Ketāb, 1973.

Pāyvar, Farāmarz. *Radif-e āvāzi va taṣnifhā-ye qadimi be revāyat-e ʿAbdollāh Davāmi*. Tehran: Māhur, 1996.

Popescu-Judetz, Eugenia. *Tanburî Küçük Artin: A Musical Treatise of the Eighteenth Century*. Istanbul: Pan Yayıncılık, 2002.

Popescu-Judetz, Eugenia and Eckhard Neubauer (trans. and ed.). *The Science of Music in Islam, vol. 6: Seydī's Book on Music*. Frankfurt: Publications of the Institute for the History of Arabic-Islamic Science, 2004.

Pourjavady, Amir Hosein. 'The Musical Codex of Amir Khān Gorji (c. 1108/1697),' Ph.D. dissertation, University of California, Los Angeles, 2005.

Pourjavady, Amir Hosein. "Negāhi be ḥayāt-e musiqāʾi-ye dawra-ye Afshāri," *Māhur* 31 (2006): 29–60.

Powers, Harold. "Mode," *New Grove Dictionary of Music and Musicians*, 6th ed. 1981.

Qāżi Aḥmad Ghaffāri. *Tārikh-e Negārestān*, ed. Morteżā Modarres Gilāni. Tehran: Ketābforushi-ye Ḥāfeẓ, 1962.

Qāżi Aḥmad Qomi. *Khulāṣat al-tawārīkh*, ed. Eḥsān Eshrāqi. Tehran: Dāneshgāh-e Tehrān, 1984.

Qāżi Mir Aḥmad Monshi. *Golestān-e honar*, ed. Aḥmad Sohayli Khᵛānsāri. Tehran: Bonyād-e Farhang, 1973.

Qāżihā, Fāṭema (ed.). *Marāsem-e darbār-e Nāṣeri: jashn-e āshpazān*. Tehran: Sāzemān-e Asnād va Ketābkhāna-ye Jomhuri-ye Eslāmi-ye Irān, 2012.

Ray, Sukumar. *Humāyūn in Persia*. Calcutta: Royal Asiatic Society of Bengal, 1948.

Reynolds, Dwight F. "The *Qiyan* of al-Andalus," in *Concubines and Courtesans: Women and Slavery in Islamic History*, ed. Matthew S. Gordon and Kathryn A. Hain. Oxford: Oxford University Press, 2017.

Reynolds, Dwight F. *The Musical Heritage of al-Andalus*. SOAS Studies in Music. London: Routledge, 2021.

Reżā-Qoli Mirzā (Ḥasan 'Abdollāh Sarābi). *Safar-nāma-ye Reżā-Qoli Mirzā Nāyeb al-ayāla*, ed. Asghar Farmānfarmā'i Qājār. Tehran: Asāṭir, 1994.

Richard, Francis. *Raphaël du Mans missionaire en Perse au XVIIe s. I*, 2 vols. Paris: L'Harmattan, 1995.

Röhrborn, Klaus Michael. *Provinzen und Zentralgewalt Persiens im 16. und 17. Jahrhundert*. Berlin: Walter De Gruyter, 1966.

Rostam al-Ḥokamā'. *Rustam al-tawārīkh*, ed. Moḥammad Moshiri. Tehran: Amir-Kabir, 1973.

Ruznāma-ye khāṭerāt-e Nāṣer al-Din Shāh Qājār (3.1309–2.1310 H), ed. Majid 'Abdeamin and Nasrin Khalili. Tehran: Āfāqgostar-e Kimiyā, 2016.

Ruznāma-ye khāṭerāt-e Nāṣer al-Din Shāh Qājār (*4.1282–3.1283 H*), ed. Majid 'Abdeamin. Tehran: Anjoman-e Āthār va Mafākher-e Farhangi, 2016.

Ruznāma-ye khāṭerāt-e Nāṣer al-Din Shāh Qājār (*1284–1287 H)*, ed. Majid 'Abdeamin Tehran: Maḥmud Afshār, 2018.

Ṣādeghi Ketābdār. *Majma' al-khawāṣṣ*, ed. 'Abd al-Rasul Khayyāmpur. Tabriz: Chāpkhāna-ye Akhtar, 1948.

Sālur, Qahremān Mirzā ('Ayn al-Salṭana). *Ruznāma-ye khāṭerāt-e 'Ayn al-Salṭana*, 10 vols. Tehran: Asāṭir, 1995–2001.

Sām Mirzā Ṣafavi. *Toḥfa-ye Sāmi*, ed. Vaḥid Dastgerdi. Tehran: Armaghān, 1935.

Sām Mirzā Ṣafavi. *Toḥfa-ye Sāmi*, ed. Rokn al-Din Homāyun-Farrokh. Tehran: Asāṭir, 2005.

Sawa, George Dimitri. *Music Performance Practice in the Early 'Abbāsid Era,132–320 A.H./750–932 A.D.* Toronto: Pontifical Institute of Mediaeval Studies, 1989.

Sawa, George Dimitri. "Theories of Rhythm and Meter in the Medieval East," in *The Garland Encyclopedia of World Music, vol. 6*: *The Middle East*, ed. Virginia Danielson, Scott Marcus, and Dwight Reynolds. New York: Routledge, 2002.

Sawa, George Dimitri. *An Arabic Musical and Socio-Cultural Glossary of Kitāb al-Aghānī*. Leiden: Brill, 2015.

Sayyed Ḥosayn Maythami, *Musiqi-ye 'aṣr-e Ṣafavi*. Tehran: Farhangestān-e Honar, 2010.
Sayyed Ḥosayn Maythami, "*Āvāz-e rāst dar dawrān-e Qājār*," *Māhur* 51/52 (2011): 127–141.
Sayyed Ḥosayn Maythami, "Nokāti darbāra-ye musiqidānān-e Qājār az 1210 tā 1264 H," *Māhur* 61 (2013): 97–101.
Sayyed Ḥosayn Maythami, "Musiqi-ye dawrān-e Zand," *Māhur* 68 (2015): 41–42.
Schofield, Katherine Butler. "The Courtesan Tale: Female Musicians and Dancers in Mughal Historical Chronicles, c. 1556–1748," *Gender and History* 24(1) (2012): 150–171.
Setāyeshgar, Mehdi. *Vāzha-nāma-ye musiqi-ye Irān*, 3 vols. Tehran: Eṭṭelā'āt, 2002.
Sepantā, Sāsān. *Tārikh-e taḥavvol-e żabṭ-e musiqi dar Irān*. Tehran: Māhur, 1998.
Sepantā, Sāsān. *Cheshmandāz-e musiqi-ye Irān*. Tehran: Māhur, 2003.
Shafi'i Kadkani, Moḥammad-Reżā. "Yek eṣtelāḥ-e musiqā'i dar she'r-e Ḥāfeẓ," *Māhur* 15 (2002): 9–14.
Shams al-Din Moḥammad b. Qays Rāzī. *Al-mu'jam fī ma'āyīr ash'ār al-'ajam*, ed. Moḥammad Qazvini and Modarres Rażavi. Tehran: Dāneshgāh-e Tehrān, 1935.
Sharaf al-Din Yazdi. *Ẓafar-nāma*, ed. Moḥammad 'Abbāsi, 2 vols. Tehran: Amir-Kabir, 1957.
Sharāyeli, Moḥammad-Reżā. "Muzik-e fawj-e makhṣuṣ," *Māhur* 66 (2015): 99.
Shaykh Reżā'i, Ensiya and Shahlā Ādhari (ed.). *Gozāreshhā-ye naẓmiya az maḥallāt-e Tehrān: Rāport-e vaqāye'-e mokhtalef-e maḥallāt-e dār al-khelāfa (1303–1305 H)*, 2 vols. Tehran: Sāzemān-e Asnād-e Melli-ye Irān, 1998.
Shiloah, Amnon. "Muslim and Jewish Musical Traditions of the Middle Ages," in *Music as Concept and Practice in the Late Middle Ages*, New Oxford History of Music, ed. Reinhard Strohm and Bonnie J. Blackburn. Oxford: Oxford University Press, 2001.
Smith, Ronald. *The First Age of the Portuguese Embassies Navigations and Peregrinations in Persia (1507–1524)*. Bethesda, MD: Decatur Press, 1970.
Soudavar, Abolala. *Art of the Persian Courts*. New York: Metropolitan Museum of Art, 1992.
Sümer, Faruk. *Naqsh-e Torkān-e Ānātoli dar tashkil-e va dawlat-e Ṣafavi* (Safevî Devletinin Kuruluşu ve Gelişmesinde Anadolu Türklerinin Rolü), trans. from Turkish to Persian by Eḥsān Eshrāqi and Moḥammad-Taqi Emāmi. Tehran: Nashr-e Gostara, 1992.
Sumits, William. "The Evolution of the Maqām Tradition in Central Asia: From the Theory of 12 Maqām to the Practice of Shashmaqām," Ph.D. dissertation, University of London, School of Oriental and African Studies, 2011.

Sumits, William. "*Tawārīkh-i Mūsīqīyūn*: the 'Histories of Musicians' from Herat and Khotan According to a 19th Century Chaghatai Treatise from Eastern Turkistan," *Revue des traditions musicales des mondes arabe et méditerranéen* 10 (2016): 127–200.

Tafażżoli, Aḥmad. "Bārbad," in *Encyclopædia Iranica*, online edition, 1988.

Tafażżoli, Aḥmad. "Fahlavīyāt," in *Encyclopædia Iranica*. online edition, 1999.

Tāj al-Salṭana. *Khāṭerāt-e Tāj al-Salṭana*, ed. Manṣura Etteḥādiya. Tehran: Nashr-e Tārikh-e Irān, 1992.

Taqi al-Din Awḥadi Balayāni, *'Arafāt al-'āshiqīn wa 'araṣāt al-'ārifīn*, ed. Dhabiḥollāh Sāḥebkāri and Āmena Fakhr-Aḥmad, 8 vols. Tehran: Markaz-e Mirāth-e Maktub, 2010.

Tura, Yalçın. "Observations on the Use of the Rhythmic Cycle *Darb-ı Fetih* ('Rhythm of Conquest') in Turkish Vocal Music of the 17th–19th Centuries," in *Rhythmic Cycles and Structures in the Art Music of the Middle East*, ed. Zeynep Helvacı, Jacob Olley, and Rolf Martin Jaeger. Istanbul: Orient Institute, 2017.

Uzunçarşılı, Ismail Hakkı. "Osmanlılar Zamanında Saraylarda Musiki Hayatı," *Türk Tarih Kurumu* XLI (161): 79–114.

Widdess, Richard. *The Rāgas of Early Indian Music: Modes, Melodies, and Musical Notations from the Gupta Period to c. 1250*. Oxford: Clarendon, 1995.

Wolfson, A. S. *Irāniyān dar godhashta va ḥāl*, Persian trans. Mirzā Ḥosayn Khān Anṣāri. Tehran: Chapkhāna-ye Khāvar, 1930.

Wright, Owen. "Ibn Munajjim and the Early Arabian Modes," *Galpin Society Journal* 19 (1966): 27–48.

Wright, Owen. *The Modal System of Arab and Persian Music, A.D. 1250–1300*. Oxford: Oxford University Press, 1978.

Wright, Owen, trans. and annot. *Demetrius Cantemir: The Collection of Notations*, pt 1, text. London: SOAS, 1992.

Wright, Owen. *Words without Songs: A Musicological Study of an Early Ottoman Anthology and its Precursors*, SOAS Musicology Series. London: School of Oriental and African Studies, 1992.

Wright, Owen. "Abd al-Qādir al-Marāghī and 'Alī b. Muḥammad Binā'ī: Two Fifteenth-Century Examples of Notation," pt 1: text, *Bulletin of the School of Oriental and African Studies* 57(3) (1994): 475–515; pt 2: commentary, *Bulletin of the School of Oriental and African Studies* 58(1) (1995): 17–39.

Wright, Owen. "On the Concept of a Timurid Music," *Oriente Moderno*, NS 15(76) no. 2 (1996): 665–681.

Wright, Owen. "Die melodischen Modi bei Ibn Sīnā und die Entwicklung der Modalpraxis von Ibn al-Munağğim bis zu Ṣafī al-Dīn al-Urmawī," *Zeitschrift für Geschichte der Arabisch-Islamischen Wissenschaften* 16 (2004/5): 283–284.

Wright, Owen. *Touraj Kiaras and Persian Classical Music: An Analytical Perspective*. SOAS Musicology Series. Farnham: Ashgate, 2009.

Wright, Owen. *Music Theory in Mamluk Cairo: The ġāyat al-maṭlūb fī 'ilm al-adwār wa-'l ḍurūb by Ibn Kurr*. Farnham: Ashgate, 2014.

Wright, Owen. "Amīr Ḫān Gurjī and Safavid-Ottoman *Usul* Parallels," in *Rhythmic Cycles and Structures in the Art Music of the Middle East*, ed. Zeynep Helvacı, Jacob Olley and Rolf Martin Jaeger. Istanbul: Orient Institute, 2017.

Wright, Owen. "The Ottoman *Usul* System and its Precursors," in *Rhythmic Cycles and Structures in the Art Music of the Middle East*, ed. Zeynep Helvacı, Jacob Olley and Rolf Martin Jaeger. Istanbul: Orient Institute, 2017.

Wright, Owen. *Music Theory in the Safavid Era: The taqsīm al-naġamat*. SOAS Musicology Series. London: Routledge, 2018.

Wright, Owen. "Bridging the Ottoman–Safavid Divide," in *The Music Road*, ed. Reinhard Strohm. Oxford: Oxford University Press, 2019.

Wright, Owen. "Persian Perspectives: Chardin, De la Borde, Kaempfer," *Rast Musicology Journal* 7(2) (2019): 2050–2083.

Zayn al-Din Vāṣefi. *Badāyi' al-waqāyi'*, ed. Alexander Boldyrev, 2 vols. Tehran: Bonyād- e Farhang-e Irān, 1971.

Recordings

Descriptive analysis of the dastgāh of Māhur by Ostād Nur'ali Borumand. Recordings and interview by Hormoz Farhat. Tehran: Māhur, 2005 (M.CD-176). Four CDs with notes (Persian and English) by Hooman Asadi.

Qajar Tasnifs by 'Abdollāh Davāmi. Tehran: Māhur, 2005 (M.CD-112). Two CDs with notes (Persian and English) by Amir Hosein Pourjavady.

Qajari Tasnifs by Rezâ-Qoli Nawruzi. Tehran: Māhur, 2010 (M.CD-296). Two CDs with notes (Persian and English) by Amir Hosein Pourjavady.

The Early Recording of Seven Dastgâhs, Māhur, M.CD-345, 2013.

Vocal radif according to the version of 'Abdollâh Davâmi. Tehran: Māhur, 2007 (M.CD-111). Three CDs with notes (Persian and English) by Hooman Asadi.

Żarbihā-ye qadimi be revāyat va ejrā-ye Ostād Yusof Forutan Tehran: Māhur, 2012 (M.CD-311). Three CDs with notes (Persian and English) by Farshād Tavakkoli.

INDEX

Note: italic indicates illustrations, n indicates notes, t indicates tables

'Abbas I, Shah, 20–1, 24, 26, 31–2, 35, 37–8, 72–7
'Abbas II, Shah, 34–5, 39, *40*, 44, 75, 77
'Abbas Mirzā, 141
Abbasid period, 96n, 276
'Abd al-Baqā, Shah, 35
'Abd al-Ḥosayn b. Mehdi al-Shirāzi, *Bahjat al-qulūb*, 207–8
'Abd al-Karim Kashmiri, 80–2
'Abd al-Mo'men Khān Bahādor, 28
'Abd al-Mu'min al-Balkhī, *Bayān al-maqāmāt al-'aliyya ma' al-furū' wa al-awzān al-aṣliyya*, 171, 208, 264, 307
'Abd al-Mu'min Ṣafī al-Dīn al-Balkhī, *Bahjat al-rūḥ*, 171, 199, 242, 246t, 259–61
'Abd al-Qāder Marāghi
  'amal, 296
  at court of Shāhrokh, *12*
  at court of Solṭān-Ḥosayn Jalāyer, 6–7
  gusha, 187
  Herat, 11
  Jāmi' al-alḥān, 6–7, 167, 200–1, 282–4
  kār, 296
  kolliyāt, 286, *286*
  manuscripts, 167–8
  maqām, 183–4
  naqsh, 298
  navākht, 294
  qawl, 280–1
  rhythm, 236–41, 250–5, 258–60
  sarband, 300
  Sharḥ-e advār, 277–9
  Timur, 8
'Abd al-Raḥmān Jāmi, 13
'Abd al-Raḥmān Qavvāl, 279
'Abdollāh Khān II, 27
abjadi (alphabetical notation), 166
Abkāriān, Hovānes (Yaḥyā), 137
Abū al-Faraj al-Iṣfahānī, 276, 278
Abu al-Fatḥ Pir Budāq, 9, *10*
Abu al-Fażl Mobārak, *Akbar-nāma*, 26, 262–3
Abū al-Ḥasan 'Alī b. al-Mas'ūdī, 177
Abu al-Ḥasan Eqbāl al-Solṭān, 150
Abu al-Ḥasan Ghaffāri, 108–9
Abū al-Karīm al-Qushayrī al-Nayshābūrī, 279
Abū Ḥāmid al-Ghazālī, *Iḥyā' 'ulūm al-dīn*, 279–80
Abū Isḥāq al-Kindī, 176–7, 231, 276
Abū Naṣr al-Fārābī, 168, 231–4, 236, 271n, 278
  Kitāb al-mūsīqī al-kabīr, 279
Abu Sa'id Bahādor Khān, 4

abu'aṭā, 209, 210–13, 216, 218–19, 229n–30n, 308
accompanists, 20, 44, 50, 92, 104, 106, 114, 122–3, 153
acrobatics, 38, *88*
Ādāb-e āvāzhā va dhekrhā'i ke dar manāber va joz ān kh'ānda mishavad, 171–2, 175t, 209
adhān (call to prayer), 149
Advielle, Victor, *La Musique chez les Persans en 1885*, 142
Afghan
  invasion, 47, 80, 201
  musicians, 3, 135, 308
afghani (*reng*), 135
African women, 134
afshāri, 203, 210–13, 218–19, 304, 308
Afsharid period, 80
Afżal al-tawārīkh, 26
āghāz kardan, 188, 190
Agra, 169
āhang, 187, 196, 280, 290
ahl-e naghma (people of music), 70–1
ahl-e ṭarab-e mardāna (community of male entertainers), 106
Aḥmad al-Rifā'ī al-Muslim b. 'Abd al-Raḥmān al-Mawṣilī, *al-Durr al-naqī fī fann al-mūsiqī*, 171
Aḥmad Kārkiyā, Sultan, 28
Aḥmadi, 106
'ajab al-zamān, 178; *see also* Moḥammad b. Maḥumud Nayshāburi
Akbar, Mughal emperor, 262
Akbar Khān, 149
Akbari, 106
Akhtar Khānom, 150
Ākhund Mollā 'Ali, 106
Akram al-Salṭana, 127
aksāk, 247, 271n
'Alā' al-Din Bokhāri, 180t, 236
  Ashjār va athmār, 180–1
ālāpchāri, 290
alḥān, 231
'Ali b. Moḥammad Me'mār (Bannā'i), 9–11, 16–17, 183–4, 238, 253, 258–9, 285, 294, 298–9
'Ali Khān-e Nāyeb al-Salṭana, 129, 307
'Ali Moḥammad Kh'ansāri, 105
'Ali Pāshā, 36
'Ali Qoli Khān Shāmlu, 26, 168
'Ali Ufuki, 249
'Ali-Akbar Mozayyen al-Dawla, 142, *143*
'Ali-Akbar Nafti, 149
'Ali-Akbar Shāhi, 130, 138, 148
'Ali-Akbar Shaydā, 146, 306, 308
'Alishāh b. Buka Awbahi, 183–4, 238–40, 247, 251–61, 285–6, 294
  Muqaddimat al-uṣūl, 17
  Uṣūl al-wuṣūl, 17
'amal
  Āqā Mo'men Moṣannef, 293
  Ebrāhim Mirzā, 27
  eighteenth century, 301
  kār-o 'amal, 307
  Mir Ṣadr al-Din Moḥammad, 24, 289–91
  Persian genres, 282–3
  Safavid period, 31–5, 287, 295–6
'amala-ye ṭarab (servants of the office of entertainment), 106, 122, 138
'amala-ye ṭarab-e khāṣṣa (special musicians of the royal court), 106–15, 124, 127–9, 138
Amasya, 11
amateur musicians, 105–6
Amir 'Alishir Navā'i, 11, *15*, 16, 301
Amir Khān, 135, 138, 199, 242–4, 251–60
Amir Khān Gorji
  āvāza, 187
  codex, 36t, 169, 242–3, 249, 261
  Isfahan, 34–6, 40, 46
  oṣul, 250–4, 257–60
  Persian and Turkish languages, 293–4
  Resāla-ye mawzun, 294
  Safavid period genres, 296–8, 300–1

Amir Khān Gorji (*cont.*)
taṣnif, 244, 317n
vocal compositions, 62n
Amir Khosraw Dehlavi, 35, 292, 297
Amira Dobbāj, 29
Amir-Qoli Dōtāri, 28
Amirshāhi Sabzavāri, 26
Amjad, 149, 306
Anaclerio, Giuseppe, 142
anāmel va kaf clap pattern, 239
Anatolia, 11, 198
ʿAndalib al-Salṭana, 115, 127
ʿAndalib-e Kāshi, 40
andarun (harem)
ʿamala-ye ṭarab-e khāṣṣa, 112
Āqā Gholām-Ḥosayn, 108
Āqā Ḥosayn-Qoli, 120
boy singers, 123
concubines, 126–9
female performers, 103–4, 126–9
Mo'men Kur, 134
multicultural environment, 38
Nāṣer al-Din Shah, 106, *128*
Solaymān, Shah, 39–40
Solṭān-Ḥosayn Bāyqarā, *66*
Zivar al-Solṭān, 115
Anis al-Dawla, *128*
Anjoman-e Okhovvat, 145–7, *146*, 152
Āq Qoyunlus court, 9, 65
Āqā ʿAli-Akbar Farāhāni, 107–9, *109*, 116, 126
Āqā Bābā Makhmur Eṣfahāni, 100–1, 172, 210–11
Āqā Gholām-Ḥosayn, 107–8, 120–2, 127
Āqā Ḥaqqi, 33
Āqā Ḥasan, 108
Āqā Ḥosayn-Qoli, 107, 108, 117, 119, 1 20–2, 129, *137*, 138, 148–9, 152, 219, 310
Āqā Jān, *133*
Āqā Moḥammad Khān, 87, 99–100
Āqā Moḥammad-Reżā, 87, 101–2, 108
Āqā Mo'men Moṣannef, 34–5, 38–9, 73, 169, 187, 193, 195, 200, 242, 244, 251–2, 255, 258, 292–3, 297–9, 302
Āqā Moṭalleb, 107, 116, 117, *119*
Āqā Reżā, 120
Āqābāyev, Pari, 150
Arabic genres, 278–81
arasbāri (Turkish vocal genre), 17, 62n, 300–1
arbāb-e ṭarab, 91
Ardabil, 75
ʿĀref Qazvini, 147, 149, 151, 306, 308
armāl, 238, 247–8
Armenia
ʿAbbas I, Shah, 77
Esmāʿil I, Shah, 37
Armenian
boys, 78
concubines and courtesans, 38, 77, 92
dancers, 3, 72
instrumentalists, 45
luthiers, 136–8
musicians, *45*
performers, 49
text, 170
Armenian Church census of houses, New Julfa, 49
Armenians, 32, 38, 49
ʿarusi, 282
ʿaruż system, 234–5
Asadollāh Khān, 149
āshpazān, *113*
aṣl, 180
ʿAṭā, *132*
ʿAṭā Malek Jovayni, *Tarikh-e jahāngoshā*, *5*
atānin patterns, 232, 234–5, 247, 249
Aubin, Eugène, 117, 130, 139–40
Aurangzeb, Mughal emperor, 243
āvāza
gusha, 199–201
maqām, 193–5
Qoṭb al-Din Shirāzi, 183
Safavid period, 206
terkib, 197

āvāz (modes)
'Abd al-Qāder Marāghi, 183
chahārmeżrāb, 310
court ensembles, 114
court music, 210
dastgāh, 208–20
Dawra Beg Karāmi, 186–7
free rhythmic, 129
instrumentalists, 269
maqām, 202–3
moṭreb, 134
non-Systematist treatises, 181, 324t, 325–6
Persian genres, 269
pianos, 144–5
Qajar period genres, 303–4
recordings, 148–51
singers, 106, 122–3
Taqsīm al-naghamāt wa bayān al-darj wa al-shu'ab wa al-maqāmāt, 168
taṣnif, 308
Timurid period, 285
treatises, 171–3
Western influence, 151
āwāzāt, 181
Awbahi *see* 'Alishāh b. Buka Awbahi
awfar rhythmic cycle, 241–2, 247, 250–2, 299
awsaṭ rhythmic cycle, 258–9
Azerbaijan, 4, 8–9, 18, 48, 138, 172, 272n
Azeri Turkish treatise, 172
'Aziz, *132*
'Aziz Shashlulband, *135*
'Ażod al-Dawla, 96–7n, 155n

Bābā Khān, 87, 100
Bābā Ṭāher Hamedāni, 304
Bābā'i, 106
Badi' al-Zamān Mirzā, 14, 29–30
badiha, 288, 300; *see also* improvisation
Baghdad, 4, 6, 8, 147, 166, 182, 234, 283
Bahā' al-Din, 4
Bahār, Malek al-Sho'arā', 147
Bahrām Mirzā, 25, *69*
Baily, John, 140
Baku, 37, 172
balabān, 13
ban on music, 67–72
bāng, 179–80, 323t
Bannā'i *see* 'Ali b. Moḥammad Me'mār (Banna'i)
Bānu 'Ożmā', 129–30
Bāqer Khān Rāmeshgar, 130, 149, 150
Bāqiya Nā'ini, 35, 169, 187, 196, 199, 297–300
Zamzama-ye vaḥdat, 35, 169, 218, 290–2
Bārbad, 177
Barbaro, Josafa, 65
bargardān, 306, 311t
basiṭ, 278, 281–3
Basra, 36
bayāt, 35, 151, 218
Bāysonghor, *13*
bāzguy, 285, 287–91, 295–302, 317n
bāzigar, 80, 82, 96n, 100–2, *103*, 105, 108, 123–4, *124*, 155n
Bazin, Père Louis, 80, *81*
bazm-e zanāna (female musical gatherings), 113
bazm (musical gatherings), 65, 84
bāznay (reed), 14
beshārat rhythmic cycle, 261–2
Bibliotèque nationale de France, 167, 169
bipartite form, 306
blind musicians, 104, 133–134
Bodleian Library, 168
Bombay, 173
bonyād ("foundation," "nucleus"), 197
Bousquet, 142
Brambilla, Marco, 142
British national anthem, 141
bugle horn, 141
Bukhara, 26, 170, 174, 236

Cairo, 182
candelabra dances, 134
Cantemir, Demetrius, 34–5, 197, 249, 252–8, 260, 301–2

Careri, Gemelli, 79
clarinets, 145
Caucasian
genres, 302–3
musicians, 293–4
Caucasians, in Isfahan, 51
Caucasus
court music, 44
influence on Safavid court music, 44
loss of, 90
Ottomans, 37–8
Ṭahmāsb, Shah, 72
Central Asia, 11, 166, 196, 200–201, 216, 227n, 251
Chahārbāgh district, Isfahan, 35
chahārgāh, 16, 148, 171–2, 214–18
chahārmeżrāb, 309–10
chahārtār, 31, 40, 44, 49
chahār-żarb, 239, 267
chālānchi, 116
Chālānchi Khān, 87, 101, 116
chālchi-bāshi (chief of the community of musicians)
Āqā Ḥaqqi, 33
Āqā Mo'men Moṣannef, 38, 169
Ḥāfeẓ Jalājel Bākharzi, 20, 33, 295
Ḥāfeẓ Moḥammad Kāżem, 36
instrumentalists, 43
nineteenth century, 115–17
Ostād Moḥammad 'Udi, 70–1
Ostād Zaytun, 29, 70
Ṭahmāsb, Shah, 72
Chalderan, battle of, 18, 67
chanbar rhythmic cycle, 7, 258, 272n
chang (harp), 11, 21, 44
Chardin, Jean, 39, 43–4, 64, 75–8
chini (set of sounding bowls), 118
Chodźko, Alexander Borejko, 101–2
chogur, 17, 137, 300–1
Chorki, 125–6
Circassian
concubines, 38
dancers, 38, 77
coffeehouses, 33, 35, 37, 43–4, 51, 304
concubines, 38, 63–97, *103*, 126–9, 155n
courtesans, 63–97
dancers, *103*
dastgāh-e bāzigar-khāna, 91
eighteenth century, 80–6
European travelers, 62n
Isfahan, *79*
kamāncha, 89
Karim Khān Zand, 49–50
long-necked lute, *74*
multicultural environment, 38
Nāder Shah, 47
recordings, 149
santur, 89
setār, 90
Shākha Nabāt, *83*
Shiraz, *85*
taṣnif, 304–5
Tehran, *86*
upper-class, 20, 51, 63, 72–3, 77–80, 82, 84, 87, 90, 93, 155n

daf (frame drum), *103*, 104–5, 114, 122, 280
Dagestan, 37
Dallāla Chizi, 73
Dalyamites, 276
Damascus, 233, 283
dancing boys
'amala-ye ṭarab-e khāṣṣa, 111
bāzigar, 123–4
dasta, 104–5, 131, *133*, 139–40
Georgian, *44*, 124
Jewish, 93, 124
Karim Khān Zand, 82
more renowned than women, 14
Muslim, 124
Nāder Shah, 48
non-Muslim, 93
raqqāṣ, 123–4
dancing girls
dasta-ye zanāna, 131
Esmā'il I, 67

Dār al-Fonun, Tehran, 142–5, *143*, 268
Dār al-Ṣanāye‘, Tehran, 137
Dar bayān-e ‘elm-e musiqi va dānestan-e sho‘abat-e ou, 170, 195–6, 199, 204–5, 301
darāmad, 188, 190, 204, 215–17, 226n, 307, 309–10
Darvish Khān, 146, 149–50, 152, 308, 310
Darvish-‘Ali Changi, 11, 26–9, 56n, 261, 294, 297–9
    Tuḥfat al-surūr, 170
dashti, 146, 203, 210–13, 218, 219, 304, 308
dastān, 176–8, 180
dasta (troupes), 104–5, 122–5, *126*, 130–3, 148
dasta-ye shāhi, 138–9, *139*
dastgāh-e bāzigar-Khāna (chamber of entertainers), 1, 87, *88*, *89*, 90–1, 100–4, 116
dastgāh, *208*, 213t, 309–10
    eighteenth century, 264, 301
    Farahani family, 120–1
    gusha, 199
    kār-o ‘amal, 307
    Persian modal system, 170–4
    recordings, 148
Dastur al-moluk (manual of Safavid government), 33
Daulier Deslandes, A., 40–2
Davāmi, ‘Abdollāh, 150, 214, 220, 265, 305
Davāzdah dastgāh, 208–9
davāzdah-band (twelve strophes), 172, 208–9
Dāvud Kalimi Shirāzi, *133*
Dawlatshāh Samarqandi, 7–8
dawr (cycle), 231, 250, 257–8, 265
Dawra Beg Karāmi, 28, 186–7, 226n, 241, 249, 251–2, 257–61, 287–8, 299–300
    Resāla-ye Karāmiya, 26, 168, 195
dāyera, 305
de Gouvea, Antonio, 38, 73, 77
De Mans, Raphael, 78
Delhi, 80–2
Della Valle, Pietro, 33, 43–4, 63–4, 72–3
dervishs, 47, 102
Dhahabiya Sufi order, 136
dhayl, 287–97, 311t
dik dak drum patterns, 232, 243, *243*, 249–50, 273n
dōbaytis (musical genre), 122, 290, 303–4
dōgāh, 34, 215
dombak (goblet drum)
    Āqā Ḥasan's son, 108
    chahārmeżrābs, 310
    dastas, 104–5, 131, *133*
    moṭrebs, 133
    recordings, 149
    rhythm, 233, 264–9
    rhythmic cycles, 275n
    sāzanda, 114, 122–3
    żarbgir, 305
    żarb, 270n
Don Garcia de Silva y Figueroa, 72–3
dōtār (long-necked lute), 31, 100, 135
dō-yek rhythmic cycle, 28, 242, 252, 300
Dust-‘Ali Mo‘ayyer al-Mamālek, 127–9, 147
Dutch East India Company, 62n
Duval, Alexandre, 144–5

Ebrāhim, Āqā, 101–2
Ebrāhim Āghābāshi, 129–30
Ebrāhim Golpāyegāni, 36
Ebrāhim Mirzā, 19–24, 26–8, 56n
Efendi Khᵛānanda, 33
Eftekhār, 149, 306
Egypt, 9
‘Emād al-Din Yaḥyā b. Aḥmad Kāshi, 9
Emām Qoli Khān, 62n
‘erāq, 204–5, 217–18, 316n
‘Erāq-e ‘Ajam, 187, 198, 295
Esḥāqvand dynasty, 28
Eskandar Monshi, 21–2, 24, 27, 29–33, 37, 67–8, 294–5
    asami-ye moṭreban va ahl-e naghma, 20–1
Esmā‘il Bazzāz, 125, *126*
Esmā‘il I, Shah, 14, 17–18, 37, 62n, 67, 91–2, 300

Esmāʿil II, Shah, 19–22, 26–7, 33, 295
Esmāʿil Khān, 107, 120
Esmāʿil Mirzā, 25
Eʿtemād al-Salṭana, 116
Euclid, *Sectio Canonis*, 167
European
  female performers, 80
  musicians, *39*
  travelers, 40–3, 63–97, 99–100

fahlaviyāt, 282
fākhta-żarb rhythmic cycle, 28
fākhti rhythmic cycle, 235, 253
farʿ, 240, 242, 249, 259
Farāhān, 108
Farāhāni family, 120–2
farmān (decree), 25–7, 68
Farrokhi Sistāni, 276
Fars, 87, 187, 198
faṣl, 11, 286
Fāṭemi, Sāsān, 96n, 298
Fatḥ Allāh al-Shirwānī, 253
  Majalla fī al-mūsiqī, 258–9
Fatḥ-ʿAli, Shah, 87–90, 96n, 100–1, 105–6, 116, 141, 144, 155n, 172, 210
Fatḥi Moṣannef, 35, 37
favākht, 238, 247–8, 255
Fāyez Dashtestāni, 304
Feldman, Walter, 197
Felfel, 72
female
  dancers, 4–6, 17, 75–6
  musicians, 4–6, 17, 75–6, *128*
  performers, 47, 67, 100, 102–4, 126–9, 134
  singers, 62n, 150
Flandin, Eugène, 104
flutes, 145, 149
folk music, 78, 134–5, 203, 304
Forṣat al-Dawla Shirāzi, 269
  Buḥūr al-alḥān dar ʿelm-e musiqi va nesbat-e ān bā ʿaruz, 173
forud (descent), 190, 204, 217
forudāsht, 281, 285
Forughi Basṭāmi, 106
foyuj (gypsies), 82
Frederick II, Duke of Holstein-Gottorp, 38–9, *39*
French East India Company, 64

Ganja, 37, 172
Georgia
  ʿAbbas I, Shah, 32
  Ṭahmāsb, Shah, 72
Georgian
  assimilated, 49
  boys, 49–50, 78, 93
  courtesans, 92
  dancers, 3, 38
  dancing boys, *44*, 124
  eunuchs, 40
  instrumentalists, 45
  musicians, 38
  Ṣafi, Shah, 38
  slave girls, 77
Gergenian, Abraham, *46*
ghaychak, 14, 21
Ghazāl, 72, 134, *135*
ghazal
  ʿAbd al-Raḥmān Jāmi, 13
  ʿAli b. Moḥammad Me'mar, 17
  Amir Khosraw Dehlavi, 35
  āvāz, 303–5
  Homāyun, 26
  kār, 285
  Persian, 282
  qawl, 281, 289, 291, 297
  Toḥfa-ye Sāmi, 30
Ghaznavid court, 178, 276, 282
Gholām Shādi, 16
Gholām-Reżā Sālār-Moʿazzaz, 308
Gilān, 20, 22, 28–9, 46–7, 69–71, 87, 101, 167, 241
Gobineau, Joseph Arthur, Comte de, 105

gofta, 280
Gol'edhār, 127
Golestān Palace, 112, *112*, 151
Gramophone and Typewriter Ltd., 307
Gramophone Company, 99, 119, 147–50, *148*
Grand Hotel, Tehran, 147, 151
Gurgenian, Abraham, 60n
gusha, 186–7, 196–206, 216–20
  'Abd al-Qāder Marāghi, 184
  Ādāb-e āvāzhā, 209
  Forṣat al-Dawla Shirāzi, 173
  kār-o 'amal, 307
  recordings, 149
  Sufi lodges, 136
guyanda, 20–1, 30, 70–1, 123, 280, 294–5, 305

Habib Samā'i, 118
Ḥabibollāh Baṣri, 36
Ḥabibollāh Samā'-Ḥożur, 108, 115, 118, 127, 138, 305, 308
Ḥabibollāh Shahrdār *see* Moshir-Homāyun
Ḥāfeẓak, 38
Ḥāfeẓ poet, 9, 303
ḥāfeẓ, 123, 295
Ḥāfeẓ title, 21
Ḥāfeẓ Aḥmad Qazvini, 20, 67, 295
Ḥāfeẓ 'Arab, 29–30
Ḥāfeẓ Dust Moḥammad Khᵛafi, 26
Ḥāfeẓ Hāshem Qazvini, 20, 22, 32
Ḥāfeẓ Jalājel Bākharzi, 20, 32–3
Ḥāfeẓ Jāmi, 33
Ḥāfeẓ Lālā Tabrizi, 67
Ḥāfeẓ Moḥammad Kāẓem, 36, 62n
Ḥāfeẓ Moḥammad Moqim, 30
Ḥāfeẓ Moḥammad Taqi, 40
Ḥāfeẓ Mohebb-'Ali, 25, 30
Ḥāfeẓ Thāni, 33
Hâfiẓ Post, 32, 298
Hairapetian, Hambartsum, 148–9
Ḥājj Ḥasan b. Ḥāji 'Ali-Naqi Ganja'i, 172
Ḥājj Ḥosayn Ẓohri Eṣfahāni, 243, 264
Ḥājj Moḥammad-Ḥosayn Amin al-Zarb, 147
Ḥājj Moḥammad Karim Khān, 138
Ḥājj Ṭāher, 137
Ḥāji Ḥakim, 120
Ḥāji Mirzā Āqāsi, 91, 102, 106
Ḥamza Mirzā, Sultan, 20–4, *23*, 32
Hangāfarin, Ḥosayn Khān, 149
Ḥarifi Moṣannef, 22
harmoniums, 134
Harutin, 48, 115–16, 170, 201
Ḥasan Chalabi, 36
Ḥasan Jān, 18
Ḥasan Kāshāni, *Kanz al-tuḥaf*, 182, 281
Ḥasan 'Udi, 241
Hāshem Qazvini, Ḥāfeẓ, 20, 22, 32
Hasht Behesht garden, 9
havā'i, 282–3
Ḥaydar al-'Ajami, 9
Ḥaydar Mirzā, 19
hazaj, 233–6, 241, 258, 271n, 282
Hedāyat, Mehdi-Qoli, 212, 215–16, 219, 269, 307, 310
  Majma' al-adwār, 172–3
Heise, Julius, 144
heptatonic scale, 166, 175–6, 180, 185, *185*
Herat, 8–18, 24–9
  Amir 'Alishir Navā'i, *15*
  arasbāri, 301
  Bāqiya Nā'ini, 35
  late fifteenth century, 65–6
  modal system, 186
  Ostād Zaytun, 71
  Persian modal system, 168–9
  pishraw, 22
  rhythmic cycles, 238
  rikhta, 299
  Solṭān-Ḥosayn Bāyqarā, *66*, 91–2
  Systematist modal theory, 166, 234, 285
  Ṭahmāsb, Shah, 68
  taṣnif, 308
  trade between Mughals and Safavids, 56n
  żarb al-fatḥ, 260

Herati, musicians, 135, *136*
Herbert, Thomas, 78
Ḥeshmat, 134
Homāyun, Mughal emperor, 25–6
homāyun, 148, 214
Hormoz Farhat, 203–4
Ḥosām al-Salṭana, 135
Ḥosayn Bālā Raqqāṣ, *140*
Ḥosayn Khān, 107
Ḥosayn Khān Esmāʿilzada, 117, 119, *146*, 149
Ḥosayn Mirzā, 168
Ḥosayn Ṭāherzāda, 149, 150, 220
Ḥosayn ʿUdi, 14–16
Ḥosaynā, 47
ḥosayni, 28, 186, 226n
Hovasap, *45*

Ibn Fażl Allāh al-ʿUmarī, *Masālik al-abṣār fi mamālik al-amṣār*, 281
Ibn Khurdādhbih, 175–7
Ibn Kurr, 182
Ibn Misjaḥ, 276
Ibn Muḥriz, 276
Ibn Sinā, 178
  Kitāb al-shifā, 105, 233
Ibn Zayla, 177, 233
  Kitāb al-kāfī fī al-mūsīqī, 167
Ibrāhīm al-Mawsilī, 276
Ikhwān al-Ṣafā, 231
Ilkhanid dynasty, 4–6
ʿilm al-adwār (theory of cycles), 165
ʿilm al-īqāʿ (science of rhythm), 231
improvisation, 177, 193, 196, 202, 217, 288, 300
India
  Bāqiyā Nāʾini, 35, 169, 297
  Ḥājj Ḥosayn Ẓohri, 243
  Nāder Shah, 48, 80–2, 209
Indian
  courtesans, 81, 92
  dancers, 48
  musicians, 3, 39, 48, 77, 135
  performers, 77
  vocal genres, 292
Indians, in Isfahan, 77
instrumental genres, 303–11, 311t
instrumentalists, 122–3
instrument-making, 27, 136–8; see also *sāztarāsh*
īqāʿ, 231, 234, 236, 247
Irān Khānom, 150
Iran Radio, 119
Iranian School of Istanbul, 149
Iraq, 20, 21
Isfahan, 32–50
  abuʿaṭā, 218
  Afghan invasion, 201
  Āqā Moʾmen Moṣannef, 244
  courtesans, 72–5, *74*, *79*, 80, 84, 87, 92, 100
  Georgian slave girls, 77
  Ḥājj Ḥosayn Ẓohri, 243
  īqāʿ, 234
  Kaempfer, Engelbert, 64
  Masʿud Mirzā Ẓell al-Solṭān, 129–30
  modal system, 186–7
  Persian genres, 282
  Persian modal system, 167–9
Isḥāq al-Mawṣilī, 233
Istanbul, 18, 147, 170

Jahānārā garden, 65
Jahāngir, Mughal emperor 35, 169
Jalāl Beg Moṣannef, 36
Jalayirid dynasty, 6, 43
Jamāl al-Din Abu Esḥāq Inju, 9
Javād Khān Qazvini, 138
Javānuya, 276
Jenāb Damāvandi, 149
Jewish
  dancers, 133
  dancing boys, 93, 124
  musicians, 87, 106, 115–16, 130, 133, 150

Kabul, 308
Kaempfer, Engelbert, 42–3, 64, 68, *70*, 75
kākoliyāt, 282

Kamāl Tawrizi, 4, 283–4
kamāncha
ʿamala-ye ṭarab-e khāṣṣa, 114
Āqā Gholām-Ḥosayn, 127
courtesans, *89*
dasta, 104–5, 131, 133
folk ensembles, 135
Ḥājj Moḥammad Karim Khān, 138
Ḥosayn Khān Esmāʿilzada, *146*
Malek Maḥmud, 30
Mawlānā Aḥmad, 33
Moḥammad Ṣādeq Khān, 117–18
Musā Kāshi, 130
Nāder Shah, 48
Nāṣer al-Din Shah, 107–8
Ostād Farajollāh, 137
Ostād Zaytun, 28–9, 69–70
Rajab-ʿAli Khān Kermāni, 87, 101
Samandar, 40
Şay Kulu, 18
violins, 144–5
kamāncha-ye farangi (European *kamāncha*), 144–5
Kāmrān Mirzā Nāyeb-al-Salṭana, 129
kār, 14, 24, 31, 260, 285, 289–97, 301, 307, 317n
Kārakiyā dynasty, 28
Karim Kur, 134
Karim Khān Zand, 49–50, 82–84, *83*
Karim Shiraʾi, 116–17, 125
Kārkiyā dynasty, 69–71
Karnā, Shaykh, 125–6
Karnal, battle of, 80–2
kār-o ʿamal (modulatory vocal genre), 206–7, 264, 287, 301, 307–8, 310
Kāshān, 30–1, 173–4
Kashmiri musicians, 135
kawli (gypsies), 71, 77–8
Kāżem Khān Bāshi, 117
khafif, 256–7
Khᵛāja ʿAbd al-Qāder, 299
Khᵛāja Moḥammad Moqim, 19
Khᵛāja Naṣir al-Din al-Ṭusi, 4
Khᵛāja Rażi al-Din Reżvānshāh, 6–7
Khᵛaja Shehāb al-Din ʿAbdollāh Morvārid, 14, 16–17
khᵛājak, 250
Khāleqi, Ruḥollāh, 116, 152
Naẓari be musiqi, 218
Khalil, Sultan, 9
khalvat (male intimate domain), 106, 112, 123
Khān Aḥmad Gilāni, 20, 28–9, 69–72
Khaṭāʾi (pen name of Esmāʿil I), 17
khayl district, Shiraz, 82–3
Khorasan
ʿAbdollāh Khān II, 27
Arabic vocal genres, 282
dastānāt, 177
Esmāʿil I, 17–18
female performers, 65
khᵛānandagi, 20–1, 295
Moḥammad b. Maḥmud Nayshāburi, 178
Nāder Shah, 47–8
non-Systematist modal theory, 166
rhythm, 258–60
Safavids, 25
Shāh-Qoli, 14
tadhkera, 170
Khorram, Prince, 35, 169
Khoshnavāz Khān, 107
Khosravāni (modulatory scheme), 177, 223n, 288, 294, 315n
Khosraw II, 177
khᵛānandagi, 20–1, 30, 294–5
Khᵛānsār, 34, 47
khᵛarazmi, 248, 261–4, 275
Khᵛorshāh b. Qobad Ḥosayni, 28
Kitāb al-adwār, 9, 50n
Kitāb al-aghānī, 281, 283
kolliyāt (modulatory composition), 24, 285–6, *286*
Kolliyāt-e Yusofi, 172, 210–11
Kotzebue, Moritz von, 141
Kretastsi, Abraham, 48
Kuhn, G., 142
Kunduz, 80
Koyuk, *5*

Lāhijān, 28–9, 46–7, 69–71
lang, 247, 267, 271n, 308; see also *aksāk*
lāzema, 287–8, 300, 311t
Lemaire, Alfred Jean-Baptiste, 142–3, *143*, 147–8
Lindsay-Bethune, Henry, 141–2
London, 149, 305
Luṭi Ṣāleḥ, 91

maddāḥ (singer of religious poems), 130
Madhāqi Nā'ini, 34
Madrasa-ye Musiqi, 143, 151
maḥalla-ye naghma (musicians' quarter), 33
Maḥāsin Isfahān, 282
maḥaṭṭ ("the ending of a piece"), 189–90, 196
Māhchubak, 14
Mahd-ʿoliyā, 126
maḥfels (literary assemblies), 48–9, 83
Maḥmud, Sultan, 29
Maḥmud Afghan, 47
Maḥmud Karimi, 220, 230n
Māhnesā' Khānom, 127
māhur, 148, 172, 210–18, 304
majles, 13–14, 26, 71, 122, 130
maktab (stylistic school), 108, 120
male
 ensembles, 104–5
 musicians, 7, *110*, *111*, *133*
 prostitution, 78
 singers, 21
Mālek Daylami Qazvini, 22, 27, 56n
Malek Maḥmud, 30
Malek Qāsem Mirzā, 104
Malek Shāh-Ḥosayn b. Ghiyāth al-Din Moḥammad, 29–30
 Iḥyāʿ al-mulūk, 29
Malekshāh b. Ālp Arslān, 261
Manisa, 11
Manuchehr Khān Gorji, 101
Manuchehri Dāmghāni, 178
Maqālīd al-ʿulūm, 9
maqām, 21, 26, 29, 168–72, 183–210, *192*, 217, 226n, 264, 295, 301
Maqṣud-ʿAli Raqqāṣ, 14
Marāgha, Azerbaijan, 137
Marāl, 134, *135*
mardomzād, 283
maʿrekagir (street entertainers), 70–1
mashākil, 282
Mashhad, 21, 22–4, 27–8, 35, 47–8, 73, 169
Mashḥun, Ḥasan, 139, 265
mashq, 102
Masʿud Mirzā Ẓell al-Solṭān, 129–30
mathnavi (poetic form), 17, 29–30, 47, 102, 136, 218, 304
Matthee, Rudi, 64–5
Mawlānā ʿAbd al-Hādi, 24
Mawlānā Aḥmad, 33
Mawlānā ʿAlishāh Buka, *Aṣl al-waṣl*, 16
Mawlānā Fatḥi, 21
Mawlānā Ḥaydar Qeṣṣa-khᵛān, 21
Mawlānā Mālek Daylami, 22–4
Mawlānā Moḥammad Khᵛarshid Eṣfahāni, 21
Mawlānā Nāji Kermāni, 18
mawludi-khᵛān (singer of religious poems celebrating the birth of the Prophet), 130
Melikhāy, 106
military bands, *141*, 147–8
Mir Aḥmad Monshi, 24, 27
Mir ʿAlishir Navā'i, 11
 Chagatai *divān*, 301
 Khamsat al-mutaḥayyirīn, 16–17
Mir ʿAzzu, 16
Mir Fayzollāh, 33
Mir Fendereski, 167
Mir Mortāz, 16
Mir Sadid Rāzi, 30
Mir Ṣadr al-Din Moḥammad
 āhang, 196
 genres, 288–90, 296–300
 gusha, 187, 200
 Ḥosayni, 226n
 maqām, 186, 195
 oṣul, 241–2, 249–61
 Qazvin, 24

Mir Ṣadr al-Din Moḥammad Qazvini, 22, 24, 168, 294
Mir Ṣawti, 35
Mir Sayyed Sharif Jorjāni, 9
Mir Shāna Tarāsh, 316n
Mir Vālahi Qomi, 22
Mirānshāh, 8–9, 50n
Mirzā ʿAbd al-Vahhāb Musavi, 48–9
Mirzā ʿAbdollāh, 46–7, 107–8, 118–22, *119*, *121*, 138, 211–15, 219, 230n, 309
Mirzā ʿAli, 49
Mirzā Ḥasan, 107, 120
Mirzā Ḥesābi Naṭanzi, 22, 30–1
Mirzā Ḥosayn Tanburi, 21
Mirzā Mehdi Asṭarābādi, 82, 261
Mirzā Moḥammad Taqi, 38
Mirzā Naṣir Eṣfahāni, 50
Mirzā Shafiʿ, 107, *119*, 173–4
Mirzā Sharaf Jahān, 24
mixed ensembles, 131–3
moʿallem-khāna (chamber of instruction), 102, 104
mobarqaʿ, 196, 207
modal system, 165–230, 307–8, 322–6
modulatory scheme, 179, 185, 188, 195, 197, 206, 211, 215, 307, 309–10
moghanniyān (male musicians), 7
Moginié, Daniel, 48
Moḥammad Kāẓem Marvi, 47–8, 80
Moḥammad, Shah, 90–1, 102, 106, 108, 116, 135, 141–2
Moḥammad Amin Khān, 16
Moḥammad ʿAwfi Bokhāri, 177
Moḥammad b. Maḥumud Nayshāburi, 178–81, 178t, 183, 325–6
Moḥammad Bāqer Majlesi, 45–6, 78–9
Moḥammad Ḥāfeẓ Eṣfahāni, 18
Moḥammad Ḥasan Khān, 107, 115–17
Moḥammad Ḥosayn ʿUdi, 28–9
Moḥammad Kamāncha'i, 20
Moḥammad Khodābanda, Sultan, 21–2, 24–5
Moḥammad Mirzā, 25
Moḥammad Moḥsen Mostawfi, 261
Moḥammad Moʾmen, 20
Moḥammad Qoli Salim, 46–7
Moḥammad Ṣādeq Khān, 107, 115–20, *119*, 127, 138, 144, 211–15, 219, 310
Moḥammad Sharaf al-Din Oghlu, 25–26
Moḥammad Shaybāni Khān, 13
Moḥammad Ṭāher Naṣrābādi, 34–5, 39–40, 46–7
Mohebb-ʿAli Balabāni, 13
moḥseni, 204–5
Moḥtasham Kāshāni, 30, 172, 208
mokhālef-e rāst, 179
mokhammas, 238, 241, 244, 247, 249, 252–3, 256–7
Mokhtāri, Rokn al-Din, 152, 310
Mollā ʿAbd al-Javād Khorāsāni, 105
Mollā Afżal Dōtāri, 31
Mollā Fāṭema, 82–3
Mollā Karim, 102
Mollā Vāṣeb, 46–7
Moluk Żarrābi, 150, 151
Moʾmen, 134
monājāt (religious chants), 149
Monarch Records, 150
monāseb-khʷāni, 82–3
Mongol period, 4–11
Mongolia, 65
Montaẓam al-Ḥokamāʾ, 119–20, 219
moqaddama, 228n
moqalled, 112, 125–6, *125*, *126*, 131, 147–8
Morād Khān, 139
morakkabāt, 183–4, 196–7; see also *tarkib*
Moraṣṣaʿ, 82–3
moraṣṣaʿ-khʷān, 295; see also *qawl-e moraṣṣaʿ*
Morteżā-Qoli Beg, 40
moṣannef (composer), 21, 34–5
Mosayyeb Khān Takallu, 30
Moshir-Homāyun, Ḥabibollah, 119, 146, 149
Moshtāq ʿAlishāh, 49
Mostawfi, ʿAbdollāh, 116–17, 307
mostazād, 281
motaghayyer, 218

moṭreb-bāshi (principal instrumentalist and chief of musicians and entertainers), 101, 116
Moṭrebi Qazvini, 32
moṭreb, 105, 114–15, 122, 124–5, 130, 133–4, 145
Moẓaffar al-Din, Shah, 29, 117, 130, 138–40, 144, 147, *148*, 167, 172
Moẓaffir Qomi, Ḥāfeẓ, 20, 32, 130, 295
Mo'ayyad al-Tojjār, 172
Mobārakshāh, 9, 52n, 284, 314n, 315n, 319
morakkab, 181–4, 195–6; see also *tarkib*
Mughals, 25–7, 56n, 73, 77, 80–2, 262–3
Muḥammad b. 'Abd al-Ḥamīd al-Lādhiqī, 260
    al-Risāla al-fatḥiyya fī al-mūsīqī, 182
Muḥammad b. Aḥmad al-Khᵛārazmī, 176–7
Musā Kāshi, 130
Musā Khān, 4
al-Musta'ṣim bi-Allāh, 4
Mustafa Paşa, 170
muzikānchi, 147–8
muzikānchi-bāshi (chief of Western-style military music), 142

Nāder Shah, 47–8, 80, *81*, 92, 170, 209
naghma (tones), 166
Nā'in, 35, 169
Najm al-Din Kawkabi, 170, 194, 197, 251, 294
Nakhjavān, 18
nakhsh, 293
nakhshayn, 293
Nakisa, 241
Napoleon, 144
naqqāra-bāshi, 116
naqqāra-khāna, 115–17
    'Abbas I, Shah, 75
    Esmā'il II, 33
    Maḥmud Afghan, 47
    Ostād Asad, 67
    Ostād Shāh-Moḥammad Surnā'i, 26
    rhythmic cycles of the, 249, 260–4
    Ṭahmāsb, Shah, 18, 72
naqqārachi (musicians of military and ceremonial bands), 70–1
naqra ("attack"), 231–2, 234–5
naqsh
    eighteenth century, 301
    Gholām Shādi, 16
    Mawlānā 'Abd al-Hādi, 24
    Mir Ṣawti, 35
    Mirzā Ḥesābi Nanṭanzi, 22
    patrons of music, 27–32
    Persian genres, 282–3
    Resāla dar 'elm-e musiqi, 171, 205
    Safavid genres, 287, 290–1, 298–9
    Shaykhi Nā'i, 14
    Ẓahir al-Din Moḥammad Bābur, 285
naqshayn, 287, 292, 299
Nārenji-Solṭān, 25
Nāṣer al-Din, Shah, 99, 106–30, *128*, 134–5, 144, 150–1, 214–15
Nāṣer-Homāyun, Arslān, 144
nashid, 278–9, 282
Nasimi, 226n, 301
    Nasim-e ṭarab, 29, 167–8, 184–5, 201, 241, 249–62
Naṣr II, 276
Naṭanz, 30–1
Nāṭyaśāstra, 239
navā, 148, 171–2, 206, 214, 217–18, 229–30n
navākht, 285, 294
Navvāb Mir Moḥsen b. Ḥaji Sayyed Aḥmad Qarabāghi, *Vozuḥ al-arqām dar 'elm-e musiqi*, 172
nawbat-e morattab, 6–7, 262–3, 277, 281, 285, 289–91, 295, 297, 313n
nawḥa (lamentation), 171–2
nawruz, 34
Nawruzi, Reżā-Qoli, 149, 265, 305
nay
    Ḥasan, 18
    Moḥebb-'Ali, 25
    patrons of music, 129–30
    played by men only, 134
    Qoli Khān Shāhi, 139

rāst-panjgāh, 214
Shaykhi Nā'i, 14
Ṭahmāsb, Shah, 68
Taqsīm al-naghamāt wa bayān al-darj wa al-shu'ab wa al-maqāmāt, 168
Western harmony, 152
Naydāvud, Morteżā, 150
Nāyeb Asadollāh, 130
nayruziyāt, 282
Ne'matollāhi Sufi order, 106, 136
Neshāṭ, 48–9
Neubauer, Eckhard, 232, 234
New Julfa cemetery, Isfahan, 45, *45*, 60n
New Julfa, Isfahan, 49, 137
Neẓām al-Din b. Ḥakim, 4
Niel, Adolphe, 142
nim-dawr, 257
Nimruz district, Sistān, 29
nim-thaqil, 255–6
non-Systematist modal theory, 165–7, 178–81, 321–6, 323t, 324t, 325t
Noqṭavi Messianic movement, 31
notations, 166, 169, 174, 181–5, 225n, 232
Nur Bay, 81
Nurā garden, 65
Nur'ali Borumand, 97n
nutak, 48

octave scale, 166, 181–5
oktoechos, 176, 220
Olearius, Adam, 38–9, 75, 77
Olivier, Guillaume Antoine, 99–100
Öljaitü, 4
'Onṣor al-Ma'āli Kykābus b. Voshmgir Ziyār, *Qābus-nāma*, 178, 282
ōrāmanān, 282
Ostād Āhu, 78
Ostād Asad, 67
Ostād Dust Moḥammad, 28
Ostād Farajollāh, 137
Ostād Ḥosayn Shushtari Balabāni, 67
Ostād Ḥosayn 'Udi, 29
Ostād Ma'ṣum Kamāncha'i, 21
Ostād Minā, 87, 96n, 100
Ostād Moḥammad Mo'men, 38
Ostad Moḥammad 'Udi, 70–1
Ostād Qāsem, 19, 26, 56n
davā-ye dard-e saram, 27–8
nāz va ghamza, 27–8
Ostād Sayyed Aḥmad Ghejaki, 13
Ostād Shāh-Moḥammad Surnā'i, 26
Ostād Shāhsavār, 20
Ostād Shams Shetorghu'i, 21, 22, 32
Ostād Solṭān-Moḥammad Changi, 21
Ostād Solṭān-Moḥammad Tanburi, 21
Ostād Yusof Mawdud, 26
Ostād Zaytun, 28–9, 69–71, 77–8, 317n
chupān-o rama, 29
Ostād Zohra, 87, 96n, 100
oṣul, 231–3, 236, 238, 240–4, 248–65, 273n, 290–1, 300–1
Ottoman
female performers, 80
musicians, 196–7
text, 170
Turkish vocal genres, 62n
wars, 37
Ouseley, Sir William, 141
ozān, 17, 300–1

panjgāh, 207
parda, 178–81, 178t, 180t, 183, 200–1, 206, 322, 323t
Paris, 148–9
Paris Academy of Music, 142
parvāna, 215, 309–11t
Parvāna Khānom, 150
patrons of music, 3–62, 126, 129–30, 140
Persian
dances, 43–4
genres, 282–4
songs and poetry, 77, 276
treatise, 168
verses, 36
Phlavān Moḥammad Bu Sa'id, 16
phonographs, 147–50

pianos, 118–19, 127–9, 144, 149, 152
Pick, Maxim, 147–8
pishdarāmad, 151–2, 310
pishraw
    Amir Khān Gorji, 62n, 317n
    Cantemir, Demetrius, 35
    dō-yek rhythmic cycle, 242, 249, 252
    genres, 288, 299–301
    patrons of music, 27–9
    popularity of, 22
    reng, 264
    rhythm, 283–4
    Shāh-Qoli, 14
    Zayn al-ʿĀbedin, 11
Powers, Harold, 193

Qābus-nāma, 178, 224n, 233, 271n, 282, 314n
Qahraman Mirzā Sālur, 124
Qajar period
    Āqā Moḥammad Khān, 87
    concubines and courtesans, 93, 96n
    court music, 98–163
    Herati musicians, *136*
    maḥfel, 48–9
    mnemonic patterns, *268*
    modal system, 210–11
    Moḥammad Shah, 90–1
    rhythm, 265–9, *266*
    vocal and instrumental genres, 303–11
Qamar al-Moluk Vaziri, 150–1
Qamar Sāleki, 134
Qandahār, 27, 47, 56n, 73, 77
qānun, 16, 19, 25–7, 48
Qara Qoyunlu, 9
qarār, 197
Qāsem (brother of Ostād Zaytun), 29
Qāsem Qānuni Herāti, 27
qaṣida, 30, 278–9, 281–3
Qaṣr-e Ṭarabafzā, 65
qavvāl-khāna, 68–9, 72, 92
qavvāl, 70–2, 279–81
    chanbar rhythmic cycle, 7
    female musicians and courtesans, 297, 305
    Luṭi Ṣāleḥ, 91
    revenues from, 75
    taṣnifs, 295
    upper-class, 92
qawl
    ʿAbbas I, Shah, 32
    Ebrāhim Mirzā, 27
    eighteenth century, 301
    genres, 279–83, 285, 288–9, 291, 293, 296–7, 299
    Mir Ṣadr al-Din Moḥammad, 24
    qavvāl-khāna, 68
    qawl-e fārsi, 292, 297
    qawl-e moraṣṣaʿ, 280, 285
    Shāh-Morād Moṣannef, 34
Qāżi ʿAbdollāh Rāżi, 30
Qāżi Jahān Qazvini, 24
Qazvin, 19–24, 30–2, 36–7, 186
Qenālizāda, 11
Qerqi, 105
qeṣṣa-khvān (storyteller), 21, 37
qeṭʿa, 152, 284
qiyan, 96n
Qizilbāsh
    ʿAbbas I, Shah, 37–8
    amīr, 25–6, 30
    musicians, 17, 293–4
Qoli Khān, 107, 115, 139
Qol-Moḥammad, 14
qomiband, 282
Qorbān Khān, 138, 307, 317n,
Qorbān-ʿAli Beg Jalawdār, *140*
Qoṭb al-Din Shirāzi, 182–3, 235–6, 254
    Durrat al-tāj, 4, 167, 280, 284
quatrains, 281–2

radif
Āqā Ḥosayn-Qoli, 121–2
Davāmi, 220
forud-e motammam, 230n
Hedāyat, Mehdi-Qoli, 173
Karimi, 220
modal system, 213–15, 219–20
Moḥammad Ṣādeq Khān, 118–19
Mirzā ʿAbdollāh, 121–2, 219
Montaẓam al-Ḥokamāʾ, 119
reng, 309
Sufi lodges, 136
taṣnif, 97n
vocal genres, 304
rāg, 35, 169, 207, 209
rahāvi, 172
rāh-e bālā, 242, 251–2
rāh-e ekhlāṭi, 262
ra'is, 116–18
Rajab-ʿAli Khān Kermāni, 87, 101, 116
rāk, 207, 209
ramal, 255, 259
raqqāṣ (dancer), 21, 82, 123–4
Rasht, 29
rāst, 171–2, 196, 206–7, 226n, 322
rāst-panjgāh, 148, 214–15, 218
ravāni, 251–2
rawża, *112*, 304
Ray, 18, 30, 276
Rayḥān, 106
recording technology, 147–50
reng, 106, 308–10
Afghan music, 135
Caucasian origin, 302–3
concubines and courtesans, 93, 106, 305
eighteenth century, 264
Moḥammad Ṣādeq Khān, 214
recordings, 148–9
Sakina, 120
żarb-e rengi, 267
reng-e afghāni, 135
reng-e afshār, 309
reng-e Armani, 303, 309
reng-e baghdādi, 303, 309
reng-e faraḥ, 106, 309
reng-e ganja, 303
reng-e ḥarbi, 309
reng-e hashtari, 309
reng-e kāboli, 303, 309
reng-e lezgi, 303, 309
reng-e lori, 309
reng-e nasturi, 303, 309
reng-e qafqāzi, 309
reng-e oṣul, 309
Resāla dar bayān-e chahār dastgāh, 171, 205–7, 307
Resāla dar ʿelm-e musiqi, 171, 205, 301
Resāla-ye davāzdah dastgāh, 172, 210–11, 215
Resāla-ye Karāmiya, 243
Reynolds, Dwight, 96n
rhythm, 231–75, 325t
rhythmic cycles, 166, 244t, 246t, 247–9, *266*, 322–6
Rifāʿī Sufi order, 9
rikhta, 35, 288–91, 299
robāʿi, 305
robāb, 171, 213, 215
Romano, Francesco, 67
Rostam, 87, 100
Rostam al-Ḥokamāʾ, 82–3, 115
Rouillon, 142
Royal Albert Hall, London, 150–1
Royal Opera House, London, 150–1
Rudaki, 276
Rudaki Institute of Language and Literature, Dushanbe, Tajikistan, 170
Rudsar, 72
Ruḥparvar, ʿAli, 241
Rumi, Nayyera ʿAẓam, 150
rusharmiyāt, 282
Rustam al-tawārīkh, 49–50

ṣabā, 34
Ṣāber Qāq, Ḥāfeẓ, 26
Ṣāber Shirāzi, 35
Ṣādeqi Ketābdār, 25, 27
Saʿdi, 303
Safavid period, 17–47
architecture, 32
court music, *39*, 44–5
courtesans, 62n
genres, 286–301
gypsy courtesans, 92
map of domains, *19*
music theorists, 168–9, 244t
rhythmic cycles, 246t, 247–9
sources, 184–7
Systematist modal theory, 166–7
trade with Mughals, 56n
treatises, 241–6
Ṣafi, Shah, 34–5, 38
Ṣafī al-Dīn al-Urmawī, 4, 168, 232, 241, 280–1, 283–4
Kitāb al-adwār, 6–7, 165, 167, 181–2, 234, 236, 319–20
Risāla al-Sharafiyya, 4, 165, 167, 234–5, 319–20
Ṣafi Qoli Beg Eṣfahāni, 39
Ṣafi-ʿAlishāh, 145
Şah Kulu, 18
Sakina, 107, 129
sorud-e anjoman-e okhovvat (fraternity's anthem), 146
Salim II, 92
Saltykov, Alexey, 141, *141*
Sām Mirzā, 22, 25, 30
Toḥfa-ye Sāmi, 19, 25, 30
samāʿ assemblies, 279, 304
Ṣamad Khān Eʿteṣām Khalvat, 117, 130, 139
samāʿi rhythmic cycle, 35, 259
Samandar, 40
Samanid court, 276
Samarqand, 8, 238, 320
Ṣaniʿ al-Molk, 108–9, *109*
Sanson, N., 42, 77
santur (hammer dulcimer)
ʿAli-Akbar Shāhi, 138
Āqā Ebrāhim, 102
chahārmeżrāb, 269, 309
Chālānchi Khān, 101
courtesans, *89*
dastgāh, 214
ensembles, 114–19, 133–4
Ḥabibollāh Samāʿ-Ḥożur, 108
Isfahan, 44
kār-o ʿamal, 307
Moḥammad Ḥasan Khān, 107
Moḥammad Ṣādeq Khān, 107, 212
Nāder Shah, 48
patrons of music, 129–30
Rajab-ʿAli Khān Kermāni, 87
recordings, 149
Zivar al-Solṭān, 127
sāqi-nāma, 136, 303, 304
sarband, 288, 300–1
sarghazal, 288
Sāru Taqi, 38–9, 77
ṣawt
Bārbad, 177
dastgāh, 171
Ebrāhim Mirzā, 27
genres, 287, 290–1, 293, 297–8, 301
Gholām Shādi, 16
Madhāqi Nāʾini, 34–5
Mir Ṣadr al-Din Moḥammad, 24
Mir Shāna Tarāsh, 316n
Persian genres, 282–3
Resāla dar ʿelm-e musiqi, 205
Zahiruddin Muḥammad Bābur Mirzā, 285
saxophones, 145
sayr, 186, 194, 196, 207, 225n
Sayyed Aḥmad Khān, 120, 148–9, 307
Sayyed Ḥasan, 120
Sayyed Mir Abu al-Qāsem Astarābādi, 167
Sayyed Rahim, 130

sāzanda (instrumentalist), 20–1, 70–1, 78, 84, 114–16, 122–3
sāztarāsh (luthiers), 70–1, 136–8, *137*, 166
scales, 175–6, *193*, 201, 202t, 303
scale degrees, 166, 175–6, 180, 182, 184–6, 192–3, 201–2, 220, 225n
segāh, 146, 148, 215, 217–18
Selim, Sultan, 18
Selim II, 72
Seljuq court, 282
seraglio, 39–40, 109
Serāj al-Din Moḥammad Ghavvāṣ, 199
setār
  Āqā ʿAli-Akbar Farāhāni, 108
  chahārmeżrāb, 309
  courtesans, *90*
  dastgāh-e bāzigar-khāna, 101–2
  Hedāyat, Mehdi-Qoli, 173
  luthiers, 136–8
  Mirzā ʿAbdollāh, 121
  Moḥammad Ṣādeq Khān, 118–19
  Moshtāq ʿAlishāh, 49
  radif, 219
  Rajab-ʿAli Khān Kermāni, 87
  Shākha Nabāt, 83
Seydi, 197
se- żarb-e sangin, *267*
shabestāniyāt, 282
shadd, 181–2, 184, 186, 200–1, 205–6
Shādi, Darvish, 11
shādiyāna rhythmic cycle, 261
Shāhedbāz, *70*
Shāhi suffix, 138–9
Shāhjahān, Mughal emperor, 169
Shāh-Morād Moṣannef, 34, 36, 51, 58n, 302
shāh-nāma, 21, 37, 47, 251
shahnāz, 172, 215
Shāhpasand (pleasing to the king), 115, 139
Shāh-Qoli, 14
shahrāshub, 309
Shāhrokh Mirzā, 11, *12*, *13*
Shāhrud, 91
Shāhverdi Khānom, 87, 102
Shākha Nabāt, *83*
Shamākhi, 37–9, 172
Shams al-Din Jovayni, 4
Shams al-Din Maḥmud Āmoli, *Nafāʾis al-funūn fī ʿarāʾis al-ʿuyūn*, 9
Shams al-Din Muhammad b. Qays al-Rāzī, 177, 282
Shams Tishi, 35
Sharaf al-Din Hārun, 4
Sharafiyya, 6–7
sharḥ (commentaries), 165
sharīʿa law, 18, 71, 136
sharva, 282, 295
Shaybāni Khān, Moḥammad, 16–18
Shaykh ʿAbd al-ʿAli Baṣri, 36
Shaykh Karnā, 125–6
Shaykh Ovays, 6–7
Shaykhi Nāʾi, 14
Shaykh Shaypur, 125–6
shetorghu (long-necked lute), 32, 44, *74*
Shihāb al-Dīn al-Ṣayrafī al-Tabrīzī, *Khulāṣat al-afkār fī maʿrifat al-adwār*, 6
Shiʿite contexts, 151, 267, 304
Shiraz
  Abu al-Fatḥ Pir Budāq, *10*
  Āqā Moḥammad Khān, 87
  Āqā Moṭalleb, 117
  courtesans and musicians, 62n, *85*
  dastgāh-e bāzigar-Khāna, 100–1
  eighteenth century, 203
  Karim Khān Zand, 49–50, 82–4
  Moshir-Homāyun, 119
  patrons of music, 9
  Shākha Nabāt, *83*
  Shams Tishi, 35
  Systematist modal theory, 166, 234
shoʿba, 168, 172, 178–81, 178t, 183, 185–210, *192*, 217, 324t, 325–6
Shojāʿ Moẓaffari, Shah, 9, 50n
Shokri, 147
shudūd, 181–2

shur, 148, 214–15, 217–18
Shurida Shirāzi, 308
Shusha, 172
single-part form, 305–6
Sistān, 25, 29–30
Siyahiç, 18
social tags, 114–15
Sohrāb, 87, 100
Solaymān, Shah, 18, 34–5, 39–42, *41*, 44, 75–7
Ṣolḥi, Mehdi, 119, 173
Solṭān-Aḥmad, 7–8
Solṭān-ʿAli Mashhadi, 65
Solṭān-Ḥosayn Safavi, Shah, 45–6, 78–9, 115, 169
Solṭān-Ḥosayn Bāyqarā, 9–11, 14–17, 24, 65, *66*, 67, 91–2
Solṭān-Ḥosayn Jalāyer, 6–7
Solṭān Khānom, 109, 126
Solṭān-Moḥammad Ṭanburi, 27–8
song-texts, 8, 32, 52n, 73, 93n, 135, 169, 193, 205, 281–6, 293–300, 313n, 315n–17n
Sorur al-Molk (euphoria of the kingdom), 115, 118, 129
Struys, J. J., 75
Sufi
  assemblies, 279, 304
  contexts, 267
  lodges, 136, 209, 218
  musician, 49
ṣufiyāna, 250
surnā, 26, 67
Syria, 9, 276
Systematist modal theory, 165–7, 170, 181–4, 285, 307, 319–20

Tabriz
  chanbar rhythmic cycle, 7, 258, 272n
  Esmāʿil I, 18
  Jalayirid court, 43
  late fifteenth century, 65–6
  Moẓaffar al-Din, Shah, 138
  Persian modal system, 172
  Solṭān-Ḥosayn Jalāyer, 6–9
  Systematist modal theory, 166, 234
  ṭanbur-e shervāniyān, 7
  varsāqi, 300
  Western music, 141–2
tadhkera, 31t, 34, 170
Ṭāherchaka, 14
Ṭahmāsb, Prince, 25
Ṭahmāsb, Shah, 18–19, 24–9, 37, 56n, 67–72, *69*, 92
Ṭahmāsb II, Shah, 47–8
taḥrir, 196, 216–17, 220, 295, 304
Tāj al-Salṭana, 140
tājiband, 282
Takiya Dawlat, 151
ṭanbur, 7, 19–21, 28, 30, 38, 39, 47, 48
Tanparvar, 241
Taqi al-Din Awhadi Balayāni, 9–11, 32, 34, 36
Taqi Kāshi, 30–1
taqlid, 125–6, 131, 149
Taqsīm, 294
Taqsīm al-naghamāt wa bayān al-darj wa al-shuʿab wa al-maqāmāt, 168, 185–6, *185*, 190–4, *192*, 201, 241, 249–60
tār
  Āqā Ḥosayn-Qoli, 129
  Aziz Shashlulband, *135*
  chahārmeżrāb, 309
  dastgāh-e bāzigar-Khāna, 101–8
  dastgāh, 174
  ensembles, 114, 133, *133*
  Farāhāni family, 120–1
  luthiers, 136–8
  radif, 219
  Rajab-ʿAli Khān Kermāni, 87
  rāst-panjgāh, 214
  recordings, 147–52
tarāna, 281, 285, 288–93, 297, 299
Tārikh-e ʿAzodi, 102
Tārikh-e Bayhaqi, 279
Tārikh-e jahāngoshā-ye Timur, *8*

tarkib (modulatory scheme), 181, 183–4, 187, 196–200, 207–8
taṣnif-kh'ān, 149–50
taṣnifkh'ān- żarbgir (singer-accompanists), 114
taṣnif
'Abbas I, Shah, 32–6
Aḥmad, Sultan, 7–8
Amir Khān Gorji, 46, 62n
Āqā Ḥosayn-Qoli, 120
Āqā Mo'men Moṣannef, 169
courtesans, 93, 317n
dasta, 134–5
dastgāh, 206–7, 210, 214
Davāmi, 'Abdollāh, 220
dō-yek rhythmic cycle, 252
eighteenth century, 264–9
ensembles, 114
female performers and concubines, 97n, 126–9
genres, 287–9, 292–5, 302, 304–8
Ḥabibollāh Samā'-Ḥożur, 108
instrumentalists, singers and accompanists, 122–3
lay musicians, 202
male singers of, 21
nineteenth century, 146–52
Persian genres, 282–3
poets, 106
qawl, 280, 297
rhythmic cycles, 244, 285
se-żarb-e sangin, *267*
Tatar dances, 43–4
ṭavā'ef, 71
taxes, 50, 64, 67, 75–6, 84, 92, 130
ta'ziya (passion play), 145, 151, 171–2
Tbilisi, 150
Tehran
acrobatics, *88*
courtesans, *86*, 87–91, *89*, *90*, *91*
dastān-e 'arab, 218
Hedāyat, Mehdi-Qoli, 173
Neshāṭ, 48–50
nineteenth century, 98–163
Qajar court, 210–11
radif, 230n
taṣnif, 304–8
Tenreiro, 62n
terkib, 197–8, 209
thaqil rhythmic cycle, 29, 238, 247–8, 256, 258, 261
Tihu, 140
Timur, 8, *8*, 50n
Timurid period, 11–17, 43, 236–40, 283, 285–6
Tolam, Gilān, 71
tombstones, *45*, *46*
torki-żarb, 241–2, 254–5, 296
Transoxiana, 65, 198, 282, 294
travel literature, 63–97
Treaty of Amasya 1555, 68
trumpets, 145
Tulem, 29
Turkish
concert, 149
Dawra Beg Karāmi, 26
dialect, 3
Madhāqi Nā'ini, 34
musicians, 3, 135, 300
treatise, 168
verses, 17, 36
vocal genres, 62n, 300
ṭuṭak (small wooden flute), 44
Twelver Shi'sim, 17, 67

'Ubayd Allāh Khān, 170
al-Ubulla, Persian Gulf, 276
'ud (short-necked lute), 4, 11, 14–16, 20, 28–9, 200, 276
Umayyad court, 276
University of Tehran, 173
urban musical life, 130–8
Urmia, 104
Uzbek dances, 43–4
Uzbeks, 11, 27, 170
Uzun Ḥasan, 9, 65

Vank Cathedral, Isfahan, 60n
Varāin district, Qazvin, 21
varashān, 236, 238, 241–2, 254
varsāqi (Turkish vocal genre), 17, 62n, 205, 292, 300, 302
vazn (meter), 265
Vaziri, ʿAli-Naqi, 151–2
Verona Arena, Italy, 151
violins, 144–5, 149, 151–2
Visnich, Hubert, 62n
vocal genres, 303–11, 311t

Waring, Edward Scott, 50, 84
    A Tour of Sheeraz, 83
Wellesz, Egon, 176
Western music, 134, 141–5, 150–2
Wright, Owen, 185, 232–3

Yaḥyā (luthier), 137, *137*
Yaʿqub, Sultan, 9
Yazd, 35
Yerevan, 141
Yusof Khān, 80
Yusof Mawdud Qazvini, 26
Yusuf bin Saka, 18

Zādur (luthier), *45*
Ẓafar-nāma, *8*
Zāghān garden, 26
Zāghi, 106
Ẓahir al-Dawla, 145
Zahiruddin Muḥammad Bābur Mirzā, 17, 285
    Bāburnāma, 11, 14–16
Zakaria Kanakertsi, 72
zakhma, 284
żarb, 134, 232, 239–40, 249, 258, 260, 265, 267, 269, 270n
żarb al-aṣl, 235, 271n
żarb al-aṣl (rhythmic cycle), 28, 245t
żarbgir (accompanists), 106, 123, 149–50, 265, 267–9, 305, 307–8
Zari, 149, 306
Zayn al-ʿĀbedin, 11
Zayn al-Din Vāṣefi, 298, 316n
    Badāyiʿ al-waqāyiʿ, 11–14
Zaynab, 127
zencîr, 238
Zivar al-Solṭān, 108, 115, 127
Zoroastrian musicians, 276

EU representative:
Easy Access System Europe
Mustamäe tee 50, 10621 Tallinn, Estonia
Gpsr.requests@easproject.com

www.ingramcontent.com/pod-product-compliance
Lightning Source LLC
Chambersburg PA
CBHW052055300426
44117CB00013B/2130

* 9 7 8 1 3 9 9 5 1 5 7 8 8 *